THE PRACTICE OF ECONOMICS

THE PRACTICE OF ECONOMICS

Economic Systems and Decision Making in Western Societies

Alex N. McLeod

Transaction Publishers
New Brunswick (U.S.A.) and London (U.K.)

Copyright © 1993 by Transaction Publishers, New Brunswick, New Jersey 08903.

All rights reserved under International and Pan-American Copyright Conventions. No part of this book may be reproduced or transmitted in any form or by any means, electronic or mechanical, including photocopy, recording, or any information storage and retrieval system, without prior permission in writing from the publisher. All inquiries should be addressed to Transaction Publishers, Rutgers—The State University, New Brunswick, New Jersey 08903.

Library of Congress Catalog Number: 92-24253
ISBN: 1-56000-083-X
Printed in the United States of America

Library of Congress Cataloging-in-Publication Data

McLeod, Alex N., 1911-
   The practice of economics: economic systems and decision making in western societies/Alex N. McLeod.
   p.   cm.
   Includes index.
   ISBN 1-56000-083-X (cloth)
   1. Economics. 2. Economic policy. I. Title.
HB171.5.M49   1993
338.9—dc20   92-24253
                                                                                              CIP

Contents

PREFACE xi

ACKNOWLEDGEMENTS xiii

Part One. Getting Started

Chapter 1.   BEDROCK FUNDAMENTALS 3

   1, What Is Economics? 3; 2, How Economists Reason, 3; 3, The Factors of Production, 5; 4, Systems of Economic Decisionmaking, 8; 5, Five Major Verities, 9; 6, An Introduction to Charts and Graphs, 11.

Part Two. Microeconomics

Chapter 2.   THE MODEL OF PURE COMPETITION 17

   1, The Two Major Branches of Economics, 17; 2. The Circular Flow, 19; 3, An Outline of the Model, 20; 4, Perfect Competition, 21; 5, Policy Implications, 22.

Chapter 3.   CONSUMER DEMAND 25

   1, Utility Functions, 25; 2, Utility and Income-Allocation, 29; 3, The Personal Demand Function, 31; 4, Elasticity of Demand, 32; 5, Changing Incomes, Tastes, and Technology, 38.

Chapter 4.   THE INDIVIDUAL FIRM 41

   1, A Typical Producer, 41; 2, The Law of Diminishing Returns, 42; 3, The Costs of Production, 45; 4, Total, Average, and Marginal Costs, 47; 5, Determining the Optimum Output, 53; 6, The Firm's Supply Function, 56; 7, Changing Prices and Costs, 58; 8, The Rôle of Profits, 60; 9, The Profit Motive, 63.

Chapter 5.   MARKETS: SUPPLY AND DEMAND 65

   1, Consumer-Goods Markets, 65; 2, The Demand for Factors of Production, 72; 3, The Market for Factors of Production, 75; 4, Long-Run Equilibrium, 78; 5, Factor Returns, 81.

Chapter 6. MONOPOLY 85

1, Monopoly by Merger, 85; 2, Simple Monopoly, 88; 3, Decreasing-Cost Industries, 92; 4, Discriminating Monopoly, 94.

Chapter 7. OTHER SUPPLEMENTARY MODELS 97

1, Joint Supply and Joint Costs, 97; 2, Complementary Goods and Substitute Goods, 98; 3, Business Cycles, 99; 4, Public Finance, 105; 5, Welfare Economics, 108; 6, The National Accounts, 110; 7, Econometric Models, 117.

Chapter 8. MONOPOLISTIC *OR* IMPERFECT COMPETITION 121

1, An Undifferentiated Product, 121; 2, Product Differentiation, 125; 3, Pricing Decisions, 129; 4, Policy Implications, 130.

Chapter 9. DISSENTING OPINIONS 133

1, Criticisms of *Laissez-Faire* Policies, 133; 2, Underconsumption Theories, 136; 3, Socialism, 141; 4, Marxism, 144; 5, Historicism in Germany and Institutionalism in the U.S.A., 148; 6, Henry George and the Single Tax, 151.

Part Three. Macroeconomics

Chapter 10. THE MACROECONOMICS OF PURE COMPETITION . 155

1, The Whole Picture, 155; 2, Real Output, 156; 3, Employment, 162; 4, Saving and Investment, 163; 5, The Interest Rate, 166; 6, Real Income, Money Income, and Prices, 168; 7, The Quantity Theory of Money and Prices, 169; 8, Stocks, Flows, and the Money Supply, 174.

Chapter 11. MODERN MACROECONOMICS 177

1, The Breakthrough, 177; 2, The Consumption Function, 179; 3, Income Determination, 181; 4, The Determinants of Investment, 187; 5, More Elaborate Models, 189; 6, An Introduction to Demand Management, 193.

Chapter 12. THE FINANCIAL SYSTEM 197

   1, Interest-Rate Theory, 197; 2, Money and Banking, 200; 3, The Rôle of Monetary Policy, 208; 4, A Double Income Multiplier, 214.

Chapter 13. THE RISE AND ECLIPSE OF DEMAND MANAGEMENT 223

   1, In the Beginning, 223; 2, Limitations on Demand Management, 226; 3, Policy Objectives and Policy Instruments, 227; 4, The Experience of Inflation, 229; 5, The Cause of Today's Inflations: A Pragmatic View, 230.

Chapter 14. THE MONETARIST COUNTER-REVOLUTION 235

   1, Monetarists and Monetarism, 235; 2, The Counter-Revolution, 237; 3, Friedman's Early Views, 239; 4, Later Monetarist Views, 243; 5, Commentary, 244. Suggested Readings, 247.

Part Four. International Economic Relations

Chapter 15. TRADE BETWEEN COUNTRIES 251

   1, The Theory of Comparative Advantage, 251; 2, Other Aspects of Trade, 257; 3, Reciprocal Demand and Supply, 258; 4, Trade between Money-and-Market Economies, 260; 5, The Determination of Exchange Rates, 264; 6, The Balance of International Payments, 267.

Chapter 16. THE INTERNATIONAL MONETARY SYSTEM 275

   1, National Monetary Systems, 275; 2, The International Gold Standard, 277; 3, Key-Currency Systems, 281; 4, The Bretton Woods System, 283; 5, The Bretton Woods System in Operation, 1945-1973, 286; 6, Generalized Floating, 290.

Part Five. Some Contentious Issues

Chapter 17. POPULATION, RESOURCES, AND THE ECOLOGY . . 295

   1, Population Fears, 295; 2, Resources and the Environment, 299; 3, Pollution, 306; 4, Disputed Conclusions, 309. Selected Readings, 312.

Chapter 18. INFLATION AND UNEMPLOYMENT 315

1, The Policy Issue, 315; 2, The Case for Focusing on Inflation, 316; 3, The Effects of a Cumulative Government Deficit, 317; 4, The Case against Focusing on Inflation, 319; 5, Some Proposed Remedies, 321; 6, Ending the Budget Deficit, 323; 7, A Modest Suggestion, 325; 8, Balance-of-Payments Problems, 327; 9, Is This Argument Persuasive? 330. Selected Readings, 331.

Chapter 19   THREE OTHER POLICY ISSUES 333

1, The Ownership of the Means of Production, 333; 2, Concentration of Ownership, 337; The Third-World Debt Problem: Who Should Pay the Piper? 342.

ABOUT THE AUTHOR 351

INDEX 355

Tables

Table 3-1. Two Hypothetical Personal Demand Functions 33
Table 3-2. A Demand Schedule with Changing Elasticities 37

Table 4-1. Hypothetical Cost Data for an Individual Firm 48

Table 7-1. Gross National Product, Income and Expenditure 112

Table 12-1. A Hypothetical Example of Deposit Expansion 202
Table 12-2. A Hypothetical Example of Combined Credit and
            Income Expansion 218

Table 15-1. A Hypothetical Balance of International Payments 268

Charts

Figure 1-1. A Sample Chart: Speed and Elapsed Time 11

Figure 3-1. Utility Functions 27
Figure 3-2. Individual Demand Functions 34
Figure 3-3. Limiting Positions of Demand Functions 36

Figure 4-1. Total-Cost Functions 50
Figure 4-2. Average-Cost Functions 52
Figure 4-3. Determining Optimum Output 54
Figure 4-4. The Individual Firm's Supply Function 57

Figure 5-1. Individual Demands and Market Demand 65
Figure 5-2. Market Demand and Supply: Stable Equilibrium 68
Figure 5-3. Market Demand and Supply: Unstable Equilibrium 71
Figure 5-4. One Firm's Demand for Labour 74
Figure 5-5. A Conjectural Labour-Supply Curve 77

Figure 6-1. Industry Revenue and Cost Curves 86
Figure 6-2. Simple and Discriminating Monopoly 89
Figure 6-3. A Decreasing-Cost Industry 93
Figure 6-4. Discriminating Monopoly: Additional Sales at Lower Prices . 95

Figure 7-1. A Simple Dynamic Econometric Model 119

Figure 8-1. Monopolistic Competition: Kinked Demand Curves 122
Figure 8-2. Equilibrium with Product Differentiation 127

Figure 10-1. A One-Man Production Frontier 157
Figure 10-2. A Community Production Frontier 160

Figure 11-1. A Consumption and a Saving Function 182
Figure 11-2. Income Determination 184

Figure 15-1. Comparative Advantage in International Trade 254
Figure 15-2. International Trade under Diminishing Returns 256
Figure 15-3. Reciprocal Demand and Supply 259
Figure 15-4. Reciprocal Demand and Supply:
                  The Foreign-Exchange Market 262

Preface

This book is addressed to readers who are making their first acquaintance with economics. Its approach is partly historical, because the path economic analysis has followed is part of the explanation of where it stands now. Also, it is primarily oriented towards the application of economic analysis to public policy decisions. This reflects my personal concern throughout my career, for my serious interest in economics began in 1932, when The Great Depression of the 1930's truncated an intended career in mathematics and physics. Accordingly, I have little patience with the direction in which many economists are now directing their efforts, as if the subject was merely an intellectual exercise or a parlour game. If it is not addressed to designing and implementing effective public policies to promote the general good, what use is it?

If you are not already aware of it, you will soon find that economists do not all agree about the conclusions to be drawn from their analysis. This has always been so—many schools of economic thought have vied for attention in the past, and they still do. In part this has been due to the complexity of the subject, and the different angles from which it can be approached. When it comes to policy conclusions, however, many of the differences do not stem from serious disagreements in analysis or disputes over facts, but from different opinions about what is desirable and about how best to achieve a given end. Most policy decisions will affect the economy in more than one way, some of which may be undesirable; deciding whether the good effects outweigh the bad usually involves complex *value judgements*, which have little to do with economics as such, and on which equally honest opinions may sincerely differ.

My presentation attempts to be as neutral as possible with respect to different schools of economic thought, and to give an account that would be acceptable to most present-day economists. This attempt breaks down somewhat in Part Three, however; nowadays the economics profession is divided rather sharply between monetarists and non-monetarists, with lesser divisions within each major group, and you will have no trouble discerning that I am not a monetarist. Nevertheless I attempt to give as fair an account of the monetarist position as I can in Chapter 14. In the end, you will have to make up your own mind about it.

Part Five is devoted to a selection of policy issues, on which you may try out your new analytical tools and see what conclusions you will come to. My commitment to such matters (other than monetarism) is kept resolutely in check in the first four Parts, because I think you should become reasonably familiar with the major tools of economic analysis before putting them to work on contentious topics. Premature excursions in this field would risk infecting you with my personal prejudices and value judgements, before you were in a position to form your own opinion of their validity. My intention was to present the issues as neutrally as possible in Part Five, too, but my resolve broke down completely as I got into it.

Section 3 of Chapter 19 is clearly partisan, for example. More importantly, Chapter 18 attacks what I consider to be the major policy challenge of this generation, every bit as serious as that of The Great Depression of the 1930's, and I do not try to disguise my opinions. In fact, as I have spelled out elsewhere, I am highly critical of most of today's economists for failing to identify and attack the problem.

Demand management gave us 20 or 25 years of unparalleled prosperity and growth after World War II, which was brought to an end by spiralling inflation. It is now clear that, as presently practiced, it has inadequate defences against this malady, despite its long record of success in difficult times. One might reasonably have expected that the economics profession would long ago have focused its best efforts on finding a remedy for inflation that did not entail severe levels of unemployment. Instead, most members have been willing to throw over all that we have learned since the 1930's and revert to the same anti-inflation techniques that would have been used 100 or 200 years ago. The only difference is that they can no longer be employed with the full rigour that would have been displayed in earlier times, because the public will not stand for the social costs that would entail.

Toronto Canada
A.N.M.

April 1992

Acknowledgements

In acknowledging his debts to others, an author faces a formidable task—he will surely be able to identify some of them, but he is equally sure to be unaware of the ultimate source of some of his ideas and inspirations. Debts to family, teachers, and former colleagues are an obvious starting point. I fondly remember my parents for starting me on my way, and I particularly appreciate the support and encouragement my wife Rosalind has given me throughout my career.

In the 1920's the Canadian Prairies still retained the optimism of an expanding frontier, and most teachers in the primary and secondary schools I attended in Regina were young, enthusiastic, able, and dedicated. At Queen's University in the 1930's I am particularly conscious of my debts to Dean Matheson and others in the Mathematics Department and Professors F.A. Knox and W.A. Mackintosh in the Economics Department. At Harvard from 1945 to 1947 the contributions of Professors A.H. Hansen, J.A. Schumpeter, and John Williams stand out.

The International Monetary Fund gave me invaluable experiences of financial institutions and international financial affairs, and international friendships. I particularly value the example set by E.M. Bernstein as an able and conscientious international civil servant, the pleasure of working with the late George A. Blowers in Libya and Saudi Arabia, and later the friendship of Frank A. Southard. My former colleagues at The Toronto-Dominion Bank and at Atkinson College also deserve thanks for their contributions.

The pages that follow incorporate some material that has already appeared in print, sometimes in almost exactly the same words. This includes articles published in one or more issues of *Banca Nazionale del Lavoro Quarterly Review*, *Queen's Quarterly*, and *Policy Options*. It also includes *The Fearsome Dilemma: Simultaneous Inflation and Unemployment*, published by University Press of America.

I would be very remiss if I did not also acknowledge the help given me by the Facilities and Support Services of Atkinson College at York University, without which publication would not have been possible. Assisted by Rita Marinucci, Hazel O'Loughlin-Vidal converted my wordprocessed manuscript into camera-ready copy.

Part One

Getting Started

Chapter 1

Bedrock Fundamentals

1. What Is Economics?

Economics may be defined as the study of how, and to what extent, mankind's wants are provided for, and how the things available to satisfy those wants are shared among the many individuals and groups that make up human society. Some of these wants consist of tangible goods such as food, clothing, houses, and automobiles, others are intangibles such as the services of lawyers, doctors, dentists, teachers, and spiritual advisers.

A further distinction may be made between tangible goods that we consume directly, such as food, and those that yield services that we enjoy, such as the shelter provided by a house. For many purposes, however, we speak of our wants being satisfied by the "goods and services" produced in the economy, without bothering to treat them separately.

2. How Economists Reason.

The functioning of even a relatively simple society of hunters and gatherers is highly complex, for it is closely intertwined with that society's cultural and social structure; in a modern money-and-market economy the complexity is almost indescribable. The technique economists use to reduce this maze of interrelationships to manageable proportions is to devise "models" of the real world, i.e. simplified schematic representations of it, limited to the features and forces that seem most important for the purpose of the particular problem that is under study.

An economic model may be likened to a diagram that a physical scientist might use to explain the structure of a molecule, or certain features of a living cell — it may not be "realistic", but it helps to explain certain features of reality. It may attempt to deal with the entire economy, or with only one small part of it, or anything in between. It may take the form of a merely literary description, a set of formal relationships like algebraic equations, or an econometric structure (i.e. a set of mathematical equations designed to give quantitative answers to specific questions).

Any model will inevitably be an *over*simplification of reality — it has to be, in order to compress the subject sufficiently for the human mind to grapple with. It must make many more-or-less-arbitrary assumptions about the working of the economy (or that part of the economy it is concerned with), which will identify the features and forces that are considered most important for the purpose of the analysis, and it will suppose that everything else in the economy is unaffected by anything that happens within the confines of the model.

This is technically known as the *ceteris paribus* assumption, literally "other things equal". We will usually refer to it as the "*if...*" assumption: *if* such-and-such conditions are met, *then* we can conclude so-and-so. The considerations that are important for one analytical purpose may not be significant for other purposes, of course. As long as their assumptions and definitions are not actually contradictory, therefore, two or more models may support and enlarge on one another, even though they do not make exactly the same assumptions or deal with exactly the same features of the economy, for each may illustrate a different facet of reality.

It is especially important to recognize that the conclusions derived from any particular model are no better than the assumptions on which the model is based — and some important assumptions may be merely implied rather than stated explicitly. Any process of reasoning is like a sausage machine: the quality of the product depends almost entirely on what goes into it, as long as the operator is reasonably competent.

All conclusions must therefore be carefully scrutinized before being applied in practice, and adjusted or qualified to take account of the factors that have been ignored in the analysis. The *ceteris paribus* or "*if...*" assumption is an indispensable tool of analysis, for it permits the effects of particular factors to be studied in isolation. However, it is a very treacherous ally when it comes to practical applications: you can't expect those other things to remain unchanged when you apply your conclusions in the real world. Perhaps your original model can be enlarged to take account of some of the missing elements, perhaps a supplementary model will cover them reasonably well, but perhaps the best you can do will be to make some sort of collective value judgement about how far your conclusions can be trusted or how they can be modified.

By the same token, a major test of any model is how closely its explicit and implicit assumptions mirror the facts of life in the real world. This raises the question of the trade-off between realism and tractability: the more realistic the model, the less tractable it is likely to be.

The most effective criticism of any model, therefore, is another model that is more realistic yet not too complex for useful applications. And of course that test involves value judgements about which opinions may greatly differ. Among other things, this helps to explain why the policy prescriptions of any two economists may diverge sharply, even though they may be in full agreement about the factual material on which they base their conclusions.

3. The Factors of Production.

One of the useful generalizations employed by virtually every economist is to classify all the human and material resources that contribute to the production of economic goods and services (i.e. all goods and services that are not free goods like air) into three categories, known as the *factors of production*: labour, land, and capital. Each of these categories can of course be subdivided into many subcategories, which may be useful for analyzing more detailed problems, but for other purposes it may be necessary to focus only on the three major categories. Individual workers or groups of workers, plots of land, or pieces of capital equipment may be identified as *agents of production*.

Labour earns wages, land earns rent, capital equipment earns interest or some similar compensation. To the enterprise that employs these factors in a productive process the payments to them are *factor costs*; to those who receive them they are *factor returns*. The enterprise may of course incur costs for the purchase of materials and supplies as well as factor costs, but all such costs can be resolved into the same components for the supplier, so ultimately the cost of all goods and services can be resolved into factor costs (or factor returns).

"Labour" as a factor of production means all services rendered by individuals through either mental or physical effort. It includes the work done by a farmer or a gardener digging up a patch of earth, planting and tending a crop, and eventually harvesting it; by a clerk or typist in an office, or the office manager, or senior staff; by a salesman or sales manager or sales officer at any level; by a worker in a factory or a retail or wholesale enterprise or by a supervisor at any level; by a proprietor, partner, or corporate executive; by a doctor or a dentist or a lawyer or a teacher or other professional; and so on.

The earnings of this factor, "wages" in the terminology indicated above, must therefore be interpreted to include not only wages and salaries but also sales commissions, the wages of management, executive bonuses, professional fees, and all forms of personal remuneration.

"Entrepreneurship" is sometimes classed as a separate factor of production. Entrepreneurs (literally, "undertakers" or "doers") are people who display initiative in setting up new business ventures or introducing new ideas or in some other way "taking charge" of an enterprise; they hire other factors of production in order to put their plans into operation. They do indeed perform an important function — especially in the model of pure competition, which we will describe shortly — but the same is true of many other types of skilled labour. Furthermore, it is difficult to decide where mere management and administration ends and true entrepreneurship begins. For the most part, therefore, we will avoid drawing a sharp distinction between the two skills.

"Land" in the sense here used really means all forms of natural resources, and therefore lumps together a lot of very different things. Farmland normally produces recurring crops that are consumed directly or that go into the production of other goods; under good management it can continue to do so indefinitely. Mineral deposits on the other hand are wasting assets that will sooner or later be exhausted; new deposits may be discovered from time to time, but they too are wasting assets. Some minerals can be re-used many times once they are produced, it is true, though even in these cases there is likely to be some unavoidable wastage.

Timber resources can be managed to produce perpetual crops when conditions are favourable, or under other conditions may be depleted like mineral deposits. Water resources may also depleted, e.g. by the drawing down of existing lakes and underground reserves, or treated as a perpetual resource, e.g. by using current flows for irrigation or power-generation.

A third important category is land used as the site of industrial or commercial activity or for residential housing. In this case convenience of location is the major consideration—nearness to markets or transportation facilities or sources of supply, for example.

The general term for the return to this factor of production is "rent"—or, more correctly, "pure rent", to distinguish it from the "rental" you may pay for a house or apartment or other property, which also includes returns to any capital structures or other improvements. "Rent" is fairly easily identified, in principle at least, when applied to farmland or the like, or to the "situation rent" paid for the use of a conveniently-located property, though even here there may be serious practical problems. In the case of the pure rent of a wasting asset, however, there are theoretical as well as practical problems. Nevertheless these concepts are useful generalizations.

"Capital" as a factor of production means "real" or physical capital, not money capital. The technical description is "produced means of production", i.e. tools or machines or buildings that are themselves the products of the overall productive system and are in turn used in further production. The term includes everything from the simplest tools to the most elaborate machinery and the specialized buildings in which it is housed. Houses and consumer durables like automobiles and mechanical refrigerators are capital in this sense—consumer capital, yielding services directly to their owners.

Returns to capital may take the form of interest, rentals, dividends, retained business profits, capital gains, or some combination of these elements. The value of the shelter obtained by the owner-occupier of a house may be considered to be an imputed rental.

Many economists have stressed the categorical difference between land and capital, primarily on the grounds that capital is man-made whereas land is not. Since capital is reproducible, the argument runs, more will be produced until the money spent for another unit would earn more if it were lent at interest instead. On the other hand, if a particular type of capital goods does not earn a return at least equal to the rate of interest, new production will cease until the wearing out of old equipment makes new production profitable again; hence the stock of capital is regulated by the rate of interest. Land on the other hand is not reproducible; the rent of land is determined by its contribution to the productive process (as explained later). The interest rate can not affect the *stock* of land, merely its *value*.[1]

Actually, there are several considerations that blunt this argument. The practical difficulty of identifying pure rent in the real world is one, though that in itself would not be sufficient grounds for rejecting it — many economic concepts are hard to identify in practice yet are useful in helping us to understand the workings of the economy. A second consideration is the fact that land *can* be created to some extent: much of the Netherlands consists of land reclaimed from the sea, and "made land" on a small scale is often a by-product of dredging harbours to improve navigation.

However, a much more telling argument arises from an ingenious model devised by a famous economist, Alfred Marshall, about a hundred years ago. He postulated that there was a fall of meteoric stones that were useful in certain productive processes (say, for grinding operations), and invented the term quasi-rents to

---

[1] The value of land is found by capitalizing its pure rent at the current rate of interest. Since a potential buyer has the option of lending money at interest, he or she will be unwilling to pay more than the capitalized rent, and the competition of other potential buyers will ensure that the payment is no less.

describe their earnings. By varying the assumptions about whether they were all found at once or more could be found by diligent search, whether they were indestructible or gradually wore out in use, and that sort of thing, his model showed that the quasi-rents of the stones could resemble the pure rent of land or the returns to capital goods or anything in between.

Marshall also showed that, once a given capital good was produced, the return on it was a quasi-rent and might remain below the interest return on the cost of producing it for some time—a useful insight into the relationship between the values of capital goods and the rate of interest. As a practical matter, therefore, there is much to be said for lumping land and capital together as productive property.

4. Systems of Economic Decisionmaking.

There are three basic economic decisions to be made in any society: what to produce, how to produce it, and how to share the products. There are many things that could be produced even in a very simple society; which, or what combination, will give the greatest satisfaction? Also, there are usually several ways of producing a given good or service, which generally involve the factors of production in different proportions (e.g., capital-intensive or labour-intensive techniques); which will be the most advantageous? And how do you decide who gets how much of each product—not forgetting that everyone does not necessarily like the same things?

History demonstrates that there are many ways of making each of these decisions, including custom or tradition, authoritarian choice, collective planning, the market mechanism, and various combinations of them. Even today there are simple societies of hunters and gatherers in which custom and tradition are the major determinants of economic activity—and the results may be very good under the circumstances, for custom and tradition perpetuate the wisdom of past experience.

In some cases the distribution of the total output seems to have been, or to still be, on the basis of personal need, more or less like the distribution of real income among members of the same family. Autocratic rulers have often dictated the allocation of resources to projects for their own advantage or glorification. Many countries in Eastern Europe and in Asia still rely largely on central planning—or did until very recently.

In most of these cases, however, the money-and-market mechanism seems to play or to have played a part: trading is an obvious way of gaining mutual benefits, and some form of money seems to have been invented spontaneously in almost every society whenever the volume of trading became great enough to make barter too cumbersome.

It would be illuminating to know more about how the three basic economic decisions were made in ancient Egypt, or in Greece, or in Babylon—or by the Incas or the Mayans or the Aztecs in the Western Hemisphere. All of these were pretty sophisticated civilizations, and the same "real" costs were incurred in their productive processes regardless of whether money or any other explicit measure of value was used, though they may not have been recognized at the time; how were they reflected in the prices of the products, or in the relative values at which they traded? How did the owners of the factors of production (including free labourers as well as the owners of slaves) get paid?

Economists and economic historians have not shown much interest in this sort of question. The study of comparative economic systems is now usually confined to money-and-market economies, planned economies, and mixed economies. This book will accept that limitation, and will be addressed to economic decisionmaking in what we choose to call Western Society — those countries in which the money-and-market system dominates the productive process, even though it is usually modified by governmental policymaking.

5. Five Major Verities.

In any economy there are five major verities. The first is that, in any given period of time, "real" income equals "real" output (the sum total of all goods and services produced, measured in physical quantities rather than money). Income consists of the additional goods and services received by or accruing to the society as a whole, excluding anything attributable to the using up of wealth or resources inherited from the past.

Strictly speaking, the capital value of newly-discovered resources should not be included in current income, even if they have been discovered as a result of conscious search or exploration, nor should there be any deduction for fortuitous losses of capital or resources due to such things as natural disasters; these should be treated as changes in capital endowment rather than as current income or loss. (However, some accounting conventions do treat them as income, and as a rule it involves no serious distortion.) On the other hand the deliberate depletion of natural resources or the amortizing of capital costs as part of the normal productive process should be shown as deductions from gross income.

The second major verity is that there are no identifiable limits to the amount of goods and services we could consume in a given period, *if* they were available to us and if we had time to adjust our habits to their availability, but there are clear and finite limits to the total output that can be produced in any period, because the human and other resources that can be put to use are limited. The workforce must be somewhat less than the total existing population; they can use only the tools, machinery, and buildings already produced; they can apply their energy and equipment only to the natural resources known and available to them.

This is sometimes called "the" economic problem, and can be summed up in a short phrase: limited means, unlimited wants. Apparently air is the only commodity that is freely available to every individual in quantities that are undiminished by the claims of others (the only "free good", as distinct from "economic goods").

The third verity is that the production of the vast majority of products requires the combined use of two or more factors of production, as already noted.

Fourth, most factors of production can be used for more than one purpose. Since the supply of any one factor is limited, it follows that increased production of any particular good or service usually means that the production of some other good or service must be reduced. Among other things, this gives rise to a useful concept known as opportunity cost: the cost of (say) planting wheat in a particular field in a particular season is that you can't plant barley or corn or oats or something else in that field that season. Presumably you choose to plant wheat because you expect it to give you a larger net return than available alternatives.

Fifth, since most products require the coöperation of more than one factor of production and most factors can be used for more than one purpose, it follows that the most efficient use of resources to satisfy human wants can only be determined in the context of the values the society puts on the many alternative goods and services that are or might be produced. This leads to the concept of "general equilibrium", which can be glibly summed up as "everything depends on everything else". In either barter terms or money terms, the value and the quantity of every product and every factor of production influences and is influenced by the value and the quantity of every other product or factor.

This is often presented as a set of simultaneous equations in which the quantities and prices of all factors and all products are determined. It means that the costs of factors A, B, and C do not "determine" the prices of products F, G, H, ..., and the quantities of the factors used in production do not "determine" the quantities of the product turned out, but that the costs and quantities of A, B, and C and the prices and quantities of F, G, H, ... are mutually determined.

6. An Introduction to Charts and Graphs.

Economists make considerable use of charts and graphs of various kinds, because the human eye is very good at judging relative sizes, so graphic representations are often helpful in explaining the relationships among *economic variables*. (A variable is an object which may *vary* numerically, either in relation to other variables or in the course of the passage of time.) Charts and graphs may look somewhat daunting at first, but it is really quite easy to make friends with them.

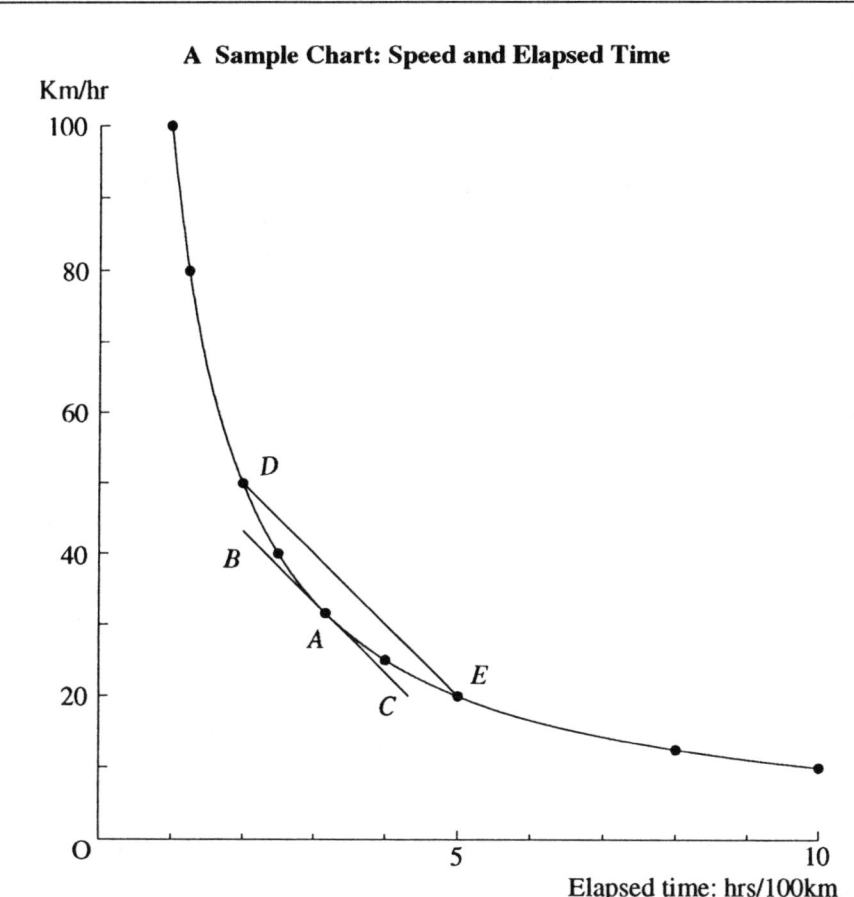

Figure 1-1. Speed is represented on the north-south axis, and the time taken to run 100 kilometers at that speed is represented on the east-west axis. The chart shows, for example, that the required time increases dramatically if the speed falls much below about 30 kilometers an hour, but on the other hand a substantial increase in speed from an already-high level does not save much time.

The three main types are bar charts, pie charts, and line charts. A bar chart uses vertical or horizontal stripes to represent two or more variables that are to be compared, either at a given point in time or at different times. A pie chart is a circle divided in segments, like the slices of a piece of pie, to show the relative sizes of the components into which a given total may be divided. A line chart uses a line to show how the size of one variable is related to the size of another, or how its value changes over time.

Most charts are two-dimensional. One axis (we will call it the north-south axis) runs from an arbitrary zero point towards the top of the page. The other (the east-west axis) runs to the east across the page from the zero point. The double-zero point is often labelled with a capital "O", meaning "Origin".

Some charts have a negative section on one or both axes, running west and south from the zero point. A few achieve a three-dimensional effect in some way; you may imagine a third axis through the zero point, perpendicular to the page.

In this book we will usually confine ourselves to relatively simple two-dimensional line charts. Figure 1-1 is an introductory sample, which needs no knowledge of economics to understand: it shows the relation between the speed at which you travel (measured in kilometers per hour on the north-south axis) and the number of hours it would take you to travel 100 kilometers at that speed (or the elapsed time), measured on the east-west axis.

Of course, you don't need the chart to tell you that the elapsed time will be one hour at 100 kilometers per hour, but ten hours if you travel at only 10 kilometers per hour. However, the chart does show you things you might not realize otherwise, without a bit of arithmetic. For example, it brings out very clearly the fact that the elapsed time will increase dramatically if you let your speed fall much below about 30 kilometers per hour, whereas speeding up from 80 to 100 kilometers per hour only saves you 15 minutes.

Also, you can visually interpolate (find intermediate values) between any two values of either variable. Thus if you want to know how long it would take you to travel this distance at 35 kilometres an hour, pick the spot half way between 30 and 40 on the north-west axis, run your eye easterly across the page until you come to the curve, then southerly to the east-west axis, and you will see that the time you want is a bit under 3 hours. If you want to know how fast you must travel to make the distance in four hours, trace a path in the opposite direction, starting at 4 on the east-west axis.

Notice the seven plotted points, and the smooth curve drawn through them. This is how most economic line charts are drawn: only a few points may be accurately known, and a continuous curve is fitted to them. In this particular case we know exactly how to calculate any number of intermediate points, so we could plot the curve to any desired degree of accuracy, but that is not always so.

In this case we know that both the speed and the corresponding travel time can be varied in indefinitely-small gradations, hence it is quite proper to show the curve as a solid line. This is not always so, either. In Chapter 3 we will note that some of the things you may want to buy are very "lumpy". For example, you can only buy radios or automobiles or that sort of thing in whole units: a curve representing various quantities purchased (as in Figure 3-1 on page 27) would be meaningless except at whole numbers of radios or autos. In such cases it is customary to plot the precise points, and either omit the curve altogether or draw it as a broken line.[2]

Now observe the line *BC*, tangent to the curve at *A*. This gives the *slope* of the curve at that point, that is the rate at which the relationship between the two variables is changing: in this case, an increase of one tenth of an hour in elapsed time for every drop of one kilometer per hour in speed. The line *DE* is a *chord* of the curve, which gives the average slope between points *D* and *E*; the two slopes happen to be the same, because the curve is symmetrical about the point *A*.

Finally, a word of acknowledgement to those of you who are familiar with mathematical concepts. You will recognize the north-south axis as the ordinate, the east-west axis as the abscissa, and that the figure is limited to the quadrant in which both ordinates and abscissae are positive. The curve itself is of course a rectangular hyperbola, the equation of which is $xy = 100$ or $y = 100/x$; its slope at any point is given by *dy/dx*.

---

[2] However, if the chart refers to a large number of radios or automobiles, it is permissible to use a solid curve. In that case interpolated figures are taken to refer to whole numbers of radios or autos, not fractional units.

Part Two

Microeconomics

Chapter 2

The Model of Pure Competition

Fatherly advice: The full implications of many apparently-straightforward statements in this chapter may not be apparent on first reading. Don't worry too much, therefore, if some things in it puzzle you, for you will probably want to look back at them from time to time as you proceed with the rest of Part Two.

1. The Two Major Branches of Economics.

Economic analysis can be conveniently divided into two major branches, microeconomcs and macroeconomics. Microeconomics is the study of how income is earned and spent. It deals with such things as the supply of and the demand for particular products, why diamonds are valued more highly than bread, what determines wage rates, why rent is paid for land, how the earnings attributable to a particular piece of capital equipment can be calculated, and that sort of thing. Macroeconomics is the study of national totals. It deals with major economic quantities like employment, income, and the general price level in a nation or region.

These terms are relatively new. They came into common use only in the 1930's, inspired by the new economic theories associated with the name of John Maynard Keynes, which are discussed in Chapter 11. However, the two lines of thought can be traced back to earliest times. They are complementary, and a proper grasp of the functioning of any economy requires an understanding of both.

In earlier days the major macro concepts were less clearly defined than they are now, and there was little or no statistical material available about most of them. By force of circumstances, therefore, most economic analysis was directed to the study of the productive process, the relative values of the goods produced, and the distribution of the benefits among the factors of production. By the 1930's the basic macro concepts had been substantially clarified, and a considerable volume of statistical material about them was being collected. New theories were built on this basis, and thereafter the glamourous policy advances they promised largely overshadowed the more prosaic achievements of micro analysis.

Until 1933 the principal model available to economists and economic policymakers was the model of pure competition, though separate models were also used to deal with pure monopoly and certain other situations thought of as special cases. ("Pure" competition means that no market participant has any power to influence the market price, "pure" monopoly means that no other seller offers the same product or any similar product.)

It will be obvious enough as we go along that this model has serious limitations. Even though it can not claim to be "complete" or "realistic", however, it does describe important forces that are identifiably at work in the real world. A modern version of its microeconomics is summarized in Chapters 3, 4, and 5, and its macroeconomics in Chapter 10.

Any microeconomic model must square its procedures with the fact that "everything depends on everything else", as noted at the end of Chapter 1. To get around this difficulty we may begin by noting that, if the economy as a whole is in a state of general equilibrium, then every particular market must also be in equilibrium — the markets in which goods and services are bought by ultimate consumers, the markets in which factors of production are bought by producers, and all the intermediate markets in which raw materials and semi-processed goods are bought and sold in the productive process.

Conversely, if every individual market is in equilibrium then the economy as a whole must be in general equilibrium. It follows that, by assuming that the economy is in general equilibrium and by invoking our old friend the *"if..."* assumption, we are entitled to examine the conditions for equilibrium in the market for any particular good or service. By a reasonable extension of this line of reasoning we may consider effects of small departures from equilibrium in a particular market, as long as those departures are within an acceptable margin of error.[1]

---

[1] This may be described as "particular equilibrium analysis". It is an example of "partial" equilibrium, in which some variables are "held constant" and only a relatively few are allowed to vary. If you are familiar with differential calculus, you will see that partial and general equilibrium resemble partial and total differentiation. If differential calculus is not your thing, first think of some three-dimensional figure—say, a sphere. Next, imagine the sphere being cut by a saw moving parallel to the ground. Finally, think of the surface created by the saw-cut: it will be a circular surface on each of the parts into which you have divided the sphere. You have just "held constant" the vertical dimension of your sphere. The size of the circular surface will depend on where

2. The Circular Flow.

Any model of a money-and-market system is most easily understood in terms of a circular flow of payments in one direction and a flow of goods and services in the other direction. As consumers spend their incomes for whatever they want, their payments put command over resources in the hands of their suppliers. These suppliers in turn use the money they thus receive to buy raw materials or partly-processed goods from other producers and to buy the services of whatever factors of production they need in order to produce the finished goods they sell to the public.

The flow of spending thus set in motion ultimately ends up as payments for the various factors of production that have participated in the productive process — i.e. as payments to the individual labourers and owners of productive resources. These people are the very same consumers we started with, and the payments they receive (their factor returns) constitute the income out of which they make their payments.

In effect, consumers use their money payments as a sort of proportional-representation system of voting for the goods and services they want. The flow of payments thus set in motion (the spending stream) regulates the productive process and the allocation of resources. Any money that is not spent on consumption is considered to be saved.

Savings may be invested directly in capital goods of some kind, as when a business firm reinvests some of its earnings in additional productive assets, or they may be held in the form of financial claims such as bank deposits, bonds, other securities, or even currency (hand-to-hand money) itself. In the first case they put resources in the hands of suppliers just like spending by consumers. In the second case the same thing is accomplished indirectly: the money is channelled through financial markets and financial institutions to borrowers who want to invest in more capital goods than their own savings will permit.

Ensuring that all savings are used to finance capital spending is important, if the circular flow of spending is to continue without interruption. In the version of the model that was generally accepted until the 1930's, it was thought that this would be done automatically by the rate of interest. We will hear more about this problem in due course, and will find that the balancing mechanism is much more compli-

---

you choose to cut the sphere, and by cutting it in a variety of different places you can get a pretty good idea of the properties of a sphere.

cated than that. For the time being, however, all we need to know is that there *is* a mechanism that ensures a match between saving and capital spending, even though it is not just the interest rate alone.

3. An Outline of the Model.

Three of the major assumptions on which the model of pure competition is based are often taken for granted rather than explicitly stated: (1) Productive resources (land and capital) are privately owned, and labourers are free to work or not as they choose (there is no slavery or serfdom or the like). (2) Everyone is free to contract out his (or her) services if he so wishes, or the services of his property, on the best terms he can find, and to associate with others for any legally-permitted purpose. (3) Contracts freely entered into are binding on all parties concerned. These three pillars of the free-enterprise system are sometimes abbreviated to private property, freedom of association, and the sanctity of contracts.

More explicitly, the model assumes that each individual offers or declines to offer the services at his (or her) command to entrepreneurs engaged in production, on such terms as his own assessment of his best interests dictates, and employs his earnings for satisfying his wants as he sees fit. Labourers (and, remember, that term includes everyone who works for any kind of remuneration) decide how long to work each day or week by balancing the attractions of additional leisure against the additional income they could earn by working a little longer.

There is free entry into all activities, in the sense that there are no arbitrary restrictions to prevent it, though not necessarily in the sense of being costless: some activities may require expensive equipment or a long period of training or other entry-fees. As for the productive process itself, the model assumes that every product is made in identical form by so many competing enterprises, and bought by so many purchasers, that no-one can influence its market price even if he (or she) withholds his entire supply or his entire demand.

Another important assumption is that all prices are flexible, and will respond quickly to "clear" all markets — that is, to bring supply and demand into balance by discouraging sellers and encouraging buyers or *vice versa*. Everyone must accept the market price for his goods or services or not sell at all, and must pay the market price for anything he buys, since he can not affect their prices in any way.

The macroeconomic system that emerges from these assumptions is a delicate balance of complex interacting forces. Consumers are sovereign — their wishes determine what will be produced and how resources will be allocated. All factors and agents of production are fully employed. As explained in the remaining chapters of this Part, they share the output in proportion to their marginal contributions to production. Competitive bidding for their services equalizes the return to each in all employments open to it, and ensures that each is used for those purposes that give the greatest satisfaction to consumers. The selfish search for profits leads to economic progress and spreads the gains among the general public.

It must be noted that the full rigour of the model of pure competition applies only in a long-run-equilibrium situation. By this is meant the situation that would exist at the end of an indefinitely-long period in which all existing distortions or disequilibria would work themselves out, and no new disturbances would be allowed to occur. The model does fully recognize that shocks and disturbances of various kinds can and do occur — workers lose their jobs because of changes in consumer tastes or technological advances and can not find new ones at once, investment mistakes are made, old plants become obsolete before their cost has been fully recovered, and so on. Equilibrating forces are set in motion automatically, however, and in due course will set matters right.

A useful technique for dealing with these adjustment problems is to identify several different time-periods—such as short-term and long-term, or perhaps a medium-term as well, the details of which can be set according to a particular purpose. This procedure helps to bring out certain important features of the model.

For example, in some cases you might want to use a very short period, in which the only possible adjustment would be for sellers to hold their products as unsold inventories in the hope of getting a higher price later, and for buyers to postpone purchases in the hope of paying less later. For other purposes you might define the short run as a period in which displaced labour could find new jobs but no sunk capital could be replaced; in that case you might identify the medium-term as a period in which certain short-lived capital goods could be replaced, and the long term as a period in which even the most durable capital would wear out and have to be replaced.

4. Perfect Competition.

We noted in section 3 of this chapter that *pure* competition means that no participant in the market has any semblance of monopoly power. Even in such a situation, however, other features of the real world may prevent the attainment of the optimum position envisaged in the model. The delays before the effects of disturbances can be eliminated is an example, in the short and medium term at least. Another example would be frictions in the adjustment mechanism itself — incomplete knowledge of available opportunities, human inertia, the cost in time and effort of making minor changes in existing practices, and that sort of thing.

Some of these features might persist even in the theoretical long-run-equilibrium position. A model that was free not only of monopolistic elements but also of these other impediments or *imperfections* used to be known as one of *perfect* competition — or sometimes as "pure and perfect" competition, for those who are meticulous in their language. The two terms are often used interchangeably nowadays, and no great harm is done thereby, but the distinction seems still worth making.

5. Policy Implications.

In the model of pure competition, consumers are sovereign. How they choose to spend their money in the satisfaction of their desires puts money in the hands of favoured suppliers and denies it to others, thus determining what will be produced and how resources will be allocated in the productive process. The clear and unmistakable implication is that any interference by government (or by any other body, such as a monopolist) could only result in harm to economic welfare.

It was recognized from the start, of course, that government had a legitimate rôle to play in police, regulatory, and other functions, but primarily as referee, to enforce the few necessary rules. Its accepted rôle did tend to grow over time, it is true, especially with the evolution of the principles of welfare economics (see section 5 of Chapter 7), but the basic presumption against government interference remained.

The fact that the returns to a given factor of production were equalized in all employments (in their final equilibrium positions) implies "equal pay for equal work", to use a modern cry for equality of pay for men and women in the same jobs — in other words, that all people with the same work-skills will be fairly treated. Similarly, it implies that the same categories of "land" or "capital" will get equivalent returns as well.

However, the implication of fairness in factor returns must not be overdone. For example, there is nothing in the model to suggest that market-determined returns to a given class of labour are fair in comparison with another: nothing to ensure "equal pay for work of equal value", to use another modern slogan. Nor is there anything to suggest that the real income jointly produced by wage-earners (in the broad sense that "wages" is used in Chapter 1) and the owners of productive property is fairly divided between the two major factors of production. The model simply says how income will be divided *if* certain conditions are met; the fairness of the division depends of value judgements, the basis of which lies outside the model and is open to various opinions.

Furthermore, in contemplating these implications we must be careful not to judge the policy decisions or recommendations of our predecessors on the basis of knowledge and experience that had not yet been accumulated. In any event our main concern should be to use the model of pure competition as a basis for more sophisticated models, and to use the best analytical tools we can devise for the analysis of current problems.

It does seem fair to observe, however, that economists long appeared to hold an overly-optimistic view of how quickly and effectively the automatic restorative forces in the economy can operate. Until the 1930's, or even later, many were prone to offer remedies for immediate problems that were based on long-run analysis. On the other hand it must be admitted that the opposite error — using short-term analysis to prescribe for long-term problems — has also been made in the past and is far from unknown today.

Chapter 3

Consumer Demand

1. Utility Functions.

The logical place to start fleshing out a description of the economy based on the model of pure competition is with the consumer, since he (or she) is seen to be sovereign. There is no room in the model for advertizing or other selling expenses by which his or her spending decisions can be influenced by others, for reasons that will become apparent when we look at the process of production. He has many needs and wants, of varying urgency; how does he decide what items to buy, and how much of each?

We usually think of food, clothing, and shelter as mankind's most basic needs, but even within each of these categories there are many things that will serve the purpose more or less adequately. Bread, oatmeal porridge, hominy grits, bologna, salt codfish, arctic char, porterhouse steaks, and caviar can all still the pangs of hunger, but different individuals consume them in very different proportions.

Two obvious reasons are differences in customs or in cultural patterns, and differences in incomes. In Scotland you would expect oatmeal to win out over hominy grits, but the other way around in southern U.S.A. In either country you would expect the rich to eat more steak than the poor. But a third important reason is differences in personal tastes: even in Scotland some people do not like oatmeal porridge, and even in Russia some people who enjoy relatively high incomes do not eat caviar.

Let us narrow things down somewhat by thinking of someone with a given income (we need not specify how much) and a given set of tastes, no doubt partly inherited from the society in which he or she has grown up but partly from his own past experience. He will find that most of these foods, and no doubt many others besides, give him some satisfaction—they have *utility* for him, or usefulness in meeting his needs, though in widely varying degree.

Now think of one particular food; say, bread of a specific type and quality. If he had no other food available, he could keep himself alive for a long time on bread alone (plus some water, of course). As long as he had at least enough bread to survive on, however, a point would come at any one meal or during any one day when each additional helping would be less satisfying (would yield less utility) than the one before. Indeed, a point might come at which consuming an additional portion would be actually unpleasant—it would yield him disutility instead of additional utility.

This illustrates what is technically known as *marginal utility*. It is our first encounter with the concept of *marginalism*, so we may as well pause to explain it, for it has wide application in microeconomics. The marginal unit of anything is the last unit added to a growing stock, including some things that can not really be stockpiled in a physical sense.[1]

The marginal utility derived from any consumable good is the utility obtained from consuming one more unit of it, measured as an addition to the total utility derived from all of it that has been consumed in the same period (say, during one meal or one day). Later we will encounter other marginal concepts, such as marginal cost (the cost of producing one more unit), marginal revenue (the revenue obtained from selling one more unit), and other applications of the marginal principle.

Before going any further, it should be noted that the phrase "the last unit added" should not be taken too literally: what we are really talking about is the effect of consuming one unit more rather than one unit less. When you are eating several slices of bread you can indeed identify the particular slice you ate last, but the utility you obtain from it does not come from the nature of that particular slice, it comes from the fact that it happens to be the last one you ate. Presumably one slice of bread is as good as another from the same loaf, so you would have gotten more utility from it if you had eaten it sooner, and some other slice would have provided the marginal addition to your utility.

Getting back to our main argument, a consumer normally has access to a wide choice of foods to satisfy his or her hunger, and access to many other things to

---

[1] The marginal concept was originally derived from a mathematical relationship, though you don't need to be a mathematician to understand it. Technically, the curve in Part A of Figure 3-1 can be derived from that in Part B by differential calculus, or that in Part B can be derived from the one in Part A by integral calculus: the value you read off at any given point in the first is the slope of the curve at the corresponding point in the second. All that matters for our purposes is the fact that the strict mathematical interpretation of marginalism applies only if the amounts of the additions are truly infinitesimal—if they "approach zero", as a mathematician would say.

satisfy other needs, wants, and whims. Nevertheless he will find that the same thing is true of each of them too: increasing consumption brings diminishing marginal utility.

Part A of Figure 3-1 illustrates our hypothetical consumer's *marginal utility function* for some particular good, i.e. the relationship between how much of it he consumes and the utility of each additional unit consumed. (The illustration is in graphic form, but alternatively it might be in the form of a schedule or table, or a mathematical expression, or perhaps in some other form.) The quantity consumed is measured along the east-west axis in physical units, the utility derived from consuming each additional unit is measured along the north-south axis on some arbitrary scale.

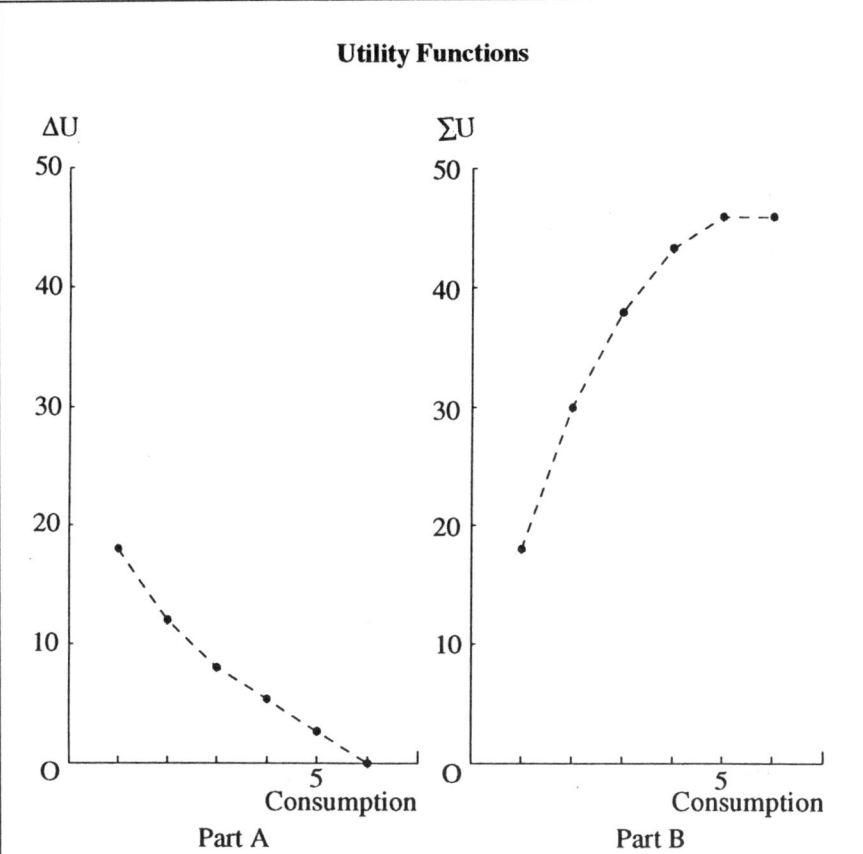

Figure 3-1. Part A illustrates Marginal Utility (ΔU); additional units of a particular good yield a hypothetical consumer less and less utility, measured on an arbitrary scale of satisfaction. Part B illustrates Total Utility (ΣU); it increases less and less rapidly, until it levels off at 46 units.

In this case we suppose the first unit consumed yields utility of 18 on this scale, and that each of the next three units yields two-thirds much as the one before it; thereafter the marginal utility drops in a straight line to zero at the sixth unit. The north-south axis has been marked "ΔU", meaning "increment of utility"; the Greek letter delta (Δ) is commonly used by mathematicians to mean a small increase in the value of a particular variable.

Part B of Figure 3-1 shows the *total utility* our imaginary consumer derives from this particular good: 18 units of utility if he (or she) consumes only one unit of it, 30 for two, 38 for three, and so on, to a maximum of 46. In this case the north-south axis has been marked "ΣU"; the Greek letter sigma (Σ) is commonly used to mean "the sum of".

There are two things to note immediately about these diagrams. First, the dots at each level of consumption indicate that the good is a "lumpy" one: you can not buy less than one whole egg at a time, or one toothbrush, one radio, or the like. On the other hand many products can be bought in fractions of a unit, perhaps almost infinitesimally small, like grains of sugar; in such cases you may legitimately draw a smooth curve through the dots, as indicated by the broken lines in the diagrams.

As a practical matter you can always use a smooth curve (or a mathematical formula, if you like mathematical formulas), as long as the product is divisible in reasonably small gradations. For lumpy products, however, the "curves" or functions are discontinuous and really exist only at the indicated points.

Second, neither figure says anything about how utility would be affected if consumption of the good were extended beyond six units. Would the consumption of each additional unit add exactly nothing to utility, indicating that the consumer was entirely indifferent as to whether he consumed more or not? In that case the curve in Part A of Figure 3-1 would be identical with the east-west axis to the east of six units, and that in Part B would be a straight line at 46 units of utility.

Or would additional consumption after six units be actually distasteful? In that case the marginal utility curve would fall below the east-west axis, and the total utility curve would turn downward.

Similar questions arise about consumption of less than one full unit, if the good is not a lumpy one. Projecting the dotted lines northwesterly from the value at one unit in Part A (or southwesterly in Part B) might give us a rough idea of what might happen for a little less than one unit, but what about the consumption of a very small quantity? Would it yield a very great utility in proportion to its size? Then the marginal utility curve might rise higher and higher as the amount consumed declined, never quite touching the north-south axis.

Or would the satisfaction from consuming such a small amount be so small as to be negligible? In that case the marginal utility curve would meet the north-south axis at a finite point, perhaps a quite low one.

There are no pat answers to these questions. You can easily imagine products for which one of these possibilities seems fairly realistic, others for which the answer would be quite different.

As a practical matter, however, these niceties are unimportant. No-one really tries to derive marginal-utility or total-utility curves for individual consumers, they are just devices to aid in understanding consumer behaviour. Even for this purpose we are usually interested in only the portion of the curve in the vicinity of the quantity actually consumed in given circumstances.

2. Utility and Income-Allocation.

Now let us endow our imaginary consumer with a given amount of income, which he or she proceeds to spend to meet not only his basic needs for food, clothing, and shelter but also his wants and desires for the enjoyment of life. As part of our general *"if..."* assumption we will suppose that he has "given tastes", i.e. a set of likes and dislikes he has inherited or acquired in the past, which remain unchanged for the time being. In addition we will specifically postulate that production is based on "the given state of the arts", meaning that the general body of technical knowledge used in the productive process is unchanged, no new inventions or innovations are introduced, and no new products appear on the market.

Let us temporarily disregard the possibility that this consumer of ours might decide to invest some of his or her money in capital equipment, or buy securities, or save in some other way, and let us look just at what he spends on current consumption. Since he spends money only in order to consume, and since the things he buys must have utility for him (otherwise why would he buy them?), we can attach utility to the money he earns. We can therefore visualize both the total utility he will obtain from his spending and the marginal utility of the last dollar or pound or franc or peso he spends. Or perhaps we should say the last cent or penny or sou or centavo—believe it or not, there was a time when these small sums could really buy something useful!

If he or she knew all about total and marginal utility and always acted logically, we would expect him to manage his spending so that the last mite spent on each item would yield exactly as much utility as the last mite spent on every other item.

Of course, few if any consumers go about allocating their incomes in this "scientific" way. Nevertheless it is reasonable to suppose that they accomplish pretty much the same thing by a process of trial and error, even though they may never have heard of marginal utility. Especially with things you buy frequently, you will soon notice it if the last few dollars spent on A would give you more satisfaction if shifted to B, so consciously or unconsciously you will tend to adjust your spending pattern to give you equivalent marginal satisfaction from your spending on each item.

The main factors that interfere with this "equilibrium" pattern are the fact that some things come in rather expensive lumps, and the fact that some lumpy things may yield services over a considerable period of time.

Money spent on lumpy non-durable items like expensive restaurant meals may be justified by comparing the total utility they yield with the total utility the same amount of money would give if put to the best alternative uses in the same pay period.

In principle, the logical comparison for durable lumpy items is the same as for non-durables, i.e. to compare the total utility derived from them with the total derived from the best alternative uses of the funds. However, the exercise is complicated by having to compare utilities or benefits in different income-periods instead of at virtually the same moment of time. Presumably the consumer must believe *at the time of purchase* that the total utility he or she will receive over time will be at least as great as the other utilities he must forego during its useful lifetime.

Furthermore, items that are both lumpy and durable are often expensive as well, and therefore bought rather infrequently. You may easily overestimate or underestimate the satisfaction they will give you, but once you have bought the item you are stuck with a "sunk cost" and may not be able to adjust your spending for some time.

Among other things, the concept of marginal utility helps to explain why you may rationally choose to spend money on steak occasionally even though you are on a hamburger budget: the marginal utility of the occasional expenditure on steak may exceed that of routine expenditure on hamburger. Variety is the spice of life, the old saying has it, so even the very poor may choose to sacrifice some necessities for the occasional luxury.[2]

---

[2] Someone once defined a luxury as something some people think some other people don't need.

Just to broaden the picture somewhat, we may rescind the temporary decision to ignore saving. "Saving" means setting a portion of current income aside in some way instead of consuming it now, and can be readily reconciled with marginal utility theory. In fact we have already recognized saving in the form of "investment" in capital goods, but it may also take other forms, such as the purchase of stocks (shares) or bonds or other securities, or putting money aside in a bank account or the like.

We may infer that the marginal satisfaction obtained from saving must be approximately equal to the marginal satisfaction obtained from current consumption, otherwise the individual could improve his or her position by consuming more and saving less, or *vice versa*. He may be anticipating important future needs, like buying a car or a house, educating his children, or preparing for his own retirement.

3. The Personal Demand Function.

So far we have been looking at how a consumer with given income and given tastes will allocate his or her income when faced with given prices for each product, if production is based on a given body of technical knowledge. Now let us look at what will happen to his spending pattern if some of these conditions change.

First, suppose that the price of some particular good changes because of the inscrutable workings of the market—say, bread. At the old price our imaginary consumer found that he or she should buy a ertain quantity of bread in each pay period, no more and no less, to get the same satisfaction at the margin from money spent on bread as from money spent on other things.

If the price of bread rises while all other prices and his or her income remain unchanged, however, he will not want to continue buying the same amount; the cost of his former marginal purchase would now be disproportionately high compared to the utility it would yield him. He can improve his satisfaction by cutting back somewhat on his purchases of bread and spending a little more on other things.

The marginal utility of bread rises as he or she reduces his consumption of it, that of other goods falls a little as their consumption increases, until the marginal dollars spent on bread and on other things again yield equal utility.[3] This implies a

---

[3] The increase in our consumer's purchases of other goods implies some changes in their output, and perhaps therefore in their prices. Remember, however, that by hypothesis he can not affect the price of any good even if he stops buying altogether. We can therefore ignore these effects on the market for now, though we will have to take account of them later when we look at how demand and supply are determined for the community as a whole.

direct relationship between the price of any particular good and the quantity a given consumer will buy, which we can set up as a schedule (as in Table 3-1 on page 33) or a curve (as in Figure 3-2 on page 34) or a mathematical relationship or *function* or in some other way.

Be sure to remember that these demand functions are subject to the usual *if...* assumption. In particular they assume that the consumer's income has not changed, that no other price has changed, and that no unspecified new conditions have arisen. Also, they specifically refer to equilibrium conditions after the consumer has readjusted the allocation of his income and after any other adjustments have been made.

It may be, for example, that the consumer believes the price rise he or she has just encountered in this particular commodity is merely a prelude to further price rises; in that case he may temporarily *increase* his purchases of it in order to stockpile it. In the first place, however, introducing the anticipation of future price changes breaches our *if...* assumption. In the second place, a temporary modification of the consumer's buying pattern does not affect the presumption that his regular purchases of the commodity in question will eventually be reduced when he achieves a new equilibrium in his spending habits.

What the demand function does is simply to tell us how much of a particular good our hypothetical consumer will come to consume on a regular basis at various prices, once he or she has adjusted his spending habits to give himself the greatest satisfaction from his given income.

By the way, it is customary in many schools of economic thought to use the word "demand" to mean the entire demand schedule or curve or function. According to this usage you should not say that, at (for example) $1.30, our subject's "demand" is for 32 units; rather, you should say that "the quantity demanded" or "the quantity he or she demands" is 32 units, or some such wording.

We have still to consider what happens if the consumer's income changes, or if his tastes and preferences change. Before looking at those matters, however, let us introduce the concept of "elasticity".

4. Elasticity of Demand.

Column 2 of Table 3-1 shows how much of some unspecified good our imaginary consumer would buy at the various prices given in column 1, and column 5 shows how much he would buy of some other good at the prices listed in column 4. Columns 3 and 6 have been added to show how much money he would spend on each of the goods in each case, and thereby illustrate the concept of *elasticity of demand*.

This particular consumer spends more on the first good as the price falls, less as it rises; the change in consumption is more than proportionate to the change in price, and his demand for it is said to be *elastic*. For example, a drop of less than 8 per cent from $1.30 to $1.20 brings an increase of 28 per cent in consumption.

The opposite is true for the second good: the consumer spends less on it as the price falls, more as it rises. In this case the change in consumption is less than proportionate to the change in price, and the demand for it is said to be *inelastic*. A drop in price from $0.80 to $0.60 (25 per cent), for example, brings a fall of only a little more than 12 per cent in consumption.

Strictly speaking, elasticity should be measured by dividing the percentage increase in consumption by the percentage decrease in price for very small (infinitesimal) changes in both. Dividing the first percentage by the second gives us the *coefficient of elasticity*.[4]

---

[4] To be precise and technical, the coefficient of elasticity at a given point on a curve may be defined in terms of synthetic geometry by the equation $e=y/mx$, where e means elasticity (in this case, elasticity of demand), m is the slope of the tangent to the curve at that point, x is the abscissa (the distance along the east-west axis), and y is the ordinate (distance along the north-south axis). In terms of differential calculus, $e=dx/dy \cdot y/x$. As with other applications of the marginal principle, however, it is acceptable to make the calculation for a short portion of the demand function. This may be illustrated by the arc between two points on the demand curve, in which case the chord that joins the two points replaces the tangent at the given point. (The chord may be seen as a sort of average of the tangents between the two points.) Elasticity so computed is known as *arc elasticity*.

Two Hypothetical Personal Demand Functions

Elastic Demand			Inelastic Demand		
Price per Unit	Quantity Bought	Amount Spent	Price per Unit	Quantity Bought	Amount Spent
(1)	(2)	(3)	(4)	(5)	(6)
$1.50	20	$30.00	$1.20	75	$90.00
1.40	25	35.00	1.00	81	81.00
1.30	32	41.60	.80	89	71.20
1.20	41	9.20	.60	100	60.00
1.10	54	59.40	.40	117	46.80
1.00	73	73.00	.20	146	29.20

Table 3-1. The first three columns illustrate an elastic demand schedule; the amount spent increases as the price falls, because consumption expands more than proportionately. The last three columns illustrate an inelastic demand schedule; the amount spent falls as the price declines.

If the relative change in quantity is greater than the relative change in price, the coefficient of elasticity is greater than one and the demand for the good is considered elastic *at that point in the demand function.* If the relative change in price is the greater, the coefficient is less than one and the demand for the product is considered inelastic. If the two percentages are exactly the same, the good is said to have unit elasticity of demand. Of course, the demand may be elastic in one part of a function and inelastic in another part.

Figure 3-2 illustrates these points graphically. Prices are measured along the north-south axis, the quantities consumed along the east-west axis. The curve

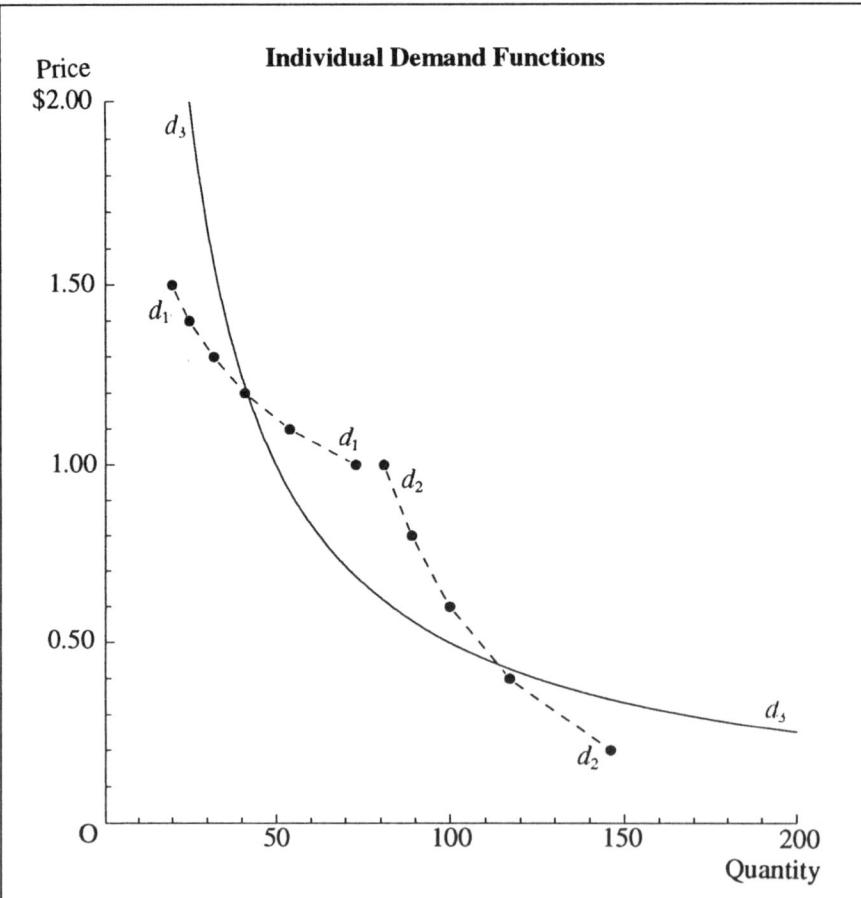

Figure 3-2. The line $d_1 d_1$ represents an elastic demand function (the quantity bought increases more than in proportion to the decline in the price); $d_2 d_2$ represents an inelastic demand function (the quantity bought increases less than in proportion to the decline in the price); and $d_3 d_3$ has unit elasticity (the quantity bought increases exactly in proportion to the decline in price).

labelled d_1d_1 has been drawn from the figures given in columns 1 and 2 of Table 3-1. It has a negative and relatively flat slope—i.e. it slopes rather gently from north-west to south-east—and represents a rather elastic demand function. The curve labelled d_2d_2 illustrates the case of inelastic demand; it has been drawn from the figures in columns 4 and 5 of Table 3-1. It's slope is also negative, but considerably steeper than the first curve.

The curve labelled d_3d_3 represents a case of unit elasticity of demand. The quantity purchased increases exactly in proportion to the fall in price, so the hypothetical consumer spends exactly the same amount of money no matter what price the market sets. It has been drawn on the assumption that the consumer always spends $50.00 on this particular good, and takes whatever quantity that will buy at the going price: at $2.00 he (or she) buys 25 units, at $1.00 50 units, at $0.50 100 units, and so on.[5]

The elasticity of demand depends mainly on two things: the urgency of the needs the commodity satisfies, and the availability of substitutes. Demand tends to be inelastic for the minimum quantities of those goods that are necessary to sustain life, and more elastic as consumption expands well beyond minimum needs or to nonessentials and luxuries. It also tends to be elastic if there are other goods that satisfy the same needs more or less satisfactorily.

If the price of beef falls while the prices of other meats hold steady, for example, consumers will buy more beef and less of other meats, and *vice versa*, so a small change in price may bring a substantial change in consumption. If nothing else will serve the same purpose, however, the price of a good will tend to be inelastic.

Figure 3-3 is designed to show the extreme range of possible elasticities, and to bring out some other features as well. The curve labelled d_4d_4 shows the maximum possible elasticity, a demand curve (or possibly only a portion of one) that is a straight line parallel to the east-west axis. Its coefficient of elasticity is infinite; it is perfectly or infinitely or completely elastic.

That does *not* mean the consumer would buy an infinite quantity of the good in question at $0.80 per unit, it merely asserts that he would buy at least 70 units at that price or any lower price, but would not buy any of it if the price were higher. (Note that the curve appears to assume a negative slope somewhere above the

---

[5] If you are interested in mathematical technicalities, the curve is a rectangular hyperbola: at very high prices it approaches the north-south axis asymptotically, at very low prices it approaches the east-west axis asymptotically. That is, it gets closer and closer to each axis but never quite gets there at any finite price or quantity.

70-unit level, as indicated by the broken continuation). Evidently something is interfering with the forces that normally give us a negatively-sloped demand curve.

One possibility is that there is a perfect substitute for this good. Let us label the good D, and let us suppose there is another good E that is identifiably different from D but can serve our imaginary consumer's needs every bit as well as, but no better than, D. Now suppose further that the inscrutable forces of the marketplace hold the price of E firmly at $0.80, but allow the price of D to fluctuate. (Perhaps D and E serve somewhat different purposes for some other consumers, and are not

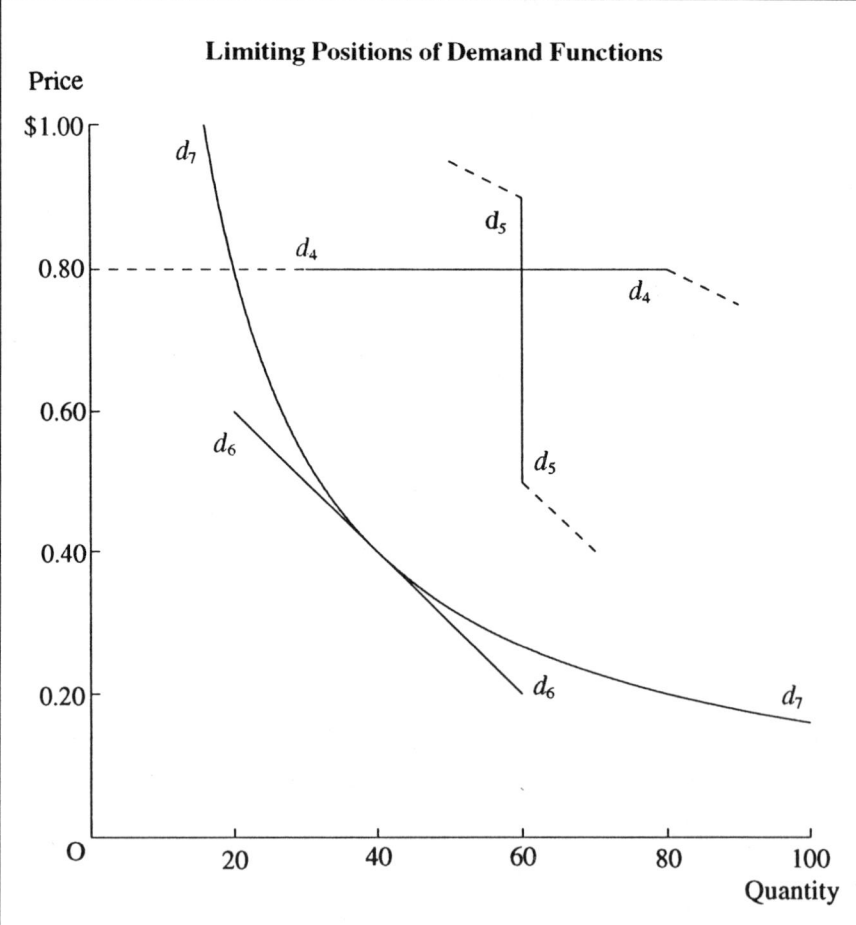

Figure 3-3. The line d_4d_4 represents a perfectly-elastic demand function; its coefficient of elasticity is infinite. The d_5d_5 function is perfectly inelastic: its coefficient of elasticity is zero. The d_6d_6 has unit elasticity at a price of $0.40 (its point of tangency with d_7d_7); it is inelastic below that price, elastic above it. The curve d_7d_7 has unit elasticity throughout (it is a rectangular hyperbola).

perfect substitutes for those people.) Clearly, our subject will buy no D at all if the price moves above $0.80, but will shift all his purchases from E if its price falls below $0.80.

The curve labelled d_5d_5 is the second limiting position, a demand function with zero elasticity or that is perfectly or infinitely or completely inelastic. As with the d_4d_4 curve, this phenomenon may occur in only a part of the function and not necessarily over its entire range.

Apparently our consumer is unwilling to do with less than 60 units at any price below $0.90, and can find no use for more unless the price falls below $0.50; above that range he (or she) may reduce his purchases somewhat, and below it increase them somewhat, as indicted by the broken-line extensions of d_5d_5.

A more plausible example would be a lumpy and expensive good, which you were prepared to buy in very limited quantities—perhaps only one, or at most two or three, in any one income period. In that case your demand curve would be a zig-zag series of straight lines. There would be one like d_4d_4 parallel to the east-west axis from zero to one at the price above which you were not prepared to buy any, and another from one to two at a price low enough to justify buying a second unit. These would be joined by a third straight line like d_5d_5, parallel to the north-south axis at the one level, and a fourth (like the third) would drop towards the east-west axis at the two level. If lower prices still would induce you to buy a third or a fourth unit, your demand curve would exhibit further zig-zags at lower and lower prices.

The curve labelled d_6d_6 (actually, like the curves d_4d_4 and d_5d_5, it is a straight line) illustrates a point made earlier, that a demand function may be elastic in one part of its range and inelastic in another part. Selected points on the line are listed in columns 1 and 2 of Table 3-2. From column 3 you can see that the curve is inelastic at prices below $0.40 (the amount paid rises as the price rises), elastic between $0.40 and $0.80 (the amount paid falls as the price rises), and completely inelastic above $0.80.

The elasticity at $0.40 is—can you guess?—unity. This is shown by the unit-elasticity curve d_7d_7 (a rectangular hyperbola in Figure 3-3), which is tangent to the

Changing Elasticities

Price per Unit (1)	Quantity Bought (2)	Amount Spent (3)
$0.80	0	$0.00
0.70	10	7.00
0.60	20	12.00
0.50	30	15.00
0.40	40	16.00
0.30	50	15.00
0.20	60	12.00
0.10	70	7.00
0.00	80	0.00

Table 3-2. Demand in this case is elastic above $0.40, inelastic below that price.

line d_6d_6 at the $0.40 level;[6] if the demand curve had been elastic at that point it would have intersected the hyperbola at a flat angle like d_1d_1 in Figure 3-2, if it had been inelastic then it would have intersected at a steep angle like d_2d_2.

5. Changing Incomes, Tastes, and Technology.

So far we have looked at the personal demand function with given income and tastes for the consumer and a given state of technology. It is now time to relax those assumptions.

If our imaginary consumer's income rises, the probability is that he or she will buy a bit more of most of the things he bought before. We can easily visualize this as a shift of each demand curve to the east, though the shift will not necessarily be in proportion to the increase in income. Presumably the increase in his spending will be greater for those goods for which his demand at lower income levels was elastic, less for those for which it was inelastic.

However, it does not follow that our consumer will increase his or her purchases of *all* goods when his income rises. He may actually purchase *less* of some things, especially at certain critical points when his income crosses some real or imaginary frontier.

For example, some goods are classified as "inferior goods" or "poor-man's goods", because people buy less of them when their incomes rise above the bare minimum required to maintain life (or to maintain what is considered a minimum standard in that society). Oleomargarine used to be considered a standard textbook example of such a good, since families typically shifted to butter as soon as they felt they could afford it. Nowadays this pattern has been confused by the widespread concern over the effects of high levels of cholesterol in typical diets; even the well-to-do may prefer oleomargarine to butter. Progress in health care has robbed textbook-writers of a good example of an inferior good.

On the other hand, as our imaginary consumer's income rises he may very well buy some products he has never bought before. These may include "superior" goods, like butter, which is (or used to be) contrasted with the "inferior" oleomargarine. Above some imprecise income-level, however, they may include "rich-

---

[6] The rectangular hyperbola that passes through any given point is relatively easy to plot. The amount spent is constant, and you can find it by multiplying the price by the consumption at your chosen point. Now divide that constant by various prices in turn to get the corresponding quantities, or vice versa, and you have a series of plotting points. If you want your hyperbola to look symmetrical, as in Figure 3-2, experiment with different scales on one or both axes until you find a combination that suits you.

man's goods" as well—items that are not only "superior" in real or supposed quality, but also expensive and very lumpy, like luxury automobiles or ocean-going yachts.

To systematize thinking on this subject, economists have devised the concept of *income elasticity* of demand. If an individual's consumption of a particular good changes more than in proportion as his income changes, the demand for that good is said to be income-elastic; if it changes less than proportionately, it is said to be income-inelastic. Later we will meet still other forms of elasticity. In general, however, the unqualified term "elasticity" means price elasticity unless the context clearly requires otherwise.

Now suppose that a substantial portion of the incomes of a certain group of consumers must be spent on a single commodity or a small group of similar commodities, as in the case of very poor people heavily dependent on potatoes or similar bulky carbohydrates because they are the cheapest foodstuffs available. These foods qualify as inferior goods, because people normally reduce their consumption of them in favour of more variety if their incomes rise.

A rise in the price of the staple food of such people will be equivalent to a *reduction* in their incomes, however, since the same amount of money will now buy less food. This may drive them to give up little luxuries like a bite of meat now and then, so the net effect may be that they buy *more* rather than less potatoes as the price rises. The adverse income- effect of the price rise offsets the substitution-effects that normally lead people to consume less of a product as its price rises.

Similar shifts will occur if tastes change, but beyond some rather vague generalities they are less predictable than income-induced changes. Demand curves will shift to the west for products that are losing popularity, to the east for those that are gaining. There may also be changes in the elasticities of individual demand functions.

In the real world, of course, such changes in taste may not be spontaneous reactions on the part of the consumer, they may be the carefully-contrived results of advertizing and other marketing initiatives on the part of sellers—but we are precluded from considering such matters as long as we stick to the model of pure competition.

Technological changes will probably alter relative prices and thereby affect the allocation of incomes, but they are also likely to mean the introduction of new products or products that have been materially changed. New or materially altered products will have new demand functions, and will affect the demand functions of old products. Some will inevitably suffer a decline (their demand curves will shift to the west) in order to make room for the new products.

Some old products may actually benefit from the introduction of new ones, however, if they turn out to be complementary. (Complementary goods are goods that tend to be consumed together, like porridge and milk.) Thus the coming of the automobile has clearly reduced the demand for the services of railways and ships, but may have increased the demand for travel in general and for travel-related services like those of travel agents.

Historically, of course, all these changes have been going on at the same time. It is difficult, and not very rewarding, to try to untangle the effects of each of these factors in the evolution of how a typical consumer spends his (or her) income today from how he would have spent it in some previous year or decade or century. Nevertheless their influence on demand functions helps us to understand the workings of the marketplace.

Chapter 4

The Individual Firm

1. A Typical Producer.

A central postulate of the model of pure competition is that each product is produced in identical form by many independent producers, so numerous that no one of them can affect the market price even if he withholds his (or her) entire production. We will speak of all producers as "firms", without specifying whether they are organized as sole proprietorships or partnerships or coöperatives or corporations. We will assume that each firm produces only one product, and we will identify all firms collectively that produce a particular product A as constituting the A industry.

The implication is that each firm operates on a relatively small scale, though you may argue that the situation could still be "purely competitive" even though each firm was pretty large, as long as no one of them was large enough to influence the market by varying its output.

Each firm is managed by an individual or a group of individuals. You may choose to identify such individuals, or the leading members of groups, as "entrepreneurs", but if so then you should distinguish between those who are initiators or innovators and those who are merely administrators or imitators.

It is sometimes argued that entrepreneurship differs from mere management in that it also involves assuming the ultimate risks in the firm. This implies that the entrepreneur is the sole proprietor. He (or she) hires other factors of production, pays them on an agreed basis regradless of whether the firm is profitable or not, organizes the productive process, and sells the product. He hopes to make a "pure" profit (explained in section 8 of this chapter) by skillfully planning and organizing production. If so it will all go into his own pocket, but by the same token he will personally absorb the loss if things go against him.

However, this argument is somewhat suspect. Entrepreneurs can often find ways of appropriating any profits that appear, while shifting the risk of losses onto others.

Many economists believe that *innovation* is a major factor in true entrepreneurship. This idea was strongly promoted by Joseph Schumpeter, an influential Austrian economist who moved to the U.S.A. between the wars and taught for many years at Harvard University.

Innovation means identifying and exploiting opportunities for devising a new or better product, or producing an old product in a new and more efficient (less expensive) way. A typical innovation may involve nothing more than a different way of organizing work patterns, or perhaps the adaptation of techniques already known and in use elsewhere. As we will see in section 3 of chapter 7, Schumpeter saw it as a key element in the dynamics of the free-enterprise system.

2. The Law of Diminishing Returns.

In establishing his firm to produce a certain product our manager will normally find that he (or she) must employ several different factors of production, and perhaps a variety of categories within each major classification. He will need "land", at the very least in the form of a site for his operation, perhaps also as a source of raw materials. (He may integrate the production of these materials into his total operation, or he may prefer to buy them from some other producer.) He will need "capital", in the form of a building or buildings, perhaps specially designed for his purposes, and probably also some machinery to be used in the productive process. And he will need the services of "labour" of some kind in addition to himself, probably including a number of different types of labour skills.

All this is true even if he wants to practice medicine or dentistry or some other profession, rather than establish a commercial or manufacturing enterprise. His first problem will be to decide what combination of factors of production will be the most efficient for his purpose, i.e. will produce at the lowest feasible cost.

At any particular time "the given state of the arts" usually offers a choice, perhaps a wide choice, of possible combinations of inputs that will enable the manager to turn out the product he wants. For example, think of the choice between capital-intensive and labour-intensive methods. In fact our manager may face a choice among an almost-continuous spectrum of methods ranging from highly automated and specialized machinery that requires relatively little labour, through semi-automatic processes that require rather more labour, to unspecialized equipment that requires much labour.

Furthermore the type of labour and the specialized labour skills he will need will be strongly affected by his choice of equipment. Generally speaking he will need a greater variety of labour skills, and more specialized skills, the less automated and specialized is the equipment he chooses.[1]

Our manager will find that his (or her) decisions on these matters will be strongly influenced by what is known as The law of Diminishing Returns—a law in the sense of being a result that is observed to occur almost invariably. Simply stated, the law says that, if you keep adding more inputs of any given factor of production while keeping all other inputs constant, a time will come sooner or later when each increment of input adds less to output than the previous increment did.

This may be illustrated by a question that used to be found in arithmetic textbooks, and perhaps still is: If it takes one man ten hours to dig a 100-foot-long ditch of a certain depth and width, how long would it take two men? (It was acknowledged that each man would have to be equipped with a shovel, of course; nowadays each would have a backhoe, presumably.) Working with shovels, one may doubt that more than about ten men could be employed at once before diminishing returns would set in—they would start getting in one another's way. With backhoes, even adding a second man might be of questionable advantage.

This is a rather crude example, but in one way it is a particularly favourable one; we have added not one factor alone, but composite units of complementary factors. Had we added men without shovels or backhoes, diminishing returns would have been obvious from the start.

In another way, however, it overdoes the case for diminishing returns. We have tacitly assumed that the second man adds exacely as much to output as the first, and so with the next few men. Actually, it is quite possible that for a while each additional input of a variable factor will add more-than-proportionately to output.

This may not seem very likely in the case of ditchdigging, but in other activities is is certainly observed quite often. Sticking to our simple example, however, it is conceivable that gangs of two or three men might work more efficiently than three men working alone, because they might be able to specialize to some extent. One might concentrate on digging, the second on throwing the dirt out of the ditch, and

---

[1] This points up a matter that is not highly important for our immediate concerns, but is of major importance in some other contexts; there is both complementarity and competition among factors of production. Any enterprise requires some combination of two or more factors, perhaps some variety of each. In that sense they are *complementary* and coöperate in the productive process. However, within limits you may be able to substitute one for another. You may substitute capital for labour by using more capital-intensive methods, or you may be able to substitute one form of labour for another, and in that sense they *compete* with one another for a rôle in the productive process.

the third on clearing the material away from the lip. As more and more gangs were added, however, diminishing returns would inevitably set in.

Essentially the same is true of adding more inputs of any factor of production to a fixed supply of all other factors employed in a productive enterprise. Think of a farmer using machinery and hired labour to work his (or her) farm, always using his resources in the most efficient way possible. If he adds more and more labour to a fixed supply of machinery and a fixed amount of land, the output gained from the employment of each additional worker might at first be greater than from the one before; each worker might be able to specialize more, and less time might be lost changing from (say) plowing one field to harrowing another. Eventually, however, he would find it increasingly difficult to find useful work for additional hands: declining returns would set in.

Suppose instead that he bought or leased more and more of the same type of machinery to work the same land with the same labour force. Each new machine might at first add more to production than the one before, especially if he had been getting along with very little machinery: tasks like seeding and harvesting could be completed more quickly, thus minimizing the risks of losses due to adverse weather. At some point, however, the increase in output due to adding another machine would begin to fall—if for no other reason then because there were not enough workers to man all the machines, or because all the land could be worked so quickly that men and machines would be idle for much of the time at every season.[2]

The same factors will be at work if the farmer adds more land of the same quality to his operations, to be operated by the same labour force with the same machinery. Each acre or hectare he adds may at first yield more output than the one before, especially if he had previously been operating with a good deal of capital equipment and labour on a small plot of land. Eventually the marginal additions to output will begin to fall off, however, as the area under cultivation gets too large for the fixed labour force or the fixed stock of machinery to handle efficiently.

You may think of this as the equivalent of *reducing* instead of increasing the amount of both labour and machinery on a given amount of land: eventually you will be back to the point at which *either* more labour *or* more machines would yield increasing returns.

---

[2] Alternatively, you might think of "machines in general" and allow the farmer to change the types of machines he uses as he adds to his total stock. (Perhaps he leases them instead of buying them, and can quickly change to more specialized equipment as his use of them expands.) Even so, he will eventually encounter diminishing returns for the same reason as before.

More generally, most productive processes use the services of more than one factor of production, and the most efficient combination of them depends on the prices of the various factors, the price the product will bring, and the technical requirements for producing the good in question. Adding more of any factor may lead to more-than-proportionate increases in output if it was previously relatively scarce compared to the other factors, but will bring less-than-proportionate increases in output once it becomes relatively plentiful.

3. The Costs of Production.

In section 3 of Chapter 2 we noted that the full rigour of the model of pure competition applies only in the long run, but that short-run and medium-term analysis is necessary for dealing with certain features of it. The management of a typical firm is a case in point: many key decisions are governed by considerations that apply only under relatively short-run conditions.

By hypothesis the manager or entrepreneur must buy his (or her) raw materials and the services of various factors of production in competitive markets at the going prices, and must sell his product at a market-set price. Costs of production are therefore of great importance to him: he must get and keep them below his selling price, or sooner or later he will exhaust his resources and have to go out of business. They can be divided into two significantly-different categories, fixed costs and variable costs.

The initial cost of a building or a machine is a sunk cost that can only be recovered over its useful life out of the income it helps to generate; some portion must be charged against operations in each successive production period thereafter until it is fully amortized, and is a fixed charge or a fixed cost in each of those periods. The rental of a leased building or leased equipment is a fixed cost for the duration of the lease.

The wages of a minimum administrative staff are also fixed costs as long as the firm continues to be a going concern, i.e. as long as it is actually turning out a product or is prepared to do so on short notice. That includes the wages of the manager or entrepreneur himself, calculated at the best rate he (or she) could earn in alternative employment (e.g., as someone else's employee). All these costs must be charged against each successive production period even if not a wheel turns and nothing is produced.[3]

---

[3] Some people prefer to restrict the term "fixed costs" to the amortization of sunk costs, which can only be recovered out of income, and to use the term "overhead costs" as a broader category that

Variable costs are those that change more or less in proportion to the volume of output: the wages of production workers, the costs of raw materials and the energy needed run the machinery, routine maintenance, and that sort of thing.

The distinction between fixed and variable costs is not rigid, for it depends in part on what timeframe we have in mind, but in any given case it is usually clear enough what category a given item belongs in. In the very short run even the hourly wage bill for production workers may be pretty inflexible: it may not be possible to reduce the labour force quickly, because of the terms of employment previously agreed to, nor to increase it materially (except by calls on the existing workforce to work overtime), because of the time it takes to interview and process new employees.

On the other hand some types of machinery and equipment have relatively short useful lives, hence their costs are variable in a relatively short timespan. And in the long run even the most durable of machinery and buildings will outlive their usefulness and have to be replaced, so all costs become variable.

Now let's consider the factors that would influence a manager in making his (or her) decisions about how much to produce. We can assume that he has already made the basic decisions about *what* to produce, what scale of operations would be best, and what organizational setup he wants, for all those matters would enter into deciding on his initial investment in capital equipment. Presumably he chose what he thought would be the most efficient size of plant, or the most efficient size he could afford with his own funds and what he could borrow from others. These decisions will have determined the fixed costs that must be charged against every production period—so much per day or per week or whatever period he plans for.

As already noted, the fixed costs of the firm should include a wage for the manager himself at the best rate he (or she) could command in alternative employment, because his venture will be a losing one unless he can get a net return of at least this much.[4] He must now tailor his other costs as shrewdly as he can to the scale of operations he has decided on. How does he decide how much of the various

---

includes true fixed costs. The basis of the distinction is the fact that many other overhead costs can be terminated in one way or another—leases and other contracts can be renegotiated, or even defaulted on (e.g., if the firm were prepared to declare bankruptcy), but a sunk cost is a sunk cost. For our purposes, however, the distinction is not important, for we will usually be discussing going concerns.

4   It may be of course that he will prefer to run his own business even though his net money income is less than he could earn in some other way, because he prefers this line of business or prefers being his own boss. In that case we must conclude that he gets at least enough *psychic income* in this activity to compensate him for the money income he forgoes; in other words he maximizes his psychic income even though not his money income.

factors of production to employ, and how do these decisions affect his variable costs?

The manager may never have heard of The Law of Diminishing Returns, but he will surely recognize that at some point he will meet rising variable costs as he strives to increase his output. This is just a different way of saying the same thing: if the output per manhour is declining as more manhours are employed, for example, then the manhour cost of additional output must be increasing. Furthermore the manhour cost translates directly into money cost, since the firm must pay the market-fixed wage rate, which in this model is unaffected by the firm's actions.

4. Total, Average, and Marginal Costs.

Table 4-1 illustrates fixed and variable costs in a hypothetical situation, and certain other concepts that can be derived from them. Let us suppose that the fixed costs attributable to each production period total 50 dollars or pounds or francs or whatever currency you prefer, as shown in column 2. The manager will expect to recover those costs, and more, from selling his output. In order to produce anything at all, however, he must also incur the variable costs shown in column 3. These will be zero if nothing is produced, $18.10 to produce one unit, $32.80 for two, and so on. Adding the figures in columns 2 and 3 gives those in column 4.

However, our manager will really want to know the average cost per unit of output, in order to compare it with his (or her) market-set selling price, though as yet we have not said what that is. Dividing the output given in column 1 into the figures in columns 2, 3, and 4 respectively gives us the average fixed cost per unit of output, the average variable cost, and the average total cost.

The next step is to derive column 8 from column 3, by taking the value at each level of output and subtracting the value at the *previous* level—or the values in column 4 instead, since they differ by exactly the $50.00 of fixed costs in column 2. Recalling the discussion of marginalism in Chapter 3, you will recognize that column 8 gives the cost of increasing output by one unit—the *marginal cost*.

You may also note that we must make the same distinction here between lumpy data and finely-divisible data as we did with consumer demand in Chapter 3. Column 9 gives the marginal costs appropriate to a finely-divisible product; it is derived mathematically from the average-variable-cost function. In that case the relationships can be properly represented by a smooth curve, as we will see shortly.

Figure 4-1 displays the same data in graphic form, which has the advantage of letting you see certain important relationships more easily. The north-south axis has been labelled "$", though we might as well have used pounds or francs or marks

Hypothetical Cost Data

Output	Fixed costs	Variable costs	Total costs	Average fixed costs
(1)	(2)	(3)	(4)	(5)
0	$50.00	$ 0.00	$50.00	$ ∞
1	50.00	18.10	68.10	50.00
2	50.00	32.80	82.80	25.00
3	50.00	44.70	94.70	16.67
4	50.00	54.40	104.40	12.50
5	50.00	62.50	112.50	10.00
6	50.00	69.60	119.60	8.33
7	50.00	76.30	126.30	7.14
8	50.00	83.20	133.20	6.25
9	50.00	90.90	140.90	5.50
10	50.00	100.00	150.00	5.00
11	50.00	111.10	161.10	4.54
12	50.00	124.80	174.80	4.17
13	50.00	141.70	191.70	3.85
14	50.00	162.40	212.40	3.57
15	50.00	187.50	237.50	3.33
16	50.00	217.60	267.60	3.13
17	50.00	253.30	303.30	2.94
18	50.00	295.20	345.20	2.78
19	50.00	343.90	393.90	2.63
20	50.00	400.00	450.00	2.50

Table 4-1. Column 1 indicates output in physical units, column 2 shows fixed costs of $50.00 attributable to the production period in question regardless of the level of output, column 3 shows the variable costs that must be incurred at each level of output, and column 4 shows the sum of the values in columns 2 and 3. Columns 5, 6, and 7 are derived by dividing the value in column 1 into those for columns 2, 3,

for an Individual Firm

Output	Average variable costs	Average total costs	Marginal costs	
			Lumpy data	Smooth curve
(1)	(6)	(7)	(8)	(9)
0	$?	$ ∞		$20.00
1	18.10	68.10	$18.10	16.30
2	16.40	41.40	14.70	13.20
3	14.90	31.57	11.90	10.70
4	13.60	26.10	9.70	8.80
5	12.50	22.50	8.10	7.50
6	11.60	19.93	7.10	6.80
7	10.90	18.04	6.70	6.70
8	10.40	16.65	6.90	7.20
9	10.10	15.66	7.70	8.30
10	10.00	15.00	9.10	10.00
11	10.10	14.65	11.10	12.30
12	10.40	14.57	13.70	15.20
13	10.90	14.75	16.90	18.70
14	11.60	15.17	20.70	22.80
15	12.50	15.83	25.10	27.50
16	13.60	16.73	30.10	32.80
17	14.90	17.84	35.70	38.70
18	16.40	19.18	41.90	45.20
19	18.10	20.73	48.70	52.30
20	20.00	22.50	56.10	60.00

and 4 respectively; column 8 is derived by subtracting the value given in column 3 (or 4) for the preceding output from that for the new level of output; column 9 is derived mathematically from the average-variable-cost function, represented graphically by a smooth curve. (The question mark in the first line of column 6 indicates that the value is indeterminate, zero divided by zero. The symbol ∞ means an unlimited amount.)

50   The Practice of Economics

or any other currency you like; it simply represents the money spent for the purposes indicated. The east-west axis indicates the level of output in a given production period (a week, a month, or whatever period the manager plans for.) The dots indicating the output and cost combinations in the first three columns of Table 4-1 have been joined by broken lines in smooth curves, to show the relationship that would obtain for a finely-divisible product; with lumpy data, the cost functions really exist only at outputs represented by whole numbers.

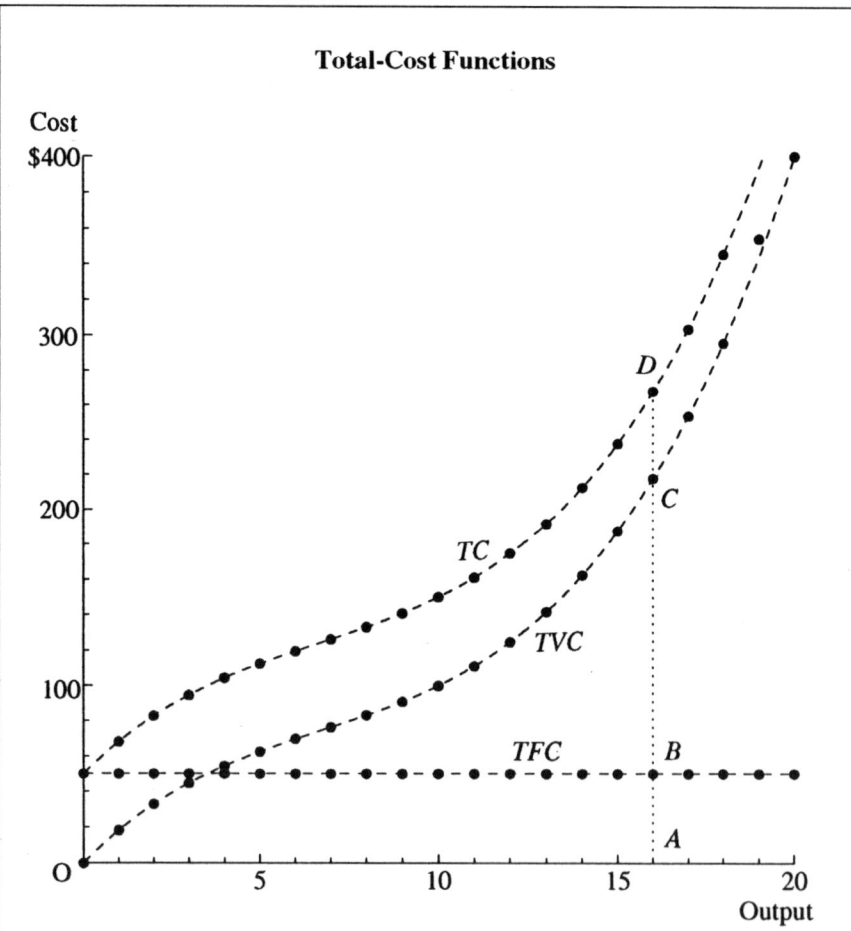

Figure 4-1. The line *TFC* represents the portion of total fixed costs that is chargeable to a given production-period even if nothing is produced at all (e.g., interest and the amortization of sunk capital). The line *TVC* represents total variable costs, i.e. the cost of labour, materials, etc. necessary to produce the output indicated on the east-west axis. The line TC or total costs is the sum of *TFC* and *TVC* at each successive output; for example, an output of A requires fixed costs of *AB* plus variable costs of *AC* or a total of *AD*.

The straight line labelled *TFC*, parallel to the east-west axis, represents the total fixed costs attributable to each production period; they are the same regardless of output. The curved line labelled *TVC* represents total variable costs. It starts at zero when no output is produced, but rises progressively thereafter. The *TC* or total-cost curve is derived by graphically adding the *TFC* and the *TVC* curves. At an output of *A*, for example, the distance *AD* is the sum of *AB* and *AC*; *CD* is equal to *AB*.

Strictly speaking we should show separate variable-cost curves for the expenditure on each separate factor of production. In order to get everything into a two-dimensional figure, however, it is convenient to lump them all together and pretend that they are all used in exactly the same proportion as output changes. The principles are the same for the combination as for each separate item of cost.

The *TVC* curve must start at zero for zero output, and the fact that at first its slope becomes less steep as output increases indicates that output is increasing more than proportionately as more variable inputs are added. At about 7 units of output the slope begins to increase, however, showing that diminishing returns have set in, and it gets progressively steeper thereafter. The *TC* curve shows exactly parallel changes, of course.

Figure 4-2 represents *average* costs per unit of output. The scale along the east-west axis is exactly the same as in Figure 4-1, so the two sets of curves can be compared directly at the same outputs. However, the scale of the north-south axis has been greatly increased in order to show greater detail, for now we want to look at costs per unit of output and compare them with various possible selling prices.

The average-fixed-cost or *AFC* curve approaches the north-south axis as output gets smaller and smaller, and approaches the east-west axis as output gets larger and larger. The average-variable-cost or *AVC* curve and the average-total-cost or *ATC* curve are both represented as U-shaped, for reasons that will be explained shortly.[5] The marginal-cost or *MC* curve for a lumpy product has been drawn as a series of straight lines joining the plotted points; for a finely-divisible product it would start at $20.00 for zero output (the same as the *AVC* curve, since these costs must be identical for the first unit produced), and would lie slightly west of the lumpy *MC* curve throughout.

---

[5] In case you are interested, the *AFC* curve is a rectangular hyperbola, like the $d_7 d_7$ curve in Figure 3-3 on page 36; its formula is $y=50x^{-1}$. The *AVC* curve is a parabola, $y=0.1x^2-2x+20$. (Hence the formula for the *ATC* curve is $y=.01x^2-2x+20+50x^{-1}$.) There is no particular significance in choosing a parabola for the *AVC* curve, beyond the fact that such curves are believed to be U-shaped as a rule, for the reasons discussed in the text, and a parabola happens to be a U-shaped curve that is relatively easy to plot.

We will use smooth curves for the charts in the rest of this chapter, as for a finely-divisible product. This allows us to determine the relationships among the various cost functions very precisely at any level of output.

The U-shape of the *AVC* and the *ATC* curves follows from the assumption that marginal costs at first decline (returns increase) as more variable factors are put to work, but then begin to increase. Average costs, both variable and total, must be declining as long as each additional unit of output is achieved at lower cost, i.e. as long as the marginal cost is less than the average cost. By the same token, average costs must be rising if the marginal cost exceeds the average.

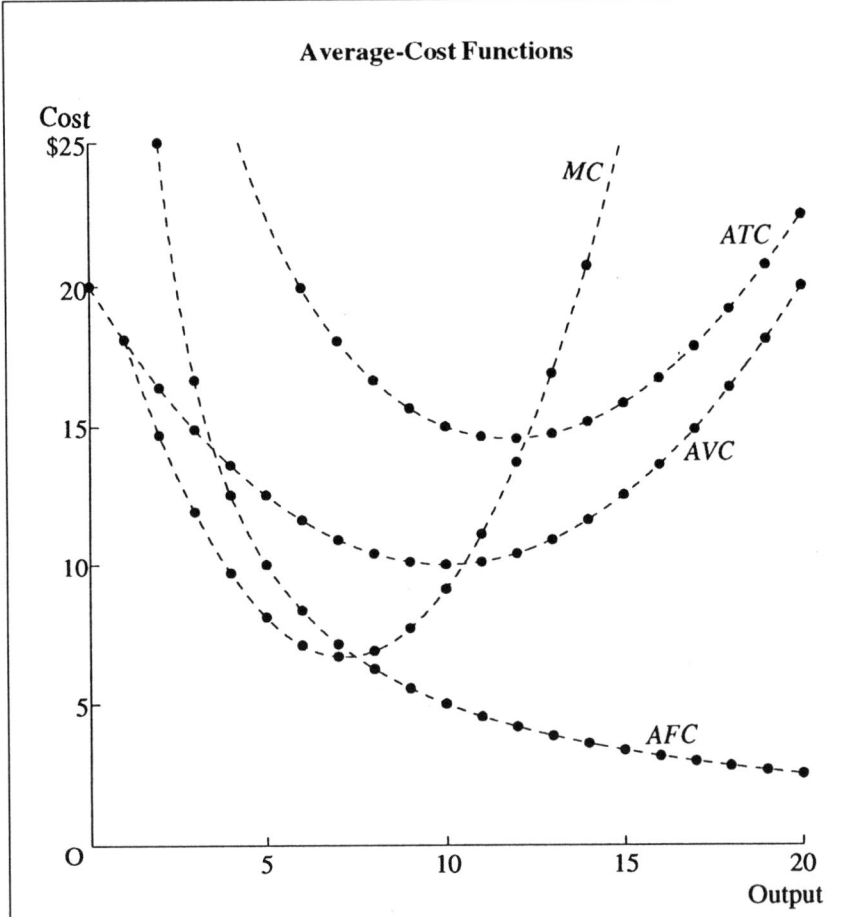

Figure 4-2. The lines *AFC*, *AVC*, and *ATC* are respectively the average fixed, variable, and total costs per unit of output; they are found by dividing each successive level of output into the corresponding total cost (as given in Table 4-1). The *MC* curve records the cost of each additional unit of output.

It follows that the average cost will be lowest when it is exactly equal to the marginal cost; the *MC* curve must cross the *AVC* and the *ATC* curves at their minimum values. However, there is no guarantee that marginal costs will in fact decline at low initial levels of output—that is merely an assumption, based on the observation that it does commonly happen. In any particular case it is quite possible that marginal costs will be constant for a while, or will rise persistently from the very start, in which case average costs will do the same.

Where is "the point of diminishing returns" in all this welter of curves? Well, it is the point at which an additional unit of input adds less to output than the previous unit did. That is equivalent to the point at which marginal cost reaches its lowest point and begins to increase—at 7 units of output in Table 4-1 and Figure 4-2 (or at 6.7 in Figure 4-3, which we are now coming to).

5. Determining the Optimum Output.

Now that we have these geometric technicalities out of the way, let's face our manager with a selling price set by a market mechanism he (or she) can in no way influence or control. Figure 4-3 repeats Figure 4-2, except for two things: we will omit the *AFC* curve, since it is included in the *ATC* curve, and we will suppose that the market-set selling price of the product is $18.00 (or 18 of whatever currency you prefer to deal in). The price is indicated by the straight line *AB* parallel to the east-west axis.

Let us also reinterpret the output scale as meaning hundreds of units instead of single units, so we are entitled to use the smooth curves we have drawn. (This also requires us to raise the fixed costs to $5,000.00 per period instead of $50.00, in order to keep the average fixed costs unchanged.)

How much should our manager plan to produce? More than 700 units, to be sure, for at that or any lower output his (or her) average total costs will exceed his selling price, whereas higher outputs will be profitable. What about an output of 1,713 units,[6] the largest at which he can cover his costs? No, he will merely break even at that point, whereas anywhere between 703 and 1,713 units will give him a profit.

His optimum output will be at the point where the *MC* curve crosses the $18.00 line, which is at about 1,281 units of output. At that level his profit will be $4,236, a maximum, represented by the area of the rectangle *ABCD*; his total revenue will

---

6 These figures have been derived mathematically from the formulas given in the preceding footnote, but you can find their approximate values by interpolation in Table 4-1 (and multiplying by 100), or by inspection from Figure 4-3.

be $23,063 and his total costs $18,827. At any lower output his marginal cost will be less than his selling price, so he could add to his profit by producing and selling a little more; at any higher output his marginal cost would be more than his selling price, and he could increase his profit by producing and selling a little less. (Note that, on the assumptions we are making, he can and will sell all that he produces.)

Now suppose that market forces reduce the price of the product to $14.00. This is less than the lowest point on the *ATC* curve, which is about $14.56 at an output of 1,180 units. If our manager thinks the new price is permanent, and if he (or she)

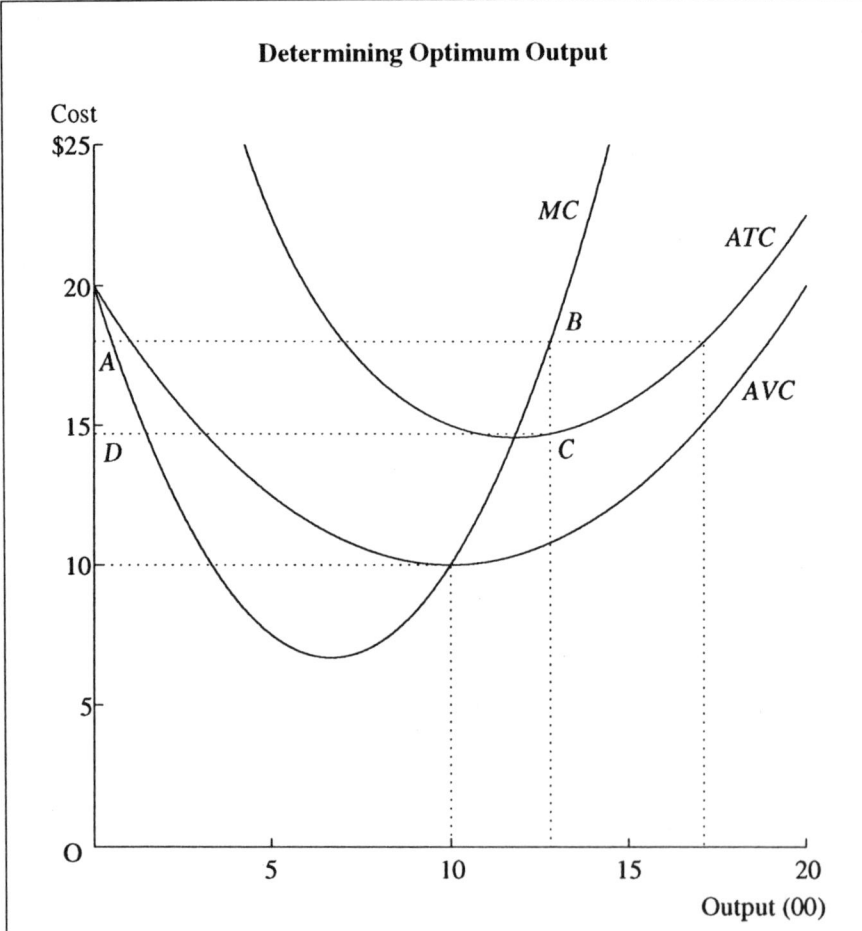

Figure 4-3. The average-total-cost (*ATC*), the average-variable-cost (*AVC*), and the marginal-cost (*MC*) curves are the same as in Figure 4-2, except that they are the "smooth" versions appropriate to large-scale outputs, and the scale along the east-west axis has been multiplied by 100. Output will be expanded until the selling price just covers *MC*; to sell one unit more or one unit less would produce less profit.

can find no way of reducing his costs, should he close up the plant and accept employment elsewhere?

Not at all, for in so doing he would lose $5,000 per period—his fixed costs. He should reduce his output to 1,161 units, the point at which his marginal costs will be just $14.00 per unit. His average total costs will be about $14.56, a loss of approximately $0.56 per unit, but his total costs will be $16,912, his total revenue $16,255, and his loss only $657 instead of $5,000. The key point is that at any other level of output his loss would be greater.

If you want to compare these alternative losses graphically in Figure 4-3, $5,000 would be the area of a rectangle bounded by 5 on the north-south scale and 10 on the east-west scale, or *vice versa*. (Remember that the east-west scale must be multiplied by 100.) The loss at a selling price of $14.00 would be a much smaller rectangle, found by drawing a line at that level from the north-south axis to intersect with the MC curve, then erecting a perpendicular to intersect with the ATC curve, then adding a line parallel to the east-west axis back to intesect the north-south axis.

How low would the price have to fall before our manager would want to close down his (or her) plant entirely? Not until it fell below $10.00. At any price above that he could cover all the variable costs needed to produce an output of 1,000 units or a bit more, and recover some part of his fixed costs. Below that he would lay off his workers and close the plant, unless he thought the price would rise again so soon that the shut-down and start-up costs would be greater than his losses in the meantime.

The closing might be temporary if the price decline was only seasonal, of course, or if the manager hoped to find ways of reducing his costs; in that case he would want to retain his key employees and maintain his firm as a going concern rather than liquidate his assets and give up the business entirely.

Notice that "the point of diminishing returns" does not enter into our manager's calculations at all—not directly, at any rate. In every-day usage the implication is that going beyond that point is counterproductive, but in our examples it has clearly been profitable to do so. As we noted in section 3, the point of diminishing returns means the point at which marginal costs reach a minimum and begin to increase. In Figure 4-3 that point is an output of 667 units, whereas the minimum operational level is 1,000 units of output (at a price of $10.00 per unit), and the plant would not be fully profitable below an output of 1,180 units (at a price of $14.56).

The real point is simply that, once a persistent and progressive decline in the return per unit of output sets in, the time will come sooner or later when marginal costs will exceed any given market-fixed price for the product. About the only way in which the point of diminishing returns and the optimum level of output could be identical would be if marginal costs were constant and equal to the market-set price for some range of output, and then began to rise.

Note also that *in this model* any money spent on advertizing or sales promotion would be wasted. The individual firm's product is identical to that of many other firms; its selling price is set by competitive forces it can not influence; and it can sell all it cares to produce by simply offering it on the open market (the demand for its output is perfectly elastic). Sales promotion would add costs that could not be recovered.

6. The Firm's Supply Function.

We can now derive a supply function for the individual firm, in somewhat the same way as we derived a demand function for the individual consumer. Like a demand function, a supply function may be expressed as a table or schedule, a curve or other graphic representation, a mathematical function, or perhaps in some other way.

Figure 4-4 offers a graphic example for any period in which the firm is unable or unwilling to alter its fixed costs, i.e. any period in which Figure 4-3 is a reasonable representation of how it should respond to price changes. The *SS* curve and its broken extension to the southwest is a portion of the firm's marginal cost curve, as in Figure 4-3, and the broken curved line south of its solid portion is a part of its average variable cost curve.

Suppose the price of the product is initially stable at p_1. The firm will maximize its profit, or minimize its loss, by setting its output at the level at which its marginal cost is equal to p_1; call that point q_1. If the price falls to p_2, the firm's output will fall to q_2. If the price rises to p_3, output will rise to q_3. And so on, defining the supply curve *SS*.

However, if the price falls below p_0 the firm will not produce or sell anything, for that is its shut-down price. Hence its supply curve is identical to its marginal cost curve at and above its shut-down price.

In the *very* short run, however, the firm's supply function may be much less elastic. It may take a few days at least, perhaps longer, to adjust even its variable costs. Until that could be done its supply curve might be virtually a straight line perpendicular to the east-west axis.

Even so, the manager would probably have some inventory of finished goods awaiting shipment, as a cushion against accidental delays. He could draw down this inventory somewhat if the market price turned favourable, and rebuild it later as opportunity offered. Or he might prefer to add to this inventory temporarily rather than sell at a price he felt was too low, while readjusting his output. His very-short-run supply curve might therefore have a slope that was much steeper than the *SS* curve but not completely inelastic, like the *S'S'* curve in Figure 4-4.

The individual firm's supply function may be elastic or inelastic, just like the individual consumer's demand function. You may wish to refer back to the discussion of elasticity in section 4 of Chapter 3.

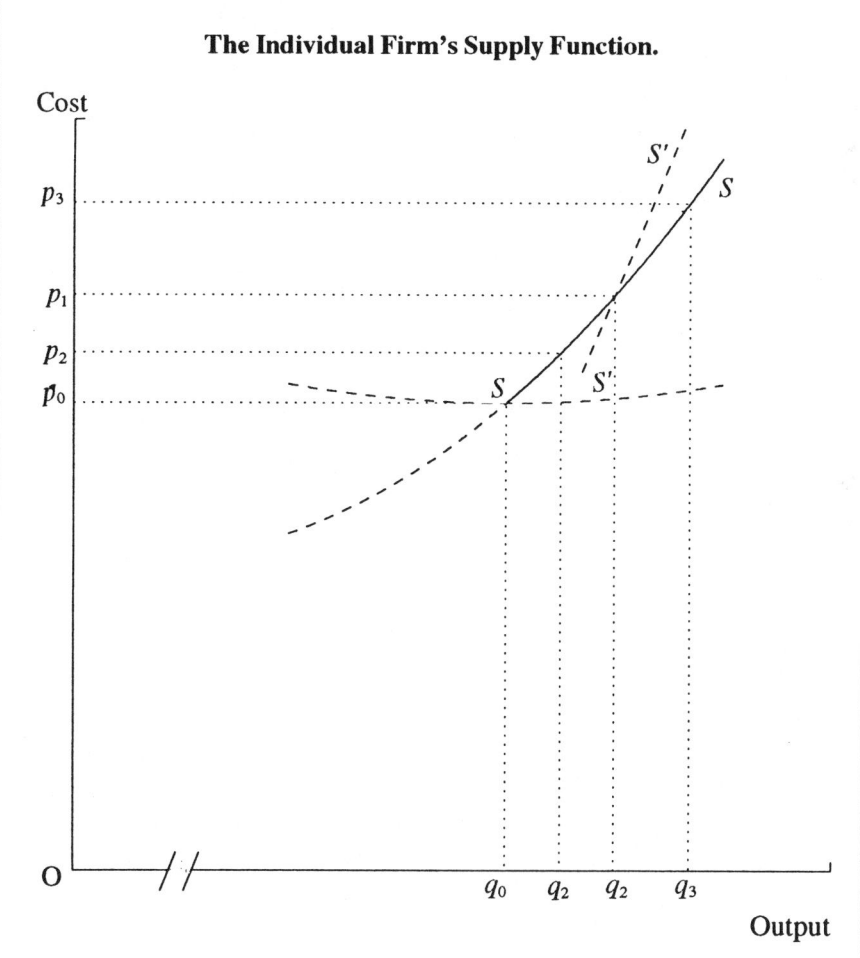

Figure 4-4. At any market-set price above its shut-down price the firm's output is determined by its *MC* curve, hence its supply curve (*SS*) is identical to the portion of its *MC* curve that extends above its shut-down price. In the *very* short run, however, the firm may not be able to change even its variable costs quickly, so its supply curve may be almost completely inelastic, like the *S'S'* curve.

One important qualification needs to be made: under some circumstances increased output may bring a *reduction* in costs instead of an increase. This is technically known as "increasing returns to scale" or "economies of scale".[7] In brief the idea is that, as a certain industry expands, it may become possible to employ cost-cutting productive techniques that are already known but are not economic at lower levels of output. Examples include such things as greater specialization of tasks, more highly automated machinery, "production line" processes, and other "mass production" techniques. These economies may be either "internal", within a given firm, or "external", benefiting all firms in the industry.

For now we may disregard economies of scale on a technicality: it is pretty hard to incorporate them into the model of pure competition, because they imply that one firm or a few firms dominate either the industry in question or an industry that is a major supplier.

If we waive that technicality, however, as we must do later when we turn to the model of imperfect or monopolistic competition, it turns out that there are also *dis*economies of scale: administrative problems, difficulties of communication among various departments or sections of the enterprise, and inconveniences of other kinds, which may eventually exceed the economies. Economies of scale are of great importance in some industries, but they are subject to limitations, and they do not negate either The Law of Diminishing Returns or the finite limits on the community's productive resources.

7. Changing Prices and Costs.

The selling price of the product is not the only price that can change in a money-and-market economy: the prices the firm must pay for the services of the various factors of production it employs may also change. (The prices of any raw materials and semi-finished goods it buys may change as well, of course, but we may look on these intermediate products as the embodiment of the factor-costs that have gone into them.) That may change both the fixed and the variable costs of the product, perhaps rather quickly. The manager's skills will be tested by the promptness and effectiveness with which he (or she) can adapt to the changes.

---

[7] This is not the same as the "increasing returns" discussed in section 2 of this chapter, which eventually turned into decreasing returns. In that case we were adding more and more of a single factor of production to a given supply of other factors. Here *all* factors may be added simultaneously, and not necessarily in the same proportions. In fact an important element in the process may be the incorporation of a rather different combination of factors, seeking the most cost-efficient mix.

A fall in the prices of all variable inputs, or in the price of any one important input, will have the effect of shifting the average and total variable cost curves and the marginal-cost curve southward parallel to the north-south axis. If the selling price is unchanged, profit will increase or any loss will be reduced, and the optimum output will increase. A rise in input prices will have the opposite effect. In either case the shift will be exactly proportionate to the change in costs.

For example, suppose the variable costs in Figure 4-4 are entirely for a uniform type of labour at $10.00 per hour. Now suppose the wage rate doubles: every point on the *AVC* and the *MC* curves will be twice as far north of the east-west axis as before. The shut-down selling price will now be $20.00 instead of $10.00, but the minimum economic output will remain at 1,000 units.

Fixed costs will not be affected—not immediately, at any rate—since they comprise the sunk costs of capital equipment and other overheads that can not be materially reduced even if the plant closes down entirely. At any given moment, however, it is probable that some firm or other will be about to replace machinery or equipment that has pretty well outlived its usefulness. A major aspect of any such decision is the need to decide on the most efficient size of new or refurbished plant.

It may be that technical advances have been made since the old plant was established, but let's defer that possibility for now and stick with the assumption that we are dealing with changes within "the given state of the arts." There are usually several alternative productive procedures available at any one time, as already noted, the choice among them depending on such things as the expected scale of production. Perhaps some of the firms renewing their capital investment at this time will conclude that a substantially larger and more costly installation will be more efficient, i.e. will produce at lower cost.

A larger plant will mean higher fixed costs, and implies a larger output in order to spread them more widely. Most likely the new machinery will require a different combination of variable factor inputs. In that case the whole set of cost curves may shift to the south and west, and may change shape materially too. Most likely, however, the two average-cost curves and the marginal-cost curve will remain in approximately the same relationship.

We may reasonably suppose that the new investment is intended to increase (or restore) profitability. It may be, of course, that the market-fixed selling price has been falling, or not rising as fast as costs, and that other managers have already introduced the new equipment; in that case the new investment is necessary to keep the firm competitive. On the other hand the manager of the firm may be a true entrepreneur, an innovator, the first to devise and introduce a new productive procedure in the industry; by doing so he hopes to gain a pure profit.

8. The Rôle of Profits.

The possibility that cost-curves might shift as a result of new investment should give you an inkling of how the firm's short-run supply function may change over time, but we are not yet ready to follow up that line of thought. Instead, look back at Figure 4-3, and suppose that the industry selling price holds at $18.00. At that level our manager is enjoying what appears to be a handsome pure profit. (Remember that his (or her) fixed costs include a managerial wage equal to what he could earn in his best alternative employment.) What could have led to this favourable outcome?

One possibility is that this is an expanding industry: consumer demand has shifted in its favour, but as yet there has not been sufficient time to shift resources to it from other industries, and competition among consumers has bid up the price. Can our manager maintain that profit indefinitely?

Not in a truly competitive environment. The other firms already in the industry may be expected to expand their output until rising marginal costs put a stop to the process, but that presumably leaves them with significant profits, too. However, new firms will be formed by managers attracted from other industries—there is no disguising the fact when an entire industry is making profits.

The normal expectation is that all this competition will in due course drive the industry selling price down till the price-line is just tangent to the marginal[8] firm's average-total-cost curve at its lowest point. No-one will get more than the normal return for the type of service he (or she) provides, or that is provided by the capital he owns (whether he uses it himself or contracts out its service to others). There will then be no incentive for any new firm to enter the industry, nor for any firm to leave it.

However, there is another way in which profits may be eliminated: by rising costs. If the industry is a relatively important user of a particular factor of production—such as soil of a particular type or a specialized labour skill not widely used elsewhere—then competition for the services of that factor will drive up its

---

[8] By this time you should not be surprised to hear that the "marginal" firm is the firm that would be the first to drop out if the price fell a little or if costs rose a little. However, it is worth pointing out that it is the *firm* that is marginal, not necessarily its manager; he (or she) may in fact be a very efficient entrepreneur, who can move easily to other industries.

returns. Also, new or expanding firms will find it to their advantage to bid a little higher to attract factors from other industries, since they can well afford to do so out of their expected profits.

Another possible explanation of the profits depicted in Figure 4-3 is that our manager is benefiting from a special supply situation. For example, he (or she) may have obtained a lease on a well-located property on specially favourable terms.[9] Once others recognize its advantages, however, they will bid for its services until all the profit attributable to its use disappears. In the process the value of the rent or quasi-rent it yields will be "capitalized": i.e. the value of the property itself will be bid up until an investor will get as much from it as from employing the same sum in other ways. The main point, however, is that the profit will be converted into a rental or some other form of factor return.

Some combination of downward pressure on selling prices and upward pressure on costs (or conversion into added factor returns) will eventually bring the price-line into tangency with the average-total-cost curve at its lowest point.

You might call this "Parkinson's Law of Costs": costs rise to absorb any profits that persist in the face of competitive forces, and become income to some factor of production or other. That factor may be some particular property that can not be duplicated, like a favourably-located plot of land. Or it may be a particular form of skilled labour, relatively scarce due either to some rare natural aptitude or to a long or difficult training period, though in the latter case the advantage would tend to disappear over a period long enough to train new personnel.

Of course, this special skill might be that of management, or entrepreneurship, or varying degrees of these skills. Managers will command wages proportionate to their demonstrated abilities, either as employees of someone else or in the form of "profits" from their own firms. A gifted entrepreneur might be able to earn a more-or-less-continuous succession of "temporary" profits from a succession of innovations.

The most important explanation of the profits illustrated in Figure 4-3, however, is that it may be an example of what economists call a "pure" profit.

In the business world, and in common conversation, the word "profit" is used in a variety of ways, but usually means the excess of revenues over expenditures in a given period of time, or the net returns to the owners or shareholders of a business,

---

[9] Pure competition does not require that the resources available to all producers be identical, merely that all have an equal opportunity to bid for the available resources. *Pure and perfect* competition would imply that everyone has the same information on which to base his decisions, so the special supply situation here postulated could not persist, but it can not be ruled out in the short run.

or "the bottom line" of a profit-and-loss statement. In this sense it includes the returns to some forms of capital, but not all. For example, it does not include the interest on borrowed funds used in a business, which is a share of the returns to capital that is paid over to those who help to finance it in this way. But it may also include a part of the wages of management, as when a sole proprietor chooses to take only nominal monthly wages (less than he could earn elsewhere) and to take most of his reward as "profit".

Economists consider such uses of the word "profit" rather muddled and untidy; they prefer a terminology that focuses on the "normal" returns to each factor of production separately. In the case of capital the returns take the form of interest, dividends, earnings retained in the business, capital gains, and any other benefit accruing to the owners of productive capital, regardless of who owns it and how it is financed. These returns must be paid eventually by every firm, at rates that must be comparable to those available in other activities, or it will be unable to maintain its capital and so will be unable to stay in business.

In principle all these returns must in the long run become equivalent to the rate of interest, since by hypothesis all risks and uncertainties would be eliminated and competition would ensure that investors would get the same return no matter how they chose to employ their money. In the short run they may differ materially, of course, but on the whole they should *tend* to be equivalent, after allowing for differences in risk and that sort of thing.

When economists speak of profit they usually specify "pure" profit, meaning something in excess of normal factor returns, in order to avoid misunderstanding. The idea is most easily understood in terms of a true entrepreneur, an innovator or initiator. A pure profit may occur when an entrepreneur introduces a new or better product, or finds a more efficient (less costly) way of producing an old product. He pays all factors of production their normal rates of return, as determined by competitive market forces, but finds some new and better way of using them to satisfy human wants.

In this case the entrepreneur makes a pure profit, because he gains an advantage over his competitors or because for the time being he has no competitors and can charge a scarcity price. His profit is a short-lived one, however, because imitators will appear sooner or later; competitors will adopt his methods or produce the new product too, and his new ideas will become the standard in the industry. The selling price will fall or costs will rise, or both, for the reasons already given. The main beneficiary will be the consumer, who will have a new or better or cheaper product.

However, the main point to be got from all this is that in the model of pure competition every manager is under constant competitive pressure to fine-tune the productive process in his (or her) firm. If he fails to do so at least as effectively as most of his competitors he will suffer losses, but if he does just a little better he may earn a pure profit. His competitors will be under the same pressure, so that any pure profit that does arise will be temporary. It is a continuing process, and ensures that everything is produced and sold at the lowest cost.

9. The Profit Motive.

The profit motive is at the heart of the free-enterprise system. However, the logic of the arguments on which it is based focus on *pure profit*, not "profit" in the sense in which that word is commonly used.

Many economists consider that Adam Smith's *The Wealth of Nations*, published in 1776, marks the start of economics as a serious discipline—at least in the English-speaking world. In an often-quoted passage he pinpoints a major feature of the *laissez-faire* economic system he advocated, which was a direct application of principles derived from what we now know as the model of pure competition:

> Every individual endeavours to employ his capital so that its produce may be of greatest value. He generally neither intends to promote the public interest, nor knows how much he is promoting it. He intends only his own security, only his own gain. And he is in this led by an *invisible hand* to promote an end which was no part of his intention. By pursuing his own interest he frequently promotes that of society more effectually than when he really intends to promote it.

In any economic system capital goods must be paid for in some way, if they are to be provided at all. In a money-and-market economy the owners of those goods are certainly entitled to a fair return for their use, and have no reason to allow them to be used by others unless they get it. Under the model of pure competition this return is determined by market forces we will explore further in later chapters, but we will not find any criterion of a "fair" return. The return in any given use must tend to equal that in other uses, it is true, but that is because of practical rather than ethical factors: capital will not continue to be available for that use otherwise.

However, the mere fact that capital must earn some imprecisely-defined return does not explain how profits motivate the free-enterprise system—not even if we (inaccurately) identify the returns to capital with "profit" in the popular sense. Essentially the same is just as true of all other factors of production—they will not be supplied to the productive process (except perhaps in a slave society) unless they too get an acceptable share in the output.

Pure profit, in contrast, can be easily identified with Smith's "unseen hand". It is the carrot before the nose of the free-enterprise donkey that induces him to pull the economic cart, as each individual seeks his (or her) own personal advantage. In the model of pure competition the reality of a pure profit is fleeting at best, but the hope of it is an effective incentive both in the model and in the real world. It attracts resources to expanding industries and thus promotes their most efficient use. It encourages innovation, and thereby makes new and better products available to the public at competitive prices. It benefits society as a whole, by reducing the cost of finished goods and by promoting the most efficient use of productive resources.

Pure profit does not accrue as of right to the owners of property, but to the skillful manager or entrepreneur or "undertaker" who manages to make the productive process more efficient. Indeed, any individual may earn a pure profit if he can spot some legitimate way of gaining an advantage. Even the much-vilified arbitrager, who makes a profit by simultaneously buying and selling the same item or commodity to take advantage of anomalies in market prices, benefits society by helping to eliminate the anomalies and thus make markets more efficient.

Chapter 5

Markets: Supply and Demand

1. Consumer-Goods Markets.

The demand function of a particular community (a town, a city, a region, or a nation) for any particular good may be seen as the sum of the demand functions of its individual members. This is illustrated in Figure 5-1, where the demand curves $d_A d_A$, $d_B d_B$, and $d_C d_C$ of three individuals with different tastes, or different incomes,

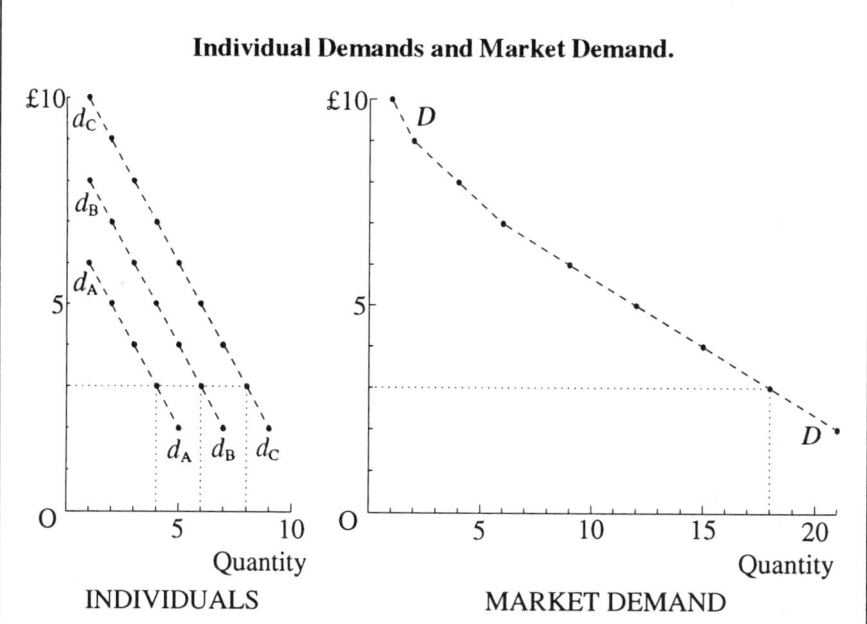

Figure 5-1. Individuals A, B, and C have different demand functions for a certain product, represented by the lines $d_A d_A$, $d_B d_B$, and $d_C d_C$ respectively, which can be added horizontally to get a combined demand function DD. At a price of 3.00, for example, A buys 4 units, B buys 6, and C buys 8, giving a total market demand of 18 units.

or both, give rise to a combined demand curve *DD*. (Note that we have used small letters for the individual demand curves and quantities, and capital letters for the combined curve.)

Individual *A* is willing to buy the product at relatively low prices, but his purchases decline if the price rises, and he drops out of the market entirely at about £6.00 a unit (or 6 of whatever currency you prefer). Individual *B* buys more at all price levels, and does not drop out until about £8.00. Individual *C* buys still more at every price, and stays in the market until the price exceeds £10.00. Their combined demand-curve is formed by adding the three individual curves horizontally. At a price of £3.00, for example, *A* buys 4 units, *B* buys 6, and *C* buys 8, giving a total market demand of 18 units.

Two things happen to the market demand curve as the price falls. First, those already in the market buy more. Second, new buyers enter the market.

Next, a market supply function can be derived in essentially the same way as the market demand function, though in this case there are additional complications to consider. These complications centre on what is known to logicians as "the fallacy of composition": assuming that what is true for each member of a group or class is, for that reason alone, true of the group as a whole.

Thus in this case the individual firm's supply function is quite valid in terms of the assumptions made (particularly that it is too small to affect the prices of either the inputs it buys or the product it sells), but it would be fallacious to conclude that the supply function of the entire industry could be derived by the simple addition of the supply curves of the individual firms.[1] For one thing, new firms may enter the industry if its selling price rises, and marginal firms may leave if the price falls. For another, it may be impossible to expand total output materially without affecting the costs of some inputs, unless the industry as a whole makes only minor claims on all productive resources.

We will have more to say about this problem in section 3 of this chapter. In spite of it, however, an industry supply function can in principle be derived from the supply functions of its member firms. When the industry's output has stabilized at a given price, adding the outputs of all firms will give the point on the industry supply function that corresponds to that price. Recalculating in the same way at

---

1 The same problem does not arise in the case of demand functions, for they may be seen as nothing more than conditional shopping lists: *if* the price is so-and-so, and *if* other things remain unchanged (including your income!), *then* you will buy such-and-such a quantity of this particular product. The effect that other people's purchases may have on the market will show up in its price, so your demand function has already allowed for it.

other outputs and prices, after costs have adjusted to each new situation, gives a succession of equilibrium points on the industry supply function.

Long-run equilibrium in the purely competitive model makes the price line tangent to each firm's average-cost curve at its lowest point, and each must sell at the same price, so each point on the long-run supply function records the average cost for the industry at that output. Therefore the supply function or curve must also be the *average cost curve for the industry.*[2]

Supply curves appropriate for short-run or medium-term periods may be constructed in the same way, within the limitations of the adjustments that can be made in those periods.

The *SS* curve in Figure 5-2 represents the supply function for a certain industry, derived as just explained. The *DD* curve is derived in the same way as in Figure 5-1. We have used straight lines for both curves, for the very practical reason that they are easy to draw. Furthermore they are merely illustrative, and any curve can be replaced by a straight line for a short distance without serious distortion. In any case we are only interested in relatively small movements around an equilibrium position, otherwise we would be trespassing on our "*if...*" assumption; we could hardly pretend that the markets for other products were unaffected if a significant transfer of resources from or to other industries was called for.

The breaks in the north-south and east-west axes of the figure, near the origin, indicate the omission of an indefinite amount of space, so we can represent the demand and supply curves on a larger scale for greater clarity without trespassing on the assumption that the changes we will introduce are relatively small movements around the equilibrium point.

Between them the *DD* and *SS* curves illustrate the "demand and supply" analysis that is a central feature of the microeconomics of pure competition. They also define the equilibrium price, P_E.

However, we do not necessarsily have to identify this equilibrium with the final long-run-equilibrium position that would be reached if all disturbances were allowed to work themselves out. For short-run analysis we are entitled to identify it with the nearest approximation that is attainable in the timeframe we have in mind—for example, the time it takes for new firms to enter the industry and get

---

2 An *industry marginal-cost curve* may be constructed in the usual way. It will differ from the marginal-cost curves of individual firms in that (a) it will take account of additional costs which an individual firm might not consider but which would become significant for the industry as a whole as its total output expanded, and (b) the firm's marginal costs really relate only to small changes in its own output when the industry's output is within a narrow range around the equilibrium level at any given market-set price.

started, or the time it takes to squeeze out marginal plants by the wearing out of their capital equipment. Thus in Figure 5-2 the supply curve has been drawn as

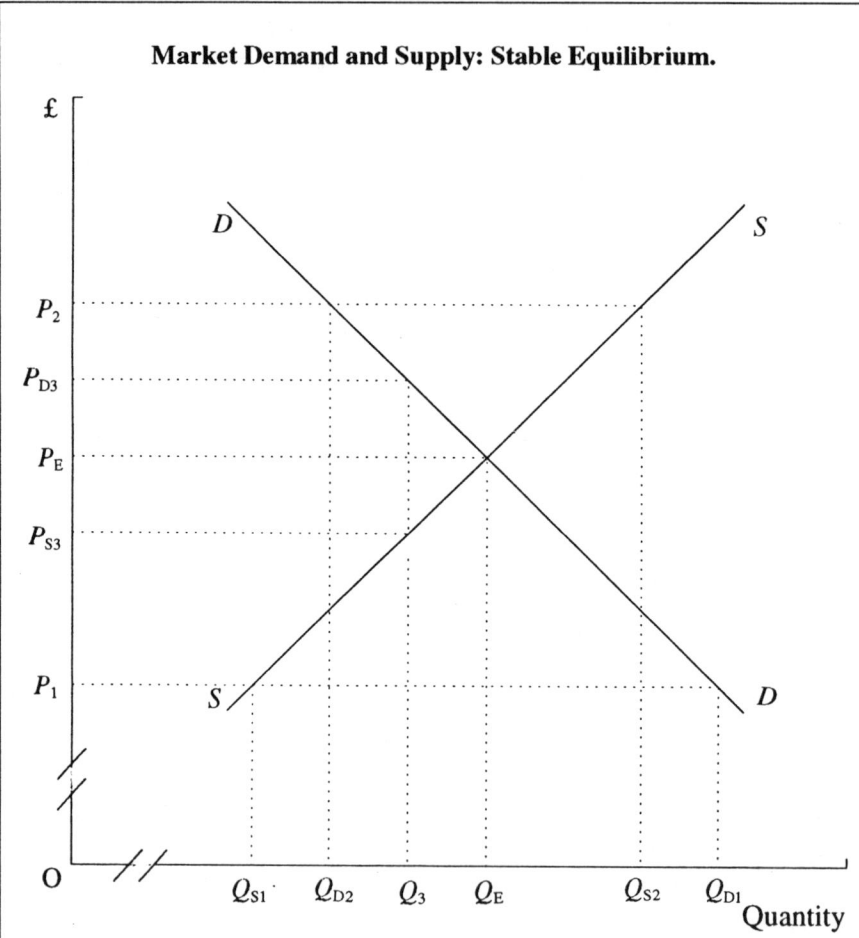

Figure 5-2. The equilibrium price is P_E; if some disturbance drives it down to P_1, then buyers will want Q_{D1} but sellers will offer only Q_{S1}, and competition among buyers will drive it up. If the price is driven up to P_2 then sellers will offer Q_{S2} but buyers will want only Q_{D2}, and competition among sellers will drive it down. Or, suppose sellers misjudge the market and offer the quantity Q_3, expecting a price of only P_{S3} (i.e. their supply-price for that output); but buyers would be prepared to pay P_{D3} if that were all that was available (their demand-price for that quantity); so the price rises, more supply is attracted onto the market, and the market tends towards the equilibrium position.

rather elastic, as might be appropriate to a rather long adjustment period; in a somewhat shorter period it would presumably be more inelastic.

On the assumptions we have made, a price of P_E and an output of Q_E is a *stable equilibrium* position, regardless of the interpretion we put on the timeframe involved. Every individual consumer can buy all he (or she) wants, every individual firm can sell all it finds it profitable to produce, no-one has an incentive to alter his (or her) behaviour, and any temporary departure will set corrective forces in motion.

Suppose that for some reason the price falls to P_1. Buyers will try to buy the quantity Q_{D1}, but sellers will be willing to offer only Q_{S1}. Any one buyer can get all he wants by paying slightly more, so competition for the relatively scarce amount available will drive the price up. As the price rises the market becomes willing to absorb less and less, while suppliers become willing to provide more and more, until at a price of P_E the amounts offered and demanded are in equilibrium.

Similarly, if some temporary disturbance drives the price up to P_2, sellers will offer Q_{S2}, but buyers will want only Q_{D2}. Any one seller would sell his full output if he reduced his price slightly, so competition among sellers will drive the price down to P_E.

Alternatively, suppose that any disturbance in the market takes the form of an imbalance in the amounts offered and demanded rather than in the price. (This may sound a little more likely, since suppliers will have to plan their output for at least a little time in advance, and might conceivably misjudge the market.)

Suppose that sellers' combined output decisions result in a market offering of Q_3, for which the supply-price is P_{S3}. If that were all that was available on a continuing basis, the demand-price would be P_{D3}. Competition among buyers for relatively scarce goods would tend to drive the price up towards the demand-price, but the willingness of suppliers to offer more as the price rose above their first expectations would counteract that tendency, so the market would move towards equilibrium at an output of Q_E and a price of P_E.

If, on the other hand, supplier miscalculations led to a market output in excess of Q_E, the supply-price would exceed the demand-price and the market price would tend to fall, but suppliers would reduce their offerings and the market would move towards equilibrium in this case also.

If the market price rose and held there, the pattern would gradually shift towards the long-run-eqluilibrium position. New firms would enter the industry sooner or later, and bring new resources with them; the entire curve would shift eastwards. If the price fell and remained low, some firms would leave the industry and supply would fall; the entire curve would shift westwards. However, it would take longer to reduce supply in this way than to increase it; a new firm may sometimes be established in as little as a few months, but (as long as it can cover its variable costs) an unprofitable plant will hold out until its fixed capital must be replaced, which may mean many years.

In any given timeframe, the equilibrium thus attained appears to be an optimum position. The price that consumers are willing to pay for the last unit purchased just covers its cost to society. No buyer and no seller can influence the market price by his own action. If the market price of any product changes, all the consumer can do is change the quantity he (or she) purchases and reallocate his spending among the various products he buys.

For his part the producer is faced with possible changes in the prices of both what he buys and what he sells, but all he can do is change the amount he produces and sells and the amounts of the inputs he buys (which of course will be interrelated), except as he may find some way of reorganizing his productive process in order to improve its efficiency.

Some economists have expended considerable ingenuity trying to visualize *unstable* equilibrium situations. It appears that this can indeed occur if the demand curve has a greater positive slope (or a smaller negative slope) than the supply curve. Perhaps you can imagine a "snob effect" in which some people (presumably pretty well-to-do) identify price with quality in a certain product and actually *prefer* to pay more for it, though you may have to take some liberties with the principles of pure competition in order to do so.

The demand curve for such a product may have a negative slope over some portion of its potential range, like the DD curve in Figure 5-3. The supply curve SS has been drawn as completely inelastic; perhaps it is some nonreproducible good, like the available supply of paintings by a long-dead master.

In this case the position defined by a price of P_E and an output of Q_S is indeed an equilibrium one, since the amount demanded is exactly equal to the amount supplied. But it is an unstable equilibrium, like a cone balanced on is apex: the slightest departure from it will be self-reinforcing. At a price of P_1, for example, sellers would offer Q_S but consumers would buy only Q_{D1}, and competition among individual sellers would tend to reduce prices farther, so a downward spiral of sales and prices would set in. Similarly, at a price of P_2 suppliers would still offer only Q_s but buyers would want Q_{D2}, and the price would rise continuously. However, such possibilities seem to demand very unusual circumstances. They seem of more interest as geometric curiosities than for economic analysis.

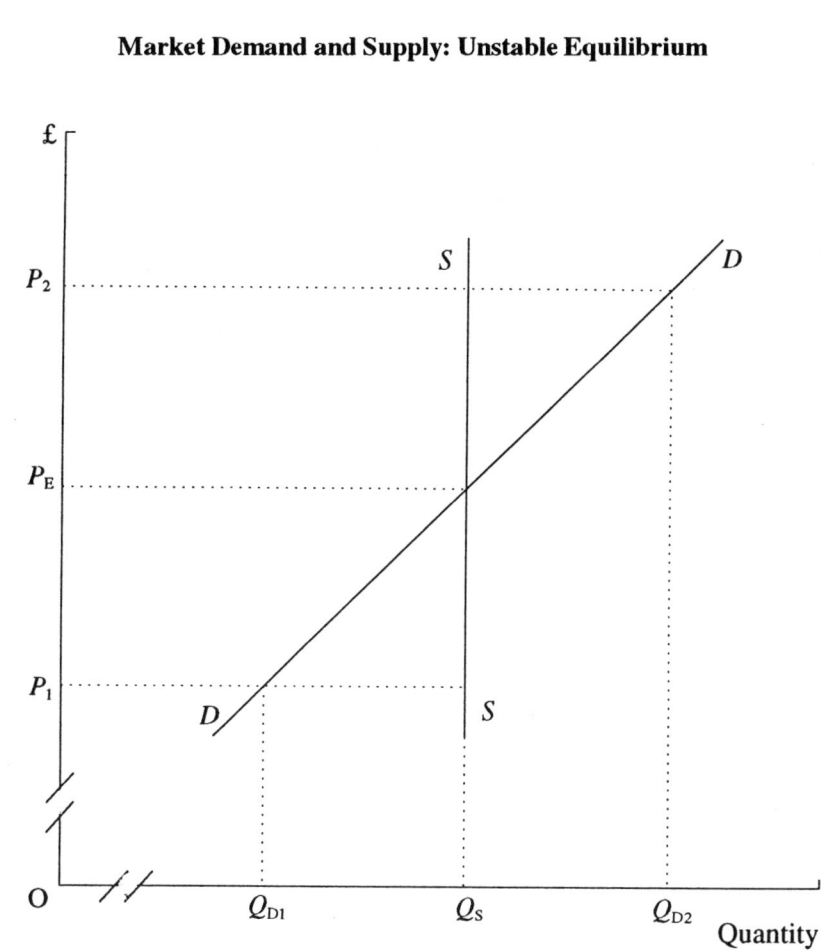

Figure 5-3. If buyers would buy *more* instead of less at higher prices, then P_E would still be an equilibrium price; the quantity demanded would exactly equal the quantity supplied. But it would be an unstable equilibrium: the slightest disturbance would drive the market *away* from equilibrium. At P_1 buyers would want only Q_{D1} but supply would be unchanged at Q_S; competition among sellers would drive the price lower and lower, buyers would want even less, and the market would move continuously away from equilibrium. Similarly, at P_2 competition among buyers for an insufficient supply would drive prices ever higher.

2. The Demand for Factors of Production.

Essentially similar markets exist for producer goods—capital equipment, land and other natural resources, raw materials and semi-processed goods, and labour of various types and skills. The demand side of these markets is linked to the utility functions of ultimate consumers, but only indirectly: it is said to be *derived demand*, because it is derived from the buyer's knowledge that he can use the good or service in a productive process that will contribute to the satisfaction of consumer needs.

There are complex interrelationships among these markets, because many industries feed other industries and may at the same time draw on the products of the same (and still other) industries for part of their own needs. Many minerals and other raw materials as well as much highly skilled labour go into the production of machinery, buildings, and other capital equipment, a good deal of which then goes into the production of other capital goods rather than consumer goods.

Food crops are of course destined for the consumer ultimately, as their designation implies, but for the most part they are subjected to anything from one to a great many intermediate processes before they reach the table. Other crops, such as cotton and other fibres, may also be destined for the consumer (after much processing), but may instead go into commercial or industrial uses where they may be incorporated in capital equipment rather than consumer goods. Other crops are used as a source of energy, for example to feed draft animals used in agriculture and other industries (as they still are in many parts of the world).

Nevertheless all these complexities can be treated adequately for our purposes within the context of the firm and the industry as we have already illustrated them. We can think of the firm buying only factors of production, since any raw materials or semi-processed goods bought for further processing may in principle be resolved into factor costs at earlier stages of the overall productive process.

In order to illustrate how the firm's demand for a factor of production is derived, let us use the same variable-cost data as we did for Figure 4-3 on page 54, except that we have so far been counting in pounds instead of dollars. (Remember also that they are the data given in Table 4-1 on pages 48 and 49, multiplied by 100.) However, we will now want to make a further change: we will want to compute production costs in manhours of labour, instead of money. Multiplying by various wage rates will then give us the money costs, which we can compare with the selling price of the product.

Let us assume that the only component of variable cost is a uniform category of labour at a market-fixed wage. If we initially assume that the wage is £10.00 per hour, we can interpret each pound of variable cost in Table 4-1 as 0.1 manhours of labour. We now want to know how many manhours the manager will buy at various wage-rates.

We now start with a selling price of £18.00 (instead of $18.00) per unit for the product. We already know from section 5 of Chapter 4 that equating the marginal cost to the selling price makes the optimum output approximately 1,281 units, and that the total variable cost will be about £13,827. We now interpret this to mean a marginal cost of 1.8 manhours and total variable costs of 1,383 manhours of labour input. That gives us one point on the firm's demand-for-labour curve: at £10.00 per hour the manager will buy 1,383 manhours.

Other points can be derived in the same way, i.e. by finding the output at which the £18.00 received from the sale of the marginal unit of output will just cover the the cost of the manhours needed to produce it, at other wage rates besides £10.00 per hour. If the wage rate is £12.00, for example, then the optimum output will be that at which the marginal cost in manhours multiplied by £12.00 equals £18.00 (or at which 1.5 manhours is the marginal labour input). This occurs at an output of 1,194 units, and requires a total input of 1,238 manhours; hence the manager will buy 1,238 manhours at £12.00. (As in section 5 of Chapter 4, these figures can be interpolated approximately from Table 4-1 or Figure 4-3.)

The function thus derived is represented by the *dd* curve in Figure 5-4. The north-south axis measures the cost of labour per manhour, the east-west axis measures the number of manhours bought. The maximum wage the firm can afford is £18.00, for that will reduce output to the shut-down level of 1,000 units, which require 1,000 manhours of labour and a marginal input of one manhour per unit of output.

You may verify this most easily by referring to section 7 of Chapter 4, where we noted that the average-variable-cost and the marginal-cost curves will shift northwards in exact proportion to a change in costs. In Figure 4-4 on page 57 the plant would shut down at a selling price of £10.00 or less; we are now counting in pounds instead of dollars, so if the wage rises from £10.00 to £18.00 the shut-down cost will do likewise. The highest wage at which the plant would cover fixed as well as variable costs is about £13.35; the output would be about 1,143, units and the manager would buy about 1,167 manhours of labour. That would yield total revenue of about £20,579 and variable costs of about £15,579, so the fixed costs of £5,000 per period would just be covered.

The firm's demand function for other factors of production may be derived in the same way. Also, just as the total demand function of the community may be derived from the demand functions of its members, so the derived-demand function of an industry (or of all industries combined) for any factor of production may be derived from the derived-demand function of individual firms.

In this case, however, as in the case of industrial supply functions, we must be careful to avoid the fallacy of composition. Firms may enter or leave the industry, and changes in the cost of the factors as industry output varies may affect the individual firms' demand functions. Nevertheless a valid derived-demand function may be constructed by the same technique we used for the industry supply function, i.e. by computing a series of equilibrium price-quantity points for a succession of possible output levels.

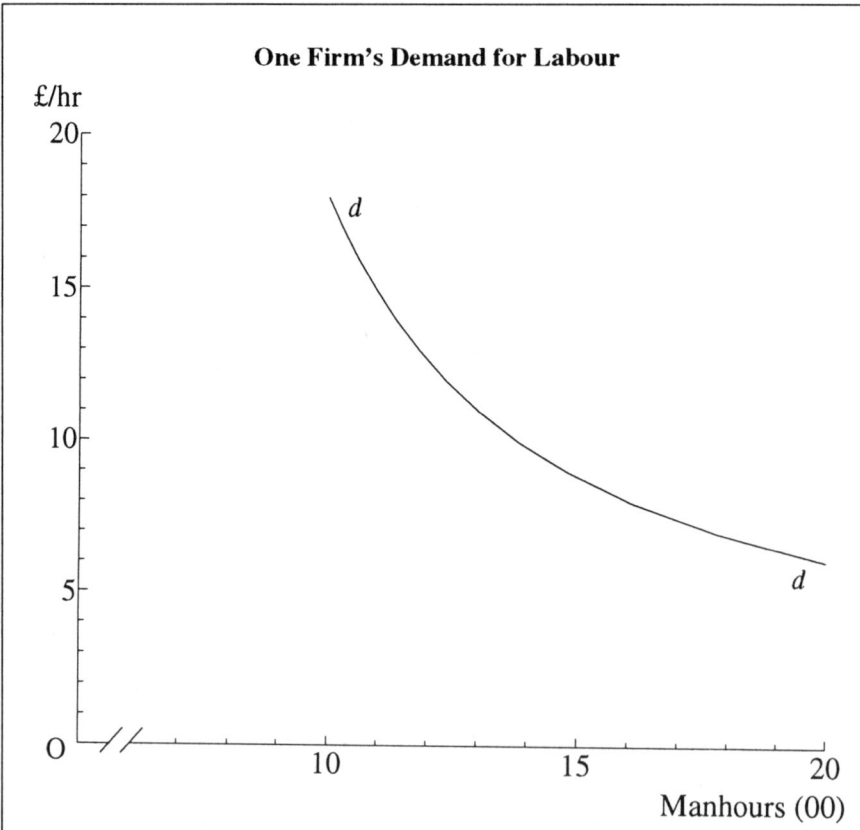

Figure 5-4. Using the same data as in Chapter 4, but substituting pounds for dollars, equating the *MC* to a selling price of £18.00 means the optimum output is 1,281 units and the *AVC* will be £13,827. If we now assume that the only element of variable cost is a uniform category of labour at a wage of £10.00 per hour, the firm's demand for labour is 1,383 manhours, and the cost of the marginal unit of output is 1.8 manhours. Now find other outputs at which *MC* in manhours multiplied by the wage just equals £18.00: the result is the *dd* curve.

3. The Market for Factors of Production.

In the model of pure competition the individual firm's supply function for any factor of production is completely elastic at the market-set wage or rent or other factor cost—the firm can buy all it can use or afford without affecting the unit cost. For the entire economy, however, and probably for any industry as a whole, the currently-available supply of every factor is rather strictly limited, and any increase in demand is likely to bid up its price. For this reason we usually think of the supply curve for factors of production as positively sloped, though this is not invariably the case. Under some circumstances increased output may generate lower costs rather than higher, due to economies of scale.

Economies of scale were discussed briefly in section 6 of Chapter 4. Typically they occur in industries that are suitable for mass production, or in large-scale public utilities, but they may conceivably occur in the supply of a factor of production. For example, an industry that makes use of a special labour skill may find that its cost begins to decline as the industry expands, because it may become feasible for someone to operate a large-scale training program to develop that particular skill.

As we have already noted, however, this sort of thing is usually rather hard to reconcile with the model of pure competition. (Thus in our example the training program would apparently be a one-firm industry.) In any case these economies are likely to occur over a limited range of outputs, after which costs will begin to rise again.

Supply functions for the various factors of production tend to be rather different from one another. "Land", or natural resources generally, is a special case in that the total supply is essentially fixed or completely inelastic, despite the possibilities noted in section 3 of Chapter 1. Its supply curve is usually represented as a straight line perpendicular to the east-west axis. The return to this factor (pure rent) may be said to be determined by the interaction between the derived-demand function for its services and the inelastic supply function, represented graphically by the intersection of the two curves, as in any other market situation.

The supply of capital equipment in general is also virtually fixed in the very short run, at whatever level has been inherited from the immediate past. It becomes more elastic as we lengthen the adjustment period we wish to consider, of course, because there are industries addressed to the production of capital goods on a continuing basis. Most of the output goes to replace older capital goods that have reached the end of their useful life, but as in other industries output can be increased or reduced somewhat even in the short run if market conditions warrant it. It is therefore reasonable to draw the supply curve for capital as somewhat elastic for most purposes, and more elastic the longer the adjustment period we have in mind.

The supply function for capital goods may change over time, in either of two senses. The nature of the community's capital equipment may change entirely, and its allocation among various industries as well, as time is allowed for the wearing out of old equipment and its replacement by new. And the total available stock may increase over historic time (the entire curve may shift eastwards), as net saving permits continuing additions.

The ultimate limit on the net rate of accumulation of capital goods in any community is the willingness of the public to save—that is, its willingness to forgo current consumption in favour of either greater consumption in the future or accumulating a cushion against adverse contingencies. In section 2 of Chapter 2 we noted the importance of this relationship, and we will have more to say about it in later chapters as well.

The nature of the supply function for labour, or for any particular category of labour, is more uncertain. The basic assumption is that everyone will work until the additional consumption an additional hour (or minute) of work per day or per week will permit will be less attractive than the additional leisure that can be had instead. (Note that this implies that everyone can decide for himself or herself how long to work each day, as if he were self-employed. Even when the workweek is determined in some other way, however, such as by negotiation between a group of workers and the management, there is some presumption that its length is ultimately determined by majority choice.)

On this basis the individual will normally be willing to work longer if the wage is higher. This is illustrated by the positive slope to the portion of the individual supply curve around the wage W_2 in Figure 5-5.

Departures from this standard pattern may occur, however, at least temporarily. If the wage-rate falls sharply, for example, an individual may respond by working more instead of less, in order to feed and clothe his family or to maintain his customary standard of living. (Perhaps his wife and children will seek work too, if they are not already working.) This will give a negative slope to his labour-supply curve, as in the section of Figure 5-5 around the W_1 wage level.

In The Great Depression of the 1930's, for example, farmers found their incomes sharply reduced as commodity prices fell while fixed costs incurred in more prosperous times remained unchanged. In many cases their first reaction was to work harder in a desperate effort to compensate—they planted larger areas and worked longer hours.

On the other hand a sudden increase in his (or her) wage may lead to a "backward-bending" supply curve, as the individual prefers to stop work and enjoy more leisure when he has earned enough to satisfy his customary wants; this is illustrated around a wage level of W_3. Thus in the early days of the industrial revolution some employers in Britain complained that raising workers' wages was counterproductive: absenteeism increased, much of the extra pay was spent on strong drink, and output suffered. These effects may have been exaggerated, but may well have occurred to some extent, in the short run at least. In the course of

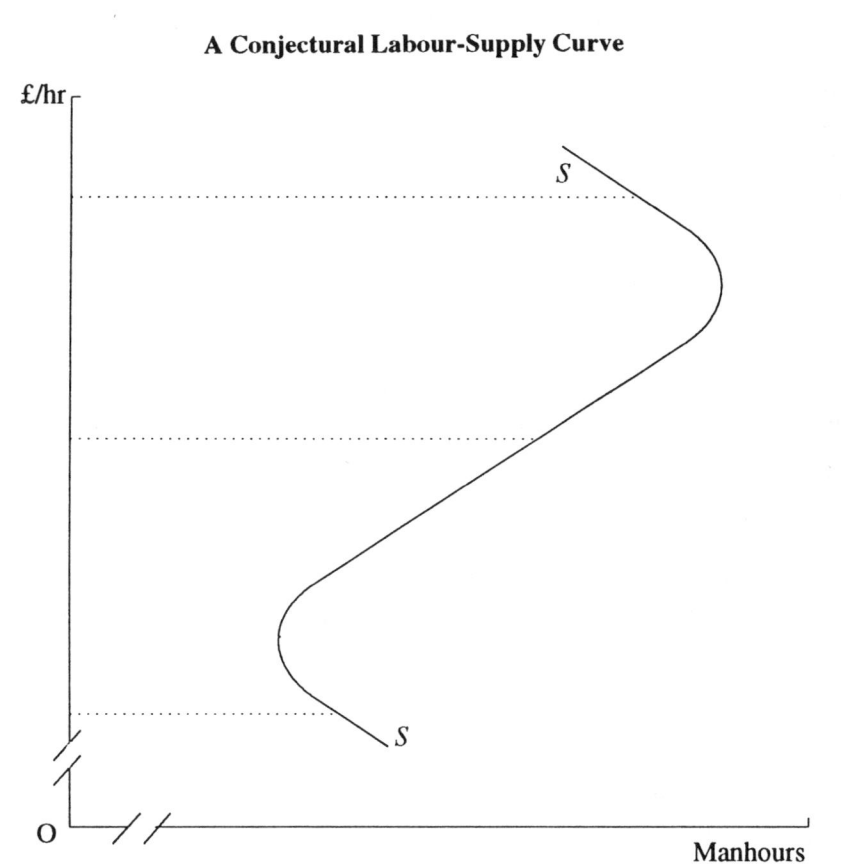

Figure 5-5. The normal supposition is that workers will work longer hours for a higher wage, so the supply curve of labour will have a positive slope, as in the vicinity of wage W_2. If wages fall sharply, however, workers may want to work more instead of less, in order to maintain their standard of living: this is illustrated by the negative slope of the segment of the curve in the vicinity of wage W_1. Or a sudden substantial increase in wages may lead workers to work less and enjoy more leisure, thus giving a "backward-bending" segment with a positive slope, as at a wage of W_3.

time, however, the attractions of increased enjoyment of the new consumer goods coming on the market obviously won out.

Nevertheless the presumption is that the individual's supply curve will normally have a positive slope, even in the fairly short run. If the wage rate has been temporarily disturbed, it will eventually return to a more normal level. If the change is permanent, then the individual will adapt by readjusting his consumption to his new level of income.

The overall supply function for labour that emerges therefore exhibits a positive slope. If higher wages attract new entrants to the labour force as well as inducing those already employed to work longer hours, the slope will be less steep than it would otherwise be, but it will still be positive. (Perhaps some individuals who have retired on their savings, or who have independent incomes, may be induced to accept employment if the wage is high enough.)

For an expanding industry the slope will probably be steeper than average, because of the need to attract labour (and other factors of production) from other industries. The overall supply and the supply available to any particular industry may change over time, of course: particular skills may be developed by experience and by training programs, and the working population will change as population changes.

In general, then, the markets for factors of production in the model of pure competition will resemble the markets for consumer goods. The demand function will normally exhibit a negative slope, the supply function a positive slope which may range up to complete inelasticity (perpendicular to the east-west axis).

The demand function for each factor may change as well as the supply function, of course, because of changing incomes or changing tastes or other developments. Technological progress, the accumulation of productive capital, and a rising level of knowledge and skills among the general population (human capital) will tend to raise incomes (and consumption), the depletion or wastage of natural resources will tend to reduce them.

4. Long-Run Equilibrium.

We have observed more than once that the full rigour of the model of pure competition obtains only in the long-run-equilibrium position to which it tends, but so far our discussion has related primarily to short-term and medium-term considerations.

Long-run equilibrium is a sort of economic nirvana in which all problems are solved and all disturbances have been given time to work themselves out. It does not really imply the lapse of a very long period of historic time, though that idea is often used to explain it. Rather, it is one of those "*if*" propositions that economists use for analytical purposes.

The long-run-equilibrium position is the way things would be *if* the natural equilibrating forces of the economy were allowed to operate freely until all "disturbances" had been eliminated, and no new disturbances were allowed to occur in the meantime. A "disturbance" in this sense is any departure from the ideal equilibrium position that could be corrected in the timeframe under consideration, anything that any participant in the productive process would be willing and able to change if time permitted, and in this case there is no time limit.

As thus understood the long-run-equilibrium position appropriate to today is not the same as that appropriate to last year or last month or last week, or even last night, because some old disturbances have been partly if not entirely corrected and some new ones have arisen, new capital has been acquired, new lessons have been learned, some productive property and natural resources have been lost or used up, irrevocable decisions have been made. The position appropriate to tomorrow or next year or at any other time in the future will be different again.

All these long-run-equilibrium positions will be quite different, since the equilibrating forces will be deemed to start from different positions. There will certainly be important similarities and continuities among positions appropriate to dates that are close together in historic time, but there will be important differences and discontinuities too.

What will be the nature of a long-run-equilibrium position? How will it differ from the short-run or medium-term equilibrium position from which it is deemed to start?

On the demand side of consumer-goods markets, the changes will be subtle but important. The prices of all goods will shift to their equilibrium levels. Each individual consumer will presumably refine the allocation of his income among the many goods and services that compete for his (or her) attention, so that his marginal spending on each is exactly proportionate to its marginal utility. In the process he will become aware of any useful products he was unaware or not fully aware of, and incorporate them in his spending pattern.

But the major adjustment that will be necessary in the consumer's spending pattern may relate to his income. If his (or her) wage or salary was not already exactly equal to the value of its marginal contribution to total output, it will become so—and of course his spending pattern will conform to his equilibrium income, not his original income. The total market demand for each product will be the sum of the individual demands as thus adjusted and refined.

There will be equilibrium in all markets for the factors of production; each factor will earn exactly the value of its marginal contribution to output in the economy as a whole, and each will be employed in its most productive uses in the economy as a whole. New firms will enter and inefficient old ones will be driven out of each industry until all are operating at the most efficient level. Each individual firm in every industry, or rather each firm that survives, will have reworked its productive arrangements to use the most cost-efficient combination of factor inputs.

Among other things that means finding the optimum scale of operations, whether measured in terms of output or capital installation or any other standard. Pure profits will disappear: the equilibrium selling price will be tangent to the average-total-cost curve of every firm at its lowest point (where it is intersected by the marginal-cost curve).

The industry's total output will of course be the sum of the outputs of all the component firms at the equilibrium price. It will be possible in principle to construct a long-run supply curve for the industry in the usual way, by finding out other price-output combinations that would just cover total costs *if* that was the equilibrium output of the industry in question and *if* all factors of production were appropriately reallocated between this and all other industries. The industry supply curve will intersect the community demand curve for the product at the price that is tangent to the average-total-cost curve of each individual firm at its lowest point, and is therefore the equilibrium selling price for the industry.

It is sometimes said that the intersection of the industry supply curve with the community demand curve for any product "determines" the equilibrium price, especially in short-run or other partial-equilibrium situations. However, it is more correct to say that all "economic variables" in the economy are mutually determined in a *general equilibrium* context. By "economic variables" we mean all factor prices, all final product prices, all prices of raw materials and semi-processed goods, the amounts of all final and intermediate products, and anything else that can be affected by how the economy uses its resources. A change in any one of them implies some reallocation of productive resources, hence will affect some or all the others.

From this point of view the ultimate determinants of the long-run-equilibrium position are limited to two: the tastes of the various members of the community, and the resources with which it is endowed at the moment for which the long-run-equilibrium position is to be determined (including, of course, the capital equipment it has inherited from the immediate past, the collective labour skills of the members, the current state of technology, and that sort of thing.)

5. Factor Returns.

In the model of pure competition, how will the output (which is the same as the real income) of the community be shared among the lenders, the other property-owners, and the wage-earners who have coöperated in its production?

It is of course impossible to say in any detail, but the general principles are clear enough. Some points were noted in section 3 of Chapter 1, but their logic should now be clearer in the light of the intervening discussion. Each factor of production will earn an income equal to its marginal contribution to total output, and that return will be the same in all industries.

The concept of "wages" as the return to "labour" should be clear enough by now. We have used the term labour to include all types of skilled and unskilled work, manual or intellectual or artistic, that commands a price in the marketplace. Wages, accordingly, includes salaries, commissions, bonuses, professional fees, the wages of management, and all forms of personal remuneration *except* the pure profit earned by an entrepreneur through some perspicacious action. Just to cover all possibilities, perhaps we should also exclude *windfall profits*, benefits that fall into someone's lap through the accidents of the marketplace. These two exclusions can be justified by the fact that they are destined to disappear in the long-run-equilibrium position to which the model of pure competition tends.

Things like charitable contributions and the welfare and other benefits paid by governments to individuals are not included in wages, of course, since they are not paid for services rendered in the productive process—they are *transfer payments* that come directly or indirectly out of someone else's income. Other transfers between individuals include those effected by fraud or robbery, which enrich the perpetrator at the expense of the victim, and claims against various types of insurance contracts.

The pure rent of land is a clear-cut concept in principle, though there are practical difficulties in identifying it in the real world and distinguishing it from the return to the capital improvements that are commonly added to land. Also, there are significant differences in the rents that are earned by land in the three major uses noted in section 3 of Chapter 1: land that produces crops (say, annually); land as a site for some industrial or commercial activity; and mineral or other exhaustible resources.

Cropland of greater fertility will yield a *differential rent* compared to land of lesser fertility. It will pay the owner to apply additional inputs of labour and capital to it until the marginal inputs yield no more than they would on the poorest land it is just barely worth farming.

Similarly, foodland near a major market will enjoy a differential return (in this case a *situation rent*) compared to equally fertile land that is farther from the market, because of the saving in transportation costs. It will pay the owner to put more labour and capital into production on the land that is near the market until the marginal inputs yield the same as they would on the most distant land it is just worth cultivating (considering the transportation costs).[3]

Rent as a return to the use of land as a site for commercial or industrial activities is a situation rent, like the differential rent of a favourably-located piece of cropland.

Mineral deposits and other wasting assets may earn similar differential rents, except that "fertility" in this case is replaced by the relative richness of the ore or other raw material and the ease of processing it. In this case, of course, some portion of the proceeds from the sale of the output must be treated as a return of capital rather than a pure rent.

Furthermore, the scale of operations will presumably be geared to exacting the maximum net return over the lifetime of the mine or other property, rather than or in addition to the sort of cost-price comparisons we have identified. That raises some interesting questions about the availability and the prices of minerals and similar products in the future, but we can not take the time to explore them now.

Turning to the returns to capital, the discussion is complicated by the fact that the use of machinery, buildings, and other capital equipment by a firm may be financed in any of a wide variety of ways, so claims against its earnings take many forms. The most important choice is between financing by what are known in financial circles as equity capital and debt capital. Since we have usually used the term "capital" to refer to capital goods like machinery and buildings, we will call these two financial categories "equity finance" and "debt finance" in order to avoid confusion.

The basic meaning of equity is the direct ownership of a property after deducting any liens or charges against it. For example, if you own a house worth $100,000 but owe a mortgage of $70,000 against it, your equity in it is $30,000. By extension the term is also applied to the direct ownership of a business firm, as in a sole proprietorship or a partnership, and to the shares issued by a corporation to finance its operations. Equity finance, therefore, means raising money for business purposes by the issuance of equity claims, such as shares of stock, or the financial

---

[3] The marginal input that is just worth applying to any piece of land illustrates the *intensive margin* of cultivation. The poorest land worth cultivating represents the *no-rent margin*. The most distant land worth cultivating represents the *extensive margin*.

claims so issued. Debt finance means raising money by borrowing from others, or the financial claims issued as evidence of the debt.

From a legal point of view equity claims are evidence of ownership, debt claims are not—they are simply evidence of a claim against someone else for the repayment of borrowed money. From the point of view of economic analysis, however, the distinction becomes of minor importance when applied to a business firm.

The owners of equity claims and the owners of debt claims jointly finance the acquisition of the capital assets the firm needs and the other commitments it must make in order to undertake its business: the main difference is in the terms on which they make their contributions available. The owners of debt claims have a prior claim on the firm for their agreed interest return, whether the operation is profitable or not, whereas the owners of equity claims must depend on net earnings. The owners of debt claims also have prior claims on the assets of the firm if their debt is not repaid according to the contract, which may be looked on as a form of conditional ownership.

It follows that the interest paid on debts used to finance productive activities is part of the returns to capital. So, of course, are the returns to equity capital—which normally take the form of dividends and any earnings retained (or reinvested) in the business. Pure rents (to the extent they can be separately identified), rentals, and capital gains are other forms.

Some returns in these categories may accrue to the firm rather than to any individual in the first instance, it is true, and be included in its dividends and retained earnings, thus further complicating matters. In substance, therefore, returns to capital include all forms of income accruing to those who directly or indirectly share in the ownership of productive resources.

Some economists emphasize the difference between interest on debt that helps finance capital used in the productive process, and interest on "unproductive" debt. By unproductive debt they mean debt used to finance consumption in excess of current income—especially, government debt incurred for any purpose except to provide public buildings and facilities that yield economically-useful services. They consider interest on productive debt a factor return, but they treat interest on unproductive debt as a transfer payment.

Other economists disagree, however. Any debt is simply a contract under which the borrower obtains the use of someone else's money for an agreed period of time in return for an agreed rental (interest payment). It can therefore be argued that any debt is "productive" in that it meets the test of the marketplace: the fact that the borrower willingly pays the agreed rate of interest shows that it yields him a service or benefit that he considers worth the price. We don't try to second-guess the consumer about his (or her) spending on anything else, however frivolous, so why do so about the rental he pays for borrowed money?

As for "unproductive" government debt, it has presumably financed expenditures deemed to be in the public interest, such as wartime activities or the expansion of employment opportunities when the economy would otherwise have been depressed, and the continuing interest payments are simply the price that must be paid for not requiring the taxpayer to repay the debt at once. It may of course be true that some of the expenditures have been ill-advised, but then some private investments for productive purposes prove to be ill-advised too.

In the long-run-equilibrium position that is the main focus of the model of pure competition, all risks and uncertainties will have disappeared. All interest rates will therefore be the same regardless of issuer or term. Furthermore, all forms of return to the ownership of property will be equivalent to the rate of interest, because competition among those with money to lend will ensure that it earns the same return in all possible uses. The values of all equity claims, including the ownership of properties yielding rentals or pure rents, will have been determined by capitalizing their yields (i.e., by bidding up their prices to whatever level makes their yields equal to the interest rate).

In any shorter timeframe rents and equity returns should *tend* to equal the interest rates on long-term debts like bonds or mortgages, allowing for differences in risks and other factors (including the possibility of capital gains), but material divergences may persist. Interest rates will vary materially according to the term of the loan, the stature of the issuer, and any other factors that are related to risks and uncertainty.

Chapter 6

Monopoly

1. Monopoly by Merger.

The word "monopoly" comes from two Greek words meaning "single seller". At the start of Chapter 2 we said that "pure" monopoly means that no other seller offers the same product or any similar product. In a broad sense, of course, all products compete for the consumer's attention, so even the monopolist does face some competition. It may therefore be wiser to define monopoly as a situation in which the demand for the product is not appreciably affected by a change in any other price.

The model of "pure monopoly" we are about to explore *contrasts with* that of pure competition in that it is at the opposite end of what we now see to be a virtually-continuous spectrum of possibilities, as discussed in Chapter 8. However, it is *complementary* in the sense that it was commonly used by earlier generations of economists to illustrate those situations (considered to be relatively uncommon) for which the competitive model was clearly inappropriate, thereby filling in an obvious gap in the analysis. A comparable situation arises when many sellers face a single buyer, as when one company is the only employer of a certain type of labour in a particular area. This is technically known as "monopsony", from the Greek words for "only" and "buyer".

Other "abnormal" situations were also recognized, of course, including duopoly (two sellers offering the same product), bilateral monopoly (a monopolist facing a monopsonist), and other variations, but economists were unable to come to as definitive conclusions in these cases as they were for pure competition and pure monopoly: a determinate solution is only possible by making a number of arbitrary assumptions about how each player reacts to the others. Indeed, that is still the situation today, though at least we can now put these cases in better perspective.

86   The Practice of Economics

The typical example of a pure monopoly is an industry in which the most efficient plant is so large that it can supply the whole market, such as a major public utility selling gas or electricity or telephone services in a particular area. We will

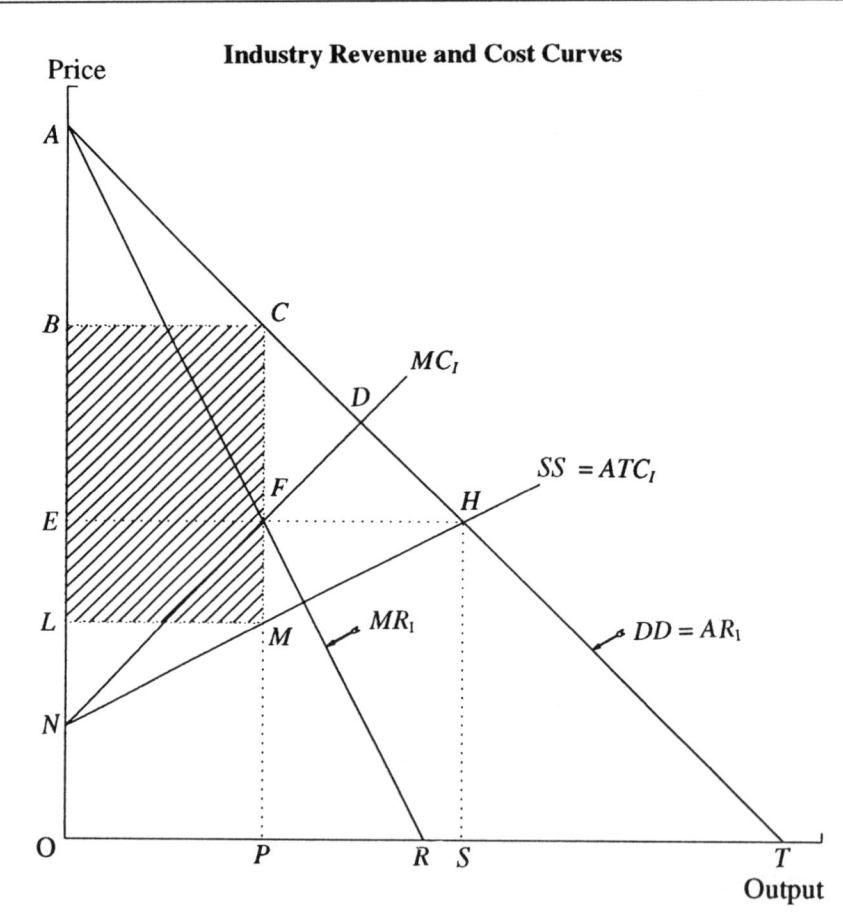

Figure 6-1. The line NH corresponds to the SS curve in Figure 5-2 on page 68, but it is also the average cost curve of the industry (ATC_I). The line ND is the marginal cost curve of the industry (MC_I), and is derived like the marginal cost curve of the firm. The line AT corresponds to the demand curve DD in Figure 5-2, but is also the average revenue curve of the industry (AR_I). The line AR is the marginal revenue curve of the industry (MR_I), derived in essentially the same way as the MC_I curve. Under competitive conditions the MC_I and MR_I curves are irrelevant to any producer's profit calculation, so the industry will produce and sell an output of OS at a price of OE. If all firms in the industry are merged into one, however, its manager will want to produce and sell an output of OP at a price of OB, i.e. the output at which MC_I just equals MR_I, in which case his monopoly profit will be measured by the rectangle BCML.

Monopoly   87

deal with this case shortly, but for now let us make use of Figure 6-1 to look at a different case, just to emphasize that other possibilities do exist.

Let us first interpret Figure 6-1 as representing an industry that is operating under conditions of pure competition. In that case it is essentially a reproduction of Figure 5-2 on page 68, which represents the total demand and supply of an entire industry, except that (a) we have changed the slopes of the *SS* and the *DD* curves as a matter of convenience (they are now the straight lines *NH* and *AT* respectively), and (b) we have added two new curves.

We may again identify the *SS* curve as the *average total cost curve for the industry* (ATC_I). You will recall that we originally identified the *SS* curve as a succession of equilibrium points, each representing the average costs incurred by all producers in the industry (which must be identical for them all under purely-competitive conditions) if that output were the equilibrium output.

It follows that we can compute the *marginal cost curve for the industry* (MC_I) in exactly the same way as we computed the marginal cost curve of the firm in Chapter 4. It is shown as the straight line *ND* in Figure 6-1—the first of the new lines.[1] It does not usually get much attention in the analysis of the determination of output and prices under purely competitive conditions, but we will soon find a use for it.

Similarly, the *DD* curve must be the *average revenue curve for the industry* (AR_I). Since it shows the price consumers are willing to pay for various quantities, and since all units must sell for the same price, it gives the revenue per unit the industry can obtain for various outputs. Also, we can derive the *marginal revenue curve for the industry* from the *DD* (or the AR_I) curve in the same way. It is shown as the straight line *AR* (or MR_I) in Figure 6-1—the second of the new curves. It shows the net added revenue the industry earns by increasing output by one unit, after allowing for having to accept a slightly lower price per unit.

Actually, there is an average revenue curve and a marginal revenue curve for the individual firm, though we did not point it out in Chapter 4. The two are identical, and coincide with the price line, since the market-determined price is both the average and the marginal receipt for the firm per unit sold. For the industry as a whole, however, they do not coincide: increased sales can only be had at a reduction in price per unit.

---

[1] Whenever an average revenue (demand) curve or an average cost curve is represented by a straight line, it can be shown that its marginal curve will also be a straight line, and that the corresponding point on the marginal curve will always be at half the output of the corresponding point on the average curve. Thus in Figure 6-1 *EF=FH*, and *OR=RT*.

Under purely competitive conditions the industry will produce an output of OS and sell it at a price of OE per unit, as in Figure 5-2. Neither the MC_I nor the MR_I curve will have any effect on the industry's output or selling price, which will be determined by impersonal market forces. Each entrepreneur or manager will be very concerned to keep his *own* marginal costs in step with his *own* marginal revenue (i.e. with the market-set price), but he can do nothing about the *industry's* marginal costs and revenue. Indeed, he may be quite unaware, or only dimly aware, that such curves or functions exist, since they are of no more than academic interest to him.

Now suppose that a single entrepreneur manages to get control of all the firms in the industry.[2] That is admittedly a rather unlikely scenario, though the merging of a small number of firms engaged in *monopolistic competition* (to which we will turn in Chapter 8) is quite feasible, and in fact has happened rather frequently in the real world. The MC_I and the MR_I curves will be of keen interest to *him* (or her), for they relate to *his firm* and he can do something about them. He will set his output so as to maximize his profit, just like any entrepreneur operating under purely-competitive conditions—unless, of course, he is restrained from doing so by government regulations or by laws against monopolies and similar practices.

If he can, the monopolist will want to limit his output to OP, for which he can charge a price of OB, and at which his marginal revenue will just cover his marginal cost. He will earn a monopoly profit equal to the shaded rectangle $BCML$—the surplus of his revenue over that for the same output under pure competition.

2. Simple Monopoly.

A more familiar example of monopoly is an industry in which the most efficient firm is so large that it can supply the entire market in an identifiable area, such as a major public utility selling gas or electricity in a given metropolitan area or even a larger region. Such a situation is commonly said to constitute a "natural" monopoly, because allowing more than one firm to operate would involve unnecessary duplication of facilities and a waste of resources.

We will now assume explicitly, as we did implicitly in section 1, that we are dealing with a case of *simple* monopoly—the firm is constrained to sell its output

---

2 Bringing several firms operating at the same stage of production (i.e., that produce the same goods) under the same control is known as "horizontal integration", in contrast to bringing together firms at different stages of production (i.e., that sell to and buy from one another for further processing), which is known as "vertical integration".

to all customers at one price. (We will have a word to say later about *discriminating monopoly*, in which the firm can sell its output at different prices to different people.)

In practice the monopolist will probably be regulated by the government or by some government-appointed body to ensure that his pricing and other policies are in the public interest, and in any case he may be expected to modify his behaviour

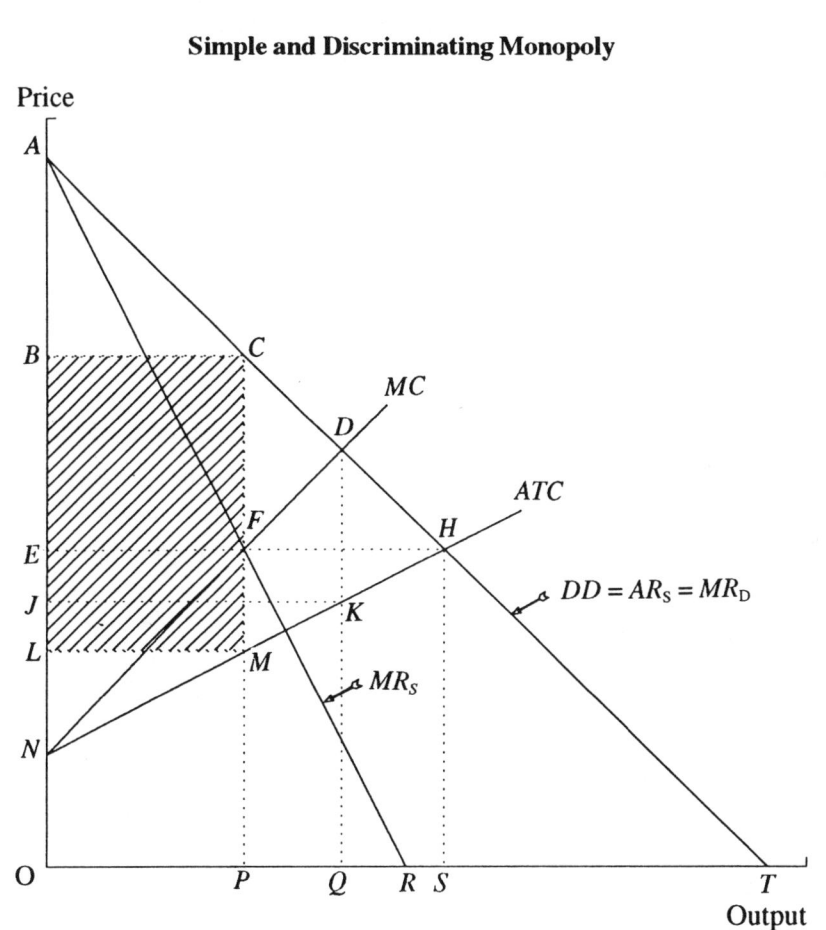

Figure 6-2. The demand curve *DD* is the average revenue curve (AR_S) of the simple monopolist, and from it we can derive a marginal revenue curve (MR_S). He (or she) sets his price at *OB* and sells the quantity *OP*, thus earning a monopoly profit equal to the shaded rectangle *BCML*. The perfectly discriminating monopolist (see section 4 of this chapter) is able to sell each unit for the value of its marginal utility to the buyer; the *DD* curve is therefore his *marginal* revenue curve (MR_D), so he will sell the quantity *OQ* and gain a monopoly profit equal to the area of the irregular quadrilateral *ADKJ*.

in the short run if that will be more profitable in the long run. However, Figure 6-2 (which reproduces Figure 6-1 with only minor changes) depicts how he would maximize his profit if he could: he would produce and sell the quantity OP at a price of OB, as before, because that would equate marginal revenue (MR_s) with marginal cost (MC).

A monopoly profit is commonly defined as a profit over and above what the firm would earn *if* it were operating under purely competitive conditions. This is an impossible stipulation, of course, since we have assumed that one firm of the most efficient size can serve the entire market: such a firm would soon drive smaller competitors out of business. The basis of comparison must therefore be somewhat arbitrary.

However, we noted in section 1 that the supply curve of a purely-competitive industry is identical to its average-cost curve, and that the consumer-demand curve is identical to the industry's average-revenue curve. We are therefore entitled to assert that the line NH (which is the same as in Figure 6-1) represents the purely-competitive supply curve in this case too, even though (unlike the example in section 1) the industry could not in fact operate under purely competitive conditions.

On that basis we may, as before, identify the monopoly profit as the area of the rectangle $BCML$, since a purely competitive industry operating at an output of OP would be selling at a price of OL. Note that in this case the monopolist gains an additional profit from the fact that the industry happens to be operating in the area of increasing cost; by restricting output he (or she) benefits from lower costs as well as higher revenues. This is not typical, however; in the usual case he will be operating in the area of decreasing costs, and his costs will be higher than the purely-competitive cost.

A word of realism is in order here. It is easy enough to draw *hypothetical* cost and revenue curves with impressive precision on a piece of paper, but no producer in the real world can identify his *actual* cost and revenue schedules nearly as clearly.

However, any entrepreneur contemplating a new enterprise must be prepared to judge the most appropriate size of plant, to make reasonably accurate estimates of the various costs he (or she) will incur, and to anticipate the probable selling price of his product. Once his firm is established as a going concern he will certainly know his costs fairly accurately, at least over a modest range around the level of output that experience shows is most profitable. Experience will also tell him the level or range of prices he can expect, i.e. his probable revenue returns. Whether his firm has a monopoly or is operating under competitive conditions, therefore, he will have a pretty good working basis for the sort of profit calculations our model exhibits. At the very worst, trial and error will show the way.

At this point you may be quite ready to accept the idea that a monopoly is a Bad Thing, but in the spirit of scientific enquiry you may very well ask just what is wrong with it. (Some wag has said that monopolies are like babies: there is nothing that makes you so tolerant of them as having one of your own.)

Well, economists find two things wrong. First, a monopolist can restrict his (or her) output and earn a larger return than he could obtain under pure competition. Since the purely-competitive equilibrium is normally taken to indicate the optimum position from the point of view of the economy as a whole, this implies an undesirable redistribution of income from consumers to the monopolist.[3]

Second, the resources of the community are not used with maximum efficiency to serve consumer needs. In the purely-competitive equilibrium, each consumer allocates his (or her) spending to obtain equal satisfaction at the margin; supply and demand in each market are equated at the equilibrium price; and the equilibrium supply-price is where the individual firm's marginal cost equals its average cost at its most efficient (i.e. its lowest) level. Hence no improvement in consumer satisfaction can be obtained by shifting resources from one product to another.

In a monopolized industry, however, the equilibrium selling price (OB in Figure 6-2) is greater than the price that would obtain under pure competition (OE) and the output is less. Consumers would get greater utility if more resources were used in that industry and output was expanded to OS.

There are several measures that could be employed by a government (or by a regulatory body appointed by the government) to correct these faults, *if* the authorities could identify the various cost and revenue functions accurately enough. The monopoly profit could be scooped up by a lump-sum tax the monopolist would be required to pay whether he (or she) operated or not; that would not alter his marginal cost, so he could not improve his position by cutting his output further, and the benefit would go to taxpayers.

---

3 Note that this conclusion depends heavily on certain value judgements and does not follow inescapably from conomic analysis. In sections 4 and 5 of Chapter 7, for example, we will encounter arguments for altering the income-distribution pattern that the purely-competitive model would bring, and in later chapters we will meet other arguments for modifying the results it would produce. Presumably the typical monopolist is no poorer and no more deserving than the average consumer, however, so has no claim to special consideration; on the contrary, he (or she) is likely to be in a privileged position and able to exploit an unfair advantage. However, measures to aid producers in industries seen to suffer unfair *dis*advantages (e.g., agriculture) may in effect create an artificial monopoly for them; in this case society evidently believes the resultant income-redistribution is justified.

However, that would leave his selling price higher and his output lower than under pure competition; the inefficient use of resources would be unchanged. Also, the benefits to individuals as taxpayers might not be the same as their losses as consumers—there might be undesirable residual redistribution effects on incomes.

Another theoretical possibility would be to levy a lump-sum tax of just the right amount to scoop up the monopoly profit, and to use the proceeds to subsidize output up to the purely-competitive level. In terms of Figure 6-2, multiply BC by BL (that is, find the area of the shaded rectangle $BCML$) to determine the lump-sum tax, divide it by FH, and offer the monopolist a subsidy of that amount for every unit increase in output above his equilibrium output of OP. That would raise output and reduce the price to the competitive levels, while just exhausting the proceeds of the lump-sum tax.

In practice, regulators usually make the best guess they can at what the comparable competitive price would be, and set that as a price ceiling. If their calculations are correct, that will force the monopolist to produce and sell the competitive output.

3. Decreasing-Cost Industries.

Mentioning the regulation of monopolies raises a related policy issue with respect to so-called "decreasing cost" industries. We have been content to use straight-line cost and revenue curves in Figure 6-2 (and will do so again in Figure 6-4), since they are simple to construct and create no serious distortions in these cases, but the fact is that the cost curves of a monopoly must be expected to show the same U-shape as those of a small competitive firm; the only significant difference is that their scale is much larger, since they cover an entire industry. Figure 6-3 illustrates the situation.

In any natural monopoly the lowest-cost output of the most efficient size of firm is likely to be somewhat greater or somewhat less than the market can profitably absorb; it would be sheer coincidence if it were otherwise. If the the demand curve intersects the ATC to the west of its lowest point, like DD in Figure 6-3, then any increase in production will reduce unit costs and we have a decreasing-cost industry. This contrasts with (for example) a purely competitive industry, in which the slope of the long-run supply curve is normally positive and unit costs increase as output rises.

Following Alfred Marshall, a famous British economist of the 19th century, most economists agree that the industry really ought to be forced to reduce its price and increase its output not merely to point H (the purely competitive level) but actually to M (at which $MC = DD$). This of course would require the industry to operate at a loss, which would be made up by a government subsidy out of general tax revenue. The concept is called "marginal-cost pricing", and the argument is that output should be expanded until the marginal utility of the last unit consumed just equals its marginal cost to society. (Some qualifying considerations are acknowledged, but the substance of the argument is as given.)

If the demand curve lies to the east of the lowest ATC, as with $D'D'$ in Figure 6-3, we have a case of *in*creasing costs. The same logic applies here: it is argued that the price-output point should be set at M', to equate MC with $D'D'$, and the excess profit should be taxed away.

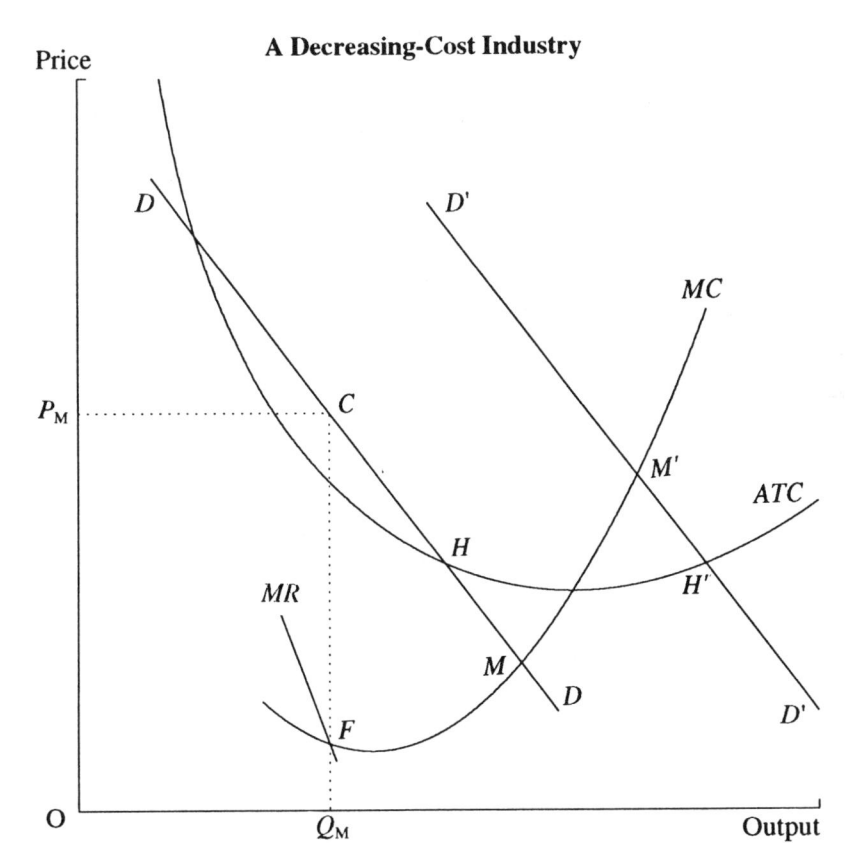

Figure 6-3. If the demand curve (which is also the industry's AR curve) lies to the west of the lowest point of the industry's ATC curve, as DD does, the monopoly price would be P_M and the output Q_M, or the point C, as shown by the intersection of MC and MR at F. Some economists would like the government to drive the price-output point to M, where $DD = MC$, and to reimburse the firm for its losses.

This may inspire you to apply the same argument to the purely competitive case, and to conclude that it is the intersection of the industry's marginal-cost (not its average-cost) curve with the demand curve that should identify the ideal equilibrium position. (In terms of Figure 6-1, when interpreted as representing a purely-competitive industry, that means point D instead of point H.)

Well, it turns out that the answer is *no*. It is too long a story to recount here, but the matter was the subject of considerable debate in an earlier generation, and the substance of the conclusion was this: the difference between the industry's average costs and its marginal costs under pure competition consists of pure rents, which are not "real" costs but merely transfers among members of the public.

Still, the last word may not yet have been said on this question. Is it not possible that some pure rents may be included in the monopolist's profit? Perhaps even in decreasing-cost conditions, as represented by the point H in Figure 6-3, but especially under increasing-cost conditions, as at point H'? If so, what are the implications for marginal-cost pricing?

Note, too, that marginal-cost pricing in decreasing-cost industries would require the allocation of additional resources, which implies some sacrifice of output in other industries. That in turn implies a comparison of the utility consumers would gain in the one case with what they would lose in the other. Also, the choice of the measures by which the revenue was raised to pay the subsidy raises still other questions, primarily concerning how particular consumer individuals would be affected.

We must leave it to the theoreticians to sort these matters out, if they deem it of sufficient practical importance. In the meantime, practical policymakers have shown marked reluctance to put marginal-cost pricing into effect. Perhaps they are right.

4. Discriminating Monopoly.

We may also note the possibility that a monopolist may be able to charge different prices for different units of output. The ideal situation from his (or her) point of view would be if he could sell every unit to each customer at exactly the money-value of its marginal utility to the buyer. In that case the DD curve in Figure 6-2 on page 89 becomes his *marginal* revenue curve (MR_D), since it shows the prices at which each successive unit of output will be sold, whereas it is the *average* revenue curve for the simple monopolist (AR_S). The point D therefore marks the intersection of his MC and MR curves, so he would produce and sell an output of

OQ. His monopoly profit would be equal to the area of the irregular quadrilateral $ADKJ$.

In practice, however, the nearest the discriminating monopolist is likely to come to this ideal is to subdivide his market into several segments having different elasticities of demand. He will then set a separate price for each segment—higher prices for the markets with lower elasticities—in pretty much the same way as in Figure 6-2; the main difference will be that he will have to allocate his costs somewhat arbitrarily among the various segments. For example, theatres, public transportation systems, and others may offer lower prices for senior citizens, students, and children, who presumably have lower incomes and therefore more-elastic demand schedules.

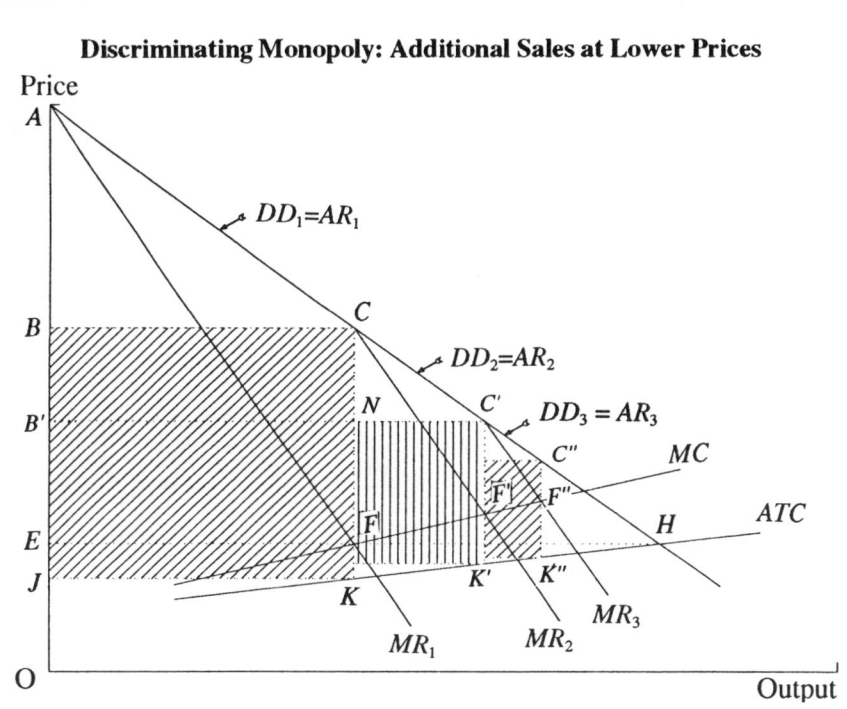

Figure 6-4. The monopoly (say, an electric utility) may set a price of OB for the first block of power to each customer, designed to give it a maximum profit at point C. However, that would tap only the portion of DD between A and C (labelled DD_1) and leave a substantial untapped market southeast of C, at prices well above MC. It could treat this as a new market, with its own MR curve (MR_2), and set a new price OB' for the DD_2 section of the market. It could then set still lower prices for additional blocks (DD_3, etc.).

Figure 6-4 shows a different possibility. The monopolist may not be able to enforce a distinction between groups whose elasticities of demand are different, but may instead be able to offer the same customers different prices for additional quantities of his product. (Thus electric utilities commonly ask a relatively high price per kilowatt-hour for an initial block of power, a lower price for the next block, and perhaps lower prices still for successive blocks.) In this case the monopolist's marginal revenue curve is initially MR_1, which intersects his (or her) MC curve at F, so he will offer an output of BC at a price of OB, like any simple monopolist, and earn a monopoly profit equal to the shaded rectangle $BCKJ$.

However, that exhausts only the portion of the demand curve northwest of C (labelled $DD_1 = AR_1$ in the figure); the discriminating monopolist will observe that there are unsatisfied demands in the portion southeast of C, at prices still above his marginal costs. He will therefore look on this as a new demand curve (labelled DD_2), with its own MR curve (MR_2), which intersects his MC curve at F'; it will pay him to offer additional output of NC' at a price of OB' to those customers who have already bought the required allotment at a price of OB.

The discriminating monopolist will then continue with a new offer for the DD_3 section of the demand curve in the same way, and as many other segments as he can reasonably contrive. He will earn additional monopoly profits equal to the shaded area to the southwest of point C'.

Chapter 7

Other Supplementary Models

1. Joint Supply and Joint Costs.

The model of pure competition was by no means a monolithic affair. Chapters 2 to 5 attempt to capture the essentials of its microeconomics in a form most of today's and yesterday's economists would find reasonably acceptable, and Chapter 10 will do the same for its macroeconomics, but they can not claim more than that. The fact is that from the first there have been several schools of thought whose models differed considerably in content and emphasis, and the views of any one school have changed over time as new insights became accepted. For the most part, however, these differences are of interest only to the specialist.

More significantly, this summary version omits some useful details that have survived more or less intact and have applications that are not confined by the assumptions of the purely competitive model. Usually they may be seen as supplementary models, or sub-models, that focus on a particular aspect of economic relationships. Some of them are addressed to microeconomic details, but some deal with macroeconomic aspects of considerable practical importance. In this chapter we will look at up-to-date versions of a few of them, but will not pretend to deal with them all—any attempt to do so would surely exhaust the reader long before it exhausted the list of potential sub-models!

Our first example deals with supply conditions. Sometimes it is impossible to produce one particular product without at the same time producing some other product or products. Mining offers many examples. Some ores contain oxides or other compounds of several different metals, such as copper, gold, lead, silver, and zinc. Crude petroleum and natural gas may contain a wide variety of complex hydrocarbons, sometimes in association with sulphur or sulphur compounds. Many industrial processes produce by-products, such as the ammonia, tar, and illuminating gas derived in the destructive distillation of coal to produce coke. These are examples of *joint supply*, situations in which the supply of one product or service necessarily involves the supply of some other product or service.

When two or more goods are jointly supplied, determining their separate costs becomes somewhat arbitrary. Some costs can clearly be allocated to one particular product, such as the cost of further refining copper once it has been separated from other metals obtained from a complex ore. As for the costs incurred up to the point at which identifiably different products appear, however, all we can really say is that they are *joint costs*.

We can do a little better when it comes to the relationships between the costs and the selling prices of jointly-supplied goods. Here we can at least derive two firm conclusions: (1) The equilibrium price of each good must equal or exceed the sum of those costs that can be directly attributed to it. (2) Among them, the equilibrium prices of the joint products must cover all the costs (joint and separate) of producing them.

In common usage the word "by-product" identifies something that is produced secondarily or incidentally in the course of producing something else. Technically speaking, a byproduct is a joint product, but the implication is that it is very much of subordinate importance: scrap metal derived from machining operations, sawdust from sawmilling, sulphur from scrubbing industrial emissions to reduce acid rain, and that sort of thing.

Nevertheless it is instructive to look briefly at this special case. At one extreme, finding a market for a by-product has occasionally turned a losing operation into a profitable one. Indeed, it has been alleged that this has happened in some cases where the by-products were pollutants the producer had previously released into the air but was forced to retrieve because of environmental damage.

At the other extreme, the by-products may be unsaleable at any price or may not even be gotten rid of by giving them away for free; they are waste products, and the producer may have to incur additional costs to haul them away and dispose of them. In this case we normally think of the disposal costs as part of the costs of producing the saleable product or products. Alternatively, however, we might identify them as *negative selling prices* for the by-products: the positive selling prices for the "products" plus the negative selling prices for the "by-products" (or less the disposal costs of the "wastes") must cover their joint costs.

2. Complementary Goods and Substitute Goods.

There is also such a thing as joint demand: the demand for *complementary goods*, things that tend to be consumed together. Porridge and milk offer a homely example. Others are tea and lemon, tea and sugar, and coffee and cream. Of course, these linkages need not be either exclusive or mandatory: milk is jointly demanded with tea as well as porridge, sugar is jointly demanded with coffee and porridge as well as tea, and milk and sugar have independent uses as well.

The demand functions for jointly-demanded goods tend to move together, but not necessarily by the same amount. For example, sugar is a relatively important constituent of sweetened tea, but has many other uses too; a shift in the demand for sugar may therefore have more effect on the demand for tea than a shift in the demand for tea would have on the demand for sugar. The effect on their prices may also be quite different, because their elasticities of demand and supply may be different.

Some other goods are rivals, or *substitutes* for one another. In a sense, of course, all goods are rivals for a share of consumers' incomes, but the rivalry becomes pretty specific when two or more goods serve very nearly the same purpose. Tea and coffee are substitutes for one another. So are beef, pork, and lamb. The demand curves (and probably the prices) of substitutes will of course move more or less together if demand increases (or decreases) for that class of goods in general, but a change in the demand for one alone will probably be largely at the expense of the other or others. And an increase in the price of one will cause demand to shift to the other, tending to raise its price in sympathy.

These same relationships are to be found in the markets for producer goods. In Chapter 4 we found that production usually requires the coöperation of more than one factor of production, and in that sense the factors are in general complementary—as we would now say, they are jointly demanded. If we turn to the details of the productive process, we also find that certain specific labour skills are jointly demanded (such as carpenters and plumbers in housebuilding). So are certain types of capital goods, and so are some particular labour skills and some particular machines (you wouldn't put an untrained operator in charge of an expensive machine).

3. Business Cycles.

By "business cycles" or "trade cycles" we mean fluctuations in economic activity that appear to be due primarily to *internal* forces operating in the process of production and trade itself, rather than *external* forces like wars or accidental discoveries or natural disasters or climatic cycles. They are characteristic of relatively sophisticated money-and-market economies.

However, the distinction between "internal" and "external" causes is not absolute. Wars, other political events, the discovery of new resources, and some other primarily-external occurrences may be at least in part influenced by economic events, and unwise husbandry may be a factor in the incidence and severity of such "natural" disasters as droughts and floods.

Mankind's economic activities have always been subject to fluctuations due to variations in the weather and to other natural causes. The most obvious examples are year-to-year variations in the yields of particular crops, or of all crops in a given area, because of normal fluctuations in rainfall, temperature, and other climatic conditions. More spectacular examples include severe floods, volcanic eruptions, and prolonged droughts such as that which afflicted great parts of North America in the 1930's or great parts of Africa in the 1980's. These fluctuations have pronounced effects on the real income of the community, whether it is a relatively simple one based on self-sufficient agriculture or a modern industrial economy, and they may *initiate* a business-cycle response in the economy, but they do not in themselves constitute business cycles.

Cycles of good and bad trade can be traced back to medieval times at least, but they appear to have become more identifiable and regular in the 19th century as industrialization gathered momentum in most of Europe and spread to other parts of the world. They posed an obvious challenge to the optimistic view that full employment should be the normal condition of the economy, as the model of pure competition implies, and therefore became an object of intensive study by economists.

Interest in business cycles rapidly waned after World War II, as the initial successes of demand-management techniques seemed to have either eliminated the problem altogether or at least to have reduced it to manageable proportions, depending on which group of economists you happened to listen to. (Demand-management techniques will be discussed in Chapter 13.) However, interest in cycles may be about to revive, thanks to the reappearance of uncomfortably high levels of unemployment in the 1970's and 1980's. The rise in unemployment is in turn due to the efforts of governments in most countries to combat inflation, which gradually grew from one or two per cent per annum in the early postwar years to double-digit proportions by about 1980.

Economists do not entirely agree on the *causes* of cycles, but their *descriptions* are broadly similar. The cycle may be divided into four distinct phases, which are repeated over and over: a period of expansion, which may or may not turn into an inflationary boom; a peak, or upper turning point; a period of recession; and a trough, or lower turning point. Which of these phases is to be viewed as the "beginning" is a sort of which-came-first conundrum, like the chicken and the egg; some theorists prefer to start at one point, others at another. There are a number of possible explanations of why a contraction or an expansion will tend to feed on itself for a while once it has begun, and why it should ultimately come to an end. Probably more than one of these forces may be operating at the same time.

Let's begin with the two main components of the spending stream, consumer spending on goods and services and investment spending on new capital goods. A sudden change in spending of either kind could start an expansion or a contraction. An increase in spending would generate more money income, which would mean more spending on consumer goods, still more money income, and so on. A decrease in spending would have the opposite effect.

If all economic resources were fully engaged in the productive process, or approximately so, the net result of more money income would be inflation with no change in real output. (Section 6 of Chapter 10 explains why this is to be expected from the model of pure competition.) However, if the business cycle were in the vicinity of the lower turning point, there would be unemployed resources. The increased spending might then bring an expansion of real output with little increase in prices.

This in turn would induce producers to buy more capital goods to supply the increased demand, since they would presumably have let their capital equipment run down during the preceding recession phase (they would not have replaced all capital goods that had reached the end of their useful life). For reasons explained in Chapter 11, the induced investment-spending thus brought about would absorb the savings generated out of the increased money income, and would generate further increases in money income. An accelerating expansion would be under way.

Consumer spending does change significantly at times, and such changes could conceivably initiate a business cycle, but in practice they are usually responses to cyclical fluctuations brought on by other causes. For example, people are likely to spend a larger percentage of their incomes (save less) when a strong boom gets under way and they get very optimistic about the future, or to spend less (save more) in a depression when the future looks bleak. However, they normally spend a fairly stable portion of their incomes on every-day purchases like food, clothing, and shelter; it is spending on durables like automobiles and major appliances that fluctuate most, both in absolute amounts and as a percentage of income.

Actually, consumer spending on big-ticket items should really be treated as a form of investment or capital expenditure, like buying a house, or like capital spending by business. That is not the customary practice, however. The established convention, as reflected in the National Accounts (explained in section 6 of this chapter), is to treat spending on consumer durables as current expenses in full; any money borrowed to pay for them is treated as negative current saving (i.e., is deducted from gross savings out of current income).

In contrast, when a consumer buys a house it is treated as a capital investment, yielding direct benefits to the homeowner in the form of shelter, instead of the interest or dividend return he would get from buying bonds or shares; money borrowed to help pay for it is treated as a *use of*, not a deduction from, current saving. The treatment of expenditures on durables is illogical, but it is the established custom, and logic often seems powerless in the face of custom.

Business investment-spending is likely to be much more volatile than current consumer spending, for it is strongly influenced by the investor's *expectations* about the future and is not so dependent on his current income. Thus in the declining phase of the cycle businessmen are inclined to *dis*invest (not replace all the equipment that is wearing out), because they do not expect to need all the capacity they have. Once a strong expansion sets in, however, they are likely to make net new investments (to acquire more than enough capital goods to replace old equipment), because they expect to need more capacity to meet the increasing demand.

The effects of net new investment may be illustrated by supposing that the economy is running smoothly at a certain output. On average its capital equipment lasts ten years, let's say, so about one-tenth of it is replaced every year; there is neither net new investment nor net disinvestment.

Now suppose that businessmen come to believe, rightly or wrongly, that there will soon be a ten per cent increase in consumer demand: they will want to increase their capital equipment by ten per cent, and their net new investment will exactly equal their usual annual orders for the replacement of equipment that has reached the end of it useful life. A ten per cent increase in consumer demand (or expected consumer demand) has brought a 100 per cent increase in orders for capital goods!

This phenomenon is so important that it has been given a very impressive name: *the acceleration of derived demand*, or the *accelerator principle* for short. You will recall from Chapter 5 that the demand for a factor of production is a *derived* demand, and we have just seen that an increase in consumer demand will have an *accelerated* effect on the demand for producer goods. We will see in Chapter 11 that the total effect on the economy may be much greater than the amount of the net new investment, if conditions are favourable, but for now we will be content to note that relatively large fluctuations in net investment may be generated by relatively small changes in consumption, or merely the *belief* that changes are about to occur.

Of course, the same thing can occur in reverse: if in our example business fails to replace its outworn capital in one year, the capital-goods industry loses 100 per cent of its sales.

Furthermore, the effects of any change may reappear in subsequent years. Thus if output suddenly rises by 10 per cent and continues at 110 per cent of the old level, then on the usual *if...* assumption one tenth of the economy's capital will need replacing in each of the next nine years, but in the tenth year (and in every tenth year thereafter) *two* tenths will need replacing.

That is not likely to happen with any precision in the real world, it is true, since "all other things" can not be depended on to coöperate so nicely, but it does show how a periodically-recurring injection of new spending can be generated by a single increase in consumption. By itself it does not "explain" the business cycle, but it does demonstrate a feature that can contribute both to expansions and to contractions in a single cycle and to the recurrence of later cycles.

There have been many theories that have attempted to explain the business cycle; none of them has been widely accepted as "the" explanation, though fluctuations in capital spending is a feature of most, and several seem to offer useful insights.

One theory is that the cycle is essentially a monetary phenomenon: it suggests reasons why bank credit overexpands at first in support of new spending (mainly for new investments), then brings on a corrective but excessive contraction. (Credit expansion is explained in section 2 of Chapter 12.) Another attributes it to infectious waves of optimism and pessimism on the part of investors or consumers or both: when conditions improve it inspires optimism, which feeds on itself until events fail to match expetations, whereupon pessimism feeds on itself in turn.

The late Professor Schumpeter emphasized the rôle of *innovations.* Innovations are often based on a new invention or new technology, but that is not necessarily the case; they may just involve an imaginative new way of organizing production, or the application of already-known techniques in a new way. An innovation or a cluster of innovations generates new capital investment, typically financed by the expansion of bank loans. This new spending stimulates output and optimism, and yields pure profits to the innovators. Eventually, however, imitators adopt the new methods or duplicate the new products, prices fall, pure profits disappear, and a contraction sets in.

Note that in this scenario the recession phase is *functional* in part at least, since the emerging competition for the innovator drives down prices and ensures that the benefits are passed on to the general public.

Any satisfactory explanation of the business cycle must offer logical reasons for (1) the cumulative expansion in one phase and contraction in another, (2) the change from expansion to contraction at the upper turning point, and (3) the change from contraction to expansion at the lower turning point.

We have identified a number of factors that support a recovery once it begins, mostly by stimulating or supporting investment: the accelerator principle, credit expansion to support new spending, growing optimism as the recovery gains strength, and feedback effects on investment as income grows. The same factors, operating in reverse, contribute to the recession phase. But, what brings on the turning points?

The ultimate limit on an expansion is set by the available supply of productive resources, if other forces do not end it sooner. Bottlenecks in the supply of certain products will appear as this limit is approached, which will slow down the rate of growth; delivery dates will stretch out into the future, some plans will be disappointed, and optimism will evaporate.

The accelerator effect eventually reverses if the expansion merely slows down, because output would have to *continually increase at the same rate* just to maintain the new higher rate of output from the capital-goods industry. (In the example we used above, a drop back to the "normal" replacement of ten per cent of all capital goods in the eleventh year would start a *negative* accelerator going.)

There are reasons for believing that a delayed "currency drain" will occur after an expansion of bank credit—the public will withdraw currency from the banks as its spending rises, which will deplete bank reserves and bring on a credit contraction. Alternatively, if the economy is overheating, the monetary authorities may find it necessary to restrict credit.

Some combination of these forces will bring a downturn, which may be either gradual or abrupt.

The main factor in the lower turning point appears to be a revival of net new investment. A major feature of the recession is likely to be net disinvestment; some capital goods are always reaching the end of their useful life, and falling consumption will mean that productive capacity is excessive and a portion will not be replaced. Eventually, however, the surplus capacity will be eliminated or greatly reduced, and the demand for new capital goods will approach the rate at which old capital is being scrapped.

Meanwhile the sharpened competition for a declining volume of business will spur the search for cost-cutting productive techniques, so the climate will be favourable for innovations, which are likely to involve new or different capital equipment. The mere ending of the recession should combat pessimism and encourage optimism, and the end of disinvestment will in itself inject a positive accelerator stimulus. A new expansion phase will begin.

So far we have spoken of "the" business cycle, but the fact is that several distinct cycles have been identified. Most economists recognize at least two, and perhaps four; they are often given the names of those who first described them.

There is a short cycle of about three years, attributed to over- and under-investment in inventories due to minor fluctuations in consumer spending, and associated with Joseph Kitchin. Next is an intermediate cycle of 8 to 10 years, caused mainly by variations in capital spending. This is the cycle the general public is most likely to know, and is associated with the name of Clement Juglar. Less commonly discussed is a construction cycle of 15 to 25 years, often identified with the work of Simon Kuznetz. Finally, there is a long cycle of 40 to 50 years, associated with Nikolai Kondratieff. This cycle is clearly identifiable in the statistical record, but its causes are not clear, and some observers have suggested that it may be due to a series of unrelated historical accidents rather than a recurring sequence.

It has been suggested that the severity of The Great Depression of the 1930's may have been due to the accidental coincidence of the low points of all four independent cycles.

4. Public Finance.

The rôle of government was originally seen to be pretty limited in the model of pure competition: primarily that of a referee, to enforce the few rules necessary to ensure fair play in the marketplace. That obviously included the prevention and punishment of crimes and fraud, or more generally the administration of civil and criminal law and courts of justice. National defence was a natural addition, since it is not feasible to "sell" it to members of a community individually: anyone who chose not to "buy" would benefit equally from the expenditures of those who did. The costs of these necessary government services were covered by levying taxes on the general public.

However, determining the proper rôle of government is primarily a matter of social relationships rather than economics: what constitutes "fair play in the marketplace" is a sort of collective value judgement by the community, and the community's views on it may gradually change over time. It should therefore occasion no surprise to note that the perceived rôle of government has tended to grow.

From time to time it has been found convenient for the government to provide new services to the community, or to apply additional restraints on market forces. Examples include child labour laws, maximum hours of work, minimum wages, safety standards, educational services, health services, income-redistribution measures, and so on. The most recent major addition is the use of fiscal policy to support output and employment, about which we will hear more in Chapters 11 and 12.[1] The comprehensive term for these services is "public goods"—things that must by their nature be produced and consumed jointly by the community, and things that the community in its wisdom chooses to supply and consume jointly.

Initially the interest in public finance focused primarily on the revenue structure by which the government raises the money to pay for the services it provides. Three distinct bases eventually became recognized: the *fee-for-service* principle, the *benefit* principle, and the *ability-to-pay* principle. The first is only suitable for services that can be provided on something resembling a commercial basis, like passport or visa fees, licences to undertake specific activities, water supplied by a municipality, and the like. The other two are principles of *taxation*, by which the bulk of public goods are paid for, namely those that can not be charged for on a fee-for-service basis or that the community chooses not to charge for in that way.

The benefit principle seeks to collect taxes from the members of the community in proportion to the benefits each is perceived to receive from government services, more or less as a substitute for the fees that would be charged if the services were amenable to the fee-for-service principle. Both the fee-for-service and the benefit principles imply a balancing of the public's demand for services with the taxes they are prepared to pay in order to get those services, and thus offer an approximation to the marginal equivalence of cost and utility that guides the spending choices of the individual consumer. Either or both may be invoked to finance certain types of government expenditure even when the ability-to-pay principle is the community's primary choice.

The ability-to-pay principle questions the possibility of determining the benefits that accrue to individual members of the community, or at any rate the ability to do so with sufficient accuracy. Some advocates stress the importance of equity or justice. A second group sees it as a matter of welfare (in the sense explained in the next section). Both these groups take the expenditure budget as given, i.e. as being determined quite independently of tax policy, but the second includes considerations of income distribution (or redistribution) whereas the first does not. A third

---

[1] Adam Smith's arguments for a *laissez-faire* economic policy were not a matter of doctrinaire morality, but of practical results: the new policy offered greater real income for the community than the feudal and mercantilist policies then in vogue. Subsequent modifications of or departures from *laissez-faire* policy prescriptions should be judged in the same way, as practical decisions that reflect changing views of social objectives.

group integrates the expenditure side of the budget with the tax side, and sees the entire budget as a general plan to maximize welfare.

This principle is now widely accepted as the major basis for a good tax structure, though (as already noted) some services may properly be financed on the fee-for-service or the benefit principle. However, there are some differences of opinion about its justification and about how ability to pay is to be measured. It is generally agreed that income is the appropriate measure, though there is some disagreement (into which we need not go here) about what should or should not be included in income, and whether some forms of income should be treated more favourably than others.

What constitutes "equity" in taxation involves some interesting questions. For our purposes the main point is to distinguish between *horizontal* and *vertical* equity. Horizontal equity means the equal treatment of people who are in essentially the same situation: for example, people with about the same incomes and comparable family responsibilities should pay about the same tax. This is pretty straightforward, and is pretty universally accepted.

Vertical equity deals with how people in different circumstances should be treated. Here we encounter a number of difficult theoretical and practical problems, to which there are no easy or universally-accepted answers. It is generally agreed that taxes should be *progressive*, that is that the marginal tax rate should increase persistently as taxable income increases, but no-one has come up with a convincing theoretical basis for deciding just how progressive they should be. Also, there are practical limits to progressivity: beyond some not-very-precisely-known point, higher marginal rates become counterproductive because they leave so little incentive to work any harder or longer. In practice, therefore, the appropriate degree of progressivity becomes a matter of judgement.

The only other aspect of public finance we can spare the space to mention is the *incidence* of taxation: the question of who ultimately pays a given tax. This question arises because the tax burden may be *shifted* onto someone other than the one who pays it in the first instance. Thus a customs import duty is paid initially by the importer, but the importer adds it to his selling price, and presumably it is ultimately paid by the final consumer (it is "shifted forward").

When a tax is intended or expected to be shifted, as in the case of customs duties, it is known as an *indirect* tax; when it is not intended to be shifted, as in the case of income taxes, inheritance taxes, and property taxes, it is a *direct* tax. A retail sales tax paid by the purchaser at the time of purchase may be legally considered a direct tax in some jurisdictions, but economists usually treat it as an indirect tax since it is collected from the merchant and is included in the price he charges his customers.

However, determining the incidence of taxation is a bit more complicated than that. Taxes may also be shifted "backward" onto suppliers or onto factors of production, and some taxes that are technically classed as direct may be partly shifted forward or backward. If the demand for an imported good is very elastic, for example, the import duty may be partly or wholly shifted to the foreign supplier in the form of a reduced price for his goods.

An income tax is usually considered to be a direct tax, intended to be paid by the person who earns the income. But a corporate income tax may in part be shifted forward to customers, or shifted backward to suppliers or to employees (as lower costs of material or lower wages), depending on market conditions. Even the personal income tax may be shifted forward to the purchasers of labour services that enjoy an inelastic demand.

5. Welfare Economics.

In North America "welfare" has become the accepted term for official subsistence grants to the indigent, but that is *not* the sense in which it is meant here. "Welfare economics" uses the word in the original sense of well-being, of faring or doing well, as in enjoying good health or prosperity. It is concerned with the good health of the society as a whole.

One approach to welfare economics focuses on optimum economic efficiency, meaning an economic equilibrium in which you can not make any individual better off without making some other individual worse off. In itself, this would clearly be a highly desirable result. Furthermore, the long-run-equilibrium of pure and perfect competition would constitute such a position, *if* its conditions could ever be met. That makes the model of pure competition a very useful standard of comparison, even though it is not attainable in practice.

However, economic efficiency in this sense would not by any means ensure that the outcome would be tolerable by the community as a whole. It might easily perpetuate great inequalities of income; it might leave physically handicapped people with no means of livelihood; it might permit some employers to live handsomely by the use of child labour or other economically-weak workers in unhealthy working conditions; it might richly reward the ruthless and penalize the compassionate. Tendencies in all of these directions, and others like them, have indeed been observed in the real world, and have commonly led to actions to eliminate or mitigate them. Optimum economic efficiency may be one requirement for an ideal concept of economic welfare, but it is not the only criterion of a healthy economy or a healthy society.

Another approach to the economics of welfare accepts the economic efficiency of the model of pure competition, but looks primarily at instances (whether in the model or in the real world) in which the results do not accord with common ideas of equity and fair play. Among other things it draws attention to the fact that economic decisions taken by one person or firm or organization in its own interests do not take account of the effects on others. The selfish action of a monopolist in maximizing his own profit, in disregard of the welfare of his customers or of the society as a whole, is an extreme but by no means an isolated example.

A central element of this analysis is the distinction between *private* costs and benefits, on the one hand, and *social* costs and benefits, on the other. In a money-and-market economy most decisions are made by individual consumers and individual producers, and this decentalizing of the decisionmaking process is the basis of the flexibility of the system.

Of course, each individual is expected to make his decisions in terms of the *private* costs he must incur, without regard to any costs that may impinge on others as a result of his decision, and the *private* benefits that he will obtain. Private costs encompass only the expenses or inconvenience incurred by the individual himself, and private benefits consist of the individual's net income from the sale of a product or service and the utility he derives directly from consumption. *Social* costs means the sum of the private costs of the decisionmaker himself and all costs incurred by others as a consequence of the decision, and *social* benefits means the sum of the private benefits of the decisionmaker and any consequential benefits to others.

This idea is sometimes discussed in terms of *externalities*, because it deals with costs and benefits that are *external* to the firm or the individual and therefore are not taken into account when decisions are made. Some of the clearest instances occur in industries dominated by one firm or a few large firms, rather than the many small firms envisaged in the model of pure competition.

For example, a smelter that emits sulphur dioxide into the air suffers only a negligible part of the damage done to the economy by the acid rain that results, so it does not consider the *social* costs of its activities when computing the profitability of its operations, and has no monetary incentive to eliminate the pollution. On the other hand a proposed dam might not only provide a means of generating electricity but might also control seasonal flooding downstream from the site, yet a public utility might conclude that the project was uneconomic since it could not exact payment for the downstream benefits and therefore would not consider them when making is decision. Clearly, some intervention in the free-market process would be in the public interest in both cases.

However, the same thing can occur under purely-competitive conditions. For example, each of many competing producers might discharge some toxic waste in an amount that would be negligible in itself, but the discharge by the industry as a whole might have serious effects; the private costs recognized by any producer, or by the industry as a whole, would not include the damage done. Beneficial externalities may also occur, such as the training of workers in useful skills, who may then find alternative employment in other industries.

The principles involved may be put very clearly in terms of marginal costs and benefits. The *marginal social cost* of a particular action may differ materially from the *marginal private cost*, and the *marginal social benefit* may differ materially from the *marginal private benefit*.

When the social cost in a given industry exceeds the private cost, there is a strong case for intervention (say, by imposing a tax on the producers) that will raise the selling price till it equals the marginal social cost; when it is less, there is a strong case for a government subsidy out of general revenues that will reduce the price till it equals the marginal social cost. Similarly, a product may be subsidized if its marginal social benefit exceeds its marginal private benefit, or taxed in the contrary case. More generally still, there is a case for intervention in any case where the market price differs materially from the price at which marginal social costs and benefits would be equal.

The case for high taxes on alcohol and tobacco is often supported on just such grounds: the consumption of these products involves the community in social costs (health care, crime, family services, etc.) that are not included in the producers' selling prices.

6. The National Accounts.

The national accounts is a statistical presentation of the generation of a nation's real income for a certain period (usually a year or a quarter). It follows a pattern agreed upon through the United Nations, subject to minor variations in some countries. There are three main components: the income and expenditure accounts, domestic product classified by industry, and the balance of international payments.

We will be primarily concerned with the first component. The second is a relatively minor modification of Gross National Product (explained below), subdivided to show totals for the major industries. The third is a detailed account of the nation's dealings with residents of other countries. We will look at this in

Chapter 15; only total exports and total imports enter the income and expenditure accounts.

If you are familiar with double-entry bookkeeping you will find that the income and expenditure accounts are organized in the same way, but you don't have to be a bookkeeper or an accountant to follow them quite easily. All you will need is to remember the description of the circular flow in section 2 of Chapter 2: goods flowing to market in one direction, money payments flowing to the factors of production in the other.

Table 7-1 is an overall summary (the equivalent of a bookkeeper's control ledger) of the income and expenditure in a hypothetical country for a particular year or quarter, in the currency of that country. Further details are given in supplementary statements (like subsidiary ledgers), as briefly described later on.

First look at the last item on the expenditure side, Gross National Product or GNP. It is the same as the last item on the income side, of course, as the circular-flow pattern tells us it should be.[2]

This (the expenditure) total corresponds to the flow of goods to various end-uses, although it really consists of the money payments for the purchase of those goods. It is derived by identifying as accurately as possible, and adding up, all the payments made in the year or quarter for the purchase of final products that someone buys to use, carefully excluding all the intermediate transactions as one producer buys goods and services from another and incorporates them in his own product. The total is subdivided in various ways, only the most important of which are shown in the table. (For some purposes the items may be grouped somewhat differently—for example, government current and capital expenditures may be combined to show the total of the government sector.)

"Personal expenditure" means the expenditure of individuals on consumer goods.

"Government current expenditure" means the expenditure of all levels of government on the goods and services necessary for the performance of their regular services to the public, excluding capital spending for public works, buildings, and the like. It does *not* include transfer payments, i.e. payments like pensions for the blind or the elderly, widow's allowances, and that sort of thing. They are

---

[2] Some statisticians prefer to limit the term GNP to the total of the income side, and (logically enough) to call the other total Gross National Expenditure (GNE); others use the same name for both. Also, some users of the National Accounts prefer to focus on Gross *Domestic* Product (GDP) and Gross *Domestic* Expenditure (GDE) instead of GNP and GNE. GDP excludes the investment income accruing to non-residents, and GDE excludes the same payments from imports.

not payments for services that contribute to current production; they do constitute income to those who receive them, but they are *transferred* in some way from the earnings of others.[3]

---

[3] Neither do they include the interest paid on public debt, which is also treated as a transfer payment. In section 5 of Chapter 5 it was suggested that even interest on "unproductive" debt meets the market test as a payment willingly made for a service rendered, but when the standard pattern for the national accounts was being formulated that view did not carry the day. If the decision were reconsidered today, would the result be the same? Well, that question seems of little practical importance; the convention that interest on the public debt is a transfer payment is firmly established by precedent.

Gross National Product: Income

Wages and salaries		580
Business profits:		
Corporations	77	
Unincorporated businesses	35	
Farm operations	13	
. . . .	125	
Inventory value adjustment	0	125
Interest and miscellaneous		
investment income		80
Net National Income at factor cost		785
Indirect taxes		115
Net National Product at market prices		900
Capital cost allowances		100
Gross National Product at market prices		1000

Table 7-1. The table should be interpreted in terms of the circular-flow concept explained in section 2 of Chapter 2. The expenditure side represents spending on the flow of goods to market, except that it excludes all *intermediate* purchases (purchases by one producer from another as part of the production process) and includes only final purchases: consumption expenditures by individuals, government spending on goods and services (such as salaries, supplies, etc., but *not* including transfer

Other Supplementary Models   113

Government capital expenditure is usually combined with private capital expenditure to give "investment" as that term is commonly used by economists.

The sum of the first three items gives *total domestic demand*. The next item, exports of goods and services, is the demand by residents of other countries for this country's products; adding it to domestic demand gives *total final demand*.

The change in inventories is actually a form of capital investment (or disinvestment if it is negative); it is likely to reflect the impossibility of precisely matching production to sales rather than an intentional investment decision, however, and hence is not considered a part of final demand. Note that this entry measures the physical change in inventories, valued at the *average* price during the year; we want

---

Gross National Product: Expenditure

Personal expenditure:		
Durable goods	75	
Other goods	245	
Services	240	560
Government current expenditure		185
Capital expenditure:		
Government	25	
Private	205	230
Domestic Demand		975
External demand: Exports		300
Final Demand		1275
Value of change in inventories		5
Total of the foregoing		1280
Less imports		280
Gross National Product at market prices		1000

---

payments and *not* including spending on capital goods like buildings), capital spending by both the government and the private sector, the net purchases of domestic goods by nonresidents, and the net change in inventories. (Net spending on inventories is also a form of capital spending, but it is treated separately for reasons explained in the text.) The income side represents the earnings of the factors of production (Net National Income), plus certain adjustments explained in the text. ("Profit" in this case means profit in the broad sense, not pure profit.)

to include only spending that reflects the production of real goods and services during the year or quarter.

By now we have a total of 1280, well in excess of GNP. How can this be?

Well, the answer is simple enough: almost all products, whether sold domestically or abroad, contain some imported materials or components or services, so we must deduct the value of imports in order to get the total value of goods actually produced in the country. (Our hypothetical country is obviously a relatively "open" economy, i.e. exports and imports are fairly large compared to GNP, so the correction is relatively large; but the deduction is necessary even in a relatively "closed" economy, in which exports and imports are relatively unimportant.) Ideally the import content would be deducted from each expenditure category and only the net domestic content shown, but that is not feasible in practice.[4]

Now it is time to look at the income side of Table 7-1, which corresponds to the flow of money payments to factors of production and others, out of which they purchase the opposing flow of goods in the circular-flow pattern. As with the expenditure side of the table, of course, it excludes that portion of all payments that merely repays a supplier for his share of the costs; you might say it is computed on a "value added" basis, i.e. it includes only the additional costs incurred at each stage of production.

In this case also we will look first at the final item, GNP. Adding up all these items should give us exactly the same total as the value of the goods produced, of course, since they record the opposite sides of the same transactions. However, the statisticians who compile these figures must be content with estimates and approximations in many cases, so it would be sheer coincidence if the two figures did come to exactly the same total in practice. The conventional solution is to identify the difference as "the residual error of estimate", add half of it to the smaller figure, and deduct the other half from the larger one. We will suppose that this has already been done in Table 7-1, and that the GNP shown is the adjusted total.

Next, look at the second-last item. It's formal title is "Capital cost allowances and miscellaneous value adjustments", but the main component is simply an allowance for depreciation. GNP measures total real output at market prices, but part of that output merely replaces capital goods that are used up or worn out as a normal part of the productive process. Depreciation is an accounting allowance for

---

4 Sometimes only net foreign trade (exports less imports) is shown, especially in relatively closed economies, but many economists consider it better practice even in these cases to add exports and deduct imports in full, since virtually all domestically-produced goods have some import content.

this fact, and deducting it from GNP gives the *net* output of the economy in the year or quarter in question.

This is the least-precise item in the national accounts, for it is determined by accounting conventions and not by market forces. Any error in it does not affect GNP, however, but instead gives rise to an offsetting error in business profits, which are calculated by deducting known and estimated costs from the value of total output at market prices.

The market prices of most goods include indirect taxes, such as customs import duties or excise taxes on tobacco and alcoholic beverages, which are expected to be shifted forward to the ultimate consumer. They are not "real" costs, i.e. they do not involve the use of productive resources and the payment of factor returns (except for relatively small administrative costs, which are included in government expenditures). Rather, they are just a device whereby money is diverted from the pockets of the public to the coffers of the government to help pay for government services. Deducting them from Net National Product leaves Net National Income at factor cost.

Now we are ready to look at the factor costs (or factor returns) that make up national money income and underlie the generation of national real income. They are wages and salaries, profits, and interest income. All are shown before the deduction of *direct* taxes.

"Wages and salaries" in the table includes "supplementary labour income" and "military pay and allowances", the latter being usually shown as a separate category in practice.

"Profits" means profits in the broad sense, not pure profits, which would be extremely difficult if not impossible to identify. It also includes some or all of the wages of management or entrepreneurship, especially in the case of unincorporated businesses and farm operations; for many purposes we would like to include these portions with wages and salaries, but that is not practicable.

Interest income excludes interest on the public debt, which is treated as a transfer payment, as already noted, but it includes some miscellaneous investment income.

Corporate profits are shown in the table net of dividends paid to nonresidents, since they are not *domestic* income. (This deduction is normally shown as a separate negative item, but the table is complicated enough as it is.) Then a further adjustment must be made to all three classes of profits, to eliminate the effects of mere price changes on the reported value of inventories.

The adjustment is shown as zero in the table, which implies that average prices are unchanged. Had prices increased during the period then the same inventory would be worth more and reported profits would have included an inventory profit that did not reflect real production, so the adjustment would be negative; had they decreased, the adjustment would have been positive. (Remember that we entered only the *value of the physical change in inventories* on the expenditure side, since we wanted to include only spending that reflects current production, so now we must include only the corresponding income.)

The national accounts also include several subsidiary income-and-expenditure statements. One of these is the sources and uses of personal income, including transfers received from governments and direct taxes paid to governments. (Among other things this statement gives "personal disposable income", a useful figure that tells how much people are able either to spend as they like or to save; it is found by deducting direct personal taxes from total personal income.)

Another statement shows the sources and uses of gross savings. A third lists government revenues and expenditures in some detail, with an estimate of depreciation allowances on government capital assets. (Many governments omit depreciation from their official accounts, because they are primarily concerned with showing that all expenditures have been properly authorized, not with "profit" or "the bottom line" like a private enterprise.)

GNP is a pretty good overall measure of the *material* well-being of the community, since it records the real income available for distribution among the populace, but it has its limitations even in this respect. For practical reasons it includes only goods that are exchanged in the marketplace for money or the equivalent, and does not attempt to include or put a value on such things as the work done by a housewife in the home, or food grown for its own use by a family, or many other activities that add to the sum total of goods and services enjoyed by members of the community.[5]

Also, it is impractical to distinguish between the purchase of certain services when they are enjoyed for their own sake, and when they are part of the cost of performing some productive activity. For example, it is clearly a matter of personal consumption when you use public transportation (or your own car) to visit a theatre, but a cost of production when you use it to get to work; in the first case the payment belongs on the expenditure side, in the second it should be deducted from gross income.

A second criticism is that GNP as conventionally measured ignores certain negative side-effects of production, such as air and water pollution due to acid rain,

---

[5] That has given rise to a standard economic joke, to the effect that GNP is reduced whenever a man marries his housekeeper: the same services are performed as before, but there is no longer any identifiable payment made for them.

and other adverse externalities of the sort discussed in section 5 of this chapter. Clearly, some deduction should be made to allow for these effects, or for the costs of correcting them.

A third criticism is that GNP focuses exclusively on material things and takes no account of other considerations that affect the enjoyment of life. For example, rising income may lead people to work fewer hours per week and enjoy more leisure; real output will decline, but total welfare will surely have risen, for the value of the additional leisure must be more than the value of the material goods forgone.

Some economists have endeavoured to correct for the perceived deficiencies of GNP by compiling an adjusted total called Net Economic Welfare (NEW). This is surely a laudable effort, and may help to mobilize public opinion in support of policies that will operate more effectively in the general interest.

Nevertheless the better-known total (GNP) serves reasonably well as an indicator of overall welfare, as long as we keep its deficiencies in mind. It may be looked on as a glorified index number, as suggested in section 6 of Chapter 10: for most purposes we are more concerned with its behaviour over time than with its absolute level at any moment. A stable or growing GNP implies a stable or growing NEW, for they have so many components in common.

7. Econometric Models.

Econometrics is the economic analysis and evaluation of massed data by means of statistical methods and devices. The word is derived from "economics" plus "metric", the latter in the sense of being related to or involving measurement. Many economic theories lend themselves to formulation as sets of mathematical relationships, often in forms that are suitable for exploration or testing by the use of available statistical data. Econometrics attempts such things as quantifying the relationships among the principal variables in a given theory, or determining the probability that changes in two or more variables either influence one another or reflect the influence of the same causal factors.

An econometric model is usually expressed as a set of mathematical equations designed to provide a quantitative explanation of the behaviour of certain economic variables. It may represent a limited section of an economy, a macroeconomic summary of an entire economy, or the economic relationships among a set of two or more economies that trade with one another. It may deal only with equilibrium relationships (a static model), or it may deal with changes in some or all variables over time (a dynamic model).

The equations that make up an econometric model may be divided into two principal types, structural and operational. Structural equations spell out the basic assumptions of the model. Operational equations describe the relationships that are to be tested, or from which numerical values for the targeted relationships are to be derived.

Both types of equation are expressed in terms of (a) variables that can be more or less accurately identified in the real world and (b) "parameters" or "operators", which are assumed to control the relationships among the variables, and are often given fixed values in order to keep the equations as simple as possible. The values of some variables may be arbitrarily assigned from "outside" the model ("exogenous variables"), and only the remainder determined from "inside" ("endogenous variables").

Perhaps an example will help to explain the matter, using a simple model of the spending stream that we will meet again in Chapter 11. The model involves one structural equation and three operational equations. The structural equation is $C_{Tn} + I_{Tn} \equiv Y_{Tn}$, which is just mathematical shorthand for saying "spending on consumption plus spending on new capital investment in any given time-period T is the only source of income in that period".[6]

The three operational equations are $C_{Tn} = kY_{T(n-1)}$, $I_{Tn} = I^*$, and $C_{T1} = C^*$; they mean "consumption in time-period T is k times the income in the previous time-period" (say, 80 per cent of it), "investment in any time-period always has the arbitrary value I^*", and "the value of consumption in the initial period has the arbitrary value C^*". C_{Tn} is an endogenous variable, except for its value in the first time-period, C_{T1}, which is arbitrarily set at C^*. Y_{Tn} is also an endogenous variable; k, I^*, and C^* are parameters (which we may arbitrarily say are constants).

These equations identify a simple dynamic model in which consumption in the initial period equals C^*, and new investment equal to I^* is introduced in that period and in each subsequent period. If we continue to assume that 80 per cent of income is consumed in the next period, and if C^* is less than 5 times I^*, income will rise persistently thereafter until it reaches that figure. Alternatively, if income in the initial period is above the equilibrium level, it will persistently decline to that level.

---

6 We use the $\equiv$ sign in this case, to indicate that it is a *definitional* equation—it defines the relationship among C, I, and Y, and it holds at all times. If we used the equal sign instead of the identity sign it might imply that the equation was merely an equilibrating condition, i.e. that it held only in the final equilibrium situation. Note, however, that structural equations need not all be identities. In a more complex model, for example, there might be additional structural equations linking spending on consumption and investment to conditions in the labour market and the capital-goods market. Some or all of these additional equations might be assumed to be mere approximations, not rigid relationships.

How do we know that? Well, if 80 per cent of income is always spent on consumption, 20 per cent must be saved. Also, investment must be equal to saving in an equilibrium situation. (If it were not, then the spending stream—and incomes—would be either increasing or decreasing, so equilibrium could not obtain.) Both conditions must be satisfied in the final equilibrium position: saving must be equal to 20 per cent of income, and must also be equal to I^*, therefore I^* must also be 20 per cent of income.

This model is illustrated in Figure 7-1, in which k, I^*, and C^* have been given the values 0.8 (or 80 per cent), 6, and 2, respectively. In time-period T_1, therefore, income is $6 + 2 = 8$. Hence in time-period T_2 consumption must be 6.4 and income 8.4.

Continuing in the same way we get 8.72, 8.976, and 9.1808 as the incomes in the next three time-periods. If we keep on, we will find that the income of each successive period gets closer and closer to 10, but never quite gets there in any finite number of time-periods.

A model like this may be used to refine a theory by trying out various assumptions designed to predict the values of certain variables, and seeking the set of

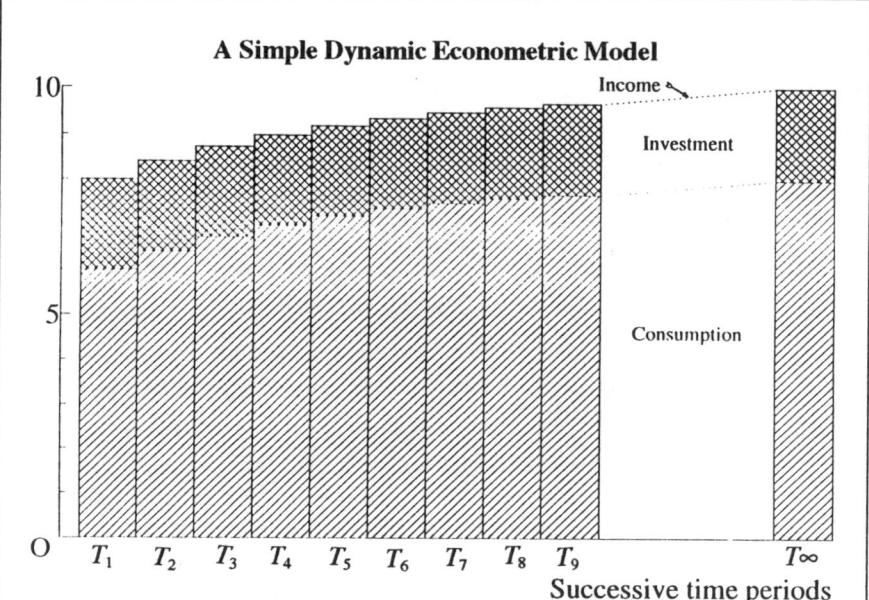

Figure 7-1. In each period income equals consumption plus investment, and consumption equals 80% of the previous period's income. In time-period T_1 income is $6 + 2 = 8$; In time-period T_2, therefore, consumption must be $0.8 \times 8 = 6.4$, and income must be $6.4 + 2 = 8.4$. The income of each successive period gets closer and closer to 10; or, in mathematical terminology, it *approaches 10 as a limit*.

assumptions that will make the predicted values closest to their known values in the real world. Another possible use is to determine approximate values for certain parameters, based on statistical data for the variables over a particular time period, and see if they give satisfactory predictions of the values of the same variables over other periods of time. Some elaborate econometric models are used to forecast the course of the economy for any number of months into the future. And there are many other specialized applications.

Chapter 8

Monopolistic *or* Imperfect Competition

1. An Undifferentiated Product.

In 1933 two quite different but complementary books, written entirely independently by Edward Chamberlin of Harvard (*The Theory of Monopolistic Competition*) and Joan Robinson of Cambridge (*The Economics of Imperfect Competition*),[1] gave economists an entirely new theoretical model in which most other models from pure competition to pure monopoly can be accommodated.

The model of pure competition recognized that there are many frictions, lags, and other features of the real world which interfere with attaining full equilibrium, but which do not alter the optimum position to which it tends. In many instances, however, the new model points to quite different equilibrium positions.

Figure 8-1 is designed to illustrate the equilibrium position of a single firm in the short run in a number of possible situations, the common feature of which is that the entire industry consists of a limited number of firms. (The technical term for this situation is "oligopoly", from two Greek words meaning "few sellers".) There is no reason to suppose that all firms are of equal size or have similar cost curves; hence there is no clear way of identifying a supply curve that would be comparable to that of a purely-competitive industry, so we can not determine the purely-competitive price.

The line *AC* represents one firm's share of the total market on the assumption that no other firm in the industry alters its price when this firm does. It is also the firm's individual demand curve and its average revenue curve on that assumption. The line *DF* is the corresponding marginal revenue curve. The point *B* indicates

---

[1] You may be amused to observe that, if the distinction noted in section 4 of Chapter 2 were to be made in this case, we would call it *impure* competition instead of *imperfect* competition.

the firm's price (*OM*) and output (*ON*) at a particular time, for reasons that will be explained shortly.

The line *GH* is the same firm's individual demand curve or average revenue curve on the assumption that all other firms alter their prices exactly in unison. The line *IK* is the corresponding marginal revenue curve.

To start with, suppose the firm produces some raw material or other for use in other industries—say, steel or copper or potash. We will also assume that the capital costs of the minimum-sized firm are substantial (the "entry fee" to the industry is high), its output is large relative to the total market, and the existing firms are strong,

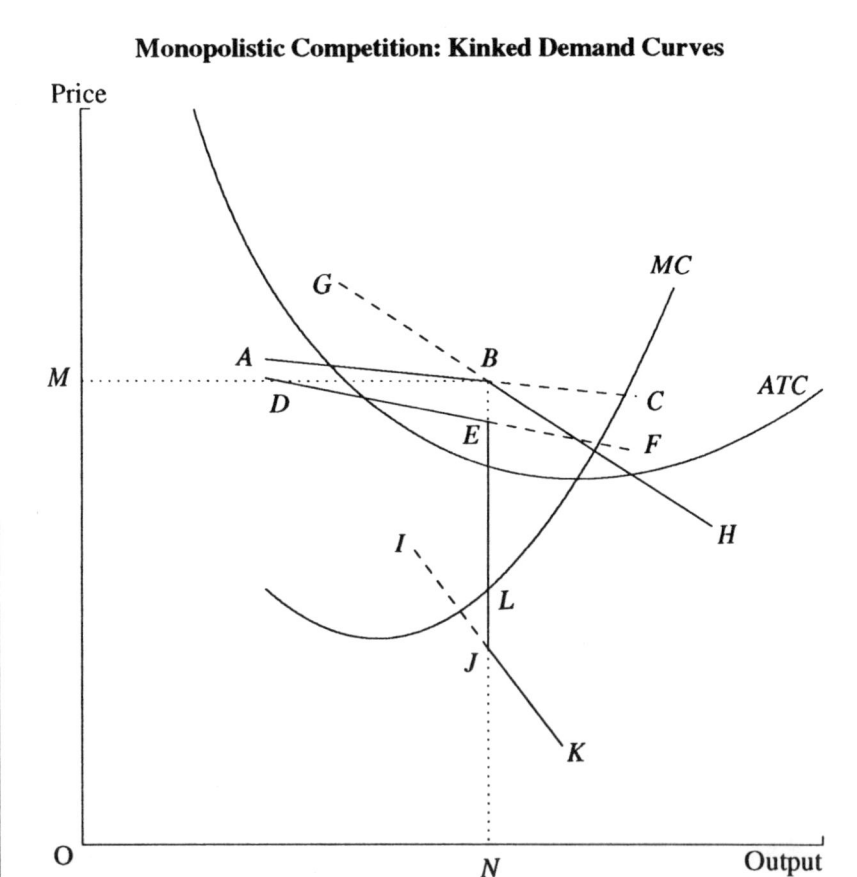

Figure 8.1. The line *ABC* represents the firm's individual demand curve or average revenue curve if no other firm changes price in response to this firm's actions, and *DEF* is the corresponding marginal revenue curve. The line *GBH* applies if all firms change prices together, and *IJK* is its marginal revenue curve. The effective *MR* curve is the dog-legged line *DEJK*.

so there is little to tempt the formation of new firms. Provided it meets their quality specifications, customer firms have no reason to prefer this firm's product over that of its competitors. Presumably the line *GH* will show the firm's proportionate share of output at various prices, i.e. it will be a reflection of the industry's demand curve.

The slope of the line *AC* will be relatively flat, but may be appreciably negative if the plant is closer than other producers to some of the customer firms and therefore benefits from a favourable differential in transportation costs in that part of the market. However, any attempt by the oligopolist to enlarge his (or her) market share by cutting his selling price (i.e., to shift the point *B* further east towards *C*) will undoubtedly provoke retaliation by his competitors, so the line *GH* is his effective demand curve for any price below *OM*.

On the other hand an attempt to raise his selling price above *OM* would result in a sharp loss of sales, as competitors would likely hold their prices in order to entice his customers away, so the line *AC* becomes the firm's demand curve in that case. Hence the firm's effective demand curve is the line *ABH*, with a kink in it at *B*.

This in turn introduces *two* kinks (or a *discontinuity*) in the *MR* curve; east of *B* it is identical with the line *DE*, west of *B* it is identical with *JK*, and the two segments are joined by the straight north-south line *EJ*. The effective *MR* curve is the dog-leg line *DEJK*, which intersects the *MC* curve at *L*, in the *EJ* segment. The firm is maximizing its profit under the existing conditions.

The other firms in the industry will be in approximately similar positions, though their cost curves may be different (either higher or lower), and so may their shares of the market and their profitability. (In this model, unlike the model of pure competition, there is no assurance that pure profit will disappear[2] or that all firms will approach uniform size even in the long-run-equilibrium position.) If their costs are higher then the point corresponding to *L* will lie farther north along the line *EJ*. If their share of the market is smaller they may find themselves operating farther above their lowest average total costs, i.e. to the west of *B*, and the *EJ* segment of their *MR* curve will lie further west.

Why do price and output settle at *B*? Well, one of the few other firms in the industry may have an *MC* curve that intersects *its MR* curve at *J*, so it would lose money at a higher price. That firm would likely be the "price leader" in the industry; probably it not only is the most efficient (lowest cost) firm, but also has a larger

---

[2] However, the *firm's* pure profit may disappear in higher factor costs, if some factors or agents of production are able to raise their charges. In other words some agents or factors of production may be able to appropriate some or all of the pure profits.

share of the market. On the other hand it may be that the current price and output pattern is simply where things have settled after a painful period of jockeying for market shares; no firm may be really happy with the result, but all may be afraid to move for fear of setting off a new price war.

In any case the manager of the price-leading firm (or of any would-be leader) may be tempted to start a price war in order to expand his (or her) share of the market, so the situation depicted is less stable than that of the true monopolist in Figure 6-1 on page 86. He may be operating in the declining-cost part of his range of potential outputs, and it may well be that his lowest-cost output would supply a much larger portion of the market demand. It may also be that he could increase his capacity and lower his costs even further with relatively moderate additional capital investment, and he may have reason to believe that some or all of his competitors have higher costs than he does.

Unless he can drive the price down below his competitors' average variable costs, however, and hold it there long enough to bankrupt some or all of them, an expansion-minded oligopolist is not likely to succeed by such a strategy; in the meantime he will be accumulating substantial losses, which he must hope to recover from increased profits in the future. Considering the costs and the risks, therefore, he may well decide to stick with his present price and output—and so may the other managers. Price and output may therefore be in unstable equilibrium: no firm will want to rock the boat, but if one does (even the price leader) it may start a price war that will hurt them all. Market stability will require either an overt agreement on prices and market shares, or a tacit agreement to maintain things as they are.

The monopolist in Figure 6-1 can react flexibly to changes in costs and demand, except as long-run considerations may offset short-run advantages. In view of his dependence on an overt or tacit agreement on the price level, however, the oligopolist in Figure 8-1 must be less flexible. If his (or her) costs rise the point L just slides north along the EJ section of the kinked MR curve; if demand falls off he may fear to cut his selling price for fear of triggering a price war; even if he senses a rise in demand, he may fear to raise his price until the price-leader does. Only if it becomes clear that the entire industry is experiencing the same pressures will it be feasible for any oligopolist to act with some confidence, and even then he must be careful to keep fairly well in step with his competitors. For example, in inflationary times both the cost curves and the revenue curves of all firms will be tending to rise, so the whole pattern will easily drift northwards.

Now let's consider the situation in a series of other industries selling undifferentiated products, but in which the optimum size of firm is smaller and smaller, progressively less capital is needed (the entry fee is less), and there are more and more firms in the industry. The slopes of the individual firms' demand curves will get progressively flatter and flatter—the more firms there are in the industry, the less effect any of them will feel from the actions of another.

Eventually we get something closely approximating a purely competitive industry. For example, think of wheat farmers in North America. Nowadays they need far more capital than they did 50 or 100 years ago (the entry fee is at least several hundred thousand dollars), but it is tiny compared to the needs of, say, an integrated steel mill. More important, there are many thousands of them; even the biggest operator could not appreciably affect the price by withholding his entire crop.

2. Product Differentiation.

Few if any consumer products are produced and marketed under conditions that even remotely resemble the model of pure competition. The typical consumer is limited to relatively few retailers as sources of any particular type of merchandise—food, clothing, appliances, automobiles, or whatever. The same applies to the medical, dental, legal, banking, or other services he may want. For many types of product (automobiles, appliances, pharmaceuticals, and many others) the retailers in turn are limited to very few alternative manufacturers for the goods they can offer their customers. Therefore, most of the analysis of the preceding section applies fully in consumer markets also.

There is one important difference, however: consumers do not and can not base their purchasing decisions on objective quality specifications in the same way that business firms can do when buying raw materials, despite the best efforts of consumer-research organizations which test and compare competing products. Oligopolists are therefore free to substitute other forms of competition for price competition—especially, efforts to persuade the public that *their* automobile or toothpaste or banking service or whatever has special qualities that make it far superior to those offered by competitors, whether there is really any significant difference or not.

Brand names, fancy packaging, advertising, and many other promotional techniques are used to *differentiate* the products of one oligopolist from those of another. These techniques add materially to the oligopolist's total costs—in some cases they may far exceed the actual manufacturing costs—but under favourable circumstances they may easily yield substantial net profits by greatly expanding total sales.

This case can be analyzed using essentially the same diagram as in the previous case. This time, however, there is no presumption that the firm's demand curve bears any particular resemblance to the industry's demand curve. Also, thanks to the effects of product differentiation, prices need not be exactly the same for all competing products, and defensive price reductions need not exactly match the change that induces them. The main difference from the first case, however, is that the slope of the firm's demand curve may be much steeper. Indeed, it may be virtually as steep as that of the industry curve, if brand loyalty is strong; a lower price for a competing product may induce few consumers to change brands.

Let's start off, as before, with the case in which the entry fee (i.e. the cost of a minimum capital installation) is high—as in the auto industry. Because the slopes of their individual demand curves are relatively steep, the *EJ* segments of their dog-legged *MR* curves may be fairly short, so most of the competing oligopolists may find that they can set their selling prices pretty much as if they were monopolists. However, they will still be vulnerable to price changes by their competitors, for the "other things" we have tacitly assumed to remain "equal" include those prices. An oligopolist may be somewhat tolerant of price differentials that favour weaker firms, but not those that favour stronger firms, and must be alert to a material *change* in any price differential.

Moreover, do not forget that this "favourable" situation is heavily dependent on advertizing and other promotional expenditures—not only the oligopolist's own but also those of his competitors. The equilibrium position depicted in Figure 8-1 tacitly assumes a given level of promotional outlays by all parties, as well as given price differentials with rival products. Any material increase in them, or the introduction of a more effective promotional technique, will call for a response by competitors.

For oligopolists with undifferentiated products the threat to market stability lies in merely competitive *price cuts* that reduce revenues for all and benefit no-one; with differentiated products, it lies in merely competitive *increases in promotional expenditures* that just offset one another and raise everyone's costs. In either case stability depends on overt or tacit agreement on prices, market shares, and promotional activities. Each oligopolist probably has some room to manoeuvre on these matters without generating retaliation, but he is unlikely to get very aggressive unless he feels strong enough to make substantial net gains or unless he is severely pressed (e.g., by the need to recoup serious losses).

Now let's see what happens if we relax the entry-fee limitation and allow more and smaller oligopolistic competitors. Figure 8-2 illustrates the situation. Suppose some innovator introduces a new product that competes successfully with existing

Monopolistic *or* Imperfect Competition   127

products, and establishes a demand represented by the line *AC*; *DF* is the corresponding marginal revenue curve. He (or she) enjoys a temporary monopoly, sells an output of *OH* at a price of *OG*, and earns a pure profit.

However, imitators will appear sooner or later, introduce similar products, and take away some of his market. In the long run his demand or *AR* curve will shift to the west or southwest until it is tangent to his *ATC* curve at *B'* and his *MR* curve moves to the position *D'F'*; he sells an output of *OH'* at a price of *OC'*. His

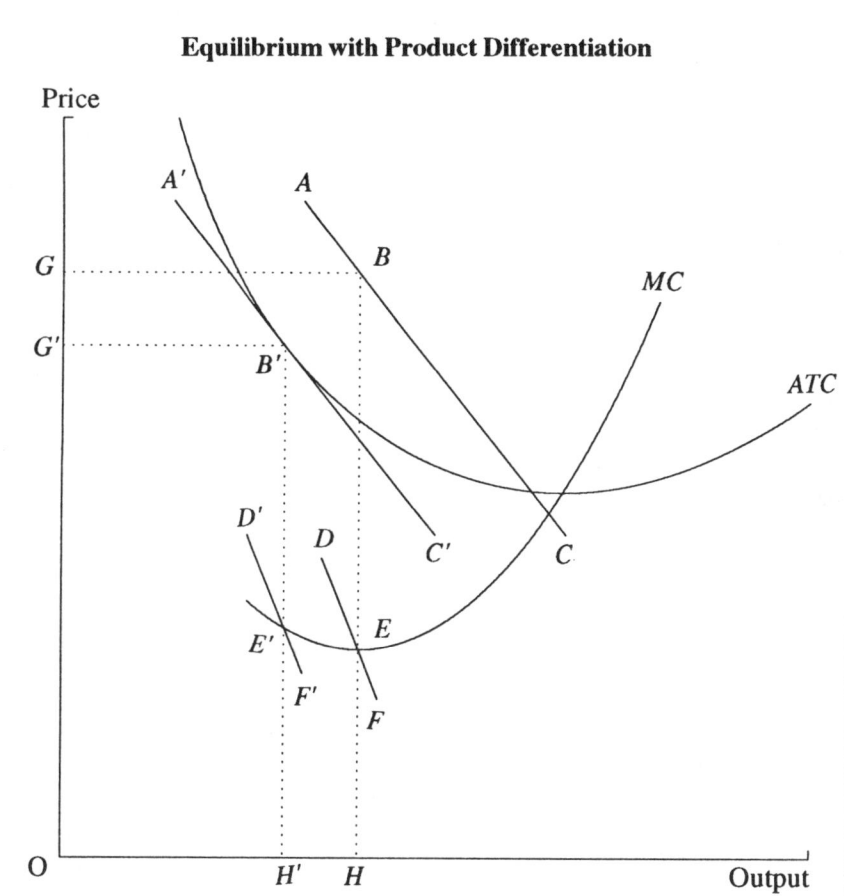

Figure 8-2. Suppose an innovator introduces a new product and wins a demand curve of *AC* for it. His (or her) *MR* curve will be *DF*, so he will set his price at *OG* and his output at *OH*; he will get a monopoly profit. Sooner or later imitators will introduce similar products, however, and capture part of his market, driving his demand curve to the south and west until it takes the position *A'C'*, tangent to the *ATC* curve at *B'*, as the *MR* curve shifts to the position *D'F'*; his price will become *OG'* and his output *OH'*.

competitors (or such of them as survive) will also end up with *their AR* curves tangent to their *ATC* curves, and none will be making an excessive profit.

Why this tangency solution? Well, to begin with, neither the innovator nor any of his imitators can have his *AR* curve any farther to the southwest, because he would have suffered losses and been driven out of business before the long-run equilibrium was reached. Nor on the other hand can it lie any farther to the northeast, because then there would be some remaining pure profit for that firm. With free entry to the industry, other imitators would have appeared until the last profit was squeezed out—*unless* the profit was due to some advantage the competitors could not duplicate, such as a favourable location or access to some unique agent of production. But in that case the firm's pure profit would have been converted into some factor return or other, so it would have disappeared anyway.

Does this tangency solution sound familiar? What about the long-run-equilibrium position of the individual firm under pure competition, as described in section 4 of Chapter 5?

But note an important difference: the equilibrium price under pure competition is tangent to the firm's *ATC* curve *at its lowest point,* thus ensuring that the consumer gets the benefit of the lowest possible cost of production. Under monopolistic (or imperfect) competition the equilibrium price is above the lowest point in the firm's *ATC* curve; all firms are operating at substantially less than the optimum output, and the community's resources are not being efficiently used for the satisfaction of human wants.

Actually, much the same is likely to happen in many cases even where entry is restricted by high capital costs or in other ways. Chains of retail stores, branch banking systems, petroleum companies operating service stations, and similar enterprises offer clear examples. They depend on strong central organizations, with many branches that deal with the public. It would take a lot of capital to duplicate the enterprise as a whole, and there may be few competitors operating in any given market, but the individual outlets that deal with the public are likely to be relatively small, so each organization can expand its capacity at relatively little cost. Adding more outlets may be profitable to the enterprise as long as each can cover its costs, so they are likely to proliferate until each is operating at the point of tangency between its *ATC* and its *AR* curves.

However, this does not constitute an open-and-shut case against product differentiation. There is little doubt that the consumer does get some benefit from a greater choice of products: different shapes, sizes, colours, smells, and packaging for cakes of soap, for example, rather than a dull utilitarian sameness. Such benefits are certainly obtained at a cost, in terms not only of other utilities forgone but also of the added inventory costs for retailers, who must carry adequate stocks of many similar products. The real question is, do the benefits justify the costs? Once more we are in the realm of value judgements, where mere economic analysis can be of little help.

3. Pricing Decisions.

Economists talk a great deal about prices, the market mechanism, price determination, and related subjects, but few economic textbooks have anything very specific to say about how prices are actually set in the real world. For that you must usually go to marketing textbooks.

Economics textbooks are usually oriented towards production, and with good reason: production is the source of all real income. They are also oriented towards the community as a whole, or even the the world-wide community. Prices enter primarily as guides to production and distribution.

Marketing on the other hand is oriented to the successful operation of individual firms, particularly the earning of sufficient income to cover all costs and yield a profit (in the businessman's sense). Marketing textbooks therefore see prices as merely one of four components of a good marketing strategy, and not necessarily the dominant one. The others are the characteristics of the product itself (which may need modification to improve marketability), the channels through which it is distributed, and promotional activities. Management is expected to find the best combination of these elements for attaining its goals. The last of them often turns out to be the most important.

In general, of course, the final price to the ultimate consumer must cover all legitimate costs, otherwise the product (and perhaps the firm) will not survive. They may be subdivided into manufacturing costs, transportation costs, and selling costs; economists recognize them all, but tend to focus on the first, whereas marketing authorities treat them all. But costs per unit are hard to estimate in advance, since much will depend on the volume of sales. Further complications arise because the typical firm produces a variety of products, and costs must be allocated among them. (Aside from a brief reference to joint costs, we have usually assumed that the firm makes only one product.)

Furthermore, estimating the probable volume of sales may be critical to choosing the right productive technique. Often there is a choice of two, three, or more known procedures, and which is the most cost-effective depends on the volume of output. A written memorandum offers a simple example. Carbon copies or photocopies may be the most economical technique if only a few people are involved.

Mimeographing or offset printing may be best for a larger circulation, but typeset copy and a high-speed press for a very large distribution.

Given these practical complexities, it is not surprising to find that the question of pricing is more likely to be approached from the point of view of "How much can we get for it?" rather than "How much must we ask in order to cover our costs?" If the answer seems to be "Not enough!", then the possibilities of modifying the product, finding new distributional channels, or mounting a bigger promotional campaign may be considered before abandoning it. Alternatively, the firm may use a standard markup over estimated manufacturing costs, the amount of the markup being based on past experience with the type of product in question.

All of which helps to explain why the oligopolists in our examples want a healthy margin of price over costs.

4. Policy Implications.

The long-run-equilibrium position to which the model of monopolistic (or imperfect) competition tends is very different from that of pure competition:

- The consumer is not sovereign, deciding what will be produced and how resources will be allocated by the purposeful use of his income to get equal satisfaction at the margin; instead he is mesmerized and misled by powerful and insidious advertizing campaigns and other devices manipulated by oligopolists for their own selfish ends.
- The resources at the disposal of sellers do not reflect an objective valuation of their wants by the consumers, but the skills of the sellers in playing on the fears and vanities of buyers or in exploiting some tactical advantage over their competitors.
- Factor returns are proportionate to their contributions to marginal revenues but not to physical output, and are not necessarily equalized in all employments, but may vary from industry to industry and from firm to firm according to the bargaining strengths of various buyers and sellers.
- Producers do not expand output and sales until the marginal cost just equals the market-fixed selling price, they limit their sales to the (lower) level at which marginal revenue just covers marginal cost.

The policy implications of this model are therefore very different from those of pure competition:

- There is no assurance that the community's resources are being employed in the most efficient way for the satisfaction of human wants; on the contrary, there is every reason to believe that resources are being wasted in unnecessary duplication of productive facilities that will not be used to their full capacity.
- There is no basis for believing that the benefits of innovations and cost reductions will be passed on to consumers in the form of lower prices; instead, they are likely to go to those factors of production that have the greatest bargaining power and are most willing to exploit it.
- There is no clear presumption against government interference in economic affairs; indeed, it appears that certain interventions would shift output and prices in ways that would spread the benefits more evenly among the general public.

Chapter 9

Dissenting Opinions

1. Criticisms of *Laissez-Faire* Policies.

It is sometimes said that the purely-competitive model and the *laissez-faire* policies originally derived from it are simply an elaborate apology for the practices of capitalistic enterprise. The start of the industrial revolution is often dated from the second half of the 18th century, Britain was the undisputed leader in the process, Adam Smith's *Wealth of Nations* was published in 1776, and the philosophy he advocated was certainly a potent factor in the subsequent ascendancy of the new industrialism over the feudal and mercantile interests that had dominated economic activity until then, so it is easy enough to see how such an accusation could be derived.

Defenders of the early British classical economists, on the other hand, argue that they had seen the enormous potential of the new industrial processes for benefiting the nation as a whole, not just promoting the interests of any particular class or group.

So it eventually proved: over the next 200 years living standards steadily rose for the general populace, though the way that was accomplished owed much to major modifications of and departures from the principles of *laissez-faire*. Even the feudal or semifeudal landowners shared the benefits, despite the loss of many of their former privileges. And Adam Smith, for one, made much of the point that the new system would promote the public good *despite* the fact that businessmen would seek only their own private profit, as we saw in section 9 of Chapter 4.

The 18th century was a century of optimism and hope, at least for philosophers and intellectuals. It was the Age of Enlightenment and Reason. People individually and society as a whole were seen as perfectible.

Adam Smith's *laissez-faire* philosophy shared this optimism. He believed in a natural harmony of interests, and that the human lot could be improved by breaking down feudal restraints, letting initiative go free, and encouraging the growth of trade, manufacturing, inventions, and the division of labour.

As industrialization gathered momentum in Britain, however, these high hopes were only partly and slowly realized. To some extent this was due to problems inherited from the past, particularly from the slow but persistent disintegration of the feudal system over a long period of time. For all its faults, feudalism had given even the poorest members of society security of a sort. The commercialization of agriculture and the enclosure of common lands set increasing numbers of landless peasants adrift. Those thus displaced were glad to find employment in the new industries, and provided a much-needed labour supply for them. It has been well said that labour was not attracted to the factories by better pay and better living conditions, but driven to them in spite of lower pay and worse living conditions.

Wages in the new factories were of course low, and certainly look low by modern standards, but that is not the essential point: the real income of the country was low, so real wages in general were of necessity low too, and those who took these jobs had few alternatives. The essential point is that the circumstances of the times permitted the new industrialists to appropriate the bulk of the increase in real income that industrialization brought. Great wealth grew alongside abject poverty—not a new phenomenon, of course, but newly expanded.

Increasing industrialization added to the problem, because independent artisans found they could not compete with the new factory methods of production and the substantial amounts of capital it required, so they too were forced to seek employment in industry. Some examples of workers organizing to improve their position can be found as much as 100 years earlier, but English common law looked on them as conspiracies in restraint of trade, and parliament had been induced to pass Combination Laws against them. These laws were eventually repealed (in 1824), but even then trade unions faced many difficulties.

Also, it became clear that the increasing use of machinery meant that nimble fingers were more important than brute strength in many lines of manufacturing, so women and children proved at least as productive as men—and at lower wages, because they had fewer alternative work opportunities. In itself, female and child labour was nothing new—it had been common from time immemorial, whether in agriculture, in homes, or in other workplaces. For that matter, it is still found in many poor countries to this day. Typically, however, it had been as part of family groups in the home or in small agricultural holdings; with the industrial revolution it was transferred to the factory, where it was at once more visible and more open to abuse.

A substantial increase in unemployment was another feature of growing industrialization. Fluctuations in employment associated with periods of good and bad trade have been identified at least as far back as the 16th century. Temporary unemployment was not entirely unknown in medieval times, for agricultural labourers and some journeymen were hired as required. The numerous accounts of vagrants and beggars are tacit acknowledgements of some chronic unemployment as well. However, the gradual replacement of feudalism by commercialized agriculture brought on what can only be described as massive chronic unemployment of those it displaced, which put severe strains on the surviving procedures for looking after the indigent. Trade fluctuations became more pronounced as industrialization proceeded, and sometimes there were prolonged periods of depressed conditions.

The slow and uncertain reduction in chronic unemployment and the recurring bouts of cyclical unemployment must be judged more disturbing than the other evils associated with industrialization, because they raised fundamental questions about the viability of the expanding free-enterprise system itself. The inequitable division of the fruits of industrialization, the abuses of child and female labour, the poverty and disease, and the other social evils evident in the early years were not inevitable; in time they could be, and were, eliminated or greatly reduced out of the increased real output the new methods made possible. In contrast, severe cyclical bouts of unemployment and depressed output seemed an unavoidable part of the new system, and called into question the confident assertion that automatic economic forces tended to bring about a stable full-employment equilibrium.

The whole history of subsequent social legislation is witness to the ability of public opinion to modify the tenets of the pure *laissez-faire* philosophy without losing the virtues of a money-and-market economy, though it clearly took a long time to make substantial progress. Important beginnings at reform were made in Britain early in the 19th century, in the form of the Factory Acts and more liberal labour legislation, and these advances were followed by others. Germany pioneered in providing pensions and insurance against sickness and accident in the latter part of the century, and Britain introduced unemployment insurance early in the 20th century. Inheritance taxes and progressive income taxes were designed to redistribute income, and at one time it was optimistically hoped that great disparities of wealth and income would gradually disappear.

2. Underconsumption Theories.

As already noted, recurring fluctuations in output and employment became an important feature of the free-enterprise system as it developed in Britain during the 18th and 19th centuries. At times there were prolonged periods of what we would now call chronic depression and unemployment. Common observation of these facts led to a commonsense explanation: with reduced sales, unsold inventories, cutbacks in production, and reduced employment, it seemed obvious that what was involved was periodic overproduction.

An important refinement of this explanation was to substitute *underconsumption* for overproduction, since output was clearly not excessive in comparison with what people (especially the unemployed) would have liked to consume. Alternatively, it can be called an oversaving theory, since saving means not spending and hence not consuming.

Many versions of this explanation, varying greatly in their sophistication, have appeared from the earliest days of the industrial revolution well into the 20th century. The analysis Keynes presented in his *The General Theory of Employment Interest and Money* (1936) may be described as the final vindication of those earlier attempts. (See Chapter 11.) However, orthodox economics vigourously rejected the possibility from the start.

After Adam Smith (1723-1790), the next leading British economist was David Ricardo (1772-1823). Thomas Malthus (1766-1834) was also a member of the British classical tradition in most respects, and enjoyed a close personal friendship with Ricardo. He is best known to the public for his pessimistic theory of population, which became part of the classical tradition and earned economics its title of "the dismal science": the belief that the bulk of the populace must always live close to the minimum margin of subsistence. However, he was also the main rebel from within the group who argued for the possibility of "general gluts" (overproduction) and an oversupply of capital. Thomas Chalmers (1780-1847) also offered similar arguments in this respect.

Even to sympathetic modern readers, Malthus's arguments for the possibility of overproduction do not appear to be any too clearly put. This may be partly because value theory in those days was rather unsatisfactory (marginal analysis did not appear until the 1870's, and most classical economists held to a labour theory of value). However, the general sense of his argument was that employers will not hire labour unless they can sell the product for more than the cost of labour, hence the workers can not buy all the product.

Obviously the employers will also buy and consume some of the product out of their profits (in the broad sense), but they normally want to save some of their income and invest it in new productive capital. So far so good, but the purpose of new investment is to produce more goods; when the new capacity comes into production there will be a glut of output on the market, Malthus said, and the supply of capital may also prove excessive.

Malthus used his analysis to argue in favour of landlords and others who have both the will and the power to consume more material wealth than they produce, because their consumption maintained output and employment. This probably helped to discredit his case, because the popular view among economists was that landlords were an unproductive holdover from feudalism; Adam Smith, for example, spoke of them reaping where they had not sown. Also, it did not really solve his problem: industrialists would not hire labour *or* pay rents unless they could sell the product for more than their costs, so apparently even the combination of consumption-prone landlords and workers could not buy the total product.

Ricardo used what is usually known as Say's Law of Markets to dispute Malthus's argument. Properly stated, the law is sensible enough. The basic purpose of production is either to consume the product directly or to exchange it for other goods and services to consume in their stead. In general, therefore, it can be legitimately said that "supply creates its own demand", which is how Say's Law is often expressed. However, Say exaggerated the rigidity of the link, and so did Ricardo. If the link were really as rigid as they said, then general overproduction would indeed be impossible. Temporary overproduction of a particular good and unemployment of some resources, yes; general overproduction and unemployment, no.

Without going into details, the substance of it is that Ricardo and Say focused exclusively on the rôle of money as a means of exchanging goods for goods. It has other rôles too, as the theory of money has long recognized. The important one for this purpose is as a store of value (i.e. as an asset in its own right), as both Keynesians and monetarists recognize. (Other rôles include those as a unit of account and as a standard of value.) The possibility that the public might decide to use some of its current flow of income to build up its stock of money as an asset means there is not necessarily a rigid link between the supply of one product and the demand for another.

Neither Ricardo nor Malthus ever persuaded the other of the error of his ways, but they remained good friends till Ricardo's death.

Some continental economists at about the same time also argued the case for overproduction (e.g., J.C.L. Simonde de Sismondi, 1773-1842). Ricardo's views carried the day with the British classical tradition, however, no doubt due in part at least to shortcomings in the arguments of the underconsumptionists, and nothing more was heard of it in that quarter until Keynes took it up in the 1930's. In the meantime the rate of interest was identified as the factor that kept saving and investment in balance, as noted in section 2 of Chapter 2 and explained in section 4 of Chapter 10, which seemed to rule out overproduction independently. However, economists continued to take comfort from Say's Law.

Hindsight is a wonderful aid to understanding, of course, but one is entitled to wonder why it was so long before the Ricardian rebuttal was questioned by orthodox economists. They devised some rather elaborate theories of the business cycle in the ensuing years, and did important work, but did not pay serious attention to the possibility of chronic unemployment despite the facts open to observation. The last quarter of the 19th century, for example, was known as The Great Depression until the 1930's appropriated that title: periods of prosperity were short and unsatisfactory, slumps were long and painful. Humans sometimes seem unable to believe the evidence of their own senses until they can find some theory to justify what they are experiencing.

In 1867 Karl Marx put forward an underconsumption argument as part of his theory of crises, about which we will have more to say in section 4 of this chapter. He rejected Say's Law, noting that the use of money means that the seller of one good need not immediately purchase another. However, his concern with crises was incidental to a far broader attack on the capitalist system. Besides, no doubt due to the revolutionary uses to which he put his analysis, it was a long time before orthodox economists were prepared to acknowledge that there was any value in anything Marx said.

In 1889 there appeared a book entitled *The Physiology of Industry*, by John A. Hobson and A.F. Mummery, which presented a new statement of the underconsumption theory, but it was criticized and derided by orthodox economists. The authors pointed out that the purpose of capital accumulation is to produce additional consumables, which implies the need for a corresponding increase in consumption in the near future when the new capacity comes into production. Also, the stock of profitable capital at any time can not exceed what is required to supply the current rate of consumption.

Hobson and Mummery argued that there is a constant tendency towards excessive saving, which is not adequately controlled by normal economic forces. Mummery died in a mountaineering accident in 1895, but Hobson continued to attack orthodox economics for many years. He believed that the central problem of society is the recurring unemployment of productive resources, human and other.

He rejected *laissez-faire* and the classical idea of a harmony of interests, and advocated reforms and government intervention, including the redistribution of income.

In the 1920's and 1930's there was renewed interest in underconsumption. Major C.H. Douglas wrote extensively on "social credit" in his *Economic Democracy* (1920), *The Monopoly of Credit* (1931), and other books in between. His presentation of the argument was not particularly able, and he was guilty of a serious misunderstanding of the nature and functions of money, but his views got rather widespread public acceptance and became of political importance in a number of countries in subsequent decades.

One memorable social-credit phrase is still applicable today. Decrying poverty in the midst of potential plenty during the 1930's, Douglas's followers made much of the cry "What is physically possible ought to be financially possible!" Then, of course, there was extensive unemployment of human labour and physical plant because of *de*flationary pressures. Nowadays we have idle people and plant because of *in*flationary pressures, but it remains true that the wit of man should be able to overcome the financial problem and make adequate use of the physical possibilities.

In *Profits* (1925) W.F. Foster and W. Catchings offered a rather sophisticated underconsumption theory of the business cycle, in which they identified "the dilemma of thrift": individuals must save, but society as a whole can not save. In subsequent writings they advocated public works, consumer credit, a tax on saving, and the use of monetary policy (especially to control the boom phase of the cycle). They were not professional economists, and tended to be regarded as cranks, but criticisms by well-known economists did not succeed any too well in discrediting their arguments. They pioneered a number of constructive ideas, and influenced official U.S. policies in the 1930's. Nevertheless, like other underconsumptionists, their arguments had serious shortcomings.

As an exercise in logic, therefore, we must rate the argument between underconsumptionists and their critics as a draw. The underconsumptionists scored many good points against received economic opinion, but were unable to present their own case in convincing form. Their critics were thus able to score many telling points in return, but they too were unable to win decisively. As a matter of influencing the opinions of the majority of orthodox economists, however, their critics were unquestionably victorious for 100 years or more.

To restate the underconsumption (or oversaving) argument in modern terms, we may start by saying that an attempt to save will *permit* the formation of new productive capital that will add to the flow of real income in future periods, but there is no automatic mechanism to *ensure* that this goal is achieved, as classical economics thought. Three possible cases may occur.

First, profitable capital projects may be correctly foreseen, and the money saved (not spent on consumption) by savers out of their current flow of income may be borrowed and used to finance those projects, so the current spending stream will be maintained for the time being. On completion of these projects the community's real income will be increased, out of which people may wish to save more than before, the same amount, or less. If the money people wish to save at their new higher levels of real income continues to be borrowed and spent on productive new capital projects, the community's real income will continue to expand. If not, the situation will revert to one of the other two possibilities.

Note that this case says nothing about whether a full-employment level of income will be achieved, as classical economists believed would occur automatically. That requires a further condition: the flow of new capital spending must just absorb all the savings people wish to make *at the full-employment level of real income*. If that condition is not met, then there will be some unemployed human and other resources even if real income is expanding. Furthermore, in that event the existence of unemployed workers will tend to depress wages, money incomes, and prices, thereby undermining the prospects for new capital investment and hence threatening the current level of real income.

The second case differs from the first only in that the current savings of savers may be used for capital projects which when completed do not prove profitable. The current spending stream is sustained as before during construction, but there is no subsequent increase in real income. If the money people wish to save at the current level of real income continues to be borrowed and spent on unproductive projects, the flow of real income will continue unchanged; if not, the situation will revert to one of the other two cases. If the current level of real income involves unemployment of human and other resources, there may again be long-run downward pressures on prices, incomes, and the expected profitability of new capital projects.

The third case is that only a part of the money savers wish to save at the current level of real income may be borrowed and spent on capital projects. The current level of the spending stream will not be sustained, but will begin to spiral downwards. This in turn will undermine the expected profitability of whatever new capital projects might be considered, so new capital spending will also spiral downwards. Stability of a sort will only be attained when income is driven so low that the portion people wish to save will in fact be borrowed and spent on new capital projects; but the amount saved and spent on new capital may now be quite small.

In fact, saving and investing might conceivably both become negative—some people might have to use up past savings in order to buy necessities, and owners of capital goods might not replace them as they wore out. But even this stability might be fragile, in the face of long-run deflationary pressures.

3. Socialism.

Socialism is the belief in and advocacy of the public ownership of the means of production, distribution, and exchange. The word was first used in English in the *London Co-operative Magazine* in 1826, and was later applied to followers of Robert Owen's coöperative ideas. It was designed to emphasize "social" as distinct from "individual" ownership of capital.

There are many variants of socialism, but it is generally accepted that public ownership may be exercised at any of several levels: by a central government, by a regional or local government, or by a coöperative enterprise (i.e., one owned and operated by its members). Socialists usually reject the *laissez-faire* philosophy and the idea of a natural harmony of interests, but retain a belief in the perfectibility of humanity. They commonly stress coöperation rather than competition, and production for use rather than for profit.

Similar ideas can be traced far back in history, but they began to have a significant influence in Britain and continental Europe early in the 19th century. This influence appears to have originated in the criticisms of the evils of the early free-enterprise system noted in the first section of this chapter, and in a search for alternative forms of economic organization, rather than in a frontal attack on private ownership as such.

The attack came from two distinct sources. One was a revolt by workers themselves against specific evils, in the form of combinations of their own that could offer a common front to their employer. As trade unions gradually evolved, they came to adopt a socialist philosophy. The second source was the same liberalism that supported the growth of industrialization: the philosophy of natural law and utilitarianism, with its emphasis on the dignity of the individual.

Freedom, equality, justice, progress, the rule of reason, and the greatest good of the greatest number were powerful rallying cries. But, when the hopes thus encouraged were disappointed, the same critical attitude that had swept away the restrictions of feudal society was turned on the new order. The rule of reason meant that the new system, too, could be called to account, reforms proposed, and agitation for a better social order set in train.

Socialist prescriptions have assumed a wide variety of forms over the years, but with one exception we need not worry about their distinctions here. (The exception is Marxism, to which the next section of this chapter is devoted, because of its practical importance in many parts of the world today.) The basic socialist philosophy spread with surprising rapidity. By the start World War I (1914) socialism in one form or another was the single most important political force in Europe. Today it is a world-wide phenomenon.

Many economists have questioned the ability of a socialist society to allocate resources and manage the productive process efficiently. In part, but only in part, this is a reaction to the proposals of many early socialist writers to eliminate interest, rents, and profits (in the businessman's sense).[1] Even if the ownership of productive property is concentrated in the state or some other social organization, however, some way must be found to incorporate the marginal rate of return to capital in the costs of production, otherwise it may be squandered on unproductive projects while more productive uses are undercapitalized.

If this problem were satisfactorily overcome, however, a more fundamental problem would remain: how would the productive process be organized, and what incentive would there be to efficiency?

Writing late in the 19th century and early in the 20th, three nonsocialist economists demonstrated that a centrally controlled socialist system does indeed have a unique theoretical equilibrium position[2], in the same sense as the purely competitive equilibrium under capitalism, and with the same qualifications and similar properties. Their ideas have been further developed by some socialist writers in more recent times, including Oscar Lange and Abba P. Lerner. However, translating these theoretical possibilities into practical reality is a separate problem, just as relating the real world of money-and-market economies to the purely competitive model is a separate problem from deriving the model itself.

The basic socialist solution to the resource-allocation problem is centralized planning. Perhaps the quickest introduction to socialist planning is through the

---

[1] In his *What Is Property?* (1840), for example, Pierre-Joseph Proudhon did not propose to abolish private property, but to do away with rent, interest, and profit.

[2] Friederich von Wieser, *Natural Value* (first German edition 1889); Vilfredo Pareto, *Cours d'Economie Politique* (1897); and Enrico Barone, "The Ministry of Production in the Collectivist State", in F.A. von Hayek, ed., *Collectivist Economic Planning* (1935; first published in Italian in 1908).

thoroughly capitalist idea of input-output analysis, pioneered by Wassily Leontief in the 1930's. It may be described as a simplified form of general-equilibrium analysis (see the last two paragraphs of section 5 of Chapter 1).

The idea behind input-output analysis is to identify the flow of goods and services from industry to industry in any economy, in order to show the relationships among them. For example, to produce an additional million dollars' worth of automobiles the U.S. auto industry would have to buy specific dollar amounts of iron and steel, nonferrous metals, chemicals, textiles, etc.; at the same time, each of those industries would need to buy specific dollar amounts of automotive products if they were to produce the indicated volumes of output required of them by the auto industry.

Input-output analysis proved useful in promoting the sudden increase in the production of munitions and military equipment when World War II broke out, by identifying the expansion of related industries necessary for increased output of any particular product. It has also proven useful for developing countries trying to expand output in any given industry. Broadly similar problems are faced by a socialist economy in organizing the production of all goods and services, and they can be solved in roughly similar ways.

Practical experience with the problems of socialist planning on any substantial scale is pretty well confined to what was until recently known as the Soviet bloc. There is ample evidence of difficulty in achieving the distributional efficiency achieved in capitalist markets, in that shortages of some consumer goods and surpluses of others seemed to be common in most members of the bloc. There is also evidence that market mechanisms can be adapted to reduce if not to eliminate these problems; most members came to use the price mechanism to some extent in allocating resources and regulating production, and those that had gone farthest in this procedure seemed to have had most success in eliminating shortages and surpluses of particular goods.

This process seems to have taken a sudden leap forward recently, with the introduction of "openness" and "reconstruction" in the U.S.S.R. and similar reform movements in other east-bloc countries. However, some internal critics had already questioned how far this trend can go without compromising basic socialist principles, and hard-line oppositon to the reforms is clearly evident.[3]

---

[3] Since this paragraph was first written, the U.S.S.R. has experienced grave problems, both political and economic, in trying to move towards a true money-and-market system; their socialist economic system has been pretty completely discredited. It should not be forgotten, however, that that system operated with considerable success for over 70 years of difficult times; it materially

However, some observers have raised basic questions about the "efficiency" test itself. First, the efficiency actually realized in free-enterprise countries may not compare all that well with that claimed for the model of pure competition, either in the allocation of resources or in the distribution of income. There is room for vast differences of opinion on that score. Second, some socialists have argued that efficiency in production is not an overriding consideration: a system that resulted in a more equitable distribution of a smaller total output might well be preferable to one that produced a very inequitable distribution of a much larger total.

4. Marxism.

Marxism is a strand of socialist thought that deserves special mention, mainly because it has had and continues to have a powerful influence on political realities in many parts of the world. Marx's own term for it was *scientific socialism*, because he believed he had established it firmly on the basis of the received classical economics of his day, and contrasted it with the "utopian" socialism of others. ("Utopian socialism" is a term usually applied to the ideas of certain writers in the early 19th century who advocated Utopia-like societies, but Marx applied it contemptuously to all forms of socialism except his own.)

Here a brief digression is necessary to provide some perspective for a central point in Marx's analysis, his quantity-of-labour theory of value. Early economists had a great deal of difficulty in deciding what it is that gives value to various products—why useless luxuries like diamonds command a great price, for example, while a basic foodstuff like bread is cheap, and an absolute essential like air is a free good. A reasonably satisfactory explanation along the lines of the supply-and-demand analysis of Chapter 5 was not worked out till the last third of the 19th century.

In Ricardo's *On the Principles of Political Economy and Taxation* (1817) he argued that the exchange values of useful products come from (a) their scarcity and (b) the amount of work required to produce them. He then concluded that their values would be in proportion to the amount of labour embodied in them. In effect, he adopted a quantity-of-labour theory of value, in which different types and skills of labour were converted to standard labour units, even though this introduced difficulties in some aspects of his analysis. An effective criticism by Samuel Bailey

---

raised the standard of living of the bulk of the populace from that inherited from their Czarist past, and put a manned space vehicle in orbit around the earth ("Sputnik") long before any other country was prepared to do so.

was published just eight years later, and substantial progress in supply-and-demand analysis was already being made, but Ricardo's prestige assured his value theory of respectful attention for many more years.

Karl Marx (1818-1883) saw socialist implications in Ricardo's value theory, but he was not by any means the first to do so. The so-called Ricardian Socialists, mostly writing in the 1820's and 1830's, had drawn similar conclusions, though they had not erected as elaborate a theoretical structure on them as Marx did.

The first volume of Marx's major work, *Capital*, was not published until 1867 (in German), and the third (posthumously) in 1895. However, he had worked steadily on his ideas from 1849 on in London, he had financed himself in part by journalism, he was politically active, and in 1859 he had published *Critique of Political Economy* (also in German), so his ideas were already spreading. His theory of value follows Ricardo's closely, with one very important difference. Whereas for Ricardo the quantity-of-labour theory was a hypothesis to explain *relative* values in a long-run-equilibrium situation, for Marx the quantity of labour in a product was identical with its *absolute* value.[4]

On the basis of his value theory Marx erected an elaborate structure of exploitation as an explanation of the capitalist's profit. Labour-power (the productive ability of workers) is a commodity, bought and sold like other commodities. Like other commodities, Marx said, its value is the number of socially necessary labour hours needed to produce it—to raise and train the worker, and to keep him or her in food, clothing, and shelter, averaged over a working lifetime.

However, an hour's labour produces more than enough to maintain the worker for an hour, so the exchange value of the product is greater than the exchange value of the labour-power that produces it. The capitalist pays the worker a wage equal to the full labour-power value of each hour worked, but in return gets the full hour's labour and retains title to the product in which it is incorporated. Profit is the difference between the full value of labour-time and the price of labour-power. Marx calls it unpaid labour, or surplus value.

Actually, one may wonder if this elaborate structure[5] is necessary. Given Marx's assumption that the value of a product is identical with the socially necessary labour time that goes into its production, any share of the output that goes to anyone else

---

[4] Marx was careful to specify that he meant *socially necessary* labour; adding unnecessary labour to a product would not increase its value.

[5] The full complexity of Marx's analysis is hardly hinted at in the brief recital given in this section. Indeed, even convinced Marxists are far from agreement about "what Marx really meant", let alone about how his theories should be revised in the light of subsequent developments.

but the workers must be the result of exploitation in some sense or other. Presumably the capitalist would be entitled to a share equal to the value of his or her labour time actually necessary for the process of production, but no more—no return for interest or rent or profit on capital, for example.

When the idea of marginal analysis made its appearence, which assigns value to the contributions of all factors of production, Marx resolutely rejected it. So do some Marxists to this day. Others (and non-Marxist socialists) accept marginal analysis, and support their criticisms of the capitalist system on more sophisticated grounds than the labour theory of value.

Profits (or surplus value) may be partly consumed by the capitalist, but may also be invested in new capital. Marx argued that the accumulation of capital brought a decline in the relative share of labour in the product, and the creation of an "industrial reserve army" of unemployed workers. Also, that it brought the concentration of capital into fewer and fewer hands, and an inevitable tendency for the average rate of profit to fall. The result of continuing accumulation was an intensifying conflict between capitalism's ability to produce and its ability to consume the products.

This is where Marx introduces underconsumption (or overproduction) into his analysis: he expected recurring crises, in which output goes unsold and capitalists incur serious losses. However, he rejected underconsumption as an adequate explanation of capitalism's troubles. He saw crises as drastic means for re-establishing harmony, though only temporarily, by wiping out the value of part of the existing capital structure and thereby arresting the fall in the rate of profit. A depression sets in, prices and wages fall, credit contracts. Eventually individual capitalists see opportunities for profit from new machines or new productive methods, so recovery begins—only to give way to a more severe crisis in due course.

This is about as far as it is worth our while to explore Marxian economics here. It remains mainly to point out two things. First, that Marx made many contributions to economic analysis, the importance of which are independent of the uses to which he put them, though acknowledgement of them by main-stream economists was long in coming.

Second, that the spread of Marxism was not due to the power of his economic theories in persuading the masses, but to a potent combination of arguments and predictions that are primarily sociological in nature—that is, they are based on a particular view of how society and its institutions evolve. There are two main elements in Marx's sociology: a materialistic (or economic) interpretation of history, and a theory of classes and the class struggle.

Marx argued that economic considerations are the key to an understanding of a given society, and of the process of historical change. Mankind earns its livelihood through a process that involves social relations, the nature of which will depend on the nature of the known productive processes of the time. Political and legal institutions will be erected as a superstructure on this economic foundation, and it will influence the ideas and the accepted modes of thought of that society. The position of an individual or a group or a class in society will depend primarily on the position occupied in the productive process. The government will be the servant of the most powerful class, and the laws will reflect its will.

According to Marx's analysis, however, society's efforts to increase and to make the fullest use of its productive powers bring economic changes which in time make the existing order increasingly inappropriate. Sooner or later the existing social relationship will have to change, and with it the political and legal institutions and the ideas and modes of thought that go with them.

Thus Marx concluded that social change eventually involves a political revolution, i.e. the replacement of the old political structure by a new and more appropriate one. The groups or classes that have evolved as part of the old productive process will have different interests, and conflicts between or among them will be an essential force in bringing about the change. But the new order will itself undergo change, and the process will continue.

Applying this philosophy of history to 19th-century capitalism, Marx reduced the class structure to two components: the bourgeois class that owns the physical means of production, and the proletarian class that provides the workforce. Their interests are naturally antagonistic (an idea that is also to be found in Ricardo, and can be traced back to Adam Smith too, despite Smith's belief in a natural harmony of interests). The resulting class war provides the economic and political mechanisms that bring about the necessary changes.

The ideas so briefly summarized here rapidly became parts of a political dogma that is still held by many with fierce and religious fervour. The belief that the eventual attainment of socialism was assured as a matter of logical necessity—that "the very stars in their courses were working for them", as someone has put it—was a powerful stimulant to workers who felt (with good reason in many cases) that they were being unfairly treated.

The zeal with which Marx propounded his sociological views, and their revolutionary implications, no doubt go far to explain the inability of orthodox economists to see any merit in his economic analysis. Bringing attention to the conflict between the conservative and the radical interpretation of classical economics was painful enough, but carrying the classical doctrine to an extreme (and in fact distorted) conclusion seems to have dislodged objective reasoning in Marx's critics.

5. Historicism in Germany and Institutionalism in the U.S.A.

The German Historical School originated when the country was still weak and divided after the Napoleonic Wars, and aspiring towards unification, which was eventually achieved when the Empire was formed in 1871 under Prussian leadership. The economies of the member states were mostly agricultural and undemocratic, and mercantilist regulations persisted at least until the unification. The Historical School began by rationalizing the existing economic structure and questioning the relevance of British classical economics for the German situation, but moved on to emphasize factual historical studies as the basis for economic analysis.

It is customary to distinguish between the Older and the Younger Historical Schools. Both used an evolutionary approach, and argued that an economic doctrine that is relevant for one country at a given time need not be relevant for another country or another time. Both were nationalistic, looking to the building up of the German economy and stressing the rôle of the state. Historical economists were generally reformers, and believed that the state should be concerned with the just distribution of real income and wealth.

Wilhelm Roscher (1817-1894) was the first economist of the Older Historical School.[6] While critical of some aspects of the economics of British classicism, his own work built on that tradition to a large extent. However, he stressed the need to inject the historical spirit into economic enquiry. He argued that, once the natural laws of political economy were recognized, reliable statistical data would solve policy controversies.

Bruno Hildebrand (1812-1878) was more consistently critical of classical analysis, and distinguished more clearly than Roscher had done between theoretical analysis and practical policy questions. Karl Knies (1821-1898) was even more critical of classical economics, and argued that historical studies are the only proper form of economics.

---

[6] Friederich List (1789-1846) is sometimes listed as a forerunner of the Historical School. He lived for some years in the U.S.A. On his return to Germany he advocated a customs union (achieved in 1834), with high tariff walls against imports. He is particularly known for supporting the "infant industry" argument for protection: a new industry may need protection to get a start, in competition with established industries abroad, but once established it should be able to compete effectively. Apparently he got this idea from Alexander Hamilton during his stay in the U.S.A.

The leading figure of the Younger Historical School was Gustav Schmoller (1838-1917). He strongly criticized the study of a particular economic relationship on the assumption that everything else remained unchanged (the "*if...*" assumption), and was quite antagonistic to the deductive method in economics; he wanted to develop the subject solely through historical monographs. Besides his academic work, he was a leader of the Association for Social Policy, which advocated social legislation and supported government intervention in the economy. The school pretty well ended at Schmoller's death, though Werner Sombart (1863-1941) carried on the argument for some time longer.

American Institutionalism was quite distinct from German historicism, though it was directly and indirectly influenced by it, and some similarities are to be seen. However, institutionalism was really more of a point of view than an identifiable school of thought; its three main representatives pursued very different objectives.

Institutionalism arose in the early 1900's, at the end of a third of a century in which the U.S.A. had grown rapidly to become one of the major industrial powers in the world. At that time the U.S. economy exhibited most of the unpleasant aspects of industrialization that had been criticized elsewhere, but lagged behind in introducing the social legislation that was gradually improving conditions in Britain and Europe. Hours of work were long, social benefits were negligible, job security was poor, health and safety regulations were inadequate, government and business ethics were deplorable.

The name of the group comes directly from the dictionary definition of "institution" as an established practice, custom, society, or organization. Thorstein Bunde Veblen (1857-1929) was the first Institutionalist. His best-known book was *The Theory of the Leisure Class* (1899), in which he scathingly depicted the "conspicuous consumption" of the captains of industry who accumulate wealth. He strongly attacked the then-new marginalist economics and the pleasure-pain ideas of economic motivation that were in vogue, and stressed the rôle of human institutions in economic evolution. He saw the development of the social structure of society as a process of natural selection of institutions.

However, the institutions Veblen was most interested in were related to human motives—habits of thought, mental attitudes and aptitudes, conventional modes of behaviour. He argued that progress comes from the survival of the fittest habits of thought and from the adaptation of individuals to a changing environment.

Veblen's theory of economic change, like Marx's, stressed the rôle of changing technology, which makes old modes of thought out of date and stimulates new ones. However, he saw the chief conflict as being between "industry", which is concerned with material improvements in production, and "business", the absentee owners of enterprises. This lead him to distinguish between industrial capital (the physical means of production) and money capital (the capitalized value of the income from capital): money capital is intangible and serves no productive purpose.

From this Veblen developed a theory of business cycles and crises. Like Marx, but for different reasons, he concluded that the conflicts were bound to get worse, and he feared the ultimate collapse of civilization.

Veblen was not a reformer; he did not hope for improving conditions under capitalism, to which he was fundamentally opposed. He was sympathetic towards socialism, but critical of it, and clearly not a socialist. Cynicism and pessimism seem to have been his main characteristics, together with a pungent wit in ridiculing the objects of his scorn.

John Rogers Commons (1862-1945) was an avowed socialist, but he worked for reforms within capitalism rather than for its overthrow. Like other institutionalists, he saw conflicts of interest rather than harmony; however, he was not unduly critical of mainstream economic theory. The institutions he was interested in were associations and corporations, through which individuals can band together for collective action. He made major pioneering contributions to labour relations, labour legislation, and social legislation. He defended labour unions and collective bargaining, at a time when they we not very popular. He argued that the government has a valid rôle as an impartial force to curb the abuse of power from large accumulations of private property.

Wesley Clair Mitchell (1874-1948) was a student of Veblen's. He became a great research economist, and pioneered what has come to be regarded as the hallmark of the Institutional School: the emphasis on factual and statistical studies. Though he approved of Veblen's views of human nature and his understanding of cultural processes, and was critical of some aspects of mainstream economics, he felt that statistical research offered the best foundation for economic analysis.

Mitchell favoured social reform in principle, but believed that intelligent reform must await adequate understanding of human behaviour and social problems. He made major contributions to the study of business cycles, and directed the National Bureau of Economic Research for many years. The Bureau has done a great deal of factual research in many fields. However, it has not produced much in the way of theoretical advances or proposals for reform.

Unquestionably, both the Historical School and the Institutional School have had a healthy influence on economic theory and economic policymaking, through their insistence on historical research and statistical studies. Most front-rank economists have always had adequate respect for historical factors and for a sound grounding in factual information. Nevertheless it is all too easy to extend theoretical concepts, however sound in themselves, to situations in which they are not appropriate, or to overlook the need for empirical verification wherever possible—that is, for objective testing by observation and experience. No doubt the profession needs to be reminded of this from time to time.

6. Henry George and the Single Tax.

Henry George (1839-1897) was a self-taught but competent American economist who won a large popular following in the late 19th and early 20th centuries, not only in the U.S.A. but also abroad. His views were strongly influenced by his experience of speculative land booms in California, based on the arrival of the first railway in the late 1860's, and similar booms elsewhere. Land values soared as settlers poured in; speculators and promoters made enormous profits without making any real contribution to economic output, while many people continued to live in poverty.

In the 1870's George discovered the British classical economists, and became thoroughly familiar with their work. He was particularly attracted to Ricardo's theory of pure or economic rent, his views on free trade, and his ideas on economic development. In 1879 George published *Progress and Poverty*, which was also printed serially in U.S. and British newspapers and was translated into thirteen foreign languages. His writings were still widely read into the second half of the 20th century, though they were no longer influential.

Although opposed to socialism, George advocated a number of economic reforms that seemed radical enough in his day. His major proposals focused on rent, which he saw as an "unearned increment" in the hands of landowners. He argued that income in this form increased more rapidly than the national income, because a growing output pressed ever more strongly on the limited supply of land. Also, rising rents meant additional benefits to landowners in the form of capital gains from the resultant rise in property values. He believed that rents rightfully belonged to society as a whole, since it was the growth and progress of society that created the property values that made rents possible. Leaving rental income in private hands, he said, enriched people who had made no contribution to production and impoverished everyone else.

George did not suggest expropriating or nationalizing land; instead, he proposed levying a 100 per cent tax on the pure rent of land and other natural resources. He wanted to leave ownership in the hands of the present holders, and to levy no tax on the value of any buildings or other improvements, thus clearly distinguishing the pure rent of land from returns to physical capital. Also, he believed that his proposed tax on rent would yield governments all the revenue they would need to fulfill their proper tasks—hence the "single tax" aspect of his arguments.

Progress and Poverty was especially influential in Britain, where anti-landlord views were already present. It strongly influenced the Fabian Society (a group of British intellectuals who sought social reforms through democratic processes) and other radicals. Orthodox economists, however, opposed George's views vigourously.

British critics argued that taxing away rent would convulse society, threaten civil war, and drive capital out of the country, so British workers would become the worst paid in Europe instead of the best. Also, that it would ruin poor widows who had put what little money they had into land. George replied that the plight of "widows and orphans" was always put forward to justify opposition to change, whereas in fact they could all be given a reasonable pension out of the proceeds of his single tax without putting much of a burden on society.

Nowadays most economists readily admit that George's single tax was economically sound enough as far as it went. A major argument advanced against it, however, is that it would no longer yield enough revenue to meet all the needs of modern government, though the statistical evidence in support of that assertion is not without its weaknesses.

Also, imposing such a tax would certainly have very disturbing effects on incomes and property values throughout the economy. There is an old adage in public finance that the only good tax is an old tax. The point is that the market mechanism will have adapted as well as it can to a tax that has been in effect for a long time, whether the tax is good or bad in itself; but a new tax, no matter how good its final effects may be, is almost certain to have some harmful immediate effects that can not be smoothed out for some time. The cost of the immediate harm must be set against the ultimate benefit expected.

George also believed that his tax on rent would bring an increase in production, end poverty, raise wages and employment, and promote peace. This seems even more doubtful than that it could displace all other forms of taxation. Whatever may have been the case in his day, the private ownership of capital is now far more important than the private ownership of land as a factor in the uneven distribution of wealth and income.

Part Three

Macroeconomics

Chapter 10

The Macroeconomics of Pure Competition

1. The Whole Picture.

A couple of generations ago critics were wont to quip, "Teach a parrot to say 'supply and demand', and you have an economist!" There was some validity in this caricature at that time. The model of pure competition was the main vehicle of economic analysis, and economists did tend to focus primarily on its microeconomic aspects, especially in the English-speaking world.

However, that is not really a fair assessment of the usefulness of the model. Supply-and-demand analysis is certainly an important part of the picture of the economy that the model paints, but it is nevertheless only a part. It is the larger picture—the macroeconomics of pure competition—that is the basis of any policy conclusions that may be derived from the model, whether they are the *laissez-faire* conclusions of the classical economists like Adam Smith or present-day revisions and reinterpretations.

You will probably find it useful to review Chapters 2 to 5 at this point. In Chapter 2 we said that macroeconomics deals with major economic totals like employment, real output, real income, money income, and the general price level. We also explained the concept of the circular flow of money payments, which regulates the process of production and allocates money incomes to the participants. Chapter 3 describes how individuals may be expected to spend their incomes in the way that gives them most satisfaction. Chapter 4 shows how producers may be expected to move persistently towards the most economical and efficient use of the resources available to them, under the conditions assumed in the model. Chapter 5 brings both sides together, and looks at the forces operating to bring about a long-run general-equilibrium situation in which no-one can better his or her position.

The model does acknowledge that serious distortions may occur in the short-to-medium term. Some goods may be unsold, some factors of production may be unemployed, and other distortions may appear. Much hardship may be experienced before equilibrium is restored, and nowadays economists are more sceptical than they used to be about how quickly the process operates. Furthermore, we now know that some of the "other things" the model ignores, or considers relatively unimportant, may sometimes be very important indeed.

However, there are still some loose ends to tidy up.

2. Real Output.

In a modern economy there is an almost-limitless variety of things that can be produced, but the resources available to produce them are pretty firmly fixed at any given moment. We depend on the market mechanism to make these decisions, and microeconomics helps us to understand the rôle of the individual consumer, the individual firm, and the individual industry in the process. So far so good, but in addition we want to know something about total real output, i.e. the total of all goods and services produced in the economy in a given period. We particularly want to know the principles that determine potential real output if all factors of production are used most efficiently, and what forces (if any) operate to achieve that potential.

The principles that determine potential real output can be illustrated easily enough if we think of a single individual living alone on a tropical island, like Robinson Crusoe. Suppose that his needs for shelter and clothing have already been met, for they would be relatively simple, and his only continuing problem is food. By trial and error he finds that he can catch an average of 3 kilograms of fish a day, or grow an average of 5 kilograms of corn (or maize, if you prefer). This must be a sustainable rate of production, of course; it must include the time spend maintaining and repairing his fishing gear in the one case and whatever agricultural tools and equipment he needs in the other case.

The line *AB* in Figure 10-1 represents the range of outputs our one-man economy can produce. His average daily production may vary from 5 kilograms of corn and no fish to 3 kilograms of fish and no corn. He may divide his time any way he likes, and his output of each product will be proportionate to the time spent producing it.

This line goes by various names, depending on how we wish to use it. If we look at it from a consumption point of view, it becomes a *budget line*. (Remember that real income is just another way of looking at output.) The lonesome producer can count his output in the number of manhours he is willing to work per day, and can budget the spending of it to "buy" whatever combination of fish and corn gives him the most satisfaction.

Looking back at Chapter 3, we can see that our man will want a marginal hour (or minute) of work to buy the same utility whether it is spent on corn or on fish. That means he wants to consume (and therefore to produce) whatever combination gives marginal utilities of fish and corn in the ratio of 3 to 5.[1] Furthermore, he will

---

[1] There are graphic techniques for illustrating the relative marginal utilities of corn and fish (or anything else), and how they interact with the budget curve to determine how consumption will be divided, but they are somewhat complicated and are not necessary for the present discussion.

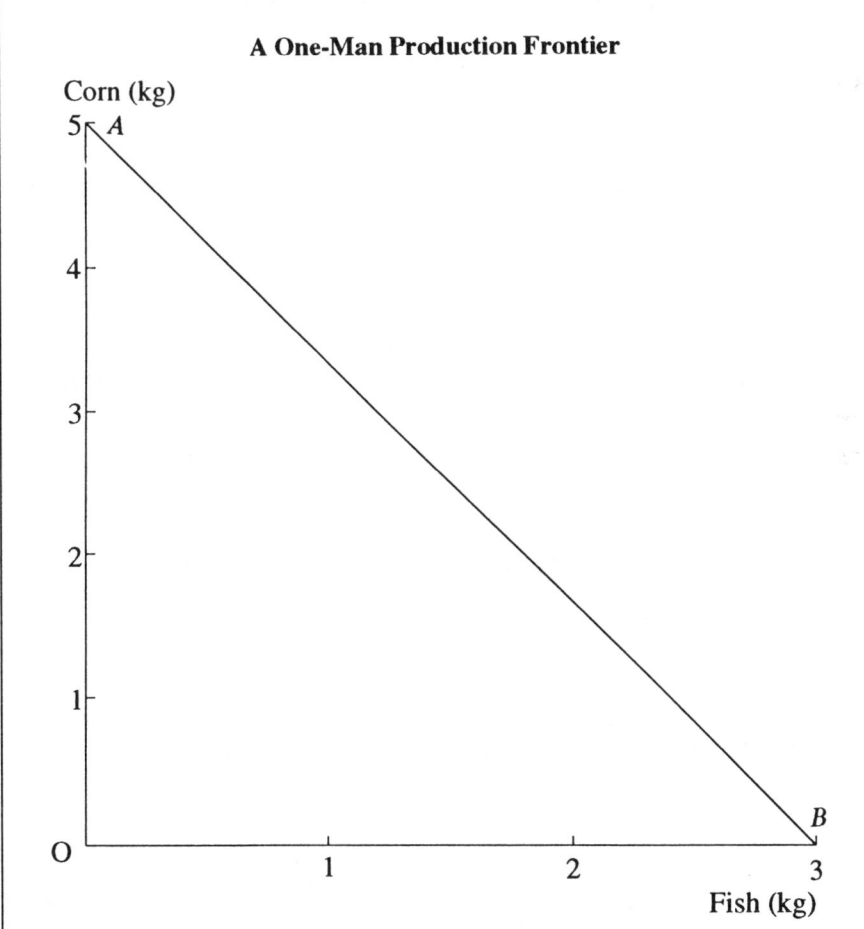

Figure 10-1. An isolated individual finds that, if he spends all his working hours fishing, his catch will average 3 kilograms a day. If he devotes all his time to farming, he can average 5 kilograms of corn a day over the growing season. Or he may divide his time any way he likes, and his output of each product will be proportionate to the time spent producing it.

determine how long to work each day in the same way: until the utility of the additional consumption made possible by the marginal man-hour of work is just equal to the marginal utility of leisure.

For now, however, we are interested in the production side rather than the consumption side of real output. From this point of view the line *AB* in Figure 10-1 may be called a *transformation function*, or a transformation curve: it shows the rate at which fish can in effect be transformed into or replaced by corn (or corn into fish) in the individual's total output. Alternatively, it may be called a *production frontier*: it shows the boundary or frontier between outputs that can be produced and those that can not. Whatever you call it, it represents the potential real output of our simple economy on the assumptions we have made. No combination north-east of the line can be produced; combinations south-west of it can certainly be produced, but indicate underemployment or inefficient use of resources.

There are several ways in which this simple model can be improved. One way is to convert it from a two-dimensional to a three-dimensional illustration, to allow our one-man economy to produce a third commodity—say, meat. If you have a good imagination, think of a new axis perpendicular to the page at the zero point of the two axes in Figure 10-1, and measure kilograms of meat along it.[2] Now imagine a second piece of paper, also perpendicular to the page, with one edge along the north-south axis. On it you may draw a new line or curve showing the trade-off between corn and meat.

Finally, imagine a third piece of paper with edges along the east-west and the vertical axes, on which you may draw a third curve showing the trade-off between fish and meat. If all three of these trade-offs are represented by straight lines, you have defined a plane surface at an angle to the page; it will cut the north-south axis at 5, the east-west axis at 3, and the vertical axis at (say) 4. If some of these trade-offs are curved lines, then you will have a curved surface—perhaps resembling the skin of a football, with the triple-zero point at its centre.

Now let's see what we can learn by varying our assumptions a bit. Suppose our castaway (as he must surely be) found eventually that he was producing more than he really wanted—that he would really prefer less food and more leisure. In that case the transformation curve *AB* would move bodily to the south-west as he decreased the length of his working day. On the other hand he might find he was not producing enough to provide a cushion against occasional poor crops, or

---

[2] If you have a *very* good imagination, perhaps you can visualize a multidimensional figure that incorporates many commodities in the economy's total output.

seasons of low fish catches; in that case he would be willing to work longer, and the curve would move to the north-east.

Another possibility is that our one-man economy might perceive that he could save himself a lot of work in the future by taking some time off from fishing and farming to construct better fishing equipment or improved farming implements. While he was so engaged his food output would decline, but it would no longer be an accurate measure of his total output, because it would omit the capital goods he was creating. These goods would presumably be worth at least as much as the food he was temporarily sacrificing, perhaps a good deal more, in terms of the utility or satisfaction he would derive from the anticipation of greater leisure (or a higher income) later on.

You can incorporate the production of capital goods into the illustration in either of two ways. One way is to identify them with one axis in the two-dimensional figure, and lump corn and fish together as "food" on the other. The second way is to set out the production of capital goods along a vertical axis in a three-dimensional figure, instead of meat.

Here we get important insights into the links between saving and investment, and into some of the reasons for saving and some of the results to be expected from it. Saving means not consuming (or not spending), and releases productive resources for the construction of capital goods. Our castaway is simultaneously saving and investing, as he reduces his consumption of food and puts his time into producing more capital goods. Once these are finished and he puts them to work, they enable him to catch more fish, or grow more corn, or both. If he continues to work as many hours per day as before, his total output will increase and the transformation curve will move to the north-east.

However, that does not exhaust the possibilities. In this two-dimensional model he will probably work *fewer* hours and enjoy more leisure, because his choice of consumer goods is so limited. Total output might actually decline, instead of increase; the transformation curve might move to the south-west. Nevertheless our single consumer's greater leisure suggests that his enjoyment of life will show an over-all increase—his psychic income (or his net economic welfare) will be greater even if his real income is not.

In any case the probability of decreased real output declines as we open up the possibility of producing additional consumer goods. Just the opportunity to branch out into other foods would make a substantial difference, for a diet limited to corn and fish would be pretty monotonous. Other creature comforts besides food could also be produced even in such a restricted environment. There is certainly a normal presumption that increased real income will increase the attraction of leisure, but

160   The Practice of Economics

it will also mean that types of consumer goods that were formerly unaffordable become affordable, and their attractions may outweigh those of more leisure.[3]

---

3 This paragraph deals with what is technically known as "effort elasticity of demand": measuring demand in terms of the effort you are prepared to make in order to enjoy the goods in question, rather than in terms of the money you are prepared to pay out of a given income. We did not use this term in the discussion of the backward-sloping supply curve for labour in section 3 of Chapter 5, but the idea is there. Sometimes the availability of attractive consumer goods may be a better incentive to work than higher money wages.

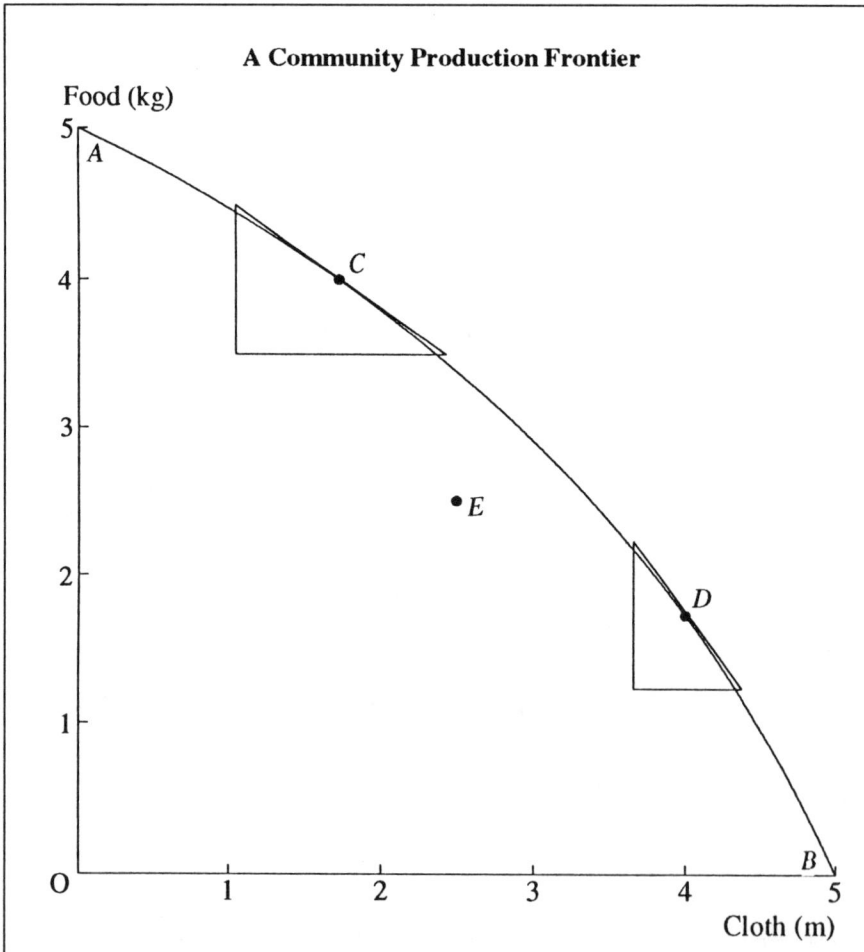

Figure 10-2. The community can produce 5 units of food if it produces no cloth, and 3 units of cloth if it produces no food. (The units are some multiple of a kilogram or a metre respectively.) Because the resources needed by the two industries are different, more and more food must be sacrificed if cloth output is increased, and *vice versa*.

The concept of a transformation function is equally applicable to a sophisticated modern economy, as in Figure 10-2. One difference you will see is that in this case we have labelled the axes "cloth" and "food", instead of corn and fish. This is simply in recognition of the fact that output will involve a much wider range of industries—not a very impressive way of acknowledging that fact, it is true, but the best we can do in a two-dimensional diagram.

Another difference is that we have represented AB as a curved line instead of a straight one. There is no deep purpose behind the change. The shape is conjectural anyway, but in a one-man labour-intensive economy it seems reasonable to suppose that there are neither economies nor diseconomies of scale of any significance, so one hour's work should be as good as another in either occupation.

In a more sophisticated economy, however, this is unlikely to be so. Different industries will employ factors of production in very different forms and proportions, and some categories may not be easily transferred from one use to another. Thanks to The Law of Diminishing Returns, economies of scale, and other considerations, we can expect bottlenecks to appear as resources are concentrated more and more on any one project. Beyond some point, therefore, any further increase in one output will require the sacrifice of more and more of other outputs. At point C, for example, the economy must give up a lot more cloth for a given increase in the output of food than at point D, as you may easily verify by looking at the little diagrams around the slopes of the curve at these two points.

Transformation functions are useful for bringing out certain macroeconomic features of many economic models, not just the model of pure competition. That happens to be the model we are concerned with now, however, and Figure 10-2 can be used to advantage.

Let us start with the point E, well within the production frontier. If this is taken to represent the current output of food and cloth in the economy, then clearly there must be considerable unemployment of some or all factors of production—or else some of them must be being used very inefficiently. (Remember that in this two-dimensional model these two industries account for the whole economy.) The diagram does not tell us whether the fault lies with the cloth industry, the food industry, or both, but it does tell us that some reallocation of resources would permit a substantial increase in total output.

The output represented by the point E is incompatible with the model of pure competition, which postulates freedom of contract for all factors of production. Probably the managers of some firms, perhaps many firms, can profitably bid for more labour, land, and capital with which to expand their outputs. If some resources are unemployed or inefficiently employed after all existing firms have raised their outputs until their marginal costs equal the market price of their product, new managers or entrepreneurs will enter the market and establish new firms.

One or both of these processes will continue until all unemployed factors have been hired and all inefficiently-employed factors have been enticed away from inefficient employers. Any firm that was using resources inefficiently will have to either raise its efficiency to the standard level of the industry, so it can afford to pay the going rates for factors of production, or go out of business. Actual output will be driven inexorably up until it rests on the transformation curve.[4]

Note the important disciplinary function of competition in this model. It ruthlessly weeds out the incompetent, the inefficient, and the lazy managers, even as it rewards the competent, the efficient, and the energetic ones as well as the innovators.

Potential output will grow with the passage of time (the transformation curve will shift to the north-east) as the public's net savings permit the supply of capital goods to expand, as technological improvements make better productive processes possible, as new sources of minerals and other raw materials are found, as the working population grows, and as the average skills of the community's members increase through training and experience.

This may of course be offset (perhaps more than offset) by the destruction of productive resources through wars or civil disturbances, by droughts and other natural disasters, by the exhaustion of known sources of raw materials, by a loss of population, or the like. Actual levels of output will follow these shifts in potential output more or less faithfully, allowing for some inevitable lags in the process by which equilibrium is approached after unforeseen accidents and disturbances occur.

3. Employment.

The number of people employed in the economy does not get much direct attention in the model of pure competition, though it is clearly an important factor

---

[4] Just where on the curve the point will be does not concern us here, any more than it did in Figure 10-1. However, we may be sure that the relative prices of food and cloth will be the same as the marginal rate of transformation (or substitution) at that point. That rate is measured by the amount of cloth that must be forgone to get an additional unit of food, or *vice versa*, and is represented by the slope of the transformation curve at the point in question. If the market price of a unit of cloth was (say) 1.5 times that of a unit of food, but the market rate of transformation (i.e., the relative cost of production) was only 1.4 times, resources would be shifted from food production to cloth production; production would shift southeasterly along the curve until some combination of rising relative costs and falling relative prices for cloth brought the two together.

in determining potential output. The reason is that full employment is deemed to be the norm. If there is an oversupply of labour, or of any particular type of labour, it will be eliminated in the same way as an oversupply of any other good: its price will fall until the amount offered contracts, the amount demanded increases, and the market for it "clears". Involuntary unemployment may indeed occur temporarily, as demand shifts from one product to another or as some firms fail and are replaced by others, but *persistent unemployment must be voluntary*—the marginal attractiveness of leisure must be greater than the marginal utility of the real income obtainable at the going wage rate.

The total population of an economy is normally taken by economists to be a "given" resource or statistic, determined primarily by noneconomic forces. (The portion that chooses to seek employment is determined, of course, by the marginal attractions of work and leisure.) Changes over time may be explained or predicted in various ways, but doing so is considered to be an exercise in vital statistics rather then economics. This is true of economic analysis in general, not just in applications of the model of pure competition.

Some economists at one time in history did attempt to explain population growth as an economic phenomenon. Thomas Malthus is probably the best-known proponent of such theories, but many other classical economists held similar opinions. The substance of it was a sort of Parkinson's Law of Population: it grows to absorb whatever food supply is available. Human beings are capable of reproducing on a geometric scale, the argument ran—if numbers doubled in (say) 25 years they could multiply by four in 50 years, by eight in 75 years, and so on. Food supplies, it was thought, could not be expanded persistently at anything like this rate, so the bulk of humanity would be condemned to existing at the minimum level of subsistence. These views earned economics the title of "the dismal science".

Dismal-science predictions have been pretty well discredited in the eyes of the public over the last 200 years or so, at least for Europe, most of the western hemisphere, and much of the rest of the world. Whether you consider it a matter of economics or vital statistics, however, some serious thinkers believe that the Malthusian problem may yet bedevil us, albeit in a more sophisticated form.

4. Saving and Investment.

We have spoken several times of the links between a community's willingness to save and its ability to expand its capital equipment. The word "investment" is commonly used by economists as a shorthand term for the creation of capital goods, as we have already done and will continue to do from time to time. Unfortunately this conflicts with the normal use of the term to mean the purchase of any property or claim in the expectation of earning an income or gain of some kind from it—stocks (shares), bonds, rental properties, futures contracts in various commodities, gold bullion, and many other things. We will *not* normally use it in the sense of buying existing properties, or mere pieces of paper, and we will promise to make it clear when we do so. Also, we will prefer to use "capital formation" or similar expressions instead of "investment" in the economist's sense. Nevertheless such expressions are often awkward, so the shorthand word is especially useful when it must be used repeatedly.

Presumably the motive for adding to capital equipment is to increase production and thereby increase one's net income. The expected benefit may be in real terms, such as the services rendered by an owner-occupied house, or in money or in some other indirect form, such as greater revenue from a business. In some cases the benefit may be purely psychological, as when a wealthy man builds a memorial to himself or his family, or commissions some useful structure and donates it to the community.

In a money-and-market economy it is important that the savings of savers and the capital expenditures of those who want to borrow those savings be kept in balance,[5] as we noted in section 2 of Chapter 2. Imagine that all money earned "today" is not spent until "tomorrow". If on-one saves and no-one invests, tomorrow's spending will be the same as today's; it will be exactly enough to buy the same total output at the same prices and will produce the same money income. The same will happen if new capital spending exactly replaces the money not spent by savers.

If investment falls short, however, then tomorrow's income will not be enough to buy tomorrow's output at today's prices; either prices must fall, or some goods must go unsold. If investment exceeds saving, on the other hand, inflationary pressures will arise. Thus saving and investment *must* be equal in any stable situation.

In the version of the model of pure competition that was generally accepted until the 1930's, saving and investment were kept in balance by the rate of interest. It was thought that savers would save more at higher rates of interest and less at lower,

---

[5] This is not a problem in a barter economy, because the only vehicles in which savings can be held are commodities of some kind—savings are automatically "invested" in those commodities. Such vehicles are sterile, however; they add nothing to productive capacity, unless they consist of flocks and herds that can reproduce naturally, and they are subject to spoilage of various kinds. They typify the sort of treasures that moth and rust doth corrupt.

whereas borrowers would borrow more at lower rates and less at higher. This is reasonable enough, of course, on the usual "*if...*" assumption. It seemed to follow, therefore, that the rate of interest could be relied on to "clear" the market for the use of savings, like the market for any other commodity. If the rate of capital spending declined, for example, then the interest rate would also decline until the flow of savings was correspondingly reduced.

Actually, this was always a rather shaky part of the model of pure competition. We have already had occasion to remark that partial-equilibrium analysis like this is not entirely satisfactory, but in this case there is more to it than that.

Individuals who save may be motivated by any of a large number of reasons. Some may save for a major future expenditure, such as a new car or extensive travel or a university education for their children. Others may want to equalize their incomes over time, for example by putting money aside in years of high earnings in order to live comfortably in lean years or after retirement. Still others may just want a cushion against possible future misadventures, or may hope to enjoy a larger income from the earnings they expect their savings to produce. Business firms may also want to save for essentially similar reasons, including the eventual replacement of their capital equipment.

There may be other good reasons for saving, too, but those just given do cover a lot of ground, and only a few of them look very sensitive to the rate of interest. Of those that do, some may respond negatively rather than positively. For example, suppose you want to save up enough to give yourself about as high an income after you retire as you expect to have just before retirement, and suppose the real rate of interest doubles. (The real rate means the rate after adjusting for inflation or deflation.) Would you now save more than before, or less? Surely less, because it will now take only half as much savings as before to give you the same interest income.

In fact, experience with inflation shows that people may quite rationally save even if the real rate of interest is negative (that is, if the rate of inflation exceeds the nominal rate of interest). It is true that people will want to anticipate their needs for anything that can be stored up for future use, and will borrow heavily (dissave) in order to do so. However, there are limits to the amount most of us can borrow, and some things you will want in the future can not be bought up in advance. For example, you can't buy today the university education your child will want in 15 years time.

There is also some doubt about how important the rate of interest is as a regulator of investment, as we will see in section 4 of Chapter 11.

However, we may take some comfort from remembering that the full rigour of the model of pure competition applies only in the state of long-run equilibrium. In that blissful condition saving and investment must indeed be in balance at the equilibrium rate of interest, even though we may nourish some doubts about how the balance is actually brought about.

In some cases the act of saving and the act of investing may be performed by the same person at the same time, as when our one-man economy in section 1 took time out from food-producing to make additional fishing equipment and farming implements. A real-life example would be a firm that plows back some of its net revenues into additional capital goods, instead of paying out all of its income to its owners.

In most cases, however, the decisions are made by different people, or if by the same people then at different times. Some investors will want more new capital goods than they can finance from their own funds. Some savers will welcome an opportunity to be paid for the use of savings they can not use directly.

Lending and borrowing contracts for suitable periods of time are an obvious way of serving the needs of both savers and investors. Normally the lender will expect payment for the use of his money, which the borrower can afford to make out of the expected returns from an addition to his capital equipment. The borrower must satisfy the lender that the contract is reasonably safe, or compensate him for any perceived risks he does take. Note also that some of the reasons for saving at one time imply dissaving (the using up of previous savings) at another time; a loan contract will permit both sides to schedule the repayment at their best convenience.

5. The Interest Rate.

Strictly speaking, "borrowing" and "lending" refer to debt contracts, and the compensation paid to the lender is interest. However, we argued in section 5 of Chapter 5 that debt finance and equity finance generate essentially similar claims to the ownership of productive resources, and that the returns to the various types of each category of claims will tend to be equal if we allow for the differences in how the risks and benefits are shared. In order to keep the discussion within manageable bounds, therefore, we will here use the term "interest" to include all returns to the ownership of productive resources.

For the same reason we will speak of "the" rate of interest. This is a gross oversimplification, of course, for in the real world there are literally thousands of different rates of interest, even in the strict legal sense. You may interpret it as a sort of average or typical rate.

Interest may be viewed as the "price" of the use of someone else's money for an agreed period of time. It is usually calculated as a per cent per annum of the sum lent (the principal). The percentage is of course negotiable between the principals, which means that in the model of pure competition it is set by market forces.

We may first distinguish between the market rate (or rates) of interest and what some economists have called the "natural" rate, i.e. the "pure" rate of interest that would obtain in the long-run-equilibrium position, when the returns to all assets would be equalized and all risks and uncertainties eliminated.

Market rates are likely to be influenced by many temporary factors, such as arbitrary changes in the money supply and other merely-monetary disturbances; at any given moment they may be either above or below the natural rate.

Market interest rates also include a risk premium, or rather two distinct types of risk premiums—against the risk of default, and against market risks. The first is the risk that the borrower may not be able to repay the loan at maturity; the main defence against it is careful evaluation of the borrower's creditworthiness before granting the loan. The second is the risk of losses due to market fluctuations. If the interest rate rises during the lifetime of a loan, for example, the lender will lose income compared to what he would have earned by keeping his money in liquid assets for a while longer. And, if he has to sell the loan (say, a bond) before its maturity, he will suffer a capital loss.

Another influence on market interest rates is the possibility that the general price level will change over the lifetime of the loan. A rise in prices means that a given sum of money will buy less goods, a fall means that it will buy more. In the first case the lender suffers a capital loss, because he gets repaid in less-valuable money; in the second case he receives a capital gain. In inflationary times, therefore, market interest rates are likely to contain an *inflation premium*; the lender will demand compensation for his expected capital loss, and the borrower will have little reason to object, for he can count on repaying in less-valuable money. In deflationary times the premium becomes negative, and market interest rates will be below the pure interest rate.

Economists also recognize *real* interest rates, usually derived by deflating the market or nominal rate by the rate of inflation. It is not the same as the pure interest rate, because it probably contains a risk premium. In practice, however, the real rate derived from the issues of a responsible government borrowing on a moderate scale is often taken to be a reasonable approximation to the pure rate of interest. In inflationary times it may become negative, especially if the current rate of inflation is not fully recognized.

168   The Practice of Economics

6. Real Income, Money Income, and Prices.

We have identified real income as real output seen from the viewpoint of those who receive it, and we have noted that real output can be visualized as the sum total of all goods and services produced in the community in a given period (say, one year). For many purposes, however, we want to compare the total for one period with that for another, so we need some meaningful way of measuring this jumble of very different things. The most common way of doing so involves the use of statistical tools known as index numbers.

Index numbers of various kinds are widely used to measure the changes over time in economic variables that lump related but dissimilar things together. You are probably familiar with the consumer price index, commonly used to measure the monthly changes in the average prices of the things a typical consumer buys. It is constructed by "weighting" the prices of the various items by the amount a typical consumer spends on them, as derived from surveys of consumer spending habits. Usually some arbitrarily-chosen year is taken as a base period, the amounts spent on each of the selected items is computed, and the total is added up. Then the total that would be paid for the same collection of items at subsequent dates is calculated, and expressed as a percentage of the total for the base date.

There are many economic variables that can be represented by index numbers, and several different ways of constructing index numbers, which we can not go into here. For dealing with real income, money income, prices, and the relationships among them, statisticians usually start by computing the money value of real output for some period (usually a year or a quarter). That is, they multiply each product by its average market price for the period, and add up the total, to get what is commonly known as the Gross National Product or GNP. We have already shown a hypothetical example of the result, in section 6 of Chapter 7.

The figures so obtained for a series of years or other periods may be viewed as a particular type of index number. Technically, they constitute an *aggregative value index*—that is, an index number expressed as a total value in money rather than as a ratio or percentage of the value in some selected base year. The full title of this series is GNP in current dollars (or pounds or francs or whatever is the national monetary unit). If the general price level did not change, it would be a reasonably good measure of the changes in real income from one period to another. (It would not be a perfect measure even then, because among other things there might be qualitative changes in some products, such as new and better models, and entirely new products might appear.)

In these days of persistent world-wide inflation, however, we know that the general price level does change; and older generations experienced prolonged periods of *de*flation as well as *in*flation. To correct for this, statisticians choose some particular year as a base year, then use the prices that obtained in that year to recompute the GNP for previous and subsequent periods. These recomputed figures are technically known as "GNP in dollars (or pounds or francs or whatever) of constant purchasing power", but more commonly they are identified as "real income".

Clearly, there is a definite relationship among real income, money income, and the general price level. Real income as just defined is an attempt to measure physical quantity; money income measures the total money value of that quantity; dividing the latter by the former gives us some sort of average price for the quantity component of money income. This is in fact routinely done year by year and quarter by quarter in the national accounts of most countries. It yields what is known as an *implicit* price index of total output (or total income), because it is derived indirectly instead of directly: since price times quantity equals value, computing the second and third *implies* the first.

7. The Quantity Theory of Money and Prices.

We have referred repeatedly to the operation of a money-and-market economy, but so far we have not brought money into the analysis in any systematic way. It is time to do so, though for now we will limit our attention to the minimum necessary for the model of pure competition. In Chapter 12 we will have more to say on the subject.

The basic function of money is to make payments and facilitate trade—the transactions function. Goods may be exchanged by barter, and still are on occasion today, but money seems to have been invented independently in most societies whenever trade became extensive enough to make it useful. Some staple commodity was commonly promoted to that rôle, by general consent or practical experience rather than any authoritarian or governmental decision. Wheat, salt, tobacco, beaver skins, and many other items have been so used at various times and in various places. Instead of looking for someone who had what you wanted and wanted what you had (technically known as a "double coincidence of wants"), you traded your product for the monetary commodity and then traded that for what you really wanted.

Metals offer certain advantages as commodity-moneys, and coins were invented to avoid repeated weighing, testing for purity, and other inconveniences. Modern money-and-banking systems gradually evolved from these simple commodity-moneys, and money is now used to effect many complex financial transactions as well as the exchange of goods and services.

The most common definition of money reflects its basic function: anything that is widely used to pay for goods and services or to settle debts or obligations, or some other set of words to the same effect. In most jurisdictions nowadays the main components are a paper currency issued by a central bank or the equivalent, and chequeable deposits at commercial banks, supplemented by coins in small denominations. The coins are tokens, i.e. they have little or no intrinsic value; they are usually issued by the government, a hold-over from the days when full-bodied coinage bearing the imprint of the sovereign was normally the standard form of money.

Sometimes chequeable deposits or close substitutes are also held at financial institutions that are not officially recognized as banks; they come within the common definition of money, although they are not always included in "the money supply" as officially reported.

Money has other functions or uses besides the transactions function. It is a logical choice as a unit of account or *numèraire*, in which records are kept and comparisons made. It is also useful as a store of value, that is as an asset, either to cover your expenditures between paydays or as a very liquid vehicle for holding some of your savings, temporarily at least. It does not have a monopoly in any of these functions—not even as a medium of exchange, since barter is still possible—but it does have important advantages in each.

The basic theory of the model of pure competition is strictly neutral about money. Despite its obvious usefulness in facilitating trade, money does not affect the equilibrium position towards which the model tends. From this point of view it is *relative* prices that are significant, not absolute prices, so any commodity will do as well as money as a unit of account. For example, you may just as well compare the values of two houses by how many kilograms of wheat it would take to buy them instead of how much money. Classical economists were fond of doing just that sort of thing, to emphasize the basic unimportance of money, though they did readily acknowledge that it certainly expedited all forms of economic activity.

For practical purposes, however, we do need to deal with absolute prices in terms of whatever is the currently-accepted form of money. One approach to the problem is through what is known as The Quantity Theory of Money, which is not actually a theory *of* money at all, but a theory *about* money. It is really a theory of the general price level, and might better be called The Quantity-of-Money Theory of Prices, even though it explicitly recognizes that other things besides the quantity of money affect the price level. We will label it The Quantity Theory of Money and Prices when a full title is necessary, but in deference to accepted usage we will usually compromise by calling it simply The Quantity Theory.

While not officially part of the model of pure competition, the quantity theory is fully compatible with it, and held sway until comparatively recent times. For several decades now it has been overshadowed by newer theories, but it is still useful in its original form as a broad generalization, and modern monetarist theories (discussed in Chapter 14) grew directly out of it. For now, however, we will be interested only in its application as an adjunct to the model of pure competition.

The essence of the theory was set out elegantly and concisely by Irving Fisher early in the 20th century.[6] His exposition is in two parts: first, the logical framework on which the theory is based; second, the theory itself. The *framework* is the proposition that the price level varies directly as the quantity of money in circulation, directly as the velocity of its circulation, and inversely as the volume of trade done by it. The *theory* is the assertion that the price level is normally a purely passive element in the relationship.

Note that the logical framework is expressed in precise mathematical language: "varies as", not merely "with". Fisher uses the letter P for the price level, M for money, V for its velocity of circulation (i.e. the average frequency with which one unit is used), and T for the volume of trade. You can therefore easily convert his statement into the algebraic equation $MV = PT$.[7] This is known as the *equation of exchange* (or the Fisher formulation of the equation of exchange). There is nothing theoretical about this equation, it is simply a flat assertion that a certain relationship exists among M, V, P, and T.

Whether the assertion that $MV = PT$ is true or false depends entirely on whether the meanings given to the four variables are consistent, and any given set of definitions can easily be tested in practice. In the commonly-accepted modification of Fisher's formulation, M is defined as currency plus chequeable deposits, i.e. those things that can be used to effect transactions. (His own definition was somewhat different.) The other terms are so defined that MV means the number of monetary units in use multiplied by the average number of times each unit is

---

6 There are several other formulations besides Fisher's, some of the cruder ones going back many centuries, but they are all in substantial agreement.

7 Fisher's framework translates into the algebraic expression $P \propto MV/T$, or $P = kMV/T$, where k is a constant whose magnitude depends on the units in which the other variables are expressed. The units are commonly chosen to make k equal to unity, and in fact a commonsense approach is virtually certain to bring this about.

actually used in a given period of time, and PT means the average price paid per item multiplied by the average number of transactions actually completed.

In other words the equation simply says that the amount paid is equal to the value of the goods bought, which is a truism. For this reason it is sometimes written as an identity, $MV \equiv PT$. It does not *in itself* identify any particular variable as "dependent on" or "independent of" any other, but it does provide a means whereby the value of any one of them can be derived from the values of the other three.

The same comments apply to other formulations of the equation of exchange, in which the variables differ somewhat from Fisher's. For this reason any of these equations may sometimes be used even by those who do not accept the quantity theory, or who find it of limited usefulness. For example, they help to explain the links between certain "real" concepts and their "nominal" counterparts, like the relationship between real income and money income discussed in the preceding section of this chapter.

The essence of the quantity theory, as already noted, is that prices are passive in relation to the other variables in the equation of exchange—they are the "dependent" variable. However, there are some complications in the relationship.

First, both V and T become constants in the long-run-equilibrium position, whatever may be the case in the short or medium term. The equilibrium value of V depends on institutional arrangements and social practices, such as the average pay period of the typical consumer, the use of credit (including credit cards, not foreseen in Fisher's day), spending and saving habits, population density, the rapidity of transportation and communication, and other factors. The equilibrium value of T is a measure of the transactions necessary to achieve the optimum level of real output, or what we would now call the full-employment level of real output, since all markets must clear if equilibrium is to obtain.[8]

Fisher emphasized that, strictly speaking, his theory holds only in the long run; during "periods of transition" it may not fully apply, and a change in one of the independent variables may not have an exactly proportionate effect on prices. He was also realistic enough to observe that, in the real world, periods of transition are the normal and periods of approximate equilibrium are the exception. (He pointed out, too, that some contracts cover long periods of time, and can only be renegotiated after a long lapse, so the equilibrating process may not be a rapid one.)

---

[8] The equilibrium values of V and T are constants only in relation to the long-run-equilibrium position appropriate to a particular moment in time. Like the equilibrium values of other economic variables, they may change over time, though the factors that control them do not normally change very rapidly.

The Macroeconomics of Pure Competition 173

This lends itself to two alternative interpretations of how the theory operates in the short or medium term. One is to identify V and T firmly with their equilibrium values, and say that the equation of exchange is *not* an identity but an equilibrating condition—it becomes fully applicable only in the long run. The other is to say that the equation is indeed an identity, but the values of V and T may temporarily but materially depart from their long-run values. Either way, however, departures from equilibrium set restorative forces in motion.

Three final points before leaving the quantity theory. First, Fisher's formulation is an example of what is technically known as the "transactions" version. His equation of exchange deals with all the transactions needed to complete the circular flow, including the intermediate transactions among producers as well as final sales to the purchasers of finished products. Other formulations may deal with a more limited range of payments, with correspondingly limited definitions of V, T, and P.

Second, there is also a very different version of the equation of exchange, known as the "income" version. It focuses on real income, on what may be described as a "value added" basis: it counts only the addition of factor costs at each stage of the productive process. In this version T must be interpreted as real income, and PT as money income. V becomes "income velocity", i.e. the number of times on the average that a unit of money paid out of income *by* someone returns as income *to* someone again. The corresponding equation of exchange is usually written $MV_Y = P_Y T_Y$, since Y is commonly used to mean income.[9] This version has nothing to do with the quantity theory, and is used for other purposes.

Third, a version of the quantity theory that evolved in England about the same time as the Fisher version deserves brief mention, because Keynes's work in this field grew directly out of it. It is known as the Cambridge, or "cash balances", version. It can be quickly explained in terms of a slightly different equation of exchange, which is commonly written nowadays as $M = KPT$, giving M, P, and T the same meaning as before. Obviously, K is the reciprocal of Fisher's V, but the meaning put on it is quite different.

Freely translated, this equation says that the stock of money M the public is willing to hold at any one time (i.e., its equilibrium holding) is some multiple K of the output T of goods and services in a standard period (say, a year), valued at the current price level P. The Cambridge economists saw the relationship of money to

---

9 Sometimes $P_Y T_Y$ is replaced by Y, meaning money income. In such cases income velocity may be defined as Y/M; the equation then becomes an identity, $MV_Y \equiv Y$, which merely repeats the definition in a different form.

prices pretty much as Fisher and his followers did, but they explicitly identified a demand schedule for money, to cope with irregularities in the timing of receipts and payments and as a protection against unforeseen eventualities.

8. Stocks, Flows, and the Money Supply.

A "stock" concept is essentially a store or inventory of something at a given point in time, while a "flow" represents movement or change over a period of time. However, the only way of dealing quantitatively with a flow is to treat it as an increase or a decrease in a stock over time. For example, we measure speed in kilometres (or miles) per hour, as if we accumulated an inventory of distance travelled per unit of time. Obviously, then, the two concepts are closely related. Sometimes there is a danger of confusion between them, however, or over their interrelationships.

These concepts enter economic relationships too. Thus real income is a flow concept, which on the spending side may be divided into an investment stream and a consumption stream. The investment stream may be seen as a flow of additions to the accumulated wealth of the community, typically in the form of increases in its stock of capital goods. The flow of spending on consumption does not result in an addition to a tangible or visible stock of goods, obviously, but the amount spent in any given period may be seen as an addition to the imaginary stock of like spending in the past. The income received in any period may also be treated as an addition to an imaginary stock accumulated in the past.

Money income may be treated the same way as real income, of course, but a new problem arises: how is the *stock* of money (more commonly known as the money supply) related to the *flow* of money income? This relationship is obviously different from those we have discussed so far, for money is neither generated nor used up in the productive process. It is like a catalyst, a substance that promotes a certain chemical change without itself being changed.

The Fisher version of the equation of exchange focuses on the relationship between the *rate of flow* of money payments and the *rate of flow* of goods and services purchased; it has been aptly described as addressing "money on the wing". The Cambridge version focuses on the relationship between the *stock* of money and the volume (stock) of transactions effected in a given period of time; it has been described as addressing "money sitting". The two approaches complement one another nicely, for the flow of goods and services for a given period of time is the measure of the volume of transactions effected.

Nowadays the money supply in virtually every country is regulated by a central bank or similar authority; in earlier days it was determined rather capriciously, by the new production of gold or in some other way. For our present purposes we must accept it as a predetermined quantity at any given time. However, changes in the money supply have important implications. History is full of examples of the inflationary troubles caused when the stock of money grows too rapidly, and the deflationary troubles caused when it grows too slowly.

These considerations are significant even within the limitations of our present model. This is not only because V and T may temporarily depart from their equilibrium values, and therefore prices may not respond "properly" and promptly to a change in the money supply, it is also because some prices respond much faster than others. Some are set under long-term contracts, for example, as Fisher pointed out long ago, and can not be changed until those contracts expire and are renegotiated. It may take a long time for equilibrium to be restored. In the meantime some people may suffer considerable hardship.

From this we may conclude that short-term equilibrium in a money-and-market economy must include equilibrium among the variables that appear in the equation of exchange. If the real output of the economy is growing, the money supply must grow in step, or distortions will arise. It is not sufficient, as the early exponents of the model of pure competition assumed, to focus exclusively on *relative* prices; absolute prices are important too.

Chapter 11

Modern Macroeconomics

1. The Breakthrough.

Historically, the credibility of the purely-competitive model and of the *laissez-faire* policies to which it seems to point has always been under attack, because conditions in the real world have seldom appeared to approach the ideal it predicts. Some of the criticisms have been directed at unintended consequences of policies based on the model, such as the abuses of child labour that occurred early in the industrial revolution, and the great disparities in the distribution of income and wealth; a few of them are noted in Chapter 9. They have led to the wide variety of social programs to be found in most countries today.

Other criticisms were directed at the validity of the purely-competitive model itself, in the light of the uncertainties and unevenness of the operation of the economy. Occasionally there were prolonged periods of depressed trade (like the last quarter of the 19th century), which raised doubts about the ability of the system to achieve its vaunted equilibrium, and the fluctuations of the business cycle called in question the stability of whatever equilibrium it did achieve.

Nevertheless the model long continued to dominate economic thought, partly because it did (and still does) contain useful insights despite its shortcomings, but mainly because no-one seemed able to devise a better one. With models, as with many other things, the only really effective criticism is to produce a better alternative.

These criticisms became virtually unanswerable as the severity and the persistence of The Great Depression of the 1930's became apparent—the most severe by far in all of recorded history. Unemployment and other imbalances undeniably appeared on a scale and with a tenacity that the best available theory said could not happen.

Eventually an intellectual breakthrough out of this impasse was achieved, which is usually called the Keynesian Revolution, honouring John Maynard Keynes and the publication of his *The General Theory of Employment Interest and Money* in 1936. However, many others contributed as well—particularly a group of Swedish economists whose work on similar ideas began somewhat earlier—and the basic concepts continued to be improved and refined for many years.

Keynesian models are addressed primarily to short-term or medium-term analysis. They do not deny that forces may be at work tending towards the sort of long-run equilibrium that pure competition envisages, they just say we needn't wait patiently to see whether that really happens, because there are things we can do to improve our lot here and now. After all, it is in the short run that we must live, make our decisions, and accept the consequences—the long run, like tomorrow, never comes. Or, as Keynes tartly put it, "in the long run we are all dead".

Like the earlier model, the newer ones focus on the circular flow of payments (the spending stream), but they identify the community's *spending decisions* as the main regulator of economic activity, and they envisage an entirely different mechanism for linking the flow of savings with new investment. Also, they do not assume that prices are flexible and that markets automatically "clear" themselves; instead, they recognize that many prices are "sticky" or reluctant to move, and that unsold goods and idle factors of production may persist for some time.

The assumption that prices are flexible and that markets always clear themselves implies that everything is always sold to the highest bidder, as in an auction sale. But even in an auction market any seller may set a "reserve" price beforehand, below which he is unwilling to sell; competing bids by would-be buyers will not clear the market unless they exceed the seller's reserve price.

Somewhat similar practices obtain in organized security markets and commodity markets: would-be buyers post their "bid" prices, would-be sellers post their "asking" prices, and no trading takes place until some buyer decides to accept the lowest asking price he can find or some seller decides to accept the highest bid price. These examples provide a more realistic approach to the behaviour of market prices.

In the consumer-goods markets in which most of us do our buying, we usually face a fixed asking price set by the seller; we may or may not be able to haggle a bit and get some reduction, but usually we face a take-it-or-leave-it situation. When we go to sell our services in the labour market it works much the same way: we may ask for whatever wage or salary we think we are worth, and we may shop around among potential employers to see what they offer, but (except in unusual circumstances) most of us must take the best offer we can find.

The "bid" prices of some would-be buyers may eventually have to be raised in a sellers' market, and the "asking" prices of some would-be sellers may eventually have to be lowered in a buyers' market, but actually-realized prices do tend to be sticky.[1] This is especially true of downward movements in price: any seller will be happy to find that his customers are willing to pay even more than he asks and will probably raise his asking price accordingly, but he may not be able to reduce his price materially without sacrificing an important part of his income.

Actually, there was an earlier intellectual breakthrough in the 1930's as well: the introduction of the model of monopolistic or imperfect competition in 1933, as noted in Chapter 8. This breakthrough owed little if anything to The Great Depression, for it grew out of work that had been under way for some years, and it played no direct role in the Keynesian revolution. It is nevertheless complementary, in that it illuminates some of the shortcomings of the model of pure competition, and helps to explain the stickiness of real-world prices.

2. The Consumption Function.

We may start our description of a simple Keynesian model with a representation of the circular flow, in which all income is earned in the production of consumer-goods and investment-goods, and is either spent on those same consumer goods or saved. Using C for consumer-goods, I for investment-goods, Y for income, and S for savings, the earnings side of the income-flow can be expressed as $C + I = Y$ ("spending on consumption and investment generates income"), and the spending side as $Y = C + S$ ("income is either spent on consumption or saved").

We need to know how the public divides its income between spending on consumer goods and saving, how the amount of spending on investment-goods is determined, and what is the mechanism that ensures that S and I will always be equal. In the course of exploring these matters we will find out how the equilibrium values of all five variables are established.

There are many reasons why individuals or families may decide to save a part of their incomes, as we noted in section 4 of Chapter 10. Most of them imply *dis*saving (using up past savings, or going into debt) at some other time—for example, saving up to make a major purchase later, or to provide income after

---

[1] Many economists assert that this is a relatively new development, and that prices used to be flexible. It may well be that increasing concentration of industrial power has increased the stickiness in recent times, but reading accounts of ancient money problems (e.g., reforms that replaced debased coins with fewer full-weight coins, or merchants complaining of falling prices and a shortage of coin) suggests that deflation has never been painless.

retirement.[2] Economists no longer assert that the rate of interest plays a dependable role in these decisions, and they have pretty well given up looking for any other single factor to replace it.

Instead, economists now rely on evidence from consumer-spending surveys, which show typical consumers' spending and saving patterns at various levels of income. From this material they derive *consumption functions* and *saving functions* for the individual consumer and for the community at large. This simply means that, at any given level of income, a predictable portion or percentage will be spent and a predictable portion will be saved. (Mathematicians say one thing is a *function of* another if the amount of the first is firmly linked to or determined by the amount of the second.)

The evidence indicates that the percentage of income saved rises as income rises, whether we compare different people on a given date or the same people at different dates. If an individual has become accustomed to a certain level of income, and then receives an increase in that income, he will spend only a portion of the increase and will save the rest. If his income declines, on the other hand, he will save less and consume more, as he attempts to maintain his accustomed standard of living, until at some point he may begin to *dis*save. Furthermore, the community as a whole reacts in much the same way, so we can derive community consumption and saving functions as well as individual consumption and saving functions.[3]

In view of our discussion of marginal costs and marginal revenues in earlier chapters, you will recognize that we are now talking about what happens to a *marginal* dollar or pound or franc of income. On that basis, what would you say determines the fraction of marginal income that is spent on consumption? The fraction that is saved? Well, the best that economists have been able to come up with are *the marginal propensity to spend* and *the marginal propensity to save*, each of which is a pretty big mouthful; but these horrendous terms just identify how a marginal increase in income is split between spending and saving.

It thus appears that decisions about how much to spend and how much to save are made primarily on the basis of the level of income, or *changes* in income, and that normally they are not affected very much by any other considerations. However, this conclusion is subject to the usual "*if...*" qualification.

---

2 Sometimes the dissaving comes first, of course, as when you borrow money to buy a car or a house and then save to repay the debt.

3 An individual may dissave by borrowing or by selling an asset in order to spend more, or by wearing out or using up physical goods acquired out of past savings (such as an automobile or an inventory of consumable goods), but the community as a whole can only do so by the third method.

For example, an increase in income that appears to be permanent, or likely to last indefinitely, will probably lead sooner or later to an increase in the average propensity to spend. That is, the entire consumption function will shift upwards—more will be consumed and less saved at each level of income. Unpredictable psychological factors may also affect the relationship: a change in hopes or fears about the future may shift the function either upwards or downwards. In either case the *marginal* propensity to spend may also change, over part or all of the range of potential incomes.

The line CC in Figure 11-1 is a graphic representation of a community consumption function. Money income is measured parallel to the east-west axis, spending at each level of income is measured parallel to the north-south axis. The 45° line is merely a useful reference device; if a point on CC is north of it then the community is consuming more than its income, if the point is south of it then the community is spending only a part of its income.

At an income of OA (or Y_3), for example, the portion spent is AB and the portion saved is BD; at OE (or Y_2) it is all spent; at OH (or Y_1) there is *dis*saving equal to JK in order to maintain spending of HK, well in excess of income. The marginal propensity to spend is shown by the slope of CC, or LB/FL; it is assumed to be constant throughout (CC is drawn as a straight line). However, CC turns abruptly vertical at income-level Y_F, for reasons explained later.

The *saving function* is shown by the line SS. Note that you can always derive the saving function from the consumption function, or the other way around, since $Y = C + S$ at every income level. Thus SS cuts the east-west axis at Y_2, where saving is zero; at Y_3 saving is AM ($= BD$); and at Y_1 it is negative and amounts to HG, which is equal to JK. The marginal propensity to save is given by the slope of SS, or AM/EA (which is the same as BD/FL).

3. Income Determination.

For now we will suppose that the economy is in the recession phase of the business cycle, so a substantial portion of all factors of production in the economy are unemployed but able and willing to work if an opportunity offers. (Note that Y_1, Y_2, and Y_3 are all well short of Y_F, which we will define as the level of income that would be consistent with full employment at stable prices.) We will also assume that prices have so far remained stable, including wages and other returns to the factors of production, because of their inherent stickiness in the short run.

Among other things this means that changes in money income will accurately reflect changes in real income, so there will be no ambiguity about the meaning of

182   The Practice of Economics

an increase in income. More importantly, it also implies that there are established firms in all or most lines of business ready to expand their ouput if demand picks up. (The problem would be much more difficult if many new businesses had to be established, new workers trained, new types of capital bought, and these new businesses turned into "going concerns", but we can't spare the space to go into that here.)

In order to get some clues about how this model works, let's try out a few arbitrary assumptions. First, let's assume that investors are currently unwilling to

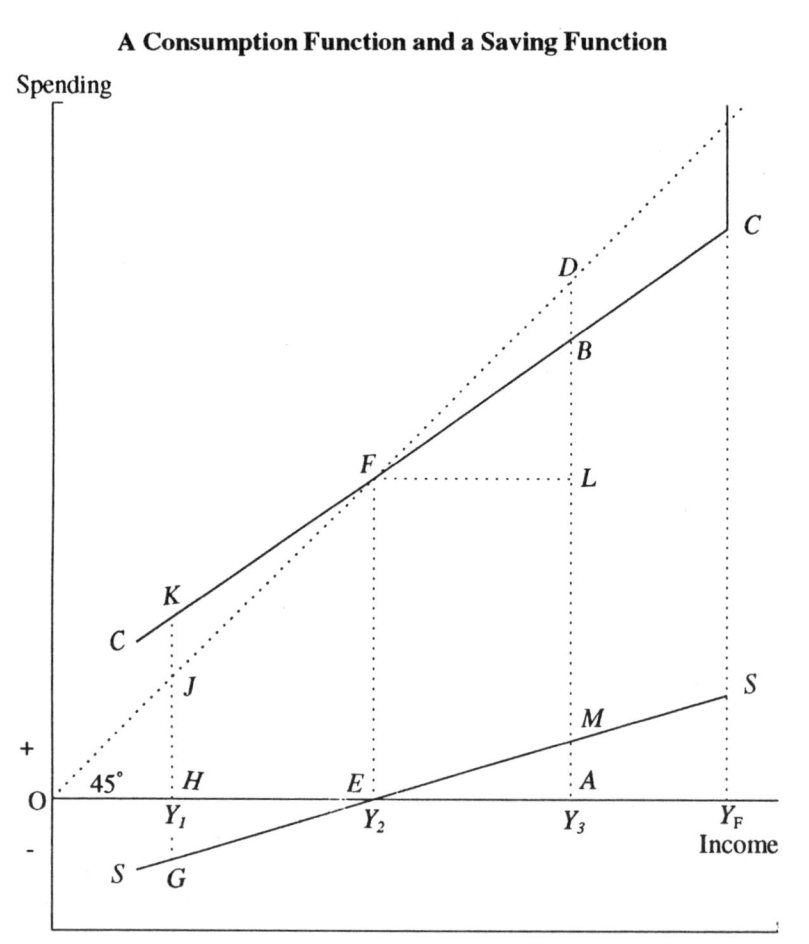

Figure 11-1. Each point on the line *CC* represents the amount that will be spent on consumption (measured northwards) at that level of the community's money income (measured eastward), and every point on the line *SS* represents the amount that will be saved. The 45° line is a useful reference device: if a point on *CC* is above it then consumption exceeds income, if it is below then consumption is less than income.

make any net investment whatever in the economy, but will not disinvest either; they simply reinvest their depreciation allowances in each income period. (Never mind *why* they so decide, we'll come to that later.) Since S must equal I, the equilibrium level of income must be Y_2, at which there is neither saving nor dissaving.

If consumers tried to save more (spend less), the initial effect would be to reduce the spending stream, and therefore to reduce income towards Y_1; but at lower levels of income there would actually be *dis*saving instead saving, the spending stream would expand again, and income would be driven back up to Y_2. If they tried to dissave in order to spend more than their incomes, the initial effect would be to raise income towards Y_3; but at any higher levels of income there would be net saving instead of dissaving, the spending stream would falter, and income would be driven back down to Y_2.

Do you find it confusing to be told that an attempt to save *more* may actually lead to saving *less*, temporarily at least? And that attempting to *dissave* may lead to saving? Well, it may be even worse than you think! Suppose most people come to believe that things are going to get worse instead of better, bad as they seem to be already, and prudently decide to save more at every level of income in order to protect themselves against possible future misadventures. That will shift the CC curve bodily southwards, the point at which it crosses the 45° line will slide to the south-west, and the equilibrium level of income will shift towards Y_1.

On the assumptions we have made, the attempt to save more has no effect whatever on savings, it merely reduces the community's total income. However, we can easily envisage conditions that would result in *smaller* savings as well as smaller income—for example, investors might choose to disinvest (not replace worn-out capital goods) at income levels below Y_2. This is known as the "paradox of thrift": under certain conditions an attempt by the community to save more may be self-defeating.

Next, look at Figure 11-2. The line CC is the same as in Figure 11-1, except that it now intersects the 45° line at Y_1. This time, however, we will suppose that investors choose to make new capital investments at the constant rate of I^* per income-period, regardless of whatever else happens in the economy. This is shown by the line I^*I^* parallel to east-west axis, and by the line $C + I^*$ north of the line CC, which is derived by graphically adding the CC and the I^*I^* curves (i.e. by adding the north-south components of the two curves at each level of income). We may call it the *spending function*. The new equilibrium level of income is now Y_2, at which $I^* = S$. Y_2 is greater than Y_1, of course, because we have added I^* to C.

184   The Practice of Economics

However, we must digress here to point out an important relationship. Take a good look the increase in income, $Y_2 - Y_1$. It is over three times the size of the new capital spending (I^*) that has been added! How can that be?

Well, the explanation is simple enough. The increase in income from Y_1 to Y_2 must raise saving from zero until it equals I^*, but only a portion of each additional dollar of income is saved. In Figure 11-2 CC is drawn on the assumption that $0.70

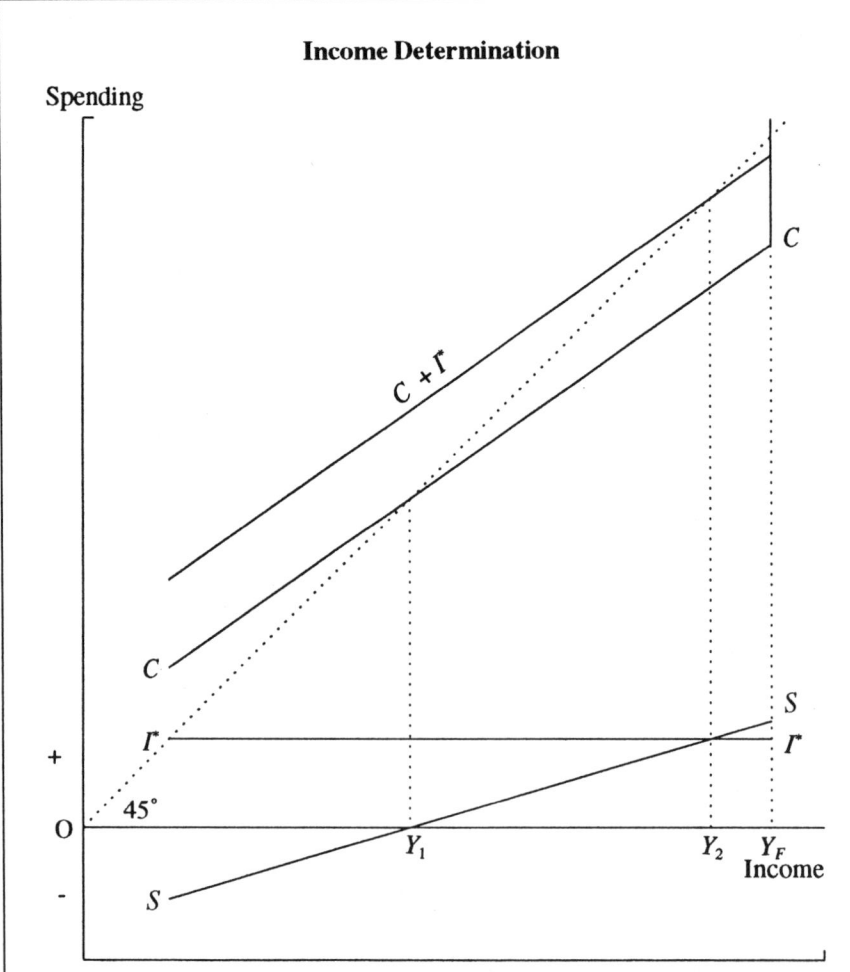

Figure 11-2. The CC and the SS lines are the same as in Figure 11-1. If there is no new investment spending in the economy then the equilibrium level of income is Y_1. Now suppose that investors decide to make new investments of I^*, regardless of what happens to income as a result, as indicated by the line I^*I^*: adding I^*I^* to CC gives a new *spending function*, the line $C + I^*$. That raises the equilibrium income level to Y_2.

is spent on consumption and $0.30 is saved, so income must rise by $3.33 in order to raise saving by $1.00.

This phenomenon is known as the *income multiplier*, or just the *multiplier*.[4] It operates on any "new" spending that arises independently from "outside" the model. In technical terms it applies to an "exogenous" increase in spending, as distinct from an "endogenous" or "induced" increase that arises out of the assumptions of the model. In our example the injection of I^* of capital spending is "new" and from "outside", whereas the increase in consumption between Y_1 and Y_2 is "induced" by the "new" spending because it stems directly from the assumption that consumption is a fixed (or at least a determinate) portion of income.

If we postulated that there was a sudden increase in the public's willingness to spend at the current level of income, for example, that too would bring an "exogenous" increase in spending and would lead to a multiple increase in income. Indeed, it might well be accompanied by an increase in the public's marginal propensity to consume, which would increase the multiplier itself. And of course the same multiplier will operate on any "outside" *reduction* in spending as well as an increase.

Actually, we had a brush with the income multiplier in section 7 of Chapter 7, though we did not spell it out at that time. Look back at Figure 7-1 on page 119, and you will see that it is an example of just the sort of thing we are now discussing: the injection of new investment spending from "outside" the model. However, we started arbitrarily with consumption of 6 and new investment of 2 in period T_1, and in so doing we short-circuited the process of expansion. To illustrate the multiplier properly we should start with income in equilibrium with (say) zero saving and zero net investment, so income is just replacing itself each period, and we should limit the chart to *increases* in income as a result of the new investment spending.

That means we must enter new income of only 2, not 8, in period T_1. In period T_2 consumption will be 1.6, investment 2, and income 3.6; in period T_3 $2.88 + 2 = 4.88$; and so on. Equilibrium will be reached as before, when income reaches 10, because only at that level will savings and investment be equal. That means the multiplier is 5—income rises by five times the new investment. Our arbitrary

---

[4] To express this multiplier in formal mathematical terms, let the marginal propensity to consume be c, and the marginal propensity to save be s, subject to the constraints that $s + c = 1$ and that $0 \leq c, s \leq 1$. In that case it can be shown that the multiplier in this simple model will be $1/s$.

starting point in Figure 7-1 brought us into the picture when the process was already 80 per cent complete![5]

Now let's see what happens as we manage to push the income-level higher and higher. Suppose a revival of net new investment brings on the lower turning point in the business cycle and the beginning of the expansionary phase, as described in section 3 of Chapter 7. In terms of Figure 11-2, the II curve shifts northwards. Rising confidence and optimism will lead to an increased willingness to spend, especially on durable goods and semidurables, as wants postponed in more uncertain times are satisfied: the CC curve also shifts northwards. With both components of the spending stream expanding, the intersection of the $C + I$ curve slides northeast along the 45° line, and income approaches Y_F, which we defined earlier as the level consistent with full employment at stable prices.

"Full employment" is a slippery concept that is not to be taken too literally. At best it is usually taken to be compatible with some minimum level of "frictional" (as well as seasonal) unemployment, in recognition of the fact that in a dynamic economy there will always be some people who have just left one job (voluntarily or involuntarily) and have not yet started another. Attempts to define this minimum level have not been too successful, however, so economists usually prefer the vaguer term "a high level of employment."

Nevertheless "full employment" is a good enough term for our simple model, as long as you understand its limitations. You may think of the full-employment level of income as equivalent to the maximum level of physical output (or real income) that is currently attainable in practice.

Of course, allowing the spending stream to keep on increasing after output has reached the maximum practicable level will provoke mere price inflation: a glance back at the old-fashioned quantity theory is enough to make that clear. Even if we don't allow the expansion to be overdone, however, a number of our assumptions become less and less realistic as output presses closer and closer to its physical limits.

It can not be supposed that unemployed factors of production can always and quickly be absorbed into existing firms. New firms may have to be formed, new capital goods put in place, new entrants to the labour force trained, and so on. Bottlenecks will appear in some lines of production, as output responds to changing

---

[5] This treatment brings out a point that is quietly evaded in Figures 11-1 and 11-2, namely that it will take a considerable time for the multiplier to be effective—apparently, an infinitely long time to have its full effect. Versions that ignore this aspect are often called "instantaneous" multipliers; they are static-equilibrium models, not dynamic models.

demand. Resort must be had to more distant or less suitable raw materials. For these and other reasons we can no longer suppose that output can be expanded indefinitely at constant cost, which we have tacitly assumed so far. In fact, as experience since the early 1970's has shown all too clearly, inflationary price rises may arise and persist even in the face of much unemployed labour and idle productive capacity.

We can't cope with all these complexities at once, however. For now we must be content to pretend that output really can be expanded at stable prices (constant costs) right up to the full-employment level, and that any further increase in the spending stream will cause prices to rise proportionately. Despite its limitations, this will prove a useful first approximation. The best we can do to depict this assumption in our diagrams is to let the spending curves become abruptly vertical at Y_F, which should be interpreted to mean that money income becomes indeterminate (dependent on the amount of inflation) while real income remains unchanged.

4. The Determinants of Investment.

So far so good, but what determines the level of I?

Anyone contemplating a new capital investment will have to decide whether the probable earnings from it are likely to justify its cost. The yield of any investment can be reduced to a single rate of return, like the average yield on a number of separate loan contracts, and the cost can be identified with the interest expenses incurred or the interest earnings forgone to finance the project.

However, Keynes argued that it will be the would-be investor's *expectations* about those future earnings that will matter, and that his expectations will be strongly influenced by unpredictable psychological factors. He called the difference between the *expected* yield and the current interest rate "the inducement to invest". Evidently the decision to invest requires a positive marginal inducement, the amount of which may change from time to time according to changing assessments of the risks, so unpredictable psychological considerations may affect this aspect of investment decisions also.

This line of argument strongly suggests that capital investments are most likely to be made when income is high and rising, because businessmen will foresee profitable opportunities for expansion, and least likely to be made when income is declining or stagnant. That inference, of course, fits neatly with the observed pattern of investment over the business cycle. When a downturn in the cycle brings a contraction in output there is likely to be not only unemployment among workers but also considerable idle plant and equipment that could be quickly put to work if demand increased, so the inducement to invest may be very low, or actually negative. As an upturn gathers strength and idle plant is reactivated, the inducement to invest may be expected to turn positive and investment activity should increase.

During a severe and prolonged downturn, output will be sharply reduced; businessmen may actually let their physical capital run down as a result, by replacing only a part of the equipment that wears out and by deferring normal maintenance. In a less-extreme situation they may merely maintain their current stock of capital goods, by just reinvesting their depreciation allowances to replace outworn capital but making no net new investments.

Normally, however, there is at least some net investment even in a recession, since experience argues that conditions will sooner or later improve, and a buyer's market for capital goods may encourage some restructuring. We may thus infer that there is some positive correlation between the level of income and the rate of new investment, even in conditions of less-than-full employment. This conclusion is supported by noting that there will be some feedback effects on investment from any increase in income that does occur, no matter what causes that increase, because any increase in income means an increase in output and implies some increase in the need for productive capital.

Instead of an unvarying line parallel to the east-west axis, therefore, as in Figure 11-2, we can at least put a modest positive slope to the curve representing net new investment.

There seems to be no simple way to include businessmens' expectations in our diagrams, however, even though they are of crucial importance in this model; the best we can do is draw a new curve further north to represent an improvement in expectations, or further south to represent a deterioration.

There seems to be no dependable way in which anyone could influence businessmens' expectations about the future in order to affect their investment decisions, but there are other techniques that may work. For example, there are ways (which we will discuss in Chapter 12) by which market interest rates can be influenced over a considerable range, thereby affecting the cost side of the profit calculation. Another possibility would be to change the rates of taxes that businessmen usually treat as part of their costs of production, as we will see a little later. *If* investment could be sufficiently stimulated in any of these ways to raise the $\Gamma\Gamma$ line in Figure 11-2, *then* output and income could be raised—perhaps to the full-employment level.

These techniques may not be fully effective in practice, however. The monetary authorities can certainly *curtail* investment if a capital-spending boom gets under way and threatens to cause an inflation, because they can raise interest rates until they exceed the expected earnings from new capital. They may also try to *stimulate* investment by reducing interest rates when output is too low and unemployment too high, but they may not always succeed; if businessmens' expectations of returns from new capital are very low (they might even be negative!), then even a very low rate of interest and a zero tax rate may not produce a positive inducement to invest.

5. More Elaborate Models.

The simple model that uses only the four variables Y, C, S, and I is adequate for explaining the principles of Keynesian income-determination, but we need something a little more elaborate to bring out its full implications. First, we need to introduce government expenditure (G) and taxation (T), in recognition of the role of government in the economy. Second, we need to introduce exports (X) and imports (M), because foreign trade also affects the spending stream. The income-generating equation then becomes $C + I + G + X = Y$, and the income-spending equation becomes $Y = C + S + T + M$.[6]

If you like, you may consider that G and T are included in C in the simple version of the model, and that government budgets are always balanced. In that case you may think of government services as being purchased by a joint community decision that they are desirable and should be paid for by taxes, instead of by individual decisions in the usual way.

Modifying this view only slightly, you may think of government *capital* spending as part of I, to be financed in the same way as private capital spending, i.e. by borrowing the savings of savers. The next step is to recognize that starting public works projects, even somewhat in advance of their need, is a sensible way of combatting the business cycle; such proposals were often made, and acted on, many years before the onset of The Great Depression.

However, Keynes and others carried this idea much further: they pointed out that a deliberately-incurred government deficit would stimulate the economy in exactly the same way as new investment, even if it was used to finance current spending rather than capital spending. (For this reason deficits in depressed times have sometimes been called "honourary investments".) In terms of the symbols we

---

6 Sometimes the first equation is rendered as $C + I + (G - T) + (X - M) = Y$, so the spending equation remains simply $Y = C + S$, as in the simple model. This constitutes a different but related definition of income, in which some spending components are netted out against the corresponding income-generating components, rather like the differences among gross and net national product and net national income in the national accounts (see section 6 of Chapter 7).

are using, a deficit becomes $(G - T)$; it is often included in this form in the income-generating equation, as in the version noted in footnote 6, to emphasize that it is the *difference* between G and T that counts.

On the other hand there is some advantage in including only G in the income-generating equation and putting T separately in the spending equation, to emphasize their separate rôles. The government's decisions to spend money, and what to spend it on, may be quite distinct from its decisions about whether to raise the money by taxation or by borrowing. A deficit may be incurred either by increasing spending or by reducing taxes, and the choice among the various possibilities may have important implications for the effectiveness of the measures taken.

Another way the government can influence the economy is by *income transfers* from one group of people to another. We have already met this idea in section 4 of Chapter 7; it is usually accomplished by taxing one group more heavily than another, or by making expenditures that benefit a particular group (such as support for the indigent, or special allowances to mothers of small children), or by some combination of the two.

Transferring income from one group to another has no direct effect on the total income of the community, of course, but there may be an indirect effect. If income is taken from individuals with a relatively low marginal propensity to spend (the wealthy?) and given to others with a relatively high propensity (the needy?), there will be a net increase in spending; and this, like any other injection of "new" spending, will increase income by some multiple of itself. (In terms of Figure 11-2, the slope of the line CC will be increased *and* the entire line will slide to the north-east along the 45° line.)

The government's decisions about taxing, spending, and incurring a deficit (or generating a surplus) constitute the making and implementation of *fiscal policy*. ("The fisc" is an old-fashioned term for the national treasury.)

Note that fiscal policy can be used just as effectively to damp down the economy as to stimulate it; if spending is getting excessive and threatens to start an inflationary price rise, the government can budget for a surplus. In effect the government can deliberately *dis*save on behalf of the general public when saving by individuals threatens to exceed investors' willingness to invest, or can *supplement* individual savings if they are inadequate to finance private investment.

We will take a more detailed look at foreign trade in Part Four, but for now we need to see something of how it affects the domestic spending stream. The production of goods for export generates domestic income, but these goods are not bought out of domestic incomes, they are bought out of the incomes of people who live in other countries. Imports are bought out of domestic incomes, but they do not generate any domestic income—not directly at any rate. We will see later that the volume of exports and the volume of imports are indeed related—in general, imports must eventually be paid for by exports—but the link is by no means precise.

There are ways in which we can hope to encourage the residents of other countries to buy more of our exports, but their chances of success are somewhat uncertain. The most dependable way is by being highly competitive in doing those things we do best. For practical purposes, however, we must usually accept the volume of exports as pretty well beyond our control and dependent largely on the incomes of our customers abroad: if their incomes rise they will usually buy more of our exports, if they fall they will buy less. Any gain in exports will result in a multiple gain in domestic income in the usual way, of course, no matter what is its explanation.

The determinants of imports are the mirror images of those of exports. The major consideration is the competitiveness of foreign products with domestic products, as determined by their relative marginal utilities and their relative prices on domestic markets. The next most important consideration is the level of domestic income: imports will normally rise as income rises, and fall as income falls.

The graphical representation of this more elaborate model offers two principal choices. First, as noted in footnote 6, we may add the government deficit $(G - T)$ and the net value of foreign trade $(X - M)$ to $C + I$ in Figure 11-2, to get a new spending function, $C + I + (G - T) + (X - M)$. This will leave the saving function as the balancing item, i.e. the difference between the 45° line and the spending function at each level of income. We may then plot $I + (G - T) + (X - M)$ in place of I alone in the lower part of the diagram; it will of course intersect the saving function at the same income level as the new spending function intersects the 45° line. In this case $(G - T)$ and $(X - M)$ are sometimes called "savings offsets", since they, like I, absorb savings that would otherwise go to waste.

Alternatively, we may add G and X to $C + I$ in order to get our new spending function, thus making use of a somewhat different but related definition of income. In this case the balancing item becomes $S + T + M$ (found by graphically adding the three separate curves) instead of just S alone. In terms of Figure 11-2, the line $C + I'$ will be replaced by a new line $C + I + G + X$, the line $I'I'$ will be replaced by a new line $I + G + X$, and the line SS will be replaced by a new line $S + T + M$.

The diagrams get pretty complicated if we try to show all these lines separately, but the idea is simple enough; you may want to get piece of paper and a pencil and give it a try.

On the income-generating side, you may start by giving the line II a modest positive slope, as already suggested. The GG line might have a moderate negative slope, on the assumption that government spending will increase somewhat less than in proportion as income increases—or rather that it will *decrease* less than proportionately as income falls, because a lower national income implies greater need for transfer payments to needy members of society. You might draw the *XX* line parallel to the east-west axis, since it depends primarily on conditions in other countries, over which the domestic economy has little influence; or you might give it a slight negative slope, like the *GG* line, on the grounds that greater domestic incomes (and consumption) would absorb some output that might otherwise be exported.

Adding these lines graphically, you may very well get a total $I + G + X$ line with a positive slope, a negative slope, or no slope at all. (By the way, notice the advantage of using straight lines in such exercises: you need only add the components at two income-levels, and draw a straight line between the two points so obtained.)

You may do the spending side in the same way. Presumably the *SS* line has a definitely positive slope, as in Figures 11-1 and 11-2. The *TT* line might be drawn at the same percentage of income throughout, as if the system of taxation were *proportional*; or with a somewhat steeper slope, if you want to represent it as *progressive* (taking a larger portion from higher incomes); or less steep, for a *regressive* system. You might draw the *MM* line proportional to income, for lack of any better idea; or you might suppose that people will spend more on imported "luxuries" as their incomes rise, and make the line a bit steeper. Adding the three lines graphically, as before, you will almost certainly get a $S + T + M$ line with a substantially steeper slope than either the *SS* line or the $I + G + X$ line.

Despite all this elaboration, the more complicated model works just like the simple one; you may just relabel the lines in Figure 11-2. The line $C + I'$ becomes $C + I + G + X$, and where it cuts the 45° line determines the level of income. The *SS* line becomes $S + T + M$; we may call it the "leakage" curve, because *S*, *T*, and *M* are often spoken of as leakages from the spending-income-respending stream, since they are not respent in the domestic economy and hence create no new income. (If it were not for these leakages, the income multiplier would be infinite!)

The $I'I'$ curve becomes $I + G + X$, and may have either a positive or a negative slope; we may call it the "leakage-offset" curve, since *I*, *G*, and *X* counteract or offset the leakages. The leakage and the leakage-offset curves will of course intersect one another at the equilibrium income level.

Note that in this more elaborate model *I* need not equal *S*—it *may* do so, but only by coincidence. The equilibrium condition is simply that the *total* of all three offsets must equal the *total* of all three leakages—in other words that $I + G + X = S + T +$

M, or that $S = I + (G - T) + (X - M)$. We have already seen that having G greater than T is a form of dissaving, and we will see in Part Four that having X greater than M means that savings are being exported (loaned to residents of other countries), so the second form of this equation is equivalent to saying that savings must be either used to finance investment, or offset by government dissaving, or loaned to foreign residents.

Note also that the income multiplier is still operative, but it is much smaller than in in section 3 of this chapter, because of the additional leakages. In Figures 11-1 and 11-2 we used an unrealistically-high marginal propensity to save, at 30 per cent, in order to make the diagrams manageable, whereas in reality something of the order of 10 per cent would be more probable. That would seem to imply a multiplier of 10. However, taxes may easily absorb 25 per cent of GNP. Imports may account for only 5 or 10 per cent in relatively "closed" (self-sufficient) economies like the USA, but 25 per cent or more in "open" economies (heavily dependent on trade). That means total leakages of over 50 per cent in many cases, so real-world multipliers tend to be around 2.[7]

6. An Introduction to Demand Management.

Demand management is the term used to identify a combination of policies designed to control the spending stream, in order to promote a high level of output and employment in the economy. (Total spending may be identified with "effective demand", i.e. the willingness and ability of the public to make its demands effective by actually making purchases in the marketplace.) It uses monetary and fiscal policies based on the sort of Keynesian models we have been discussing in this chapter.

If unemployment threatens, one possible remedy is to encourage new investment, usually by monetary expansion or by reducing taxes that are considered as costs of production by businessmen, or some combination of the two. Another is to encourage export sales, or to encourage domestic producers to replace imports, but there are pitfalls here that we will consider when we discuss foreign trade. Government spending may be increased, or various taxes may be reduced to encourage spending by the public.

---

[7] In formal mathematical terms the multiplier becomes $1/(s+t+m)$, where s (as before) is the portion saved out of a marginal increase in income, t is the amount paid in taxes, m is the portion spent on imports, and c is the portion spent domestically—subject to the constraints that $s + t + m + c = 1$ and $0 \leq s, t, m, c \leq 1$. The denominator is larger than that in footnote 4 because of the additional leakages, hence the multiplier is smaller.

The immediate effects of these various measures may differ considerably, so the choice will depend partly on what secondary effects seem most desirable. And of course the same techniques can be used in reverse, to cool down the economy if it threatens to overheat and produce inflation.

Using the community's savings to finance capital investments that will increase production and real income in the future is clearly preferable to using them merely to finance current spending on goods and services, even though the immediate effect on employment may be exactly the same. In principle, therefore, monetary policy should be used first, and production brought as close as possible to the optimum level by this means. Fiscal policy should preferably be neutral (the budget should normally be balanced), because the presumption is that the market mechanism will then put the nation's savings to work most efficiently.

Nevertheless, deficit-financed spending is in turn clearly preferable to letting potential savings go unused and thereby accepting a reduced level of output and employment—in which case no new capital would be generated anyway, so no sacrifice of future income would be involved.

However, fiscal policy is too unwieldy to be used for delicate adjustments; budget planning is a complicated exercise, usually performed only once a year, and must be based on uncertain projections and forecasts of how the economy will perform over the next twelve months or so. Monetary policy is more flexible, and can respond rapidly to changing conditions. In practice, therefore, fiscal policies are set first and only changed with some lag if conditions change; monetary policy copes as best it can in the meantime.

Although demand management is concerned primarily with maintaining full employment in the short or medium term, it is neither unconcerned about nor incompatible with long-term considerations. Thus we have already noted the presumption in favour of policies that would promote greater productive capacity for the future.

For another example, successful demand management must recognize that continuing technical progress and innovation at home and abroad is persistently altering the conditions of production and the appropriate allocation of resources. *Structural* changes will be necessary from time to time, perhaps constantly, in order to effect these reallocations, and may result in the obsolescence of capital and some temporary unemployment of workers.

Merely expanding the spending stream will not be an appropriate way of eliminating any unemployment that stems from such readjustments, for extensive retraining may be necessary, and some skills (like some capital) may have become obsolete. What demand management *can* hope to do is to minimize non-structural unemployment. That will not only cushion the immediate loss of output and income, but also provide a climate in which the necessary structural adjustments can be accommodated with the least disruption.

Chapter 12

The Financial System

Fatherly advice: Some of the material in this chapter is fairly complicated. The main thing is to get the general idea of what is set out in each section, even if you do not follow every argument in detail at first.

1. Interest-Rate Theory.

There are at least half-a-dozen lines of thinking about interest rates by theorists of the past that have a valid place in interest-rate theory today, some of which we have already had occasion to refer to.

The British classical school, and their followers until quite recent times, approached the subject primarily from the point of view of equating the supply of and the demand for savings in real terms, as part of a long-run-equilibrium position. They argued that the supply of savings involved a real cost, in terms of refraining from the current consumption the saver might otherwise enjoy, which had to be covered by the payment of interest as a reward. They identified the demand for savings as coming from the use of capital in production, which yielded a return out of which the necessary reward to savers could be paid. Applying standard partial-equilibrium microeconomic analysis, the interest rate became the "price" that equated supply and demand. In equilibrium, therefore, the interest rate was identified with the marginal return to capital.

The Austrian school emphasized the greater productivity of more "roundabout" (more capital-intensive) methods of production, which made it profitable for producers to pay interest in order to call forth the necessary supply of savings. They saw lenders as being influenced by "time preference"—a natural preference for the enjoyment of goods now rather than later. This may be explained in part by a lack of foresight, insufficient self-control, the basic uncertainty of one's remaining life expectancy, and the presumption of greater marginal utility from consumption now rather than later. If you expect your income to rise in the future but your needs to remain the same, you may prefer to borrow now rather than save; but if you expect your income to decline (say, after retirement), you may wish to save even with no (or a negative) reward.

Gustav Cassel described interest as the price of capital-disposal, that is the price of the use of a given amount of capital for a given period of time.

Knut Wicksell was not the first to distinguish between the "natural" rate of interest and the "market" or "money" rate, but he integrated the idea effectively into a "cumulative process" by which purely monetary factors, particularly a change in the money supply, could affect the money rate of interest and influence the aggregate level of economic activity.

Wicksell, other Swedish economists, and D.H. Robertson in Britain introduced important additional modifications in neoclassical interest-rate thinking, which led to the "loanable funds" theory. They argued that the amount of current savings available to finance investments is apt to be modified in two ways: by the actions of the monetary authorities, and by hoarding. Official actions to increase the money supply (in ways explained later in this chapter) increase the amount of investment that can be financed currently, actions to contract the money supply reduce it. On the other hand both current savings and newly-created money may be hoarded instead of being made available to finance investments; or, on the contrary, previously hoarded money may be dishoarded and used to supplement current savings.

The theory identified the money available for investment as "loanable funds". They consist of current savings plus new monetary expansion (or minus monetary contraction) plus net dishoarding (or minus net hoarding). It also held that relatively high interest rates will encourage dishoarding, while relatively low rates will encourage hoarding. The net effect was a significant modification of the classical demand-and-supply analysis of the setting of the interest rate, by the introduction of additional factors linking real and market rates.

The term "hoarding" subsequently came into disrepute, because its meaning is not clear. Despite childhood stories of misers holding gold coins in hidden caches and taking them out secretly to gloat over them, does the word really mean anything different from "holding"? In a sense, therefore, all money is hoarded by someone at all times. However, we may identify "hoarded" money as used in the loanable-funds theory with balances held idle for precautionary or speculative purposes, so many aspects of the loanable-funds theory anticipate Keynes's ideas on interest rates, to which we now turn.

An important innovation in J.M. Keynes's *The General Theory of Employment Interest and Money* was his liquidity-preference theory. He saw three distinct reasons why the public wants to hold money: the transactions motive, that is to carry out day-to-day purchases; the precautionary motive, to provide against unforeseen contingencies; and the speculative motive, to permit seizing good opportunities for acquiring valuable assets. He argued that the first was relatively insensitive to changes in interest rates, but the second and third were sensitive. (The last two may be treated together for some purposes, as the money-as-an-asset motive.)

Keynes described the interest rate as the price that equates the portion of their wealth people wish to hold in the form of cash (money as an asset) with the available supply of cash. In simple models the public's choice of financial assets is limited to "money" and "bonds", but his treatment is adaptable to more complex models offering a wide selection of portfolio assets. Taken literally, his presentation implies that the interest rate is purely a short-run partial-equilibrium monetary phenomenon; however, his analysis does take account of real as well as monetary factors, and subsequent modifications are even more explicit on this point.

A simple illustration of Keynes's theory of the interest rate in the very short run may be presented in terms of a supply-and-demand diagram like Figure 5-2 on page 68, with the interest rate measured on the north-south axis and the money supply on the east-west axis. You may take the *DD* curve to represent the public's "liquidity-preference function", that is its demand for money as an asset: money is the most liquid of all assets, and the public will only reduce its holdings if it is paid a higher and higher interest rate in compensation.

The *SS* curve is interpreted as the supply of money, arbitrarily decided by the monetary authorities, and therefore represented as a straight line parallel to the north-south axis. The interest rate will settle at whatever level will induce the public to hold the quantity of money the authorities choose to provide.

Now suppose something happens to make the public more wary about the future, so its *liquidity preference* rises: the *DD* curve moves bodily northward, and the interest rate must rise. If on the other hand the public becomes more optimistic, the *DD* curve will move southward and the interest rate will fall. However, the monetary authorities may offset either of these movements by altering the money supply. Or they may either raise or lower the interest rate if liquidity preference remains relatively stable, by supplying less or more money.

As suggested at the start of this chapter, all these ideas about the interest rate have some validity; their main limitation is that they are all based on partial-equilibrium analysis. In a long-run general-equilibrium position the market interest rate must be equal to the natural rate; the natural rate must be equal to the marginal productivity of capital; the public's saving-consumption and time-preference patterns must be in balance; saving and investment must be equal; the public's preferences not only between "money" and "bonds" but also among the enormous variety of real and financial assets must be satisfied at the ruling interest rate; and so on. If any of these conditions were not satisfied, then it would not be an equilibrium position.

2. Money and Banking.

The principal aspects of money were described in sections 6 and 7 of Chapter 10, but some important features of modern monetary and financial systems need further attention. What has been said so far would apply equally well if pieces of money consisted solely of some commodity (such as full-bodied metallic coins, i.e. coins whose bullion value was equal to their monetary value), as was actually the case for much of recorded history. In most countries nowadays, however, money consists primarily of (1) paper currency notes issued by a central bank or similar authority and (2) chequeing accounts at a commercial bank or similar institution. Coins are used only for small change, and the authorities maintain their value by exchanging them freely for currency notes or chequeable deposits.

The essential relationships can be quickly grasped through a model that in fact rather crudely summarizes what actually happened in many countries. Suppose the productive techniques of an isolated community gradually evolve until self-sufficiency gives way in substantial measure to specialization and trade, and a commodity money becomes established to replace barter.

The monetary commodity might be anything that could not be easily manufactured—perhaps a rare form of shell, perhaps kernels of grain, perhaps an agreed weight of some metal. Some economists have gone into great detail about what qualities would be most desirable for the monetary commodity, but the main point is that the quantity available for monetary use should not change too rapidly.

To be specific, let's say they choose a cowrie shell, and that the total known supply in the community is 1000 cowries. (Perhaps more could be found by diligent search, but we will suppose no more are found in the period we will consider.) There is some borrowing and lending of money between individuals, but the amount is small, because many would-be borrowers want the money for a longer time than the would-be lenders are prepared to offer, so there is virtually no *financial* asset except money.

Relying on the quantity theory, we will suppose that the community's output is stable from year to year and that appropriate (and stable) prices in terms of cowries are established for all the products traded. If the community sets aside some savings at one season for use at another, or some net savings every year, most of it must be in the form of commodities or net additions to capital (new houses, more fishing equipment, or the like). Some people may choose to keep a cowrie or two in reserve for emergencies, and we may suppose that the equilibrium price level reflects the holding of a small portion of the total money supply of 1000 cowries in this way, but any attempt to increase that portion would put enough downward pressure on prices to discourage the idea.

Now suppose that some enterprising individual with a reputation for reliability observes that some of his (or her) fellow citizens who hold a few cowries as emergency reserves are a bit concerned lest they be stolen, and offers to keep them in a secure place for a fee. His service proves successful, he builds a reputation for returning depositors' money on demand, and eventually he comes to hold 100 cowries in safekeeping.

Then the innovator notices that the amount of money on deposit with him is remarkably stable; frequently someone does withdraw all or part of his money for some purpose, but just as frequently someone else adds to his deposit. Cautiously he begins to lend out some of his depositors' money, secure in the knowledge that if worse comes to worst he can repay them out of his own resources.

Economists sometimes use a bare-bones balance sheet to illustrate the assets and liabilities of a firm at a given point in time. (Don't panic, all you will have to know is which is your left hand and which is your right.) It is called a T-account, because it consists of a bar across the top and a line down the middle like the capital letter T. We will put the firms assets (things it owns and debts it is owed) on the left-hand side, and its liabilities (debts it owes) on the right, though you may reverse them if you like—in some countries they do.

When our enterprising individual takes in 100 cowries in deposits his T-account will look like this:

Actual shells	100	Due to depositors	100

After he has lent out (say) 20 cowries it looks like this:

Actual shells	80	Due to depositors	100
Loans receivable	20		

The trouble with T-accounts is that they require a lot of space to show a series of changes over time. One way around this is to turn the T on its side and make it into a T-square account, like a draughtsman's T-square, as in Table 12-1, and let successive columns represent either successive points in time or the changes that occur between two points. This also allows us to stack several T-square accounts on top of one another, so we can see the corresponding positions or changes in several balance sheets at once.

Now let's get back to our newly-established depository for cowrie shells. Column 1 represents the public's balance sheet at the start. The public's financial assets are limited to the 1000 cowries in circulation, if we ignore any debts one person may owe to another, and we have added an item called "net worth" on the liability side so total assets equal total liabilities.[1]

---

[1] It is not really a liability, unless you count it as a liability of the cowrie-holders to themselves, but bookkeepers and accountants get very upset if balance sheets don't balance, so they enter an amount equal to the excess of assets over liabilities on the right-hand side and call it "shareholders' equity" or "net worth" or something like that.

A Hypothetical Example

Sector assets and liabilities	Time sequence: (1)	*	(2)	*
General Public				
A Actual cowries	1000	− 100	900	+90
Shell deposits	—	+100	100	—
Total assets	1000	—	1000	+90
L Debts	—	—	—	+90
Net worth	1000	—	1000	—
Depositories				
A Actual cowries	—	+100	100	− 90
Loans receivable	—	—	—	+90
Total assets	—	+100	100	—
L Due to depositors	—	+100	100	—

Table 12-1. Numbered columns are balance sheets at successive points in time, asterisks indicate changes between balance sheets. Column 1 is the starting point; once the public decides to put 10 per cent of its assets on deposit with the depository,

The Financial System 203

The following column, marked with an asterisk, represents what happens when some cowrie-holders decide to leave, say, 10 per cent of their assets with the depository: they give up 100 cowries in exchange for the depository's promise to repay them in full on an agreed basis—perhaps on demand, perhaps on a fixed date, perhaps after giving an agreed amount of notice. For its part the depository gains 100 cowries, and incurs a liability to repay the same amount. (All numbered columns are balance-sheet positions at a particular moment, all columns marked with asterisks represent changes between balance sheets.)

Column 2 shows the two balance sheets after the deposits have been made. This is the point at which the enterprising individual who started the depository begins to experiment with lending some of the money to others. His experiments prove successful.

Being an honest man (or woman), he confides his new discovery to his depositors. He offers to pay them interest on their deposits instead of charging a safekeeping fee, and still repay them on the same terms, if they will let him lend out a portion of their deposits. They agree, and he finds by experience that a reserve

of Deposit Expansion

(3)	*	(4)	*	(∞)
990	-9	981	+8.10	989.01
100	+9	109	—	109.89
1090	—	1090	+8.10	1098.90
90	—	90	+8.10	98.90
1000	—	1000	—	1000.00
10	+9	19	-8.10	10.99
90	—	90	+8.10	98.90
100	+9	109	—	109.89
100	+9	109	—	109.89

its portfolio is out of equilibrium in odd-numbered columns. When the depository finds it can safely lend 90 per cent of its deposits, its portfolio is out of equilibrium in even-numbered columns.

of 10 per cent in actual cowrie shells is enough to protect him from the risk that withdrawals might temporarily exceed deposits.

Before proceeding further, let's make a slight change in our assumptions: instead of a single depository, which might abuse its market power, let's suppose a large number of similar competing depositories are established. (Our 1000 cowries might actually be 100,000 cowries or some much larger figure—1000 is convenient in order to save space in the table, but it is not very realistic.)

Let's suppose there are many creditworthy businessmen and others who would like to employ more capital than their own funds will permit, or who have other good reasons to borrow, so the depositories have no trouble lending out their 90 cowries of free funds. The result is represented by the second column marked by an asterisk: as the loans are spent, these 90 cowries go back into circulation among the general public.

The public's financial assets rise from 1000 cowries in column 2 to 1090 in column 3—990 in actual cowries, 100 in deposits. At this level of assets, however, the public now prefers to hold 109 cowries on deposit instead of 100, so it redeposits 10 per cent of the additional 90 cowries (as in the column marked by the third asterisk). This gets us to column 4, where the depositories have cowrie reserves of 19 against deposits of 109, and are in a position to lend another 8.1 cowries (90 per cent of the public's redeposit).

So the process continues. In each odd-numbered column the distribution of the public's portfolio is not what it wants, and its efforts to correct the situation put more resources in the hands of the depositories. That in turn means that in each even-numbered column the depositories have free lendable funds, and their efforts to employ their funds profitably put the public's portfolio out of balance once more. Equilibrium for both groups is achieved when the public's deposits expand to 109.89 cowries and its total assets to 1098.90 cowries. At that point the public circulation of cowries is 989.01, and the 10.99 held by the depositories is just enough to provide reserves of 10 per cent against their deposit obligations.

What does all this do to the circular flow of money in one direction and goods in the other?

Well, for one thing it is clear that the spending of the new loans granted by the depositories must mean an increase in the spending stream, but we will not be able to follow that lead very well until we have explored some of the ideas in the last section of this chapter. However, we can get the general idea by the use of the quantity theory of money and prices.

At the outset we assumed that real output was stable from year to year, that prices were also stable, and that the money supply was fixed at 1000 cowries; in terms of the equation of exchange, *T*, *P*, and *M* were all constant. That means that the velocity of circulation, *V*, must also have been constant. Presumably the original 100 cowries placed with the intermediaries were being held idle as precautionary reserves, since the holders were willing to let the depositories hold them in safekeeping, so the *active* money supply was only 900 cowries. Now, however, 89 of those 100 cowries are as active as the original 900, and only 11 are held idle (as reserves by the depositories).

Obviously, the active circulation has gone up by nearly 10 per cent; or, if you prefer, you may say that the *average* velocity of the *total* money supply (1000 cowries) has gone up by nearly 10 per cent, since nine-tenths of the previously-idle money has now become active. If the community's output has indeed remained constant then the price level must have risen about 10 per cent too—the net effect has been an inflation proportionate to the amount of previously-idle money that has been activated.

However, the assumption that output and prices were initially constant is arbitrary and unrealistic. If some net savings were being put aside each year and invested in additional productive capital goods, and if full employment was maintained (as the model of pure competition indicates), then there must have been a persistent increase in real output. With a constant money supply and nothing to suggest a change in its velocity of circulation, the price level must have been steadily declining.

If you are prepared to doubt that price deflation is as painless as the model of pure competition and the quantity theory imply, you should be prepared to believe that the effects of the deposit expansion could be *beneficial* instead of harmful. In fact it is conceivable that the expansion of deposits (and the accompanying expansion of loans or credit) might just exactly match the growth of output and bring a persistently stable price level, though that is highly improbable in a monetary system based rigidly on some commodity money. All we can say for now is that the credit expansion may partly offset, fully offset, or more than offset any deflationary tendencies that would otherwise occur with a fixed money supply and a growing real income.

So far we have said nothing about what sort of evidence the depositories give their depositors in acknowledgement of their indebtedness to them. Perhaps it is a simple receipt. Perhaps it is an entry in a booklet the depositor keeps in his possession, initialed by an employee of the depository, like a savings-account passbook. Or perhaps it is a promissory note, stipulating the maturity date and other details. A note would be appropriate for deposits payable on demand: the depositor would only need to present it to the depository to get his money, or any part of it he wanted.

By this time the depositories are looking more and more like the institutions we now call banks. The next logical step is for the depositor to use his bank's promissory note to pay some third party, by endorsing it over to him. This would save trouble for both parties, especially for large transactions. The one would avoid making a special trip to his bank, carrying off actual cowries, and counting them out in payment; the other would avoid verifying the count, carrying the cowries to *his* bank, and depositing them there.

As this practice spread, the banks might decide to facilitate it (and incidentally reduce their own workload in handling deposits and withdrawals) by issuing notes in round amounts payable to bearer on demand. Presto! They have just invented the banknote, which is simply an IOU of the issuer. In time banknotes become accepted as a substitute for cowries for making payments, because they are lighter and more convenient.

Other depositors may find another way of doing pretty much the same thing: they may simply write a note to their banker asking him to deduct so many cowries from their account and add it to so-and-so's account. Presto! Two more inventions, the cheque and the chequeable deposit!

These inventions provide the public with important alternatives to cowries as financial assets, and in fact greatly expand the money supply once they became widely used. (Remember that we defined "money" as anything that is widely used to pay for goods or to settle debts or obligations.) The evolution of various types of depositories greatly expands the public's choice of financial assets, and the potential size of its total portfolio; but the invention of new types of money has especially great potential for asset expansion, for good or ill.

How great is this potential? Well, that depends mainly on two things: the the portion of its financial assets the public chooses to hold as bank deposits (or banknotes) rather then actual cowries, and the ratio of actual cowries to their obligations the banks find it necessary or prudent to keep as a reserve against unexpected withdrawals.

The first of these ratios depends on the habits, likes, and dislikes of the public; we will call it the "acceptance ratio" of deposits (or notes), though that term is not in common use. The second is known as the reserve ratio, and what constitutes a prudent ratio is found by experience: banks that maintain an insufficient ratio go bankrupt.

You will now see that both the acceptance ratio and the reserve ratio were 10 per cent in Table 12-1. That meant that a deposit of 100 cowries gave rise to loans of 90, redeposits of 9, new loans of 8.1, new redeposits of 0.81, and so on; total deposits rose to 109.89, and total loans to 98.90. Presumably the redeposits came from savings out of the income generated by the spending of the borrowed money, though we are not yet in a position to explore how this could happen.

If the acceptance ratio had been 90 per cent instead of 10 per cent, however, then a reserve ratio of 10 per cent would have given rise to initial deposits of 900, loans of 810, redeposits of 729, and so on. Total deposits would have been 900 + 729 + 590.49 + ... or over 5,263, and loans nearly 4,737. Quite a difference!

How could the acceptance ratio reach 90 per cent? Surely no community is likely to save 90 per cent of its income. No, the only reasonable explanation is that the new financial asset can substitute in part for actual cowries in the making of payments. Banknotes or chequeable deposits, or some combination of the two, are the obvious answer. In fact they could conceivably substitute for actual cowries in all uses (an acceptance ratio of 100 per cent). That, plus a reserve ratio of 10 per cent, would let deposits expand to 10,000.

By now we have got about as much out of our hypothetical example as we can, so we may as well look briefly at money and banking in the real world. Gold, silver, or some combination of the two was the basic commodity money in most countries through most of recorded history, and the gold standard of the late 19th and early 20th centuries was the most sophisticated example.

In English-speaking countries banks that issued banknotes or accepted chequeable deposits eventually became known as *commercial* banks, because the most successful early banks focused primarily on serving commercial enterprises. (Success depended mainly on the quality of the bank's loans, and experience soon showed that goods on the way to market were the safest available security under the conditions that then obtained, since they could be seized and easily sold if the debtor was unable or unwilling to repay.) Similar banks arose in other countries, differing mainly in their names. They all accepted non-chequeable deposits too, of course—including deposits payable after a fixed term or after a stipulated notice.

Other depositories also developed, serving other needs—savings banks, building societies, savings and loan associations, and many other types. Banks and other depositories are collectively known as "financial intermediaries", because they *mediate between* primary lenders (holders of banknotes or deposits, who in effect lend to the depository) and ultimate borrowers (who borrow directly from the depository but indirectly from the noteholders and depositors).

For reasons we can not take time to recount, note issues became the monopoly of official banks of issue virtually everywhere, and these banks of issue became central banks (i.e. banks with the responsibility of regulating the money supply in the best interests of the country). Their notes have completely replaced gold or other commodity moneys for domestic purposes, and other banks must use these notes for their cash reserves. They can therefore exert a strong influence on the entire financial system, as explained in the next section of this chapter.

Lending by intermediaries (especially by commercial banks) is commonly called "credit creation", because their granting of loans (or credits) seems to generate an almost-equal amount of new deposits. However, "credit expansion" is a better term, because it is really a sequence in which loans and deposits expand together, and it involves decisions by the public as well as by the intermediaries. Note also that the sequence is only possible if the intermediaries have acquired "free" reserves (more than they actually need) in some way—typically, by some action of the central bank.

This gives rise to the concept of a "deposit multiplier" and a "credit multiplier", because both deposits and loans will ultimately rise by some multiple of the free reserves that start the process going.

Clearly, commercial banks have a great advantage in this procedure. Note carefully where the advantage lies, however. It does not lie in the mere *fact* that they can "create" credit, for we have seen that other depositories can do that too. Their advantage lies in the *greater scope* they have, because the public uses their obligations as money. Comparatively little of the loans by others returns to them immediately by way of redeposits; for most part they depend on new savings for their expansion. But virtually all loans, by banks or by anyone else, are redeposited immediately in a chequeing account, regardless of whether they are to be held there for a while, spent soon, or exchanged for some other asset.

3. The Rôle of Monetary Policy.

> *Fatherly advice:* Note that there are just four main points in this section: (1) the central bank can expand the money supply, thereby *tending* to reduce interest rates *and* to make new loans available to the public; (2) it can control "the" money supply, or "the" interest rate, but not both independently; (3) the spending of new loans generates new income; (4) *but* under some circumstances the monetary expansion may not bring new spending.

A major feature of any modern financial system is a central bank (or its equivalent), whose activities revolve around the issue of the banknotes that constitute its principal liabilities and provide the general public with hand-to-hand currency. Its principal assets usually consist of a mixture of foreign exchange and government securities, though they may include some promissory notes or other obligations of private enterprises. (Sometimes most of the foreign-exchange reserves are held by the government itself, rather than the central bank.) Usually it does not deal directly with the general public, but only indirectly, through other banks. It plays an important rôle in the operation of the economy, by influencing the performance of the financial system as a whole.

A second important feature is a number of competing commercial banks, i.e. those financial institutions that hold most of the public's chequeable deposits. (Remember that a common definition of money is anything that is widely used as a means of payment, which usually comes down to "currency plus chequeable deposits"; the providers of these deposits therefore play a key rôle in the financial system.) However, commercial banks also hold many types of non-chequeable deposits, which may greatly exceed their chequeable deposits, and their total deposit obligations constitute their principal liabilities.

The principal assets of the commercial banks are a wide variety of loans and marketable securities, and cash reserves. Their loans are typically repayable on demand or in the near future, and are not normally confined to commercial enterprises; nowadays they probably should be called department-store banks instead of commercial banks. Their cash reserves consist mainly of central-bank notes.[2]

Then there is a host of other financial institutions, sometimes lumped together as "non-bank financial intermediaries" (or "non-banks" for short). Both the liabilities and the activities of some of then (sometimes called "near-banks") closely resemble those of commercial banks; for example, they may offer transfer privileges on some of their deposits that make them virtually identical with chequeable deposits, though usually the total of such accounts is relatively small.

The liabilities of non-banks may take any of a wide variety of forms, including such diverse items as the "shares" or deposit-like obligations offered by credit unions, the cash surrender values of life-insurance policies, and pre-paid premiums for casualty insurance. Their assets may vary greatly in nature, and may include both loans and securities with maturities ranging from very short to very long. Their

---

[2] In practice most of their cash reserves may be held as demand deposits with the central bank, rather than actual notes, but the effect is the same.

total assets and liabilities may be relatively small in some countries, but may far exceed those of the commercial banks in others.

In effect, the central bank buys its assets by tendering its own notes or the equivalent (i.e. its IOU's) in payment; they are readily accepted because experience has made everyone confident that they will be accepted in turn by everyone else for all payments.

In a somewhat similar way the commercial banks buy their assets and make their loans by tendering their own IOU's (credits to chequeable-deposit accounts) in payment, while the others do it by means of cheques on their accounts at the commercial banks. The public accepts payment in this form for the same reason it accepts the notes of the central bank; if people do not want to add all of their receipts to their chequeing accounts, they transfer some of them to other types of accounts at commercial banks or other financial institutions, or buy other assets, because they offer some advantage or other (such as interest income).

By law or by prudent convention, the cash reserves of commercial banks are set at a modest but fairly definite percentage of their deposit obligations, so their total liabilities (and therefore their total assets) are several times as large as their cash reserves; hence any increase in their cash holdings permits a multiple expansion of their deposits ("the deposit multiplier") and loans ("the credit multiplier"), as explained in section 2 of this chapter.

The assets of the "other" financial institutions will usually include at least some small amount of till-money in central-bank notes, but most of their cash and contingency needs will be met by chequeable and non-chequeable deposits at commercial banks and by readily-marketable securities. They may or may not be subject to a legal requirement to observe some set ratio of specified liquid assets to liabilities, but they too share the benefits of the credit multiplier to the extent that they can attract a portion of the public's financial resources.

Because of the key rôle its banknotes play as cash reserves for the commercial banks, and the key rôle chequeable deposits play in the economy, the central bank is able to exert a strong influence over the entire financial system. For example, suppose it wishes to expand the spending stream in order to increase the income of the economy. It can hope to do so by making more loans available, by reducing interest rates, or by some combination of the two. That constitutes the devising and carrying out of what is known as *monetary policy*, because it involves the manipulation of the money supply and related variables.

One way the central bank can hope to stimulate the spending stream is by buying up some securities in the marketplace—usually but not necessarily government securities. If it buys the securities from commercial banks then the banks get added cash reserves immediately; if it buys them from the general public the sellers will probably deposit the proceeds in their commercial banks, so the banks get the central bank's IOU's anyway. Thus the commercial banks get "free" reserves, i.e. more than they are required or find it prudent to keep, so they will be willing to increase their lending to the public.

Even if a seller deposits the central bank's IOU's in a near-bank or uses them to acquire some other asset, the near-bank or other recipient will promptly redeposit them into its own chequeing account with a commercial bank. In this case too, therefore, the banks get free cash reserves and will be able to increase their lending. However, any part of the money that is first placed with some other financial institution will give that institution additional free reserves as well (i.e. an addition to its chequeable deposits with commercial banks), so it too will have new money to lend.

The increased willingness of lenders to lend is only a part of the story, however; potential borrowers need some incentive to borrow. Here a second aspect of central-bank expansion comes into play. Market interest rates respond to changes in demand and supply in much the same way as any other price—in this case, to changes in the demand for and the supply of borrowed money.

Providing the commercial banks and other lenders with free reserves will therefore tend to weaken market interest rates, improve the "inducement to invest", and stimulate new capital formation. The result should be a sequence of new loans and redeposits that will expand the assets and the liabilities of all financial institutions, as explained in section 2, in whatever proportion the public chooses to distribute its assets among them. The spending of the newly-borrowed funds, whether on new capital formation or for consumption,[3] should activate the income multiplier and generate increased income.

This, of course, is exactly what the central bank wanted when it decided to expand its note issue. The immediate effect of that action is to temporarily upset the balance between the public's holdings of banknotes and its holdings of other financial assets. The public's efforts to restore that balance put free reserves in the hands of the financial institutions and thereby set off a sequence of loans, redeposits, and new loans. The spending of these loans sets off a multiple expansion

---

[3] The central bank's action to expand credit may stimulate more spending on consumption (less saving or more dissaving) as well as or instead of new capital formation. The combination of greater availability and lower cost of credit may induce some people to borrow in order to buy such things as automobiles and major appliances. It may also persuade others to use up some savings they have accumulated in the past as emergency reserves; they may conclude that they can count on borrowing if an emergency does occur, instead of providing for it in advance.

of income, already noted. It also generates new savings, by a sequence that is explained in section 4 of this chapter.

However, although the central bank can thus exercise a potent influence over the entire financial structure and over market interest rates, it is by no means all-powerful. In fact, you might say that it *proposes* but the general public *disposes*—over a considerable range of options, at least.

If the central bank decides to increase its note issue, as in this example, the public decides how much of it to keep as additional hand-to-hand currency, how much to deposit in chequeing accounts, how much in interest- bearing accounts, and how these accounts will be apportioned among commercial banks, near-banks, and non-banks. Then in due course it may decide to convert some of its new assets into bonds or equity shares or rental property, or to use them in some other way. All these decisions will determine how much (if any) credit expansion will occur. The effect on interest rates will also depend on public attitudes and preferences, including the state of its liquidity preference.

Specifically, the central bank can indeed *control* the money supply within a narrow margin of error, in the sense that it can increase and decrease its note issue in a succession of moves until the public is manoeuvred into holding just the "right" total of banknotes and chequeable deposits, but that means it must let interest rates find their own level. Alternatively, it can *control* the interest rate in the same way, but it must then accept whatever level of money supply is necessary to make that rate effective. It can't control both at the same time.

More generally, the central bank can rigidly control any "monetary aggregate" it chooses. (The definition of money we have favoured so far is not the only possibility, and in fact there is a good deal of dispute these days over what is the best one; hence the term "monetary aggregates" has been coined, to accommodate a variety of definitions.) Alternatively, the central bank can maintain any given interest rate (say, the treasury-bill rate) at any level it likes, or several selected rates (say, the rates on all government securities), or even the entire structure of interest rates. Or, it could rigidly control the total amount of lending by the commercial banks, or by any group of financial institutions it chose. But it can't achieve more than one of these things independently.

In practice, therefore, the central bank must accept some compromise between the structure of the public's financial assets and the structure of interest rates it would like at any given point in time. However, its choice of which of these intermediate target variables to pursue may not make a great deal of difference in the end, for its ultimate objective is to promote a high level of employment at stable prices, and it will probably have to revise its tactics more or less continuously in the light of evolving conditions.

Successful attainment of that objective implies the achievement of equilibrium in the public's portfolio of financial assets, in the structure of interest rates, and in the balance between the two; whatever guide the central bank chooses for is monetary policies, therefore, the results must ultimately converge on the same equilibrium position.

Furthermore, the expansion of income by monetary policy is a pretty iffy proposition. Monetary expansion will only generate new income *if* willing borrowers can be found, *if* the potential lenders consider these would-be borrowers creditworthy, and *if* the borrowed money is actually spent. In a deep depression there may be a shortage of willing borrowers because it may not be possible to drive interest rates low enough to create a positive inducement to invest. Even if willing borrowers can be found, they may not be able to persuade the lenders they are creditworthy; not everyone who is prepared to take risks with other people's money can be trusted with it. And some people who are indeed creditworthy may be willing to borrow, but only to increase their readily available cash balances as a precaution against possible misfortunes, so their borrowing may not result in any new spending.

The link between the money supply and the interest rate is also somewhat iffy. The interest rate (or the return on any other asset) must be sufficient to compensate the lender for giving up liquidity—for making a term deposit or buying a bond or a share or a rental property instead of holding cash, for example. Thus the decision to acquire any income-yielding asset, like the decision to spend rather than save and the decision to invest, has a major psychological component and is therefore potentially volatile. In good times the public's liquidity preference may be low, and people may be easily persuaded to buy bonds and other income-yielding assets; but in bad times liquidity preference may be very high, and people may be reluctant to hold anything but very-short-term obligations.

The state of the public's liquidity preference may put practical limits to how low the central bank can reduce the interest rate. In any given situation each successive reduction will require a greater expansion of the money supply. If liquidity preference is high, however, a point may eventually come at which it would be virtually impossible to reduce the rate any further no matter how much the money supply was expanded.

The extreme case is known as the "liquidity trap", and may occur if there is some minimum level to the interest rate the public can be induced to accept. The liquidity function becomes perfectly elastic at this level: any further monetary expansion adds to the public's cash balances, but no longer reduces the interest rate.

Some economists deny that any such situation can develop, and it is certainly not a necessary part of Keynesian models; the real point is just that monetary policy, like many other things in this imperfect world, is subject to diminishing returns.[4]

4. A Double Income Multiplier.

In Chapter 11 we met the "income multiplier", and in this chapter we have met both a "deposit multiplier" and a "credit multiplier". By now you probably suspect that there is a link between the income and the credit multipliers, since we have already noted that the spending of borrowed money will swell the spending stream and generate new income. If so, you are quite right. In order to head off some possible confusion in terminology, however, let us hereafter replace the term "income multiplier" by "spending multiplier", thus identifying it with the multiplicand rather than the product.

Before we explore the link between the credit and the spending multipliers, we should note that there are many multipliers that can be identified in economic analysis, and we should take a look at some of the characteristics of multipliers in general. Some are clearly related, like the credit and the deposit multipliers, in that they are generated as part of the same expansionary sequence, and may therefore be seen as members of a family of multipliers.

The spending multiplier is also a member of a family, since a given injection of new spending will produce not only a stream of further additions to domestic spending (and therefore additions to income) but also a stream of additions to savings out of the new money income and (in an open-economy model) a stream of additions to spending on imports.

---

[4] There is an interesting historical case that does seem to verge on a liquidity-trap situation. In Britain the interest rate was easily held at 3 per cent during World War II and into the post-war era, but in 1946 the Treasury, under Dr. Hugh Dalton, tried to force it down to about 2 1/2 per cent ("The Dalton Drive"). Government securities became unsaleable, holders dumped them on the market, and official efforts to support their prices (in order to establish the new interest rate) merely brought a rapid and continuing increase in the money supply. In February 1947 the authorities gave up, the interest rate rose to 3 per cent again, and held there for a considerable time. Apparently people thought a rate of 2 1/2 per cent could not be held, and feared capital losses if they bought bonds at that yield and had to sell later at higher yields. (If the interest rate falls, the price of any bond will rise until the yield becomes the same as the new interest rate; if the interest rate rises, the price of any bond will fall; hence you will want to sell any bonds you have rather than buy new ones if you think the interest rate will soon rise, because you will expect to buy them back at a lower price later.)

Alternatively, some of the products of a multiplier sequence may be looked on as "leakages" from the process. This can be clearly seen in the case of a credit expansion generated by the appearance of redundant cash in the hands of the financial intermediaries or the public: it ends when the initially- redundant cash is either absorbed by the intermediaries' increased need for reserves, or held willingly by the public in view of its expanded portfolio of financial assets (and, as we will see, its increased money income). However, the same thing may also be seen in the case of the spending multiplier.

Imagine an economy that saves 10 per cent of each additional franc (or mark, or whatever is the national currency) of income and spends 20 per cent of it on imports (its marginal propensity to save is 10 per cent, its marginal propensity to import is 20 per cent). Now suppose new spending of 1000 francs is somehow injected in a certain income period, and produces new income in that period. In the second period 700 francs from this new income will be spent domestically and produce new income, 300 will leak away as savings or imports; in the third period 490 francs will be sent and 210 will leak away; and so on.

The sum of 1000 + 700 + 490 + 343 + ... is 3333, and the sum of 300 + 210 + 147 + ... is 1000. That is, the spending multiplier is 3.3[5], and the sum of the leakages is exactly equal to the injection of new spending that started the expansion going. Furthermore, the savings and the import leakages are exactly in proportion to their marginal propensities: 100 + 70 + 49 ... = 333 and 200 + 140 + 94 + ... = 667 respectively.

Now that we have introduced open-economy conditions, however, we must note that they have an effect on the credit multiplier as well as the spending multiplier. We can not spare the time to go into it in detail, but the essence of it is that, as explained in Chapter 15, imports must be paid for by exports, either directly or indirectly; failing that, some way must be found to pay foreign suppliers in their own currencies.

Credit-induced spending will stimulate import demand, and presumably it will also reduce exports, because it will absorb production that might otherwise be sold abroad. The excess demand for foreign currencies must be supplied out of the central bank's external reserves, and paid for by cancelling out some of the domestic money supply.

---

[5] If you are mathematically inclined, look back at footnote 7 on page 193 and you will see that this conforms to the expression $1/(s+t+m)$, since in this case t is obviously zero.

The net effect is to reduce the central bank's foreign reserves and its domestic monetary obligations by the same amount, thereby partly negating its efforts to expand credit and sharply reducing the credit multiplier. Furthermore, although the authorities may be willing to allow their external reserves to run down for a while, and may also borrow abroad to support the import drain, sooner or later they must either cut back on the credit expansion (probably reverse it) or let the exchange value of the domestic currency depreciate sharply on foreign-exchange markets.

Now at last we are in a position to look at the double (or compound) income multiplier. There it is, clearly enough: anything that will increase the free reserves of the financial system will lead to a multiple expansion of loans, and the spending of the proceeds of those loans will lead to a further multiple expansion of money income. However, we must be careful in how we compute the compounding effect.

If the typical cash reserve ratio of financial intermediaries is 10 per cent, not an unrealistic figure, you might be tempted to expect a deposit multiplier of ten, and therefore a credit multiplier of nine. (Deposits equal loans plus reserves; if reserves are 10 per cent of deposits, loans must be 90 per cent.) You might also be tempted to look for a high spending multiplier to compound with the credit multiplier, thus getting a really impressive compound income-multiplier to apply to the central bank's credit-expansion efforts. If so, you would be wrong.[6]

The first possible source of error is the confusion of the ratio the *final level* of deposits to the *final level* of reserves with the ratio of the *expected increase* in deposits to the *initial level* of free reserves. Even in a closed economy some of the initial free reserves will be lost to increased circulation among the public (technically known as the "currency drain"), so only a part of the initial free reserves will remain with the intermediaries.

In a typical open economy a much greater portion of any initial free reserves will be lost to pay for increased imports (the "external drain"). Remember that the two leakages are proportional to the two marginal propensities, and note that imported parts, supplies, and services account for an important portion of many final products. Your marginal propensity to add to your bank balance may be pretty small compared to the marginal propensity of your spending to spill over into imports. That means the growth of financial assets (the savings leakage) will be small compared to the external drain, so the credit multiplier may be pretty low.

---

6 Remember that we are assuming that the authorities are not prepared to let the exchange value of the currency fall unduly. If they are prepared to ignore balance-of-payments considerations and let the exchange rate go free, however, then the compound income-multiplier will be free to rise as dramatically as it would in a closed economy. The implications for domestic inflation are obvious.

The spending multiplier itself may not be very large, for the same reason—the marginal propensity to add to financial assets is likely to be small compared to the marginal propensity to import. Attempts to compute it empirically in actively-trading countries have often come up with a figure in the vicinity of two.

Despite the need for caution in computing the compound income-multiplier, however, there are many constructive things to say about the links between the credit multiplier and the spending multiplier. Unless these links are explicitly recognized, the expansion of financial assets appears to go on in a vacuum, with no necessary relationship to the community's money income, let alone its real income. Recognizing them helps to explain how it is that, under favourable conditions, the mysterious manipulations of merely *financial* variables through the exercise of monetary policy can have powerful effects on *real* economic variables like employment and output.

Table 12-2 offers a schematic example of how the combined expansion works. It is based on a closed-economy model in which the various financial intermediaries that deal directly with the public maintain a cash reserve ratio of 10 per cent on the average. The public keeps 20 per cent of its liquid assets in banknotes, and 80 per cent in deposits of various kinds with financial intermediaries. The banknotes are issued by a central bank, which deals only with other financial intermediaries and so is not included in the table. (The public gets its banknotes from the intermediaries they deal with, which get them from the central bank.) To keep things as simple as possible—they are complicated enough as it is—we will limit ourselves to a closed-economy model.[7] This exaggerates the possible expansion, of course, but the basic principles are not affected.

In the preceding section we noted that the immediate effect of an expansion of the central bank's note issue is to temporarily upset the balance between the public's holdings of banknotes and its holdings of other financial assets. (The same is true of a contraction of the note issue, of course.) We have now seen that the actions to restore its desired combination of financial assets sets off a sequence of redeposits, new loans, new deposits, and more new loans that does not end until the new banknotes are entirely absorbed either by the public (to service a higher

---

[7] If you want to expand the table to open-economy conditions, you will have to introduce a central bank and its balance sheet (which must include some foreign exchange among its assets), and subdivide money income into spending on domestic goods, spending on imports, and saving (say, in the ratio of 7:2:1). Spending on imports will not only reduce the new income generated in each period by the respending effect, it will also reduce the redeposit of banknotes with the intermediaries, because the public will have to use some of them in each period to buy foreign exchange from the central bank (or rather from the other intermediaries, which must then replenish their own supplies from the central bank).

Item	Start	Period T_1		
		(1)	(2)	(3[1])
BALANCE SHEETS				
Depositories				
A Free reserves	+1000	−1000	+ 720	(720)
Required reserves	—	—	+ 80	(80)
Loans[2]	—	+1000	—	(1000)
Securities	−1000	—	—	(−1000)
L Deposits	—	—	+ 800	(800)
General Public				
A Banknotes		+1000	− 800	(200)
Deposits		—	+ 800	(800)
L Debts		+1000	—	(1000)
INCOME AND COMPONENTS				
Money income		+1000		
		+1000		
Spent on consumption[3]		+ 900		
		+ 900		
Saved[4]		+ 100		
		+ 100		

A Hypothetical Example of Combined

[1] These columns represent the cumulative effect of all the preceding changes.
[2] Loans are spent and become income in the same period.
[3] Spending on consumption becomes income in the next period.
[4] Savings are included in the redeposit in the same period.

Table 12-2. The depositories obtain free reserves of 1000 francs, due to a central-bank open-market purchase of securities from them. In Period T_1 they make cash loans of 1000 francs to some members of the public, who acquire banknotes in exchange for debts and spend the proceeds, thereby generating additional income of 1000 francs, 900 of which is spent and 100 saved (all this in column 1). In the course

Credit and Income Expansion

	Period T_2			Period T_3		T_∞
(1)	(2)	(3^1)		(1)		
− 720	+ 518.40	(518.40)		− 518.40	....	—
—	+ 57.60	(137.60)		—	....	+ 285.71
+ 720	—	(1720.00)		+ 518.40	....	+ 3,571.43
—	—	(−1000.00)		—	....	− 1,000.00
—	+ 576.00	(1376.00)		—	....	+ 2,857.14
+ 720	− 576.00	(344.00)		+ 518.40	....	+ 714.29
—	+ 576.00	(1376.00)		—	....	+ 2,857.14
+ 720	—	(1720.00)		+ 518.40	....	+ 3,571.43
+ 900				+ 810.00	....	+10,000.00
+ 720				+ 648.00	....	+ 7,200.00
				+ 518.40	....	+ 5,184.00
				....	....	...
+1620				+1976.40	....	+35,714.29
+ 810				+ 729.00	....	+ 9,000.00
+ 648				+ 583.20	....	+ 6,480.00
				+ 466.56	....	+ 4,665.60
				....	....	...
+1458				+1778.76	....	+32,142.86
+ 90				+ 81.00	....	+ 1,000.00
+ 72				+ 64.80	....	+ 720.00
				+ 51.84	....	+ 518.40
				....	....	...
+ 162				+ 197.64	....	+ 3,571.43

of spending the borrowed money and their increased income the public makes net deposits of 800 francs (column 2), in order to maintain their preferred 20:80 division between notes and deposits (column 3), thus giving the depositories 720 francs of new free reserves. In Period T_2 new loans generate another 720 francs in income, and in the meantime the 900 francs spent on consumption in Period T_1 has also generated new income (column 1). In Period T_3 the depositories are able to make new loans of 518.40 francs. Eventually the process ends with an expansion of about 3,571 francs in loans by the intermediaries and 35,714 francs in increased money income.

money income) or by financial intermediaries (as cash reserves in support of increased liabilities). Accompanying this expansion of credit and financial assets, and intimately related to it, there is a multiple expansion of income as the new loans are spent.

The process starts with free reserves in the hands of the intermediaries, as a result either of open market purchases of securities by the central bank, or of the intermediaries rediscounting some of their own loans. ("Rediscounting" means selling the loan contracts to the central bank, or borrowing from it on the security of their customers' debts.) Central-bank open-market purchases may be made either from the intermediaries or from the general public; in the first case the intermediaries get free reserves directly, in the second case they get them indirectly because the public will deposit some or all of the proceeds with them.

Now look at the first column of Period T_1. The intermediaries make loans of 1000 francs (their free reserves) to their customers, which we have represented as being done by handing over banknotes. In practice it would normally be done by just crediting the customer's deposit account, but the lender loses the full amount from its free reserves anyway, as the loan proceeds are chequed away to make whatever payments the loans were intended to finance. The borrowers get cash, and of course their debts increase by the same amount. They spend their newly-acquired money, thereby generating new money income of 1000 francs in that period. Of this, 900 francs is spent (becoming income in the next period) and 100 is saved.

The public wishes to hold 20 per cent of its liquid assets in banknotes, and 80 per cent in deposits. The spending of the new loans and the new income blends with other components of the spending stream, and in the normal course of business the public therefore makes net deposits of 800 francs with the intermediaries, which causes the latter to add 80 francs to their required reserves. All this is indicated in column 2 of Period T_1. These deposits include the 100 francs the public has added to its willingly-held savings, but also include the money it intends to spend in the next period.

Column 3 shows that the public has indeed reshuffled its liquid assets according to its wishes. (The figures in this column are enclosed in parenthesis, to indicate that they are the cumulative total of all previous changes.) But in restoring its own desired asset mix the public has given the intermediaries new free reserves of 720 francs.

The same sequence is repeated in Period T_2: another 720 francs of new loans is granted, and generates new money income. This time, however, there is an additional increase of 900 francs in money income, from the money spent on consumption in the previous period. By period T_3 there are three income streams going—one from the respending effects of the 1000 francs lent and spent in the first period (810 francs), another from the 720 francs lent and spent in the second period (648 francs), and the start of still another (518.40 francs) from new loans. In each successive period a new (but smaller) sequence begins.

The last column in the table shows the final equilibrium position. (If you learned the formula for summing a converging infinite series in high-school algebra, you may easily verify the totals.)

Look closely at the figures. The loans granted by the depositories have increased by 3,571 francs, and of course the debts of the public (or some members of it) have gone up by the same amount. But the public's liquid assets have gone up by exactly the same amount, which exactly mirrors what the public has saved out of its increased money income!

There are several important implications of this analysis. For one thing, look back at section 8 of Chapter 10, where we concluded that the money supply must grow in step with the growth of real output if trouble is to be avoided. If you wish, you may identify all the deposits in Table 12-2 as chequeable deposits at banks, and the public's liquid assets as identical with "the" money supply. In that case it becomes clear that even money balances, which can apparently be created out of thin air by the authorities, must eventually be saved out of income.

Also, "savings" out of income as recorded in the table must refer solely to *savings in the form of money balances*; presumably additional savings have been accumulated, in the form of other types of financial claims as well as in physical assets.

On the other hand you may view the deposits in the table as a composite of a great many types of obligations of all sorts of intermediaries, representing the public's entire portfolio of financial assets. This interpretation is particularly acceptable for relatively long-run applications, for it is in immediate short-run applications that money-proper (money in the sense implied in the equation of exchange) enjoys its greatest advantages over other liquid assets. It is indeed the view that has been suggested in most of this section.

In that case the "deposits" in the table certainly include chequeable deposits and other forms of money-proper, as well as many other kinds of deposits and other vehicles in which people may choose to employ their savings. It therefore remains true that an increase in the supply of "money" (here represented by banknotes and chequeable deposits), like any other financial claim, must eventually be saved out of income. Furthermore, a long-run-equilibrium position implies that the money-supply is just appropriate to the current flow of money income under equilibrium conditions, and that the public is at the margin of indifference between holding money and holding any other asset.

Chapter 13

The Rise and Eclipse of Demand Management

Fatherly Advice: Note that the views of other economists on these matters may greatly differ.

1. In the Beginning.

As noted in section 7 of Chapter 11, the term "demand management" identifies a combination of economic policies designed to manage the total spending (or "effective demand") in the economy, in order to promote a high level of output and employment. It is based on the sort of Keynesian models briefly summarized in that chapter, and is interventionist in philosophy—that is, it reflects a belief that unaided market forces can not be relied on to maintain satisfactory levels of employment and real output, and that certain actions by the government can improve on the performance of the economy. The theory was reasonably complete by the end of World War II, though it continued to be improved and refined in the light of experience in the decades that followed.

The principal instruments of demand management are monetary policy and fiscal policy. Both of these instruments operate by expanding or contracting the spending stream, i.e. the flow of money payments that regulates economic activity in a money-and-market economy, including the flow of money income.

Monetary policy is the use of the powers of the central bank (or its equivalent) to influence both the level of market interest rates and the availability of loans from banks and other financial institutions. As explained in sections 3 and 4 of Chapter 12, reducing market interest rates and making loans more readily available is expected to encourage more borrowing-and-spending, especially on new capital projects, thus adding to the economy's money income. Raising interest rates and restricting lending is expected to have the opposite effect.

Fiscal policy uses the taxing and spending powers of the government to inject money directly into the spending stream or to withdraw money from it. Its essential feature is the deliberate creation of government deficits to stimulate the economy, or surpluses to restrain it.

One of the great virtues of demand management is that it is completely compatible with the money-and-market system. Monetary policy and fiscal policy operate at a very general level by regulating the spending stream, and do not interfere in any way with the spending decisions that allocate resources and generate money incomes.

Of course, that means they can not operate directly on "real" economic targets such as real income (or output) or the number of people employed. As a first approximation, however, we may use changes in money income as an indicator of changes in real income. How close the approximation is will depend on how stable the general price level happens to be; in the early years after World War II prices were pretty stable in many countries, but by the 1970's inflationary pressures were serious virtually everywhere.

Changes in real income in turn provide a reasonable indication of changes in employment, in the short run at least. Technological changes and shifts in the composition of output may cause employment to grow more rapidly or less rapidly than real income over time, but they usually occur rather slowly. Under favourable conditions, therefore, changes in money income can be taken to reflect changes in both output and employment.

Monetary policy had begun to be used in the 1920's, but had proven disappointing—especially in the 1930's. Market interest rates had eventually fallen quite low, but that had not proven very effective in promoting the capital spending necessary to stimulate an expansion of output and employment. Majority opinion did not expect much stimulus from monetary policy after the war either, but firmly believed in keeping interest rates low for whatever good they could do; they had been kept low throughout the war for a variety of reasons that need not detain us now, and remained so for many years thereafter. (A *restrictive* monetary policy, on the other hand, can be highly effective in reigning in a rate of spending that is considered excessive—that has frequently been demonstrated.)

The conventional wisdom of the day therefore put its main faith in fiscal policy. The argument, valid enough as far as it went, was that monetary policy can *permit* private borrowing-and-lending that *may* expand the spending stream, but deliberate government borrowing-and-spending will *ensure* its expansion. In terms of Figure 11-2 on page 184, and on the assumptions they made, low interest rates *may* lead to a rise in I^rI^r (and therefore in $C + I^r$), but injecting a deliberate government deficit of $(G - T)$ will certainly lead to a higher total spending function $C + I^r + (G - T)$.

As noted at the end of Chapter 11, taxing and spending plans must usually be fixed some time in advance, typically for a year or so at a time. This limitation on fiscal policy can be reduced to some extent by devising discretionary taxing or spending measures, which can be varied at short notice by the fiscal authorities. However, it was soon recognized that some *automatic stabilizers* were present in the government's financial affairs, and others could easily be introduced.

If output declines, tax receipts will automatically decline as a result—especially revenues from sales taxes and pay-as-you-earn income-taxes. Some expenditures will automatically increase too, such as unemployment insurance payments and other forms of social assistance. Similarly, a too-buoyant economy will generate a government surplus through increased tax revenues and reductions in social-assistance payments.

Eventually the idea of "full-employment budgeting" evolved, though it was never satisfactorily achieved in practice: a budget that would automatically balance at full employment, generate stimulative deficits if the spending stream faltered, and generate deflationary surpluses if the economy threatened to overheat.

Of course, there was at first no practical experience with demand management. Nevertheless the governments of several major countries bravely issued statements in which they undertook to put the new theory into practice. A United Nations committee issued a report favouring it. The Articles of Agreement of the International Monetary Fund listed as one of its purposes "To facilitate the expansion and balanced growth of international trade, and to contribute thereby to the promotion and maintenance of high levels of employment and real income ... as primary objectives of economic policy". So began 20 or 25 years of unprecedented and persistent growth of world trade and real income.

A number of policy objectives were recognized in most countries, of which three were deemed to be of particular importance: high levels of output and employment, price stability, and a viable balance-of-payments position.[1]

Evidently the first two of these objectives are of prime importance, because if they can be satisfactorily achieved by most countries then the third should not be difficult to reach. At worst it would require some reallocation of resources from

---

1   The balance of international payments will be discussed in section 6 of Chapter 15. A viable balance-of-payments position may be described as a combination of the nation's ability to earn its way in international trade in the medium and long term with the ability to contain short-run imbalances within internationally acceptable limits.

domestic to export and import-competing industries in the deficit countries, and the other way around in the surplus countries. A mutually agreeable change in exchange rates might be all that was required. There should be no more than temporary unemployment of human or other resources in any one country while these changes were being made, and the pains of adjustment could be eased by measures such as unemployment insurance and other social programs.

It should be noted, however, that "price stability" was interpreted rather differently then than it is now. It was recognized, of course, that serious inflationary pressures would arise if expansionary demand-management policies were pressed too strongly once full employment was reached or closely approached. However, most economists were more afraid of a relapse into the unemployment and *de*flations of the 1930's, still so fresh in everyone's mind; some actually advocated a deliberate though moderate *in*flation as a defence against this possibility.

A few economists did warn against the risk of inflation, but others countered that progressive income-taxes would automatically produce surpluses in government budgets as the average money income rose with inflation, which would defuse the problem. (Evidently they overlooked the ability of governments to spend any money they get.)

Under the circumstances, therefore, it is quite understandable that first priority was originally given to maintaining high levels of output and employment, and rather low priority was given to defences against the risks of inflation. Nevertheless the origin of later problems lay in the fact that official policies from the first were "soft" on inflation.

2. Limitations on Demand Management.

Powerful though they are in their general impact on the spending stream, monetary and fiscal policies have serious limitations. They are blunt and imprecise. They can not be used to give selective stimulus to a depressed region or sector of the economy. They can not by themselves do much to induce the expansion of production into new and untried fields, even if potential productive capacity is available.

Furthermore, both instruments have limitations of their own. Monetary policy is subject to lags and uncertainties in attaining its full impact on the spending stream. It takes time for the authorities to identify the nature and severity of a problem and to implement suitable measures, and additional time for the public to react to those measures. To some extent these lags can be allowed for, but this can not be depended on. For example, psychological and other factors may cause the public to respond more sluggishly or more promptly some times than others.

Fiscal planning is rather inflexible, as already noted, because of the constraints of budgeting. Abrupt changes in taxes may be disturbing, either in themselves or because the public may accelerate or delay decisions if a tax change is expected. It is not always feasible to bring forward suitable new spending projects on short notice, and once begun they may be difficult to terminate on demand. Also, the general public must agree that deliberate fiscal deficits are justified under the current circumstances; if they believe the deficits are not justified, they may be stampeded into actions that will defeat the policy (e.g., cancelling private capital spending that would otherwise be made).

Balance-of-payments considerations put a further limit on demand management in actual practice. We have already encountered this problem in section 4 of Chapter 12, but so far in this chapter we have side-stepped it on the grounds that it would be easily managed if all countries were reasonably successful in maintaining full employment at stable prices. Unfortunately, however, conditions in the world today do not remotely approach that ideal, so balance-of-payments problems are very real for most countries.

If one country did succeed in stabilizing its domestic prices while others suffered from both unemployment and inflation, and tried to use demand-management techniques to expand its output and employment to their full potential, it would soon run into trouble. Some of its increased money income would spill over into increased imports, while its exports would continue to languish because its foreign markets would still be depressed. Either it would continually lose exchange reserves, or its currency would continually depreciate on world markets, as long as it persisted with its expansionary policies.

However, the most serious limitation on demand management as presently practiced is the fact that neither monetary policy nor fiscal policy can effectively and independently control either real output or the price level. Between them they can indeed control the flow of money income, but not its separation into its "real" and "price" components.

3. Policy Objectives and Policy Instruments.

As demand management evolved, it became recognized in due course that two major conditions must be met if two or more policy goals or objectives are to be attained at the same time: (1) there must be at least as many independent *policy instruments* as there are independent *policy goals*;[2] and (2) the achievement of each independent policy goal must be influenced by at least one policy instrument.

Furthermore, achieving economic policy objectives does not involve a mere yes-no success-failure test; rather, it involves quantitative and qualitative measures of achievement, underachievement, or overachievement. A little thought should therefore convince you of a third requirement: (3) some policy instrument must be able to influence the achievement of each policy goal *independently of the achievement of any other goal*. For example, if one policy instrument influences two policy goals then it must be possible to use some other instrument to neutralize or reinforce the effect on one without affecting the other, in order to be sure both goals are satisfactorily achieved.

Applying these principles to demand management, we may note that we have two major domestic goals (full employment and price stability) and two major instruments (monetary policy and fiscal policy), so the first requirement is met. Also, the achievement of both goals is influenced by the spending stream, and both instruments act directly on the spending stream, so the second requirement is well met, too.

However, we run into trouble with the third requirement. In the first place, monetary and fiscal policies tend to be complements or alternatives. We need both, for each may be effective in circumstances in which the other is not. But they are not entirely independent either, because they act on the spending stream in broadly similar ways and have similar effects on both major goals. And no other policy instrument or group of policy instruments has yet been devised that will satisfactorily reinforce or offset the combined effects of fiscal and monetary policies either on prices or on employment, without affecting the other.

You may ask, what about price controls? Can't they be used to hold prices stable, so demand management can focus on maintaining full employment?

Various forms of wage and price controls have been tried on many occasions in many countries in the past, but with only limited and temporary success. Sometimes, it is true, they were poorly designed or badly managed. However, it is extremely hard to devise a program that is clearly fair to everyone. The Canadian effort in the 1970's was better conceived than most, was at least moderately successful in achieving its announced goals, and was not followed by a spurt of catch-up wage and price increases, yet its end was widely welcomed.

---

[2] This is rather like needing as many independent equations as unknowns in order to solve certain algebraic problems. However, in the world of economics it may take two or more coöperating instruments to achieve a single goal in some cases.

But controls have a much more serious fault still: they are not really compatible with the free-enterprise money-and-market system, which is profit motivated. Recall the discussion of "pure" profit in sections 8 and 9 of Chapter 4. Price controls are incompatible with the money-and-market system because they are unable to respect pure profit. It is easy enough to recognize the idea in the abstract, but how could you ever identify what part of a businessman's "bottom line" is pure profit?

The public could not be expected to accept wage and salary controls without effective limits on bottom-line profits, and the price controllers would have to make use of some standard accounting definition for them—probably a "fair" markup over cost (a subjective concept at best). There would be no way of identifying pure profit and rewarding the innovator, so time and money spent seeking it would be wasted. Inflation would presumably be slowed down, but not ended; the result would be a cost-plus inflation.

Cost-plus inflation? Well, during World War II a story was told about three businessmen who met for lunch in Ottawa while negotiating war contracts with the Canadian government. One reached for the bill and offered to pay for them all. "I can put it on my expense account", he said, "and I'll get 50 per cent of it back on my corporate income-tax." "Oh no!" said the second, "Let me have it! I am in the excess-profits-tax bracket, I'll get 85 per cent of it back!" "No indeed", said the third, "I am on a cost-plus contract, I'll make money on it!"

4. The Experience of Inflation.

For the first decade or so after World War II the price levels in most countries did indeed hold fairly stable, considering the circumstances, while international trade and the world's real income were expanding rapidly. Initially, therefore, it was possible to hope that price stability would become the rule, as the inflationary pressures and other distortions inherited from the war and from prewar years were gradually overcome. From the first, however, so-called "creeping inflation" of 1 or 2 per cent per annum appeared in even the most fortunately-situated and best-managed economies. Many people came to believe this was, if not actually beneficial, at least harmless, or a small price to pay for prosperity.

Unfortunately, the various national inflations seemed inclined to get worse instead of better as time passed. Also, it became apparent that the usual instruments of demand management could not control the situation satisfactorily, because fiscal and monetary restraint were more effective in reducing employment than in curbing inflation. By the 1970's inflations were clearly getting out of hand almost everywhere, and the full-employment goal was compromised as fiscal and monetary restraint became the main element of the anti-inflation strategy. In the early 1980's the annual inflation rate soared into the double-digit range in most countries, and only with great difficulty has it been brought back down to or below 5 per cent.

The unemployment rate, measured as a percentage of the labour force, has followed a similar course. A typical rate in the 1950's was around 3 per cent, but in the early 1980's it too got into the double-digit range in many countries. There has been some subsequent decline, at least in the industrialized countries, but even there it is still far above its best postwar level.

However, the objective of supporting the level of output and employment has not been entirely abandoned. There is no doubt that the current inflations could be quickly ended in the same way that many past inflations have been, that is by sufficiently tight money and by balancing government budgets. Undoubtedly the reason this has not happened is that the public will not accept the social suffering it would bring, and insists on some easing of the anti-inflation strategy.

The net effect, therefore, is that demand management as presently practiced can not achieve either of its main goals. Instead, it is condemned to seeking uneasily for the position of minimum total discomfort from two painful maladies.

5. The Cause of Today's Inflations: A Pragmatic View.

Economists are by no means agreed about the causes of inflation, though some general points are widely accepted. For example, it is clear that there must be a too-rapid growth of the money supply in order for inflation to occur, and that this in itself is enough to produce it. (In technical terms, the overexpansion of money is both a necessary and a sufficient condition for inflation to develop.) However, that in itself does not explain much, unless we know why the overexpansion is allowed to occur in any given case.

In some historical instances the overexpansion was clearly caused by foolish or irresponsible decisions by governments, or failure to grasp the potential for the growth of credit-based money, or other policy mistakes. More commonly it was the pressures of war finance or some other sudden and urgent demand, with which more orthodox financial policies either could not cope quickly enough or could not cope adequately.

But, why should responsible governments with efficient modern tax structures and banking systems permit the overexpansion of money in normal peacetime conditions, knowing full well that it spells inflation? That is what needs explaining about inflation in the postwar era.

What is sometimes called "the validation thesis" seems to make use of the greatest amount of common ground to be found among various schools of thought on the causes of today's inflations. It is based on two points. First, it acknowledges that the overexpansion of money is an essential feature of inflation. Second, virtually all governments nowadays are committed to supporting a high level of output and employment; that support is now badly compromized by efforts to suppress inflation, but public opinion will no longer tolerate its complete abandonment, because of the high social costs. Hence the authorities are compelled to *validate* a significant portion of all incipient price increases by increasing the money supply and money incomes.

Today's inflations are therefore categorically different from those of the past, because of this combination of circumstances. They are not caused by weakness or incompetence of administration, nor by a surge of private spending financed by an inadequately-controlled banking system, nor by a sudden increase in urgently-demanded government expenditures pressing against an insufficiently-elastic revenue system, as was the case with most inflations in the past. Rather, they are caused by the need for socially-responsible officials to make a difficult choice between two equally-desirable social objectives: less inflation, or less unemployment.

But, why do upward pressures on prices develop in the first place? This is where differences in opinion among economists are most notable.

The classic explanation used to be what we now call the "demand-pull" version, which focuses on the overexpansion of the money supply without much concern for why it occurs. A number of fresh versions have been offered since World War II, and much ingenuity has been shown in devising economic models that formalize them. Some emphasize cost-push factors (in contrast to demand-pull), others stress the rôle of expectations, or structural factors (such as differences in productivity between the industrial and the service sectors), or autonomous shifts in demand or supply functions. They offer useful insights into some aspects of inflation, but none has won general acceptance as a comprehensive explanation. Only a few attempt to explain the simultaneous appearance of unemployment.

Lacking any version that can claim wide acceptance within the economics profession, a pragmatic explanation can be fashioned on the basis of the "bid" and "asked" prices found in organized markets for securities and commodities, as briefly described in section 1 of Chapter 11.

The same principles apply to any sale-and-purchase transaction, whether it is a merchant selling physical goods, a doctor or other professional selling a service, or an individual selling his or her labour to an employer. No trading takes place until some buyer accepts some seller's asking price, or some seller accepts some buyer's bid price. *Realized prices* thus depend on market conditions. If you are a seller and conditions are favourable, you may easily get your asking price—and may then wonder if you should have asked for more. But if they are unfavourable you may not be able to find an offer you are prepared to accept at all.

As an individual, your welfare is strongly bound up with your money income. You can add to the total real income of the community as a whole by working harder, turning out more goods per hour or getting more done, but your own real income may not increase one iota—the immediate benefit may go to your employer or to someone else. If you can get more money for the same amount of work, however, then your real income will rise almost exactly in proportion; any conceivable increase in your personal money income can add only infinitesimally to inflation. Thus we all have an incentive to push our asking prices ever higher, so we all share the responsibility for inflationary pressures.

The authorities will of course be reluctant to let the money supply increase enough to satisfy all these asking prices. Some output or potential output will go unsold, production will be cut back, and unemployment will increase. But asking prices may continue to creep up despite these pressures, because costs will be rising as previous price increases at earlier stages of production work their way through the economy, overhead costs must be spread over a smaller volume of sales, and interest expenses will probably be rising. At best it may be a long time before realized prices ease materially, if they ever do, since those who still have jobs will find that their money incomes are rising more or less in step with prices.

You may object that this seems to explain too much. If that is really how the market system operates, why did prices stay as stable as they did for the first postwar decade?

Persistent fears of relapse into chronic depression undoubtedly had a sobering effect on everyone's asking prices at first, but these fears were gradually replaced by growing confidence in the new system. Growing wealth and improved social-security benefits have raised most people's bargaining ability. And rightly so—a major function of accumulated savings is to provide a cushion against adversity, and the very purpose of social-security systems is to provide a safety net against economic misfortunes. Then it gradually became clear that the authorities could not crack down too hard on prices, so price demands got bolder and bolder.

Also, policy mistakes by major governments (and by their economic advisers) certainly played major rôles. The U.S.A.'s decision in the 1960's to fight the Vietnam War without a tax increase—to have butter as well as guns—has often been cited as a major factor in the subsequent rise not only of U.S. prices but also of world prices, thanks to the dollar's key rôle as the major international currency.

Another example was the continued insistence on low market interest rates as an article of almost religious faith in many countries, even after it became clear that persistent inflation was a fact of life and was actually making some real interest rates negative. Interest rates are prices, and as such have important rôles to play in a money-and-market economy. Artificially low rates induced spending on projects that were not basically economic; that added to immediate inflationary pressures, and eventually caused great hardship on borrowers when the inevitable adjustments occurred.

As well, the fact that government policies almost everywhere continued to be soft on inflation had serious international repercussions. As will be noted in Chapter 16, it gave rise to persistently divergent national price trends, which led to the collapse of the Bretton Woods System between 1971 and 1973.

In turn, the abandonment of the attempt to maintain normally-fixed exchange rates had feedback effects on the domestic inflations of the individual nations. Plot price indexes for just about any country over the postwar period, and you will find a sharp break in the trend line between those two years. There can be no denying that the shift to a regime of generally fluctuating rates greatly reduced balance-of-payments disciplines on domestic policies.

Chapter 14

The Monetarist Counter-Revolution

Fatherly Advice: This chapter deals with policy issues that are both complex and controversial. Be prepared to suspend judgement, and don't allow yourself to jump to premature conclusions. The opinions expressed or implied here may not be shared by other economists, particularly those in section 5.

1. Monetarists and Monetarism.

"Monetarism" is a term used to identify the views of a group of economists that centres on the University of Chicago and on the person of Professor Milton Friedman. It was first applied in 1969 by Karl Brunner, one of the group, but the views themselves have been in continuous evolution since at least the 1920's. Monetarists are at pains to emphasize their links to the quantity theory described in section 7 of Chapter 10, of which Irving Fisher was the leading North American exponent early in the 20th century. Prior to 1969 they usually referred to themselves as "quantity theorists", in deference to this link. However, their views have come to differ materially from the old quantity theory.

There are differences of opinion among monetarists, of course, just as there are among adherents to Keynesian-type analysis. For the most part we will limit ourselves to Friedman's views, however, since he is the principal monetarist, and this chapter must be kept within reasonable bounds. Not surprisingly, his views have changed somewhat over the years, in response to changing conditions and the results of further work.

Monetarism (or the new quantity theory, whichever you wish to call it) appears to have begun primarily as a criticism of certain aspects of early models of the sort discussed in Chapters 11 and 13, but it has evolved into an alternative to those models as an analytical framework for deriving policy decisions. While it tends to emphasize its disagreements with them on the theory of money, these disagreements are mainly of interest to monetary specialists. The really fundamental difference between the two analytical frameworks is one of basic economic philosophy. Keynesian-type models see a necessary interventionist rôle for governments; monetarists are firm believers in *laissez-faire* principles.

In the monetarists' view, the private sector of the economy is inherently stable, and a full-employment equilibrium is restored automatically (and apparently quite quickly) after any disturbance. They assert that unemployment is largely voluntary, and that it will always return to its "natural" level (again, apparently, fairly promptly). They conclude that under most circumstances discretionary intervention will do more harm than good; they particularly oppose fiscal-policy interventions. Their principal policy recommendation is that the money supply should be allowed to expand at a fairly steady rate, in order to accommodate the growth in output and population and to ensure relatively stable prices.

Friedman himself is well-known as a believer in a rather extreme *laissez-faire* philosophy. His economic writings cover many fields besides the theory of money, and many other aspects of money besides monetarism. Following a University of Chicago tradition, he is a strong advocate of the proposition that adherence to automatic rules should replace reliance on the discretionary decisions of the monetary and fiscal authorities.

Monetarists place great emphasis on empirical work, and they have thereby injected some much-needed realism into the study of the theory of money and monetary policy. In this they are following the earlier traditions of the German Historical School and the American Institutional School.

There is also distinct evidence of the influence of the Austrian School of economic thought on monetarism. The Austrian School was one of the originators of the marginalist analysis in the last third of the 19th century, which is the foundation of microeconomics as we know it today. Twentieth-century members of this school have included Ludwig von Mises and Friederick A. von Hayek, whose views were pretty right-wing. Hayek's *The Road to Serfdom* (1945) stirred up considerable debate at the time. He argued that modern democracies are travelling a road that will lead to fascism, because since about 1870 they have reversed the older liberal trend, abandoned the individualistic tradition that created Western civilization, and embraced socialism and planning. In subsequent years he wrote further along similar lines.

It should be noted that the essence of the *laissez-faire* remedy for depressed output and employment is for real wages to decline until the costs of production fall far enough to make new investment in productive capacity profitable again. To be blunt about it, this means forcing wage-and-salary-earners to underbid one another in unrestrained competition for existing jobs. The labour market would then "clear", involuntary unemployment would end, and recovery would begin.

Unfortunately, declining wages and salaries means a declining spending stream, so total sales (and total output) might have to fall pretty low before things turned around. However, it is not clear whether monetarists as a group, or any monetarist, would be prepared to see the process carried to that extreme, nor how long they really think it would take to reach a new equilibrium after a serious disturbance.

2. The Counter-Revolution.

A brief and non-technical but incomplete description of monetarism is to be found in the First Wincott Memorial Lecture, which Milton Friedman gave in London in 1970. It was published as Occasional Paper 33 of the Institute for Economic Affairs, under the title *The Counter-Revolution in Monetary Theory*. His justification for the title was the assertion that, as Keynes had made the revolution against the old quantity theory of money in the 1930's, so the monetarists had made a counter-revolution against Keynesianism. He then remarked:

> A counter-revolution, whether in politics or in science, never restores the initial position. It always produces a situation that has some similarity to the initial one but is also strongly influenced by the intervening revolution. That is certainly true of monetarism which has benefited much from Keynes's work.

By the time of his lecture Keynesian demand-management techniques were everywhere in trouble. Bursts of inflation in many countries had led to substantial retrenchment on employment-maintaining commitments, and the depressing combination of inflation with unemployment had become evident, though neither was yet on the scale faced subsequently. In the international sphere the Bretton Woods System was experiencing serious problems, which came to a head soon after.

Lacking any better solution, many governments had already given priority to combatting inflation, and had embarked on restrictive fiscal and monetary policies. Monetarists did not necessarily accept these measures as proper applications of their doctrines, but they were clearly influenced in large measure by monetarist thinking. As a practical matter, therefore, monetarism was already in the ascendancy over Keynesianism. A substantial defection of professional economists from the

Keynesian to the monetarist camp had also occurred, which gathered further momentum in subsequent years.

Most of the lecture was devoted to a review of the preceding 40 years of U.S. economic history from a monetarist perspective. Then followed a section entitled "Key Propositions of Monetarism", which may be summarized as follows:

1. "There is a consistent though not precise relation between the rate of growth of the quantity of money and the rate of growth of nominal income" [i.e. income measured in money, not real income].

2. "On the average, a change in the rate of monetary growth produces a change in the rate of growth of nominal income about six to nine months later."

3. "The changed rate of growth of nominal income typically shows up first in output and hardly at all in prices.... On the average, the effect on prices comes about six to nine months after the effect on income and output, so the total delay between a change in monetary growth and a change in the rate of inflation averages something like 12-18 months."

4. "In the short run, ... monetary changes affect primarily output. Over decades, ... [they affect] primarily prices. What happens to output depends on real factors ...."

5. "It follows from the propositions I have so far stated that *inflation is always and everywhere a monetary phenomenon* in the sense that it is and can be produced only by a more rapid increase in the quantity of money than in output. However, there are many different possible reasons for monetary growth, including gold discoveries, financing government spending, and financing private spending."

6. "More rapid monetary growth at first tends to lower interest rates. But later on, as it raises spending and stimulates price inflation, it also produces a rise in the demand for loans which will tend to raise interest rates. In addition, rising prices introduce a discrepancy between real and nominal interest rates. This ... explains why monetarists insist that interest rates are a highly misleading guide to monetary policy."

In a final section entitled "Concluding Cautions" Friedman observes that some monetarists believe that monetary policy can be used to "fine tune" the economy, but he does not. Because of the lags he has mentioned, he believes that such discretionary changes do more harm than good. "A steady rate of monetary growth at a moderate level can provide a framework under which a country can have little inflation and much growth. It will not produce perfect stability ... but it can make an important contribution to a stable economic society."

It is interesting to note that an early concern of monetarists was to insist that money is important—that is what explains the adoption of the term "monetarism". No serious economist had really said categorically that "money doesn't matter", but some professing Keynesians had come rather close—they had pretty well given up on monetary policy under any and all circumstances. As we have noted before, many economists and policymakers had espoused low interest rates as a matter of unquestioning faith, and persisted in that opinion even after it became clear that inflation was actually making some real interest rates negative.

It is also true that in the concluding chapter of *The General Theory* Keynes spoke cheerfully of "the euthanasia of the rentier", and looked forward to the indefinite continuation of low interest rates. But even in the midst of this passage there are a number of cautionary qualifications, including the proviso "that we do not stimulate [investment] in this way beyond the point which corresponds to full employment".

In any case, and regardless of what he himself said or thought, there is nothing in the logic of Keynes's analysis that denies a useful rôle to interest-rate policy in encouraging capital formation under favourable conditions, as when there are unemployed resources and profit expectations are marginal, or in discouraging it when demand is excessive. It is really impotent only when the prospect of a profit on new capital goods is negligible.

As it turns out, however, monetarists themselves assign only a limited rôle to monetary policy. One of their important contributions to practical policymaking has been the documentation of the lags between an easing or tightening of monetary policy and the impact on output and prices, as Friedman reported in his Wincott lecture. This leads him to deny any short-term function to monetary policy and relegate it to promoting a stable long-run trend in prices and output.

3. Friedman's Early Views.

We may start a fuller account of Friedman's views with a reference to "The Quantity Theory of Money—A Restatement". This is his introductory chapter to *Studies in the Quantity Theory of Money*, a collection of research studies published in 1956. He linked his restated theory to a more subtle version of the old quantity theory that was sustained by an oral tradition at the University of Chicago through the 1930's and 1940's. It was a theoretical approach which insisted that money matters, and that sound short-term analysis must consider the reasons people are willing to hold the existing nominal quantity of money.

The revised theory is in the first instance a theory of the demand for money, not a theory of output or money income or the price level. Money is one kind of asset or one way of holding wealth, a capital good that yields useful services. The demand for it can be analyzed in the same way as the demand for a consumption service, and depends on three major sets of factors: the income and the total wealth of the holder ("the budget constraint"), the costs and benefits of holding money compared to holding other forms of wealth, and the tastes and preferences of the holder. The theory was thereupon developed in considerable technical detail.

Friedman then raised the question of what it means to say that someone is or is not a "quantity theorist" (read "a monetarist"). He noted that most economists could accept the general lines of his analysis, but that there would be fundamental differences of opinion over its importance for understanding economic activity. He then offered three identifying points.

The first of Friedman's identifying points was that "The quantity theorist accepts the empirical hypothesis that the demand for money is highly stable—more stable than functions such as the consumption function that are offered as alternative key relations". Not only that it is stable, but also that it plays a vital rôle in determining such things as the level of money income or of prices. The second and third points were that a quantity theorist rejects two specific conclusions about the demand for money that are espoused by some Keynesians, but are mainly of technical interest and need not detain us here.

Friedman was elected president of the American Economic Association in 1967, and he devoted most of his presidential address to monetary policy. He began by listing what he thought monetary policy can *not* do. First, it can not peg market interest rates for more than a very limited period. Attempting to keep them below their "natural" level means expanding the money supply, which does initially reduce market interest rates, but then sets forces in motion that expand spending, income, loan demand, and perhaps prices, and thus ultimately raise market interest rates. (The idea of a "natural" interest rate, distinct from the market rate and set by "real" economic forces, has long been accepted by most economists.) If the public comes to expect that prices will continue to rise, market interest rates will definitely rise above what they would otherwise have been.

Second, Friedman argued that monetary policy can not peg the rate of unemployment for more than very limited periods. Exactly paralleling the natural rate of interest, he introduces a "natural" rate of unemployment, and argues that any departure from it will tend to set forces in motion that will restore it. In his presidential address he identifies it with equilibrium in the structure of real wage rates. A lower rate of unemployment implies an excess demand for labour, so real wage rates will tend to rise; a higher level implies an excess supply of labour, so real wage rates will tend to fall. (In later writing he identified the natural rate with the "non-accelerating rate of inflation": attempts to reduce the actual unemployment rate below the natural rate will merely result in a higher rate of inflation.)

More generally, Friedman asserted that the monetary authorities can not effectively peg real quantities—real interest rates, the rate of unemployment, real income, the real quantity of money (i.e. the quantity of goods and services the public's cash balances will buy), or the like. An increase in the rate of growth of the money supply will temporarily increase the rate of growth of real output, decrease market interest rates, and decrease the unemployment rate, but these effects then vanish and leave only a permanent increase in the rate of inflation. (At least, that is what he was saying into the 1970's; later he seems to have become less certain of even a temporary effect on output and employment, and some other monetarists reject it altogether.)

What Friedman said the monetary authorities *can* do is peg nominal quantities—the money supply by any given definition, the exchange rate, the price level, and that sort of thing. Monetary policy can prevent money itself from becoming a source of disturbance (for example, by bringing on an unnecessary deflation). It can provide a stable background for the economy and ensure that the average level of prices will behave in a known (and preferably stable) way. Finally, it can help offset *major* disturbances within an economy for other reasons, such as resisting an excessive bout of spending by temporarily raising interest rates, or easing a substantial shift of resources by a higher rate of growth of the money supply than would otherwise be desirable. However, Friedman was doubtful that such uses could be kept within proper limits.

Turning to how monetary policy should be conducted in the light of these limitations, Friedman first concluded that the money stock is the best immediate instrument to use. (He felt that the particular definition of money to choose is less important than that one be chosen.) He then concluded that relatively stable prices in the future will require a fairly steady growth in the money supply, to accommodate the growth in output and population—a proposal he had previously made to a U.S. congressional committee in 1958, and was to repeat in his Wincott lecture. This would not achieve perfect price stability, but because of the uncertain lags in the response to monetary policy he felt that any attempt to offset other disturbing factors might make things worse instead of better. (In 1958 he had added a second-best proposal: it would be a major improvement if the monetary authorities were to avoid wide swings in the rate of growth of the stock of money.)

Three key elements in this summary of Friedman's views must be stressed, for they appear at different points in the story and their combined significance may easily be overlooked: (1) the emphasis on the links among money, income, and wealth; (2) the insistence on the stability of the demand for money; and (3) the insistence that basic economic decisions are based primarily on real rather than nominal comparisons.

This combination leads logically to the monetarist conclusion that changes in the money supply do indeed have powerful effects not only on spending patterns but also on the composition of asset holdings, and that "natural" forces will always overcome discretionary attempts to manipulate the money supply. For example, an arbitrary increase in the money supply will temporarily upset the balance among money and other assets, among various interest rates and other asset returns, between the nominal value of the money supply and nominal income, and between the apparent attractions of work and leisure, but the public will act to restore its desired relationships in real terms.

Mention should also be made of a long study of U.S. monetary history by the National Bureau of Economic Research. The first results were published in 1963 under the title *A Monetary History of the United States, 1867-1960*, by Milton Friedman and Anna J. Schwartz. The authors conclude that the evidence supports many major monetarist beliefs, such as the stability of monetary relationships and the dominant rôle of money in the long run. Particular interest attaches to a long chapter (Chapter 7) about the U.S. monetary experience between 1929 and 1933, designed to refute the assertion that monetary policy was bound to be ineffective under such conditions.

The major theme of Chapter 7 of *A Monetary History* is that inappropriate policies followed by the Federal Reserve System (the U.S.A.'s central bank), not inherent deficiencies of monetary policy, were to blame for the severity of The Great Depression in the U.S.A., which had serious repercussions on the rest of the trading world. The substance of the authors' criticism is that the Fed (as it is familiarly known) failed to effectively perform the lender-of-last-resort function that is to be expected of any central bank in such circumstances.

The failures of the Fed that the authors criticize were errors of omission rather than commission: there is no suggestion that any bank was improperly denied rediscount facilities (that is, the ability to sell sound assets to the Fed in order to meet its obligations). But the Fed did not take the initiative, as it should have, to ensure that the financial system as a whole had adequate liquidity. The authors argue that more skillful actions would have greatly moderated, and perhaps prevented, the sharp and prolonged contraction of the money supply. Given monetarist beliefs about the rôle of money in the economy, this implies greatly reducing the severity of the depression, if not quickly producing full recovery.

4. Later Monetarist Views.

Monetarist views have changed somewhat as time has passed, and some offshoots of monetarist thinking have appeared. They differ on certain points of doctrine, but their prescriptions are broadly similar.

Two main streams of monetarism have developed, sometimes called "Monetarism Mark I" and "Monetarism Mark II". The Mark I version, to which Friedman adheres, differs from the views already summarized mainly in that it accepts a short-run trade-off between inflation and unemployment. The three key propositions already identified are retained: (1) the private sector is inherently stable; (2) a change in the rate of growth of the money supply initially alters output and employment, but in the long run this real effect vanishes; and (3) long-run policy rules for monetary and fiscal policies are preferable to demand management. However, a new proposition, which was perhaps implicit before, is now made explicit: (4) any rate of growth of the money supply is compatible with a full-employment equilibrium, but different rates produce different rates of inflation.

Monetarism Mark II is sometimes called "the new classical economics". It rejects even a temporary effect on output and employment from a change in the rate of monetary growth. The difference focuses on the "rational expectations" assumption—that economic operators make no systematic errors and rationally project the future on the basis of all the available facts, including a relevant economic theory. The net result is that there can not be even temporary departures from equilibrium. "Full information" becomes the means of achieving an economic optimum.

Advocates of "supply-side" economics were a somewhat more distant offshoot of monetarism. Their name suggests that they would attack inflation by raising the output of goods and services available to the consumer rather than by reducing demand — presumably by reducing costs or increasing productivity or improving work incentives, rather than by reducing demand. Instead, however, they looked rather narrowly at the government sector, and sought to reduce both government spending and taxes. The argument was that taxes were so high as to be counterproductive, and that lower tax *rates* would produce more tax *revenues* because they would restore work incentives.

The supply-side prescription was that government spending should be reduced, partly by cutting down on social services and partly by reducing government controls over business. The budget was to be balanced, or brought more nearly into balance, thereby releasing market funds to finance private investment and increased employment. Early in his career President Reagan introduced a phased reduction of taxes in the U.S.A. as a direct application of this philosophy, but the net effect was to increase the deficit instead of to reduce it.

5. Commentary.

Monetarists have made major contributions to economic analysis and to practical policymaking. They have helped to discredit some of the more extreme policy prescriptions that purported to be derived from Keynesian analysis, such as the almost religious belief in low-interest-rates-at-any-cost. They have made positive additions to the understanding of monetary affairs, such as the demonstration that there are likely to be major lags before monetary policy can be effective. These and many other contributions must be applauded by all who wish to promote sound theories and policies as instruments for the public good, rather than subvert them to support some preconceived model of the economy. Nevertheless there are a great many differences between monetarists and their critics that still need to be resolved.

In evaluating the present position of monetarism, it is important to note that its ascendancy over Keynesianism has been achieved in the field of practical policymaking and not as an intellectual defeat by one of the other. Monetarists do have an answer to the inflation-unemployment dilemma, unpalatable though it may be: give priority to eradicating inflation, and ignore the unemployment, which they claim is largely voluntary anyway. Non-monetarists remain convinced that there are logical weaknesses in monetarist analysis and prescriptions, and that there is still substantial validity in Keynesian-type analysis; but they have not come up with a credible alternative solution to the inflation-unemployment dilemma, so they no longer get much of a hearing from practical policymakers.

An important aspect of the monetarist counter-revolution has been the assembling of a great deal of statistical information, and the carrying out of empirical testing of various monetarist hypotheses. Monetarists believe that they have been able to verify a number of their beliefs in this way. However, drawing valid conclusions from statistical comparisons is a tricky business. Monetarists as a group are quite as well aware of the limitations and pitfalls of these procedures as anyone else, and have tried conscientiously to avoid errors, but in a number of important cases their critics are not persuaded that they have succeeded.

Monetarists are surely right in asserting that real economic forces "fight back" and tend to restore the market interest rate to its "natural" level in the face of any disturbance, including the intervention of the monetary authorities. Surely, too, any *major* change in the rate of growth of money will ultimately have more effect on changes in prices than in output and employment. But those two points, singly or in combination, do not discredit the belief that sensitive day-to-day adjustments of monetary policy can promote the smooth operation of the financial system and of the economy as a whole. At least *some* monetarists (not including Friedman) agree that monetary policy can be effective in the short run.

The criticisms by Friedman and Schwartz of the U.S. Federal Reserve System's actions in the 1930's undoubtedly have considerable validity. The Fed's failure to act aggressively to provide liquidity under the circumstances was a derogation from traditional central-banking practices. As reported in a famous passage in Walter Bagehot's *Lombard Street*, the Bank of England learned in 1825 how to deal with such a problem. According to subsequent testimony by a Bank spokesman, "We lent ... by every possible means consistent with the safety of the Bank, and we were not on some occasions over-nice. Seeing the dreadful state the public were in, we rendered every assistance in our power." The panic had promptly subsided.

More sensitive actions by the Fed would surely have eased the U.S.A.'s banking crisis in 1933, but of course it is impossible to tell for sure whether that would have materially shortened or alleviated the depression. In other countries, where more appropriate central-bank policies were followed, monetary policy proved no more successful in stimulating recovery.

Incidentally, however, the Fed's failure to act decisively at that time is no doubt the explanation of the persistence of excess reserves in the U.S. banking system for many years thereafter, which has puzzled most observers. That would be a logical reaction for bankers in troubled times, when their central bank had failed to act resolutely to combat past crises.

A more fundamental problem relates to the very basis of monetarist analysis. Monetarists merely *assume* that something very like the long-run-equilibrium position of the model of pure competition is fairly quickly approached in the real world. Despite the emphasis they usually put on empirical verification, they do not appear to have attempted it in this case. (Remember the emphasis in section 2 of Chapter 1 on the link between assumptions and conclusions.)

The Keynesian philosophy does not deny that there may indeed be forces tending to bring about a full-employment equilibrium in the long run. However, it stresses the historical evidence that they operate very slowly and painfully, and it argues that there are things that can be done in the here and now to speed up the adjustment process and to reduce the pain.

Their basic assumptions are particularly important for monetarists' views on unemployment. When identified with a long-run-equilibrium position for the economy as a whole, their natural rate of unemployment seems remarkably like the minimum level of frictional and seasonal unemployment that most other economists easily recognize. Now add the assumption that equilibrium is rather quickly attained after any disturbance, and the obvious conclusion is that the actual unemployment rate can never be far from the natural rate. The net effect, therefore, is to rationalize whatever unemployment rate happens to exist at any given time (or the rate that would exist if official interventions to influence it were abandoned) as being the inescapable minimum rate.

These same assumptions are also involved in reaching the conclusion that most unemployment is voluntary.

A clear example of voluntary unemployment is search unemployment, which refers to people who find themselves without a job for any reason but who will decline any offer at a wage or salary much below the going rate for the skills and experience they possess, in the expectation of finding something better without undue delay. Typical involuntary unemployment, in contrast, consists of workers who face too few vacancies (there is excess supply of labour), and who have little prospect of being offered a job (even at wages materially lower than the going rates) unless the demand for labour increases. Intermediate categories may also be identified, of partly voluntary and partly involuntary unemployment; and members of the higher categories may be pushed into lower categories if their search proves fruitless.

Involuntary unemployment is typical of a situation characterized by inadequate aggregate demand, though it could also be the result of unduly high wage demands. The minimum frictional and seasonal unemployment associated with a full-employment equilibrium may be identified with search unemployment of modest duration. By assuming that long-run-equilibrium is quickly attained, therefore, monetarists are assuming away all involuntary unemployment and leaving little but search unemployment. Hence their conclusion that most unemployment is voluntary.

Do monetarists really believe that most of today's unemployed would refuse a job that was compatible with their skills and experience, even if it were at or only slightly below the going rate? If they do believe that, do you?

Or do monetarists really mean that wage-and-salary-earners should be forced to engage in unrestrained competition for existing jobs, until wages fall sufficiently to make new investment profitable again and to "clear" the labour market in *laissez-faire* fashion?

And is monetarism really a counter-revolution, that has permanently replaced Keynesianism, except for such elements of it as it may choose to incorporate in a new order? Or is it a rebellion, which will force material changes in Keynesianism but will not overcome it?

The distinction between a revolution (or a counter-revolution) and a rebellion is that the former is successful in overthrowing the previously recognized authority and replacing it with another, whereas in the end the latter fails to do so. But a rebellion, even though it ultimately fails, may also bring about changes and reforms in the old order; in this respect the two differ in degree rather than in kind. Whether monetarism finally proves to be a rebellion or a revolution will depend ultimately on the ability of Keynesians to devise a solution to the inflation-unemployment dilemma that is more satisfactory than the monetarist solution.

However, you should not make up your mind about monetarism solely on the basis of a description by someone who is obviously opposed to it, and perhaps biased. First, read some of the writings of convinced monetarists and see what you make of them. A few suggestions are included in the reading list at the end of this chapter. They range from the popular to the rather advanced.

Suggested Readings

Friedman, Milton. *The Counter-Revolution in Monetary Theory.* London; Institute of Economic Affairs, Occasional Paper 33, 1970. [A good non-technical introduction.]

―――――. "The Quantity Theory of Money—A Restatement", in *Studies in the Quantity Theory of Money*, M. Friedman (ed.). Chicago; University of Chicago Press, 1956. [Technical, except from section 18 on.]

―――――. "The Role of Monetary Policy", *The American Economic Review*, vol. 58, no.1, March 1968, pp. 1-17. [Presidential address, December 1967; non-technical.]

Millon Friedman and Anna J. Schwartz. *A Monetary History of the United States, 1867-1960.* Princeton N.J.; Princeton University Press for the National Bureau of Economic Research, 1963. [Moderately difficult.]

―――――. *The Great Contraction, 1929-1933* [a reprint of Chapter 7 of *A Monetary History of the United States, 1867-1960*]. Princeton N.J.; Princeton

University Press for the National Bureau of Economic Research, 1965. [Largely non-technical.]

Frisch, Helmut. *Theories of Inflation.* Cambridge; Cambridge University Press, 1983. [Mostly technical, but with simplified introductory summaries of most chapters.]

Hoover, Kevin D. "Two Types of Monetarism", *Journal of Economic Literature*, vol. XXII, no. 1, March 1984, pp. 58-76. [Moderately difficult.]

Laidler, David E.W. *The Demand for Money: Theory and Evidence*, 3rd ed. New York; Harper & Row, 1985. [Moderately difficult.]

Part Four

International Economic Relations

Chapter 15

Trade between Countries

1. The Theory of Comparative Advantage.

For the most part it is just a figure of speech to say that nations trade with one another; sometimes a national government will indeed buy or sell abroad on behalf of its residents, but usually it is individuals in one country that trade with individuals in other countries. Basically, the reason they do so is the same as the reason they trade with other residents of their home country, namely because specialization and the division of tasks makes for greater productivity. Both partners (or all participants) gain because they can share in the increase in total output thus brought about, compared to what they could produce if they tried to be self-sufficient in everything.

The most obvious example is when each country produces something the other can not possibly duplicate. If one country has iron ore but no coal, and another has coal but no iron, it is clear that both can benefit by exchanging one product for the other. Almost as obvious are cases in which both countries can in fact produce the same commodities, but at glaringly different costs. It is possible to grow bananas and other tropical fruits in hothouses in northern climates, and to grow temperate-zone crops in tropical lowlands, but the costs will be high or the quality low or both. Regions with outstanding natural resources, like the forested areas of North America or Scandinavia, or with outstanding suitability for certain crops, like the grain-growing potential of the Russian steppes or the plains of North and South America, can be expected to specialize in those products and trade them for their other needs.

However, a substantial amount of world trade takes place among countries with skills and natural resources that seem surprisingly similar—among equally industrialized countries, for example. It turns out that *comparative advantage* is more important than *absolute advantage* in determining the benefits to be obtained from trade. It may be that one of two trading countries has superior productivity in all traded products (perhaps because of superior natural resources, perhaps because it has accumulated more and better capital equipment, perhaps because its workers are more highly skilled). Even so, both countries can benefit from trade. The first should specialize in that product or those products for which it has the *greatest* advantage, the second should specialize in those for which it has the *least disadvantage*.

In order to avoid having to deal with too many complications at once, we will use a simple example of two hypothetical countries that trade in only two commodities. (They may each produce other commodities too, but consume them entirely at home.) We will also speak of *relative* prices rather than *absolute* prices, i.e. we will use one commodity as a standard in which to measure the value of the other, instead of using money as you might expect us to do.

Classical economists liked use relative prices in order to emphasize the essential unimportance of money and to focus on the "real" relationships that underlie most economic analysis, but our reasons are somewhat different. We do want to emphasize "real" factors all right, but we don't mean to suggest that money is unimportant; we just want to avoid the confusion that can arise when you mix the two. In this case the risk of confusion arises because the two countries will normally have two different moneys, linked by an exchange rate, and we don't need that additional complication just now.

Let's call the two countries Redland and Blueland, and suppose that until now they have not traded at all but have maintained high tariff walls to protect their domestic markets. Now, someone persuades them both of the advantages of trade, and they agree to try it out with cloth and wheat, but as yet neither is willing to lend to or borrow from the other: all transactions are on an immediate barter basis. We may also suppose they are of about equal size, are industrialized to about the same degree, and enjoy about the same levels of income and wealth, just to emphasize that trade can be beneficial between similar countries as well as dissimilar. However, Redland happens to have better resources for producing both cloth and wheat.

In Redland one hour of labour will produce 4 units of cloth or 4 units of wheat, so the price of a unit of cloth has been 1.00 units of wheat (or the price of a unit of wheat has been 1.00 units of cloth). Resources can be readily transferred between these industries but not others, at constant cost; the maximum output of wheat is 400 units, of cloth 400 units. In Blueland one hour of labour will produce only 1.00 units of cloth or 2.00 units of wheat, so the price of a unit of cloth has been 2.00 units of wheat (or the price of wheat has been 0.50 units of cloth); the maximum output of wheat is 500 units, of cloth 250 units.[1] What will be the new price structure after trade begins, how much of each commodity will each country produce, and what will be the pattern of trade?

We may say at once that Redland will produce only cloth and Blueland only wheat. The clue lies in the fact that one hour of work in Redland produces four times as much cloth as in Blueland but only twice as much wheat. Redland has a comparative advantage in cloth (i.e. a greater absolute advantage), Blueland has a comparative advantage in wheat (i.e. a lesser absolute disadvantage).

To see why this is so, and how both countries benefit from trade, we may make use of the transformation functions or production frontiers and consumption-possibility curves we introduced in section 2 of Chapter 10. Before trade begins their consumption possibilities are, of course, limited to their production frontiers.

Redland's production frontier is represented by the straight line *AB* in Part A of Figure 15-1, which has a slope of 1 (the marginal cost of a unit of wheat is 1.00 units of cloth at any level of output). Blueland's production frontier is represented by the line *DE* in Part B, which has a slope of 2 (the marginal cost of wheat is 0.50 units of cloth at any level of output). In each country the two products will exchange at their marginal costs, and the price line will be identical with the production frontier.

We don't have enough information to tell us exactly where on these frontiers actual pre-trade output (and consumption) lay, but we know from Chapter 3 that they would be at whatever point made the marginal utilities of cloth and wheat proportionate to their prices, that is 1 to 1 in Redland and 2 to 1 in Blueland. Let's say that means points *C* and *F* respectively—150 units of cloth and 250 of wheat in Redland, 175 of cloth and 150 of wheat in Blueland.[2] World production totals were 325 units of cloth and 400 units of wheat.

When trade opens, consumption patterns and prices in both countries will change until marginal utilities match a new world price structure; if prices were not the same in both countries (neglecting the costs of transportation between them),

---

[1] You may of course interpret the units of output as actually being multiples of some basic unit—perhaps 1,000 or 100,000 or 1,000,000 kilograms or metres or whatever. We need small numbers to keep the diagrams compact, but large numbers to give us small marginal changes. The figures used have been chosen with a view to making the diagrams readable, not for realism.

[2] Actually, as noted in footnote 1 on page 158, there are graphic techniques for illustrating the relative marginal utilities of two (or more) goods, and thereby locating the points *C* and *F* in the diagrams. However, these techniques introduce additional complexities that are not really necessary here. They just amount to a more complicated way of saying that the marginal utilities of wheat and cloth must be proportional to their prices if the position is one of stable equilibrium.

arbitragers would buy in one and sell in the other until the difference disappeared. But, what will the new price structure turn out to be?

Well, the new price of a unit of cloth will not be more than Redland's price of 1.00 units of wheat (the slope of *AB* in Figure 15-1A, or *DH* in Figure 15-1B), because producers in Redland could continue to "transform" local wheat into local cloth at that price by shifting productive resources, and would spurn the export sales. And it won't be less than 0.50 units of cloth (the slope of *DE* in Figure 15-1B, or *GB* in Figure 15-1A), because producers in Blueland would continue to "transform" local wheat into local cloth at that price in preference to imports.

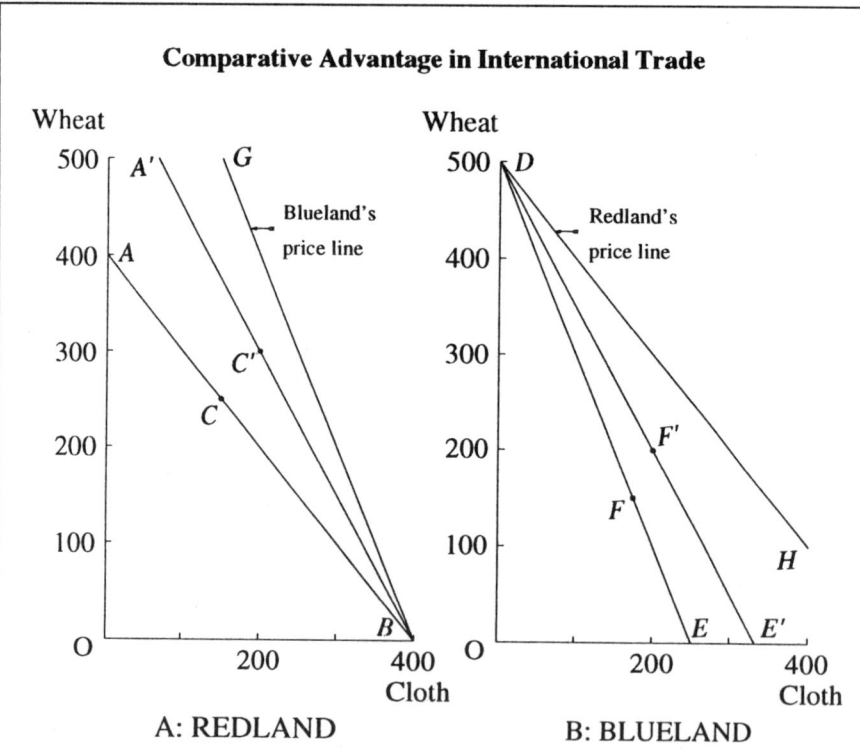

Figure 15-1. Redland's production frontier is the line *AB* in Part A, Blueland's is *DE* in Part B. Before trade opens, both production and consumption in Redland will be at (say) *C*, 150 units of cloth and 250 units of wheat, and one unit of cloth will trade for 1.50 units of wheat. The Blueland production and consumption will be (say) at *F*, 175 units of cloth and 150 units of wheat and one unit of cloth will trade for 2.00 units of wheat. World output of cloth is 325 units, of wheat 400 units. After trade opens a new equilibrium will be reached—say, one unit of cloth will trade for 1.5 units of wheat in both countries, as shown by the lines *A'* in Part A and *DE"* in Part B. Redland specializes in cloth and produces 400 units, Blueland specializes in wheat and produces 500 units; world output rises to 400 units of cloth and 500 units of wheat, so both countries can consume more of both products.

We can also say that, if output and consumption in (say) Blueland were very much smaller than in Redland, the new price could not be very different from the old Redland price—Blueland would sell part of its output of wheat in order to satisfy its cloth needs at a price of 1.00 units of wheat instead of 2.00 per unit of cloth, and scoop out most of the gains from trade. (Sometimes it pays to be small!)

In any case, however, the new price ratio in the now-internationalized market (and in each country too) must be proportionate to the new marginal utilities of cloth and wheat, just as the old price ratios were in the separate markets in the individual countries before trade began. Since we have said that they are comparable in size and income, however, let's say the new price is 1.50 units of wheat per unit of cloth, or about 0.67 units of cloth for a unit of wheat, roughly half way between the old prices; it is shown as $A'B$ in Figure 15-1A and DE' in Figure 15-1B. The total amount of production (and consumption) of both products will be determined as part of the same process of adjustment that brings about the new price, and so will the amounts exported and imported.

To see how this is brought about, look again at Figure 15-1. Redland's *consumption-possibility* curve now becomes $A'B$, even though its *production frontier* curve remains $A'B$. It could conceivably sell (or try to sell) 333 units of its cloth output for 500 units of wheat (all Blueland's maximum output) at the new price, so in principle it could consume any combination between 67 units of cloth and 500 units of wheat and 400 units of cloth and no wheat. Let's say that its utility functions are such that its consumption settles at C' once all the adjustments to the new situation have been completed: 200 units of cloth and 300 units of wheat.

It turns out that, by arbitrarily selecting the point C', we have answered all our remaining questions! First, we know that world production of wheat is now 500 units (all in Blueland) and world production of cloth is 400 units (all in Redland). Second, since Redland consumes 300 units of wheat and 200 units of cloth, it must import all that wheat and export 200 units of cloth. Third, Blueland must therefore import (and consume) 200 units of cloth, and must also consume 200 units of wheat—it must be at point F' on its new consumption-possibility curve DE'. Also, the marginal utilities of cloth and wheat in Blueland at that point must be the same as in Redland, and proportionate to the new price ratio; otherwise consumption, exports, and imports in both countries, as well as the price ratio itself, would have to change until they were.

The increased specialization of production made possible by trade has increased the world output of cloth by 75 units and wheat by 100 units from the same resources, so both Redland and Blueland have been able to improve their real incomes. Redland now consumes 200 units of cloth and 300 units of wheat instead of 150 and 250. Blueland consumes 200 units of cloth and 200 units of wheat instead of 175 and 150.

Now for one final refinement. We noted in section 2 of Chapter 10 that a country's production frontier is likely to be bowed out towards the north and east, because of the Law of Diminishing Returns and other factors, instead of the straight-line constant-cost functions we have used so far. Figure 15-2 adapts our illustration to this situation. We will just point out the major differences, without going through the analysis again. (If you insist on all the details, you have two choices: you may work them out for yourself, or you may consult a more elaborate economics textbook!)

First, the marginal costs of transforming cloth into wheat or wheat into cloth are not constant (the slopes of the production-frontier curves change as the production mix changes). Second, the before-trade price lines are tangent to the corresponding production-frontier (and consumption-possibility) curves at C and F, respectively, instead of identical with them. This enables us to identify the points clearly, without

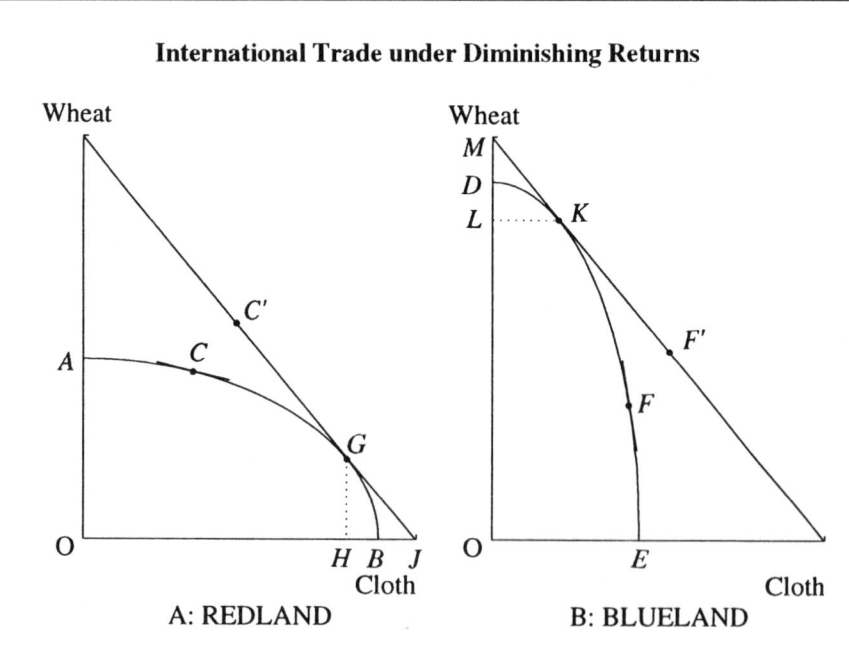

Figure 15-2. Increasing the output of cloth will cost more and more wheat, in both countries, and increasing the output of wheat will cost more and more cloth. Before trade, the national price lines will be tangent to the production frontiers at C and F respectively. After trade, the new international price will be tangent to the production frontiers at G' and K' respectively. *Consumption* after trade shifts to C' and F' on the new *consumption-possibilities* curves.

having to speculate about marginal utility (though it remains true that marginal utility and price must be proportionate). Third, the after-trade price line is tangent to the production-frontier curves at G and K respectively.

Fourth, it may be that neither Redland nor Blueland will find it advantageous to specialize completely. One or both may continue to produce some of the imported product, because the marginal costs of domestic producers at low levels of output may be lower than those of foreign producers at high levels of output and diminishing returns. Thus in Figure 15-2A Redland continues to produce GH units of wheat, which is worth HJ units of cloth at the world market price, whereas giving it up in favour of complete specialization would produce only HB additional units of cloth. For its part Blueland continues to produce LK units of cloth, equivalent to LM units of wheat in market value, whereas it could obtain only LD additional units of wheat if it were to give up all cloth production and specialize completely in wheat.

2. Other Aspects of Trade.

The theory of comparative advantage (or comparative costs) is not the only explanation of how nations can benefit from trade. A second factor is differences in the marginal utility they obtain from the same goods. If Redland and Blueland had identical endowments of resources and skills, but Redland had a much colder winter and needed more warm clothing, trade would benefit them both. The pre-trade price of cloth would be higher in Redland, because warm clothing would yield more utility than in Blueland; its after-trade price would fall in Redland, rise in Blueland. Consumers would gain utility by taking more of the now-cheaper commodity (cloth in Redland, wheat in Blueland). Redland would export wheat to pay for the additional cloth it would now consume, and Blueland would export cloth to buy additional wheat.

Or it might simply be a matter of tastes or preferences, not climate. Perhaps Redlanders are very fond of stylish and fancy dress, so they are forever making new clothes and discarding the old, whereas Bluelanders are more informal and relaxed in dress. In that case, too, the pre-trade price of cloth would be higher in Redland, and the after-trade price would fall there but rise in Blueland. Consumption in both countries would shift to the newly-cheaper commodity, and both would enjoy a net gain in utility.

Another possibility has to do with decreasing-cost industries. If either of the two potentially-tradable products is produced at decreasing cost (or increasing returns to scale), then it is clear that trade will be doubly beneficial: specialization will be reinforced by increasing returns.

In fact trade would then be beneficial even in the unlikely event that the two countries had identical resources, climates, tastes, and skills, as long as some way could be found to decide which country would specialize in which product. The world consumption-possibility curve would be at a maximum if one country (it would make no difference which) took over the decreasing-cost industry and the other took over the increasing-cost industry. And of course the advantage would be greater still if both industries operated at decreasing cost.[3]

3. Reciprocal Demand and Supply.

Note that we are assuming that there is no borrowing and lending between Redland and Blueland, so each country's imports must be paid for by exports. Thus Redland buys imports of 300 units of wheat with 200 units of cloth in Figure 15-1, and Blueland buys 200 units of cloth with 300 units of wheat, since one unit of cloth is worth 1.50 units of wheat on both domestic markets and in the international market. Similarly, in Figure 15-2 Redland's exports of cloth must be worth the same as Blueland's exports of wheat.

More generally, this points up a relationship that has been given the rather daunting title of *reciprocal demand and supply* (or just reciprocal demand for short). The basic idea is simple enough, however: any given *demand* for wheat imports by Redland is also an offer to *supply* cloth exports to Blueland. Also, Redland's *demand price* for wheat imports necessarily converts into an equivalent *supply price* for its exports of cloth, and the two prices are reciprocals of one another. The same is true of Blueland's exports and imports. An offer to pay two units of wheat for one unit of cloth is an offer to sell one unit of wheat for half a unit of cloth, and an offer to pay one unit of cloth for one unit of wheat is an offer to sell one unit of cloth for one unit of wheat.

Figure 15-3 illustrates how this works out in terms of the supply and demand functions we used in Chapter 5. Suppose that the D_wD_w curve in Part A represents

---

[3] If cloth were a decreasing-cost industry then the line AB would be concave towards the north-east as it approached the east-west axis, instead of convex as with the increasing-cost situation depicted in Figure 15-2A; the after-trade price line would therefore intersect the axis at point B, as in Figure 15-1A. The line DE in Part B would likewise be convex as it approached the east-west axis, and one country or the other would specialize completely in cloth. If wheat were a decreasing-cost industry as well then AB and DE would also be concave to the north-east as they approached the north-south axis, and both countries would specialize completely.

the demand for Blueland wheat by residents of Redland in exchange for cloth, and the $D_C D_C$ curve in Part B represents the demand for Redland cloth by residents of Blueland in exchange for wheat, after trade has opened up and consumption patterns have adapted to the new situation. The principle of reciprocal demand allows us to calculate the supply curve of cloth to Blueland from Redland's demand curve for wheat, and the supply curve of wheat to Redland from Blueland's demand curve for cloth.

The $D_W D_W$ curve tells us that, at a price of 1.00 units of cloth for a unit of wheat, Redland would purchase no wheat at all; at that price it could produce wheat domestically, so the supply of cloth to Blueland would be zero. That gives us point A on Blueland's supply-of-cloth curve: zero at a price of 1.00 units of wheat for a

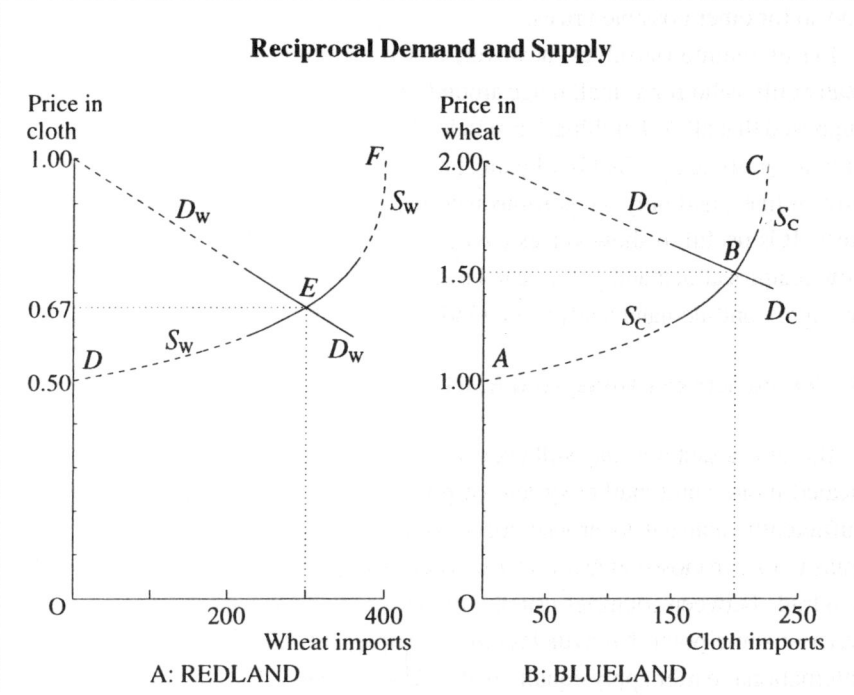

Figure 15-3. Redland's demand for wheat in terms of cloth ($D_W D_W$ in Part A) constitutes Blueland's supply curve of cloth in exchange for wheat ($S_C S_C$ in Part B). Thus at a price of 1.00 units of cloth for a unit of wheat Redland would buy no wheat, since it could produce it locally at that price; this gives point A on its $S_C S_C$ curve. At the equilibrium price of 0.67 units of cloth for a unit of wheat Redland supplies 200 units of cloth and receives 300 units of wheat, which gives point B on Blueland's supply-of-cloth curve, and other points can be found in the same way. Similarly, Blueland's demand for cloth ($D_C D_C$ in Part B) constitutes Redland's supply curve for wheat ($S_W S_W$ in Part A).

unit of cloth. At the equilibrium price of 1.50 units of wheat Redland offers 200 units of cloth, or a total value of 300 units of wheat, which gives us point B on Blueland's supply-of-cloth curve. At a price of 0.50 units of cloth for a unit of wheat Redland would be prepared to buy 450 units of wheat (50 units to the east of the edge of Part A), so the supply of cloth to Blueland would be 225 units; this gives us point C on Blueland's supply-of-cloth curve. Other points on the curve can be found in the same way.[4]

Redland's supply-of-wheat curve can be derived from Blueland's demand-for-cloth curve in the same way. Blueland will pay no more than 2.00 units of wheat for a unit of cloth, because it could produce cloth domestically at that price, so Redland's exports would be zero if it offered only 0.50 units of cloth for a unit of wheat. At the equilibrium price of 0.67 units, however, it gets 300 units of wheat; and so for other possible prices.

Let us remind ourselves, however, that these demand and supply curves are really only valid for a small range around the equilibrium value, in which it can be supposed that all "other things" can indeed "remain equal", or at worst can change only insignificantly. That is why most portions of each curve have been drawn as broken lines, and only the portions near the equilibrium point are shown as solid lines. It is useful to show values over a larger range, because that helps us to see how reciprocal demand curves can be drawn, but we need to keep the limitations of supply-and-demand analysis in mind or we may be led astray.

4. Trade between Money-and-Market Economies.

Barter transactions may still take place on occasion even under today's sophisticated money-and-market system of production and consumption, but they are sufficiently unusual to arouse special interest when they do occur. Domestic transactions in most countries are usually carried out in whatever is the local money, and trade between countries usually involves an exchange of one currency for the other at some point. Nevertheless the principles we have expounded in terms of international barter apply equally well to trade conducted for money, and we will find important advantages in now shifting to a more realistic approach.

---

[4] Redland would presumably buy more and more wheat if the price fell lower and lower, but below some point the total payment in cloth would be worth less and less in terms of wheat, because the lower price would more than offset the higher volume. If the price were to fall to zero, for example, the total value in terms of wheat would be zero no matter how much free wheat Redland would consume. A lower price for wheat means a higher price for cloth, hence beyond some point (C in Figure 15-3B) Blueland's supply-of-cloth curve will curl back towards the north-south axis.

We may begin by noting that "comparative advantage" is not by any means confined to two commodities, but includes all the goods and services produced in both Redland and Blueland, including various types or grades of each. Perhaps Redland has a substantial comparative advantage in woollen cloth and a lesser advantage in cotton cloth, but Blueland has a comparative advantage in cloth made from nylon and other man-made fibres. Similarly, Blueland may have a comparative advantage in hard spring wheat suitable for breadstuffs, and also in barley and several other grains, but Redland may have a comparative advantage in soft winter wheat suitable for pastry or pastas, and in corn (maize) and some other grains. In addition, the comparative advantages of each country in the whole range of their products will enter the picture, including services—such as those rendered by lawyers, doctors, banks, insurance companies, tailors, carpenters, and many others.

All these goods and services can in principle be ranked in terms of their comparative advantage from the point of view of (say) Redland, starting with the one in which it has the greatest comparative advantage and ending with the one in which it has the greatest comparative disadvantage. Of course, not all these goods will actually be traded internationally; so far we have ignored transportation costs and the like, but they make it clearly impracticable to export or import some things except on a very limited scale.

If you like, you may reinterpret "wheat" and "cloth" in Figures 15-1, 15-2, and 15-3 as bundles made up of the many different goods actually exported by Blueland or Redland, the controlling factor being that the total value of the two bundles must be identical. Redland's export bundle will obviously include all those commodities and services in which it has a relatively high comparative advantage, but the dividing line between its exports and its imports will also depend partly on how strong the demand in both countries (i.e. in the two-country "world" as a whole) is for the various tradable products.

You may think of Redland adding new export items, in which it has less and less advantage, until its total supply of exports just equals its total demand for Blueland products—supply and demand being both measured in terms of some standard commodity, such as wheat of a certain grade. Or you might think of Blueland doing the same thing in relation to Redland products.

However, a much better alternative is to think of the *money value* of each country's exports and imports in terms of its own domestic currency. The demand for foreign currencies in exchange for the local currency is equivalent to the demand for a package of imports in exchange for a package of exports.

This immediately raises the question of the exchange rate between Redland's currency (let's call it a dollar or a $) and Blueland's (a pound or a £). An exchange rate is essentially a price—the price of one currency in terms of another. It can therefore be treated by conventional demand-and-supply analysis like any other commodity. Instead of speaking of the price of wheat in terms of cloth or cloth in terms of wheat, therefore, we will speak of the dollar-pound exchange rate: either the price of the pound in dollars (dollars per pound, or $/£) or the price of the dollar in pounds (pounds per dollar, or £/$). As before, the two are reciprocals of one another, and hence equivalent.[5]

---

[5] In the actual exchange markets of the world it has become customary to quote the exchange rate for most foreign currencies in terms of the amount of local currency needed to buy them, though the dollar-exchange-rates of the British pound and some other currencies are usually quoted in U.S. dollars in all markets.

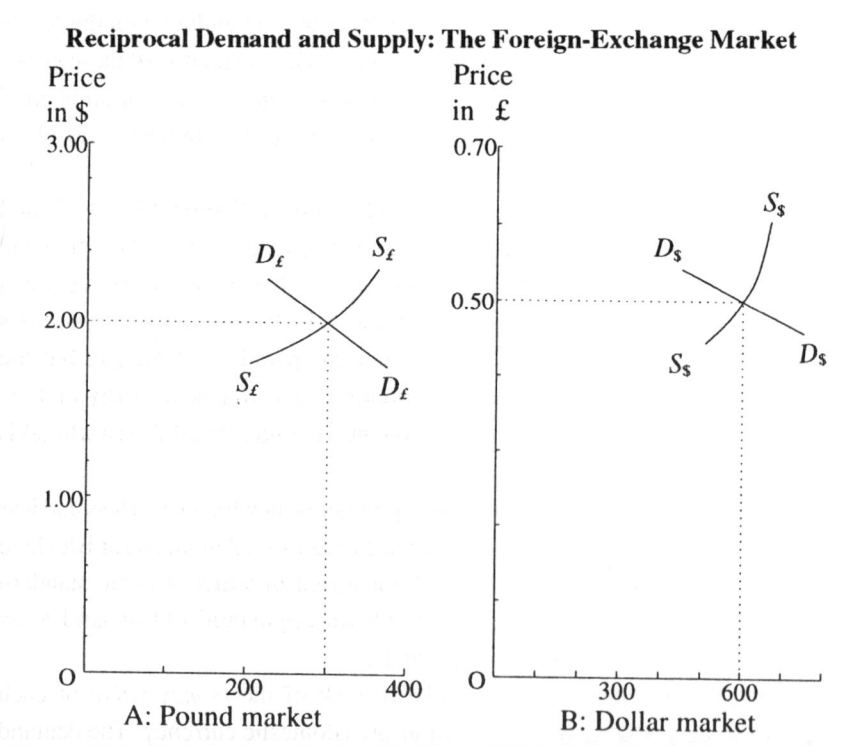

Figure 15-4. The principles illustrated in Figure 15-3 for barter transactions operate in foreign-exchange markets too. The demand for foreign currencies in exchange for the local currency is equivalent to the demand for a package of imports in exchange for a package of exports of equivalent money value. Thus in this illustration the exchange rate must be £1.00 = $2.00, so Redland offers $600 for £300, and Blueland offers £300 for $600.

Figure 15-4 illustrates the market for pounds in exchange for dollars, and the market for dollars in exchange for pounds. It is essentially similar to Figure 15-3, since it is again a case of reciprocal demands: a demand for pounds means a supply of dollars, and a demand for dollars means a supply of pounds. If this is an equilibrium position then the values of each package must be equal at the current exchange rate; thus the exchange rate must be £1.00 = $2.00, so Redland offers $600 for £300, and Blueland offers £300 for $600. Also, the composition of each package of imports and exports and the prices of all the individual items must be at their equilibrium values; otherwise some or all of these variables would change until a general equilibrium was reached.[6]

However, shifting to money payments instead of barter introduces important differences. For one thing, the dollars or pounds demanded and supplied represent the total value of all the various goods and services that are to be traded, so we get away from the limitations of barter and labour-cost interpretations of value. For another, we can include lending, borrowing, and other capital transfers in our model, since they are effected in terms of money just like trade in goods and services.

A third difference between a barter model of trade and a money-payments model is that the origin of the demand for a currency is not confined to the other country. (This is not significant for our analysis, but it is of some importance in real-world exchange markets.) In the barter model the demand for wheat imports originates solely in Redland, and the demand for cloth imports originates solely in Blueland. In the money-payments model, however, a part of the demand for each currency may occur in each country.

Some residents of Redland may want pounds to spend in Blueland, but others may earn pounds in Blueland and will want to exchange them for dollars to use at home. Similarly, some residents of Blueland will want to buy dollars, but others will have dollars to sell. Thus there may be an active market for pounds in Redland, and an active market for dollars in Redland. In principle the exchange rates in the two countries may differ, temporarily at least, but in practice *arbitrage* will normally reduce the differences to negligible proportions—sharp-eyed traders will buy one currency in the market where it is cheaper and sell it in the other.

---

[6] However, as with all discussions of equilibrium, much depends on the timeframe you have in mind: given a longer adjustment period, some or all the values appropriate to a short-run equilibrium might change appreciably.

5. The Determination of Exchange Rates.

If an exchange rate is viewed as the price of one currency in terms of another, the *equilibrium* rate in any particular timeframe is commonly said to be "determined" by supply and demand in the same way as the equilibrium price of any other commodity. In both cases the equilibrium price in the short run may not be the same as in the long run, and in the medium term it may be different again—presumably somewhere in between the other two. The reason is the same in both cases, of course: the longer the timeframe under consideration, the greater is the possibility of resources being shifted from less productive to more productive employments, thereby tending to correct any initial misallocation.

This interpretation is straightforward enough in terms of our simple two-country world. It is also readily adaptable to the exchange rate of one currency against all others in a multi-country world, since "the rest of the world" may be lumped together as a single entity for analytical purposes and some sort of average value determined for the exchange rates of their various currencies.

Even the exchange rate between any two currencies in a multi-currency world can be incorporated without serious problems of principle: the direct demand for one currency in terms of another is complemented by indirect demands through the use of third currencies obtained in trade, and the direct supply of the local currency in exchange will be supplemented in the same way. Thus, if Redland has a surplus of Blueland's currency in a three-country world in which trade is in or near equilibrium, then it must have a shortage of Brownland's currency, which it can expect to purchase with its surplus holdings of Blueland's currency.

We will see later that international flows of capital can only be effected by the transfer of goods and services. In a world which is enjoying peace and prosperity, and in which trade is in or near equilibrium, therefore, the bulk of the demand for various currencies stems from the desires of residents of one country to buy things in other countries.[7]

Reverting to our two-country model of the world, Redland's residents want Blueland's currency to buy things there, and their total purchases there must equal the total purchases Blueland's residents want to make in Redland. Redland will value these purchases in dollars, Blueland in pounds. In Figure 15-4 the total value of exports and imports come to $600 in Redland's terms and £300 in Blueland's

---

[7] In the real word, however, merely speculative transfers of money capital may at times greatly exceed the trading in currencies for normal trade purposes.

terms; obviously, as we have already noted, the exchange rate between the two currencies must be £1.00 = $2.00.

We have just derived a relationship of historic importance, which goes by the imposing name of the Theory of Purchasing-Power Parity. The purchasing power of a currency is the quantity of goods and services it can buy, and the theory says the equilibrium exchange rate between two currencies should be in proportion to their purchasing powers: if the pound can buy twice as much as the dollar, then the pound should be worth two dollars.

In practice, however, purchasing-power parities are usually computed by comparing *price levels* in the countries in question. The price level is actually the reciprocal of the purchasing-power of the currency; it is measured by a price index that records the cost of a given basket of goods in each currency, rather than how much a unit of that currency will buy. (Remember that under free trade the *relative* prices of everything must be the same in both countries—for example, in Figure 15-1 the after-trade price of cloth is 1.50 units of wheat—so we want to compare the cost of the same basket of goods in each country.) Usually a base year is chosen, in which the exchange rate is believed to have been in equilibrium, and the purchasing-power parity for subsequent periods is calculated by the relative changes in the price indexes.

However, although purchasing-power-parity calculations can be very useful, they do have important limitations that have to be taken into account. First, if the world economy is deemed to be in or near equilibrium, the parities so calculated are essentially long-run-equilibrium values; there may be powerful market forces that will tend to generate short-run-equilibrium market rates that are very different. Second, as already noted, some goods and services can not be effectively traded internationally, for a variety of reasons, including prohibitive transportation costs. Third, even for those goods that are traded internationally, prices in various countries may not be strictly comparable because of the cost of transportation from one country to the other, import tariffs, differences in domestic competitive conditions, and other factors. There is some disagreement among economists about how serious these limitations are, and how they can best be offset.

Furthermore, it must be remembered that both the purchasing-power-parity and the more general supply-and-demand approach to exchange-rate determination are examples of partial-equilibrium analysis. Ultimately, of course, all such exercises must be reconcilable with general-equilibrium considerations: "everything depends on everything else", as we noted in section 5 of Chapter 1. It is therefore more appropriate to say that the equilibrium values of exchange rates, domestic prices, output, employment, and all other economic variables are *mutually deter-*

mined, rather than that the value of any one variable is *determined by* another or by a small group of others.

Under some circumstances the link does seem to run strongly from domestic prices to exchange rates, but under other circumstances it seems to run more strongly the other way, and in either case there are likely to be important feedback effects from the second to the first. For example, a large speculative flight of capital out of a country may overwhelm normal commercial transactions on the exchange market and cause the currency to be grossly undervalued in terms of normal purchasing-power considerations (that is, foreign currencies will buy much more than the equilibrium amount of the local currency). This in turn will temporarily make export industries seem highly profitable, and may ultimately set off a bidding war for local resources that will bring domestic price increases which may ultimately "justify" or "validate" the now-depreciated exchange rate.

On the other hand, speculative capital movements may cause a particular currency to be grossly *over*valued in terms of normal purchasing-power considerations (that is, the local currency will buy more than the equilibrium amount of foreign currencies). That will put deflationary pressure on the economy, since domestic producers will be put at a disadvantage compared to foreign producers, and this situation may last for a long time.

In this connection the relationship between exchange rates and domestic prices under the classic gold-standard system deserves brief mention, because the effect was to make the exchange rate control prices rather than the other way around. This system (described more fully in Chapter 16) defined the value of each national currency as a fixed weight of pure gold, and each country was expected to maintain that value by both supplying and redeeming its currency for gold on demand.

Accordingly, the "mint parities" of gold-standard countries were precisely set by the gold contents of their currencies, and market rates could only move in a very narrow range around parity. The exact limits, known as the "gold export and import points", were determined by the cost of physically shipping gold from one country to the other; if the market rate for the currency you wanted got too high, you could always buy and ship gold instead of paying what the exchange dealer asked. Domestic prices were set by market forces, and the domestic authorities were expected to maintain the convertibility of the the currency into gold at par; the net effect was to make domestic prices conform to world prices.

A different regime of normally-fixed exchange rates (also described in Chapter 16) was established after World War II, but ran into increasing difficulties, and broke down by 1973. Since then most major currencies have traded at fluctuating rates, which have varied substantially from year to year and even from day to day.

6. The Balance of International Payments.

The statistical services of most countries compile the receipts and payments of the nation's residents in transactions with the residents of other nations, which they report on a regular basis, usually annually and quarterly. With only minor differences, these reports follow a standard internationally-agreed form, which is an adaptation of double-entry bookkeeping. They are entitled "The Balance of International Payments" or something similar, and are usually treated as a part of the National Accounts (described in section 6 of Chapter 7).

The statements are divided into two parts, the "current account", which covers transactions relating to the income of the period in question, and the "capital account", which covers lending, borrowing, investing, and the exchange of assets. Sometimes the change in external reserves (which is really a subdivision of the capital account) is shown separately as a third part. As in other double-entry systems, the two sides should balance exactly; in practice, however, there are inevitable errors and omissions, so a balancing item has to be added.

Before proceeding further, however, a warning is in order. Contrary to our usual usage, the term "investment" in this section of this chapter will be used in the sense of purchasing an asset, usually a financial claim of some kind; it will not necessarily imply the creation of new physical capital. Similarly, terms such as "capital", "capital account", and "capital transactions" will be used in a bookkeeping sense, and will not necessarily imply that capital formation is involved. The reason is that we are here dealing with accounting procedures for recording the financial effects of certain economic transactions, not with the underlying economic phenomena themselves.

Table 15-1 shows the major entries from an imaginary balance-of-payments statement for (say) Redland for a certain period, presumably a year, under reasonably "normal" conditions. In particular, we will assume that Redland is not engaged in or threatened by war, there is no flight of "hot money" from Redland in search of a haven in Blueland (which we will now identify with "the rest of the world"), or in the other direction either, and there is no significant speculation against either country's currency in the foreign-exchange market; international capital movements are for conventional lending-and-borrowing or investment purposes only.

Receipts are customarily identified as "credits", and payments as "debits".[8] Also,

---

[8] If you are familiar with double-entry bookkeeping, this usage of "debit" and "credit" may seem perverse: the statement in the table appears to be a sort of cash account, in which receipts are normally classed as debits and payments as credits. You may rationalize the accepted usage by

receipts are commonly given a plus sign and payments a minus sign. This is logical enough, but it results in a rather confusing situation when applied to the change in official reserves: an *increase* in reserves is a debit (i.e. a use of funds or an offset to receipts), and thus would normally appear with a *minus sign* in front of it! Separating the change in official reserves from other capital items, as in this table, makes it possible to avoid any such confusion.

The pattern of entries in the table is typical of a country that is importing capital to supplement its own savings, as is shown by the fact that Redland's total current payments exceed its total current receipts. Like an individual, a country can only spend more than it earns by either liquidating some of its assets or borrowing, so the excess of current payments is approximately balanced by net receipts of capital.

thinking of the statement as a summary of the ledger accounts to which the various items are posted, in which payments become debits and receipts credits.

A Hypothetical Balance of

I. Current Account

Receipts		Payments	
Merchandise exports	8,414	Merchandise imports	7,750
Services:		Services:	
Travel	373	Travel	489
Interest and dividends	161	Interest and dividends	859
Freight and shipping	419	Freight and shipping	395
Other	533	Other	1,225
Total services	1,486	**Total services**	2,968
Transfer receipts	306	Transfer payments	146
Total current receipts	10,206	Total current payments	10,864

Balance on visible trade   + 664
Balance on invisible trade   -1,482
Balance on transfers   + 160
Balance on current account   - 658

Table 15-1. **Redland's Balance of Payments.** Redland's current-account receipts (credits or +'s) are its exports of goods and services, its current-account payments are its imports of goods and services (debits or -'s). The balance on current account must

(It would be *exactly* balanced by deducting the increase in official reserves from the net capital inflow, were it not for the net errors and omissions; see the reconciliation at the end of Part III.) Also, for reasons that will be explained shortly, it appears that Redland has been importing capital for some years.

Now look at the details of the current account. Redland's merchandise exports exceed its merchandise imports—it has a "favourable"[9] balance on merchandise (or visible) trade.

---

[9] This terminology is an inheritance from the Middle Ages, when the links among trade, capital movements, and monetary movements were not widely understood. It was commonly argued that an excess of receipts had the "favourable" result of increasing the country's reserves of gold or the equivalent. This is now seen to have been a fallacy, since the inflow of gold would have feedback effects on domestic prices and incomes (and therefore on exports and imports as well), but the old terminology is now firmly entrenched in the language because nothing better has succeeded in replacing it.

International Payments

II. Capital Account
(net changes)

Long-term capital:	
Nonresident direct investment	− 530
Resident direct investment	− 490
Trade in outstanding issues	+ 11
New domestic issues	+ 1,356
Retirements	− 278
New foreign issues	− 20
Retirements	+ 10
Other long-term capital	+ 75
Total	+ 134
Short-term capital:	
Resident holdings abroad	+ 604
Nonresident domestic assets	+ 119
Other short-term movements	− 6
Total	+ 717
Net capital receipts	+ 851

III. Change In External Reserves

Allocation of SDR's	+ 21
Net monetary movements	+ 143
Increase in reserves	+ 164
Reconciliation:	
Current-account balance	− 658
Capital-account balance	+ 851
	+ 193
Net errors and omissions	− 29
Increase in reserves	+ 164

be covered by net capital movements (including the change in official reserves), except for undetected errors and omissions, as shown in the reconciliation at the end of Part III.

However, this is more than offset by an "unfavourable" balance on trade in services (invisible trade). Redland earns some money from Blueland's tourists and other travellers, but its own residents also spend money on travel in Blueland. As well, they earn some interest and dividend income from loans and investments in Blueland, but they owe considerably larger sums to residents of Blueland for the use of capital they have previously imported from there; this suggests that they have been importing capital for some time, though by now they have found some opportunities of their own to invest in Blueland or lend to some of its residents. They earn something for freight and shipping services to Bluelanders, too, but also buy similar services from Bluelanders.

"Other" services is obviously a catch-all item; it includes such different things as payments by governments for membership fees and contributions to international organizations, receipts by Redlanders and payments to Bluelanders for royalties, engineering services, consultancy fees, and various financial services, and so on. The fact that Redland's payments in this category substantially exceed its receipts in Table 15-1 is consistent with its net importation of capital: for that implies the need to import foreign technology and expertise to go along with the capital.

Transfer receipts and payments cover items that are neither income nor capital transactions in the normal sense. They include the remittances made by Redland emigrants to Blueland (or Redland residents temporarily working in Blueland) to support relatives left behind. Also, they include things like the value of inheritances by Redlanders from relatives in Blueland, or the other way around, and the value of assets owned by immigrants or emigrants, where the residency status of the assets changes with the residency status of the owner even though no actual transfer of assets occurs. In some countries they are relatively important, but in most cases they are not big enough to concern anyone but the statisticians who must try to make the balance-of-payments account balance.

Some balance-of-payments statements show only net receipts or net payments for service items, but many experts decry the practice. Travel receipts, for example, are earned by particular Redlanders who happen to find employment in that field, and travel payments are made mostly by a quite different group of Redlanders out of incomes earned in a wide variety of ways. There seems to be no special significance in the net difference between the two figures, except perhaps to someone studying the comparative advantages of the travel industries of Redland and Blueland.

Now look at the capital account. To help keep the pluses and minuses straight, think of buying and selling pieces of paper. If a Redlander borrows abroad or liquidates an asset he is selling a note, bond, share, or other asset to a Bluelander, so it is a plus (credit, receipt) from Redland's balance-of-payments point of view, just as if he had sold some export commodity. If he repays a loan he is buying back his IOU, like buying an import, so it is a minus (debit, payment). If a Bluelander lends to a Redlander or buys an asset from him he is buying a piece of paper that identifies his ownership, so again it is a plus for Redland's economy; if his loan is repaid in any form he gives up the piece of paper to a resident, like selling a Blueland export, so it is a minus for Redland.

The two main divisions of the capital account are long-term capital movements and short-term capital movements. However, the distinction is somewhat arbitrary, for it has to be based on the *form of the contract* (e.g., the purchase of a ten-year bond instead of a three-month Treasury Bill) rather than the *intent of the purchaser*. Thus one Bluelander might buy a ten-year Redland bond in the belief that the interest rate was about to fall and give him a quick profit on its resale, whereas another might keep his money in a portfolio of Redland Treasury Bills for years on end because he had business interests there and wanted a liquid emergency reserve. The changes in the first person's portfolio would be counted as long-term capital movements for balance-of-payments purposes, the second as short-term, whereas in reality their intentions would be the opposite. On the whole, nevertheless, the distinction is a useful approximation.

Long-term capital movements may be further divided into changes in *direct* investments and changes in *portfolio* investments. Direct investments involve ownership or control, as in a subsidiary firm or a branch plant. Portfolio investments, as the name implies, are made primarily at arms length as a matter of choice among alternative assets, and typically involve the purchase of security issues (either debt or equity) in the open market. Here too, of course, the distinction is somewhat arbitrary but useful, since evidence of ownership can take a wide variety of forms (including issues of marketable equity securities), and the amount of ownership required to give effective control is hard to quantify with precision, especially if ownership is widely dispersed.

In Table 15-1 the net payment (capital outflow) for nonresident (Blueland) direct investment in Redland implies that Redlanders have been buying out the interests of Bluelanders in direct investments the latter had earlier made in Redland. (To be more precise, it means that such buy-backs have exceeded new Blueland direct investment in Redland.) The net outflow for resident (Redland) direct investment means that Redlanders are making net new direct investments in Blueland. The third item means that Redlanders have sold more previously-issued securities to Bluelanders than they have bought; but it does not tell us whether they were originally Redland or Blueland issues, or some of each.

New domestic (Redland) issues sold abroad may include the refinancing of some of the maturities included in the next heading, "Retirements" of earlier Redland issues. Likewise, new foreign (Blueland) issues on the Redland market may include the refinancing of some issues included in "Retirements" of previous Blueland issues. "Other long-term capital movements" includes the purchase (-) or sale (+) of Blueland assets by Redlanders, or the purchase (+) or sale (-) of Redland assets by Bluelanders.

The main short-term movements are changes in Redland holdings of bank balances and similar assets in Blueland, and changes in Blueland holdings in Redland. In Table 15-1 both are shown as credits (pluses). Perhaps Redlanders had raised long-term loans in Blueland towards the end of the previous year, but had not been able to use all of the proceeds right away, and had left part of them in short-term deposits with Blueland banks; then this year they drew these balances down (sold pieces of paper back to the Bluelander banks), as well as floating new long-term loans. Perhaps some Bluelanders, for their part, have acquired balances in Redland banks because they expect to be making purchases there (or buying securities) early in the next year.

The last item is "Other short-term movements", which is shown as a small net payment. It would consist mainly of minor things like open-book credits between commercial firms. Some countries may quietly tuck away the "net errors and omissions" item here, on the assumption that it is probably made up mostly of unrecorded capital movements. This hides the embarrassment of the country's balance-of-payments statisticians if the errors and omissions happen to be large, but many authorities argue that current-account errors and omissions are just as likely as capital-account errors, and that anyway it is better to show the gap openly rather than hide it away.

Note, by the way, that the table suggests Redland is paying off equity obligations to Blueland and substituting debt obligations, even while making net additions to its total obligations. This is not certain, for the item for new domestic issues may include equity as well as debt issues, but the repatriation of Blueland direct investments almost certainly involves a reduction in equity obligations.

There are only two items in Part III, aside from the reconciliation of the totals in the three parts. The first one (the allocation of Redland's share of a distribution of Special Drawing Rights in the International Monetary Fund) does not occur every year. Familiarly known as SDR's, they are a sort of international money issued by the Fund and useable for international payments, subject to certain rules and obligations, as explained in Chapter 16; they are only distributed to members when the Fund decides they are needed for the good of the international community.

These allocations add to Redland's official reserves in the year in which they are made, but they are quite distinct from normal changes in those reserves, which reflect the ebb and flow of receipts and payments in the ordinary course of trade.

"Net monetary movements" means changes in Redland's official external reserves. These consist of official holdings of gold (if any), SDR's, foreign currencies that are useful for international payments, and Redland's "position in the International Monetary Fund". That means its total contributions to the Fund, less any drawings against the Fund and any use of SDR's in transactions with Blueland.

Finally, combining the current-account and the capital-account balances shows that they do not quite explain the increase in Redland's external reserves. The difference is the balancing item we have already mentioned, "net errors and omissions".

Chapter 16

The International Monetary System

Fatherly Advice: Most chapters so far in this book are intended to help you understand why things happen in any economy (typically, a national economy), but this one is different: it is primarily a historical account of how the international monetary system evolved over the years, and is designed to help you understand how it got into the mess it is now in. Also, it touches on important policy issues; you should be warned that they are very complex and contentious, that they are treated very sketchily here, and that the views of other economists may be very different from those expressed or implied hereunder.

1. **National Monetary Systems.**

The so-called "international monetary system" is actually a rather *un*systematic assemblage or federation of separate and distinct national monetary systems, each of which jealously guards its independence. The features that justify applying the term "system" to it have evolved gradually over time, more often as a result of practical adaptations by traders than by explicit international agreement, and their nature has changed in response to changing conditions in world trade as well as to changes in man's understanding of that trade. Accordingly, the evolution of the international monetary system has been closely linked both historically and logically to the evolution of domestic monetary systems.

As illustrated in section 2 of Chapter 12, national monetary systems typically grew out of the promotion of some particular commodity (such as gold or silver) to the role of "money" for domestic trading purposes. In principle, such a commodity-money system is automatic or self-regulating: it does not have to be managed by anyone. This is at once its main strength and its main weakness.

Automaticity is the main strength of a commodity-money system, in that no-one can manipulate it for his own advantage; the principal exception is that the sovereign (or the government) may occasionally be able to change the content of the monetary unit itself, as when medieval kings debased the coinage by calling in the old coins and replacing them with new coins bearing the same name but having less bullion content. It is its main weakness, in that the available supply of the monetary commodity may not grow in step with "the needs of trade"[1]: too rapid growth will bring inflation, too slow growth will be a drag on the economy.

Even the most sophisticated commodity-moneys, which were based on gold or silver or both and made use of standard-weight metallic coins, encountered other practical difficulties as well. The rise of note-issuing and deposit-taking banks, together with other specialized financial institutions, alleviated some of these problems but generated new problems of their own. The belief that all these notes, deposits, and other financial claims were ultimately convertible into the standard commodity-money served to keep the system operating smoothly enough most of the time. Every now and then, however, something would set off a scramble to actually convert these substitutes into the commodity-money, and would threaten to bring the economy to a halt.

Central banking as we know it today (briefly described in Chapter 12) gradually evolved in response to these difficulties, and pretty well ended the financial panics that used to disrupt the domestic economy periodically. Their note issues replaced whatever commodity-money had previously been held by the public, they came to hold the nation's external reserves of gold or foreign exchange or whatever, and they learned to use their control over the note issue to regulate the financial system in order to anticipate trouble and avoid excessive reactions. In most major countries this process was well advanced by the beginning of the 20th century. In practice, therefore, there came to be important discretionary elements in the operation of what were still essentially automatic systems.

Opportunities for trade with other countries naturally led to the rise of markets in which various national currencies could be exchanged for one another, and exchange rates among them established. If two countries happened to use the same basic commodity-money, then the exchange rate between their currencies would tend to be rather stable, for reasons we will shortly see. If their currencies had different foundations, however, then the exchange rate between them might fluc-

---

[1] "The needs of trade" is a rather vague but useful term that refers basically to the growth of the economy, but allows for possible changes in the financial system that economize on the use of whatever is currently accepted as money.

tuate rather widely and rapidly in response to changing supply and demand—which is to say, in response to changing tastes, fortunes, circumstances, and seasonal patterns in the two countries.

2. The International Gold Standard.

The classical gold standard was a prime example of a commodity-based international monetary system. It was virtually automatic, for it required relatively little of the authorities in each country: just that they define their monetary units in terms of a fixed weight of gold, that they provide domestic gold coins on demand in exchange for gold bullion or foreign gold coins (subject to only a modest charge for minting or reminting them), and that they permit domestic coins or bullion to be freely exported.

However, these principles were not consciously designed to produce an integrated international monetary system; initially they evolved in response to concerns that were primarily domestic. In those days they were thought to be the basis of any sound currency, in order to ensure that the monetary unit was worth no more and no less than its bullion value. The essence of a fair exchange is the giving and receiving of equivalent value, and the value of the monetary unit was identified exclusively with its bullion content; the value of a banknote or a bank deposit was seen to stem from its convertibility into full-weight gold coin.[2]

Nevertheless one result of two or more countries adopting the gold standard domestically was the automatic creation of an international monetary system that in effect fused their domestic monetary systems together. Defining their respective currencies in gold meant setting their "mint parities" at the ratio of their gold contents. For example, the fine gold content of the pound sterling was set at 113 grains, and that of the U.S. dollar at 23.22 grains, so their parity was £1 = $4.48665.

Furthermore, the market exchange rate could not depart from parity by more than a relatively small amount, determined by the costs of physically moving gold between the financial centres concerned (mainly freight, insurance, packing, and the interest lost while the gold was in transit). If the price of foreign exchange rose above the "gold export point" it became worth someone's while to ship gold abroad

---

[2] Nowadays it is widely agreed that the acceptability of any form of money is primarily due to the confidence of the public, based on past experience, that it will be readily accepted by other people in their turn. In other words, it is the assured convertibility of money into goods and services in general, not into gold or some other specific commodity or into foreign exchange, that gives money its value. It is only in the last stages of a run-away inflation that people try to reject their customary forms of money and seek substitutes.

and convert it into the other country's currency instead of buying that currency; if it fell below the "gold import point" it became worth someone's while to bring in gold from abroad and turn it into domestic currency.

In 1816 Britain became the first country to formally adopt the gold standard, and a newly-issued gold sovereign or 20-shilling piece became the standard coin. Before that, like a great many other countries, Britain had been legally on a bimetallic standard (gold and silver); for all practical purposes, however, it had already been effectively on the gold standard for about 100 years, by accident rather than design. London was the world's leading financial centre in those days, and sterling was the major international currency—that is, a currency widely used for international transactions, in preference to the less-well-known and less-actively-traded currencies of other countries. The prestige this gave the gold standard helped to promote its widespread acceptance in the international community by the end of the 19th century.

The gold-exchange standard was a variation of the gold standard in which a country held all or a major part of its external reserves in a chosen foreign currency that was convertible into gold, instead of in stocks of physical gold. This variation played an unexpected rôle in the subsequent history of the international monetary system, but it was a logical development at the time, when economic growth and the spread of the gold standard were putting pressures on the world supply of monetary gold.

For a country newly assuming the responsibilities of the gold standard, this version avoided the need to accumulate a substantial gold stock. Also, it was administratively simple; it avoided the costs of holding, protecting, and shipping gold; and it meant that the country's external reserves could be invested in interest-bearing securities. Since sterling was the leading international currency, it was a logical choice as the reserve medium for countries on the gold-exchange standard.

Of course there were disadvantages to the gold-exchange standard too. With the wisdom of hindsight, we can now see that the most obvious was the risk that the government of the gold-holding country might some day devalue its currency (reduce its gold content), or simply cease to redeem it in gold. In that case the country on the gold-exchange standard might have little choice but to follow suit. To the holders of sterling at the end of the 19th century, however, that risk presumably seemed small.

The gold-bullion standard, which differed from the gold-coin standard only in that gold coins did not circulate, evolved after World War I. Hand-to-hand currency consisted of currency notes or banknotes and subsidiary coin, and gold could only be obtained from or sold to the national authorities in the form of standard gold bars or the equivalent. The principal advantage was that it economized on the monetary use of gold; all monetary gold was held by the central bank or some similar authority, and none of it was dispersed among the general public.

It is important to note that any system of stable and reliable exchange rates, such as that engendered by the international gold standard, offers the maximum advantage from international trade: producers in every country can compete in world markets without fear that an adverse movement in exchange rates might enable producers in some other country to undercut them unfairly.

On the other hand all varieties of the gold standard implied a willingness to adopt domestic policies that were compatible with fixed exchange-rates. To be specific, that meant contracting the money supply and damping down the economy when the exchange rate threatened to go above the gold export point, or expanding the money supply and stimulating the economy if it threatened to go below the gold import point.[3] Under the circumstances of the times, this seemed a modest price to pay for a great advantage.

Remember that the principal analytic tool of economists then was the model of pure competition. And don't forget our old friend the *"if..."* assumption from section 2 of Chapter 1. *If* all the conditions necessary for the long-run-equilibrium position of the purely competitive model were met throughout the world, *if* all countries followed free-trade policies, and *if* stable exchange rates were maintained, *then* all the world would enjoy full employment and a maximum level of real income. *Under those conditions*, or any reasonable approximation of them, the burden of maintaining fixed exchange-rates would not be too severe, because natural equilibrating forces could be relied on to bring about any necessary readjustments in case anything occurred to upset the balance.

Unfortunately, the real world is not entirely like that. Before The Great Depression of the 1930's the most serious flaw most economists saw in the model of pure competition was that it did not explain the business cycle. By the 1920's it had become widely believed that the cycle was primarily caused by distortions in the price structure, and that it could be largely tamed if not eliminated by manipulating the money supply and thereby stabilizing the general level of prices.

That policy prescription soon proved ineffective, but the attempt to implement it marks the start of modern monetary policy, i.e. the management of the money

---

[3] Actually, all this was supposed to happen automatically as a result of gold movements; but in practice central banks found they had to monitor the financial system in order to anticipate trouble and avoid excessive reactions, as already noted.

supply as a means of influencing the general performance of the economy. This eventually lead to the much broader use of monetary policy as part of demand management. But that is getting ahead of the story.

Laudable as the price-stability objective was, it often conflicted with the gold-standard objective of keeping the exchange rate stable. For example, there might be an inflow of gold while inflation threatened. (Perhaps other countries were suffering even worse inflations and were therefore importing more than they were exporting—the gold standard did not really prevent either inflation or deflation, it merely prompted all countries to inflate or deflate in unison.) The exchange-rate objective would say to expand the money supply, but the price-stability objective would say to contract it.

Or there might be an outflow of gold when the economy was going into a recession and prices were tending to fall. (Perhaps the country's trading partners were already in recession and adversely affecting its exports.) In that case the exchange-rate objective would call for a contraction of the money supply, but the price-stability objective would call for an expansion. The inevitable result was considerable confusion in official policies, even before the end of the 1920's.

A case can be made for saying that the gold standard ended in 1914, at the outbreak of World War I: gold payments were suspended by the belligerents, and by the time of their resumption in the 1920's nations were no longer willing to subject their economic policies unequivocally to exchange-rate requirements.

What finally brought the gold-standard era to a close, however, was the onset of The Great Depression of the 1930's. It struck various countries unevenly in both timing and severity. The gold standard could not cope with the strains imposed on exchange markets as the repercussions spread from one country to another and back again. Existing economic theories were unable either to explain what had happened or to prescribe an effective remedy.

If you want to pick a precise date for the demise of the gold standard, then 21st September 1931 will do as well as any. That is the day on which Britain formally suspended the obligation of the Bank of England to sell gold. It is admittedly an arbitrary choice, however. On the one hand the U.S.A. and some European countries continued formally "on gold" for a long time thereafter. On the other hand the system as it had hesitantly resumed operation after World War I had a new and potentially fatal weakness, as already noted. But after that date it was clear that gold could no longer be said to be the foundation of the international monetary system.

3. Key-Currency Systems.

A "key" currency is one that is widely used as an international money and is therefore generally acceptable to the residents and governments of other countries in settlement of obligations or as an international asset (e.g., as all or part of another country's external reserves). This status is awarded by the practical decisions of market operators, not by any formal international agreement of any kind, and typically goes to the currency of a major country with a strong economy. Before World War I sterling was far and away the dominant key currency, though the term was not then in common use. After World War II it has been the U.S. dollar. However, its position has been weakened by a number of factors in recent years.

When Britain suspended gold payments in 1931, the gold-exchange standard based on sterling became the sterling-exchange standard. Countries holding their external reserves in sterling could conceivably have maintained their gold parities by buying gold with their sterling, or buying other currencies still convertible into gold, but they would have suffered a severe capital loss in so doing and would have added greatly to the stresses already evident in exchange markets.

In addition, Britain was still a major source of many of the industrial products they needed, a major market for their exports, and a major financial centre. And, since many countries found themselves in the same situation, they found they could continue to trade with one another and settle in sterling as before: the only obvious difference was that their external reserves were held in inconvertible sterling instead of convertible sterling. Much of their past trade and financial connections could therefore continue virtually unchanged.

So was born the Sterling Area, mostly but not entirely composed of members of the British Commonwealth,[4] bound together by practical considerations rather than ideology. They had extensive opportunities for multilateral trade and capital movements at stable exchange rates within the area, subject to a minimum of interference by the exchange controls and the other limitations that sprang up because of the disturbed times.

Their trade with countries outside the area was certainly hampered, especially with countries still "on gold". Exchange rates for these currencies fluctuated uncertainly, exchange controls on their use had to be coördinated with Britain's, and earnings in them surrendered to a central pool; but the same currencies could

---

[4] Not including Canada.

be obtained from the central pool for approved payments. Nevertheless the members continued to enjoy the advantages of a broadly-based international monetary system of their own.

Other somewhat similar groupings arose, such as that of France and its overseas dependencies, based on the French franc and having formal or informal links to other gold-bloc countries (European countries still "on gold"). There was also a dollar bloc, of countries rather more loosely linked to the U.S. dollar. There was a measure of stability within each of these key-currency systems, though not without some jockeying for advantage among them through unilateral devaluations and the like. Exchange rates among the various currencies in one system and those in another tended to fluctuate rather unpredictably, however.

Still other countries found themselves suspended uncomfortably between key-currency systems. Canada, for example, in those days sold much of its exports in Britain but bought most of its imports from the U.S.A. When sterling was depreciated sharply against the U.S. dollar the Canadian dollar held somewhere in between, so export earnings were depressed while import costs were increased.

It fairly soon became apparent that unilateral actions aimed at gaining a trade advantage were self-defeating, for they merely invited retaliation in kind and benefited no-one. For example, one country might hope to gain export sales (and thereby stimulate its economy) by devaluing or depreciating its currency[5]; but if its competitors followed suit their devaluations or depreciations became merely competitive, a "race for the bottom". The same was true of merely competitive import tariffs or exchange controls or deflations—no-one could win. Until the Keynesian breakthrough in economic analysis, the only hope was that the depression would eventually bottom out and a revival begin through new investment spending.

Some beginnings of international coöperation did occur. In 1936, for example, Britain, France, and the U.S.A. signed the Tripartite Agreement, wherein they undertook to consult one another before altering their exchange rates. However, the practical effects were not obvious; all nations continued to act independently for the most part. It was primarily the rearmament boom of the late 1930's that set recovery in motion. The irony of that fact was widely noted then and later: money

---

[5] A devaluation is a reduction in the established value of a currency, measured in terms of its gold content or its parity with a key currency or the like. A depreciation is a reduction in the market value of a currency, whether or not it is attempting to maintain a fixed parity with some other currency; it is brought about my market forces, with or without the approval of the national monetary authorities.

was readily found for spending for *de*structive purposes but not for *con*structive purposes.

4. The Bretton Woods System.

Strictly speaking the term "Bretton Woods System" refers to all the financial arrangements worked out the United Nations Monetary and Financial Conference in Bretton Woods, N.H., U.S.A., from 1st to 22nd July 1944. Those arrangements included the establishment of the International Bank for Reconstruction and Development (the I.B.R.D. or the Bank) as well as the International Monetary Fund. (the I.M.F. or the Fund).[6] However, the term has come to be used primarily to mean the international monetary system formalized in the Articles of Agreement of the International Monetary Fund.

As World War II drew to a close the western allies began to prepare for greater international coöperation in various fields. The proposals in the monetary field culminated in agreement on the structure of the I.M.F. at the 1944 conference at Bretton Woods. The Articles of Agreement there devised were not an exercise in dogmatic theory but an attempt by practicing administrators and their advisors to devise realistic rules and procedures for the future. They hoped to retain the good features of the gold standard, yet avoid not only its inflexibilities but also the merely competitive exchange-rate depreciations, devaluations, and deflations of the 1930's, which were vividly fresh in the minds of most participants at the conference. The structure they devised was designed to produce fixed exchange rates as the norm, but to permit changes where justified by the course of events, subject to scrutiny by the Fund on behalf of its member countries.

The declared purposes of the new institution were to promote international monetary coöperation, to facilitate the balanced growth of international trade and thereby promote high levels of employment and real income, to promote exchange stability and a multilateral system of current-account payments, and to assist members in correcting maladjustments in their balances of payments.

The substance of the new system was a pooling of a portion of each country's external reserves, out of which loans were to be made to members who experienced balance-of-payments difficulties. These loans were to be strictly temporary, in

---

[6] The I.B.R.D. is a pool of funds contributed by its member nations and supplemented by borrowing in world capital markets. Its original purposes were to help finance the reconstruction of war-damaged economies and to promote development in what we now call the Third World; the first of these eventually lapsed.

order to cushion the necessary domestic adjustments the borrowers were expected to make; they were to be repaid when balance was restored. Contributions and borrowings were to be in terms of individual quotas for each member, which took account of such things as its economic strength and the volume and variability of its external trade.

Par values for the currencies of original member countries were based on the rates prevailing on the 60th day before the Articles of Agreement came into effect, with some exceptions; for subsequent entrants they were prescribed as part of the terms of membership. They were expressed in terms of gold as a common denominator, or in terms of the U.S. dollar of the weight and fineness in effect on 1st July 1944, which was just another way of saying the same thing.

A proposal to change its par value could only be make by the member country itself, and only to correct a fundamental disequilibrium. A cumulative change of not more than 10 per cent could be made without Fund approval, but greater changes did require approval. Members also undertook to avoid restrictions on current payments, to avoid discriminatory currency practices, and to convert balances held in their currencies by other countries when needed for current transactions.

The *form* of this new international system was that of a determinedly symmetrical treatment of all currencies; only the U.S. dollar is specifically mentioned anywhere, and that solely as an alternative way of identifying gold parities. The *substance* of the system, however, was essentially a codification and institutionalization of the key-currency system, based on the U.S. dollar. It was not the Articles of Agreement of the International Monetary Fund, but the marketplace, that made the dollar the foundation of the new system—just as the marketplace had already made it the dominant key currency without asking the permission of the U.S. Congress, and just as the marketplace had made sterling the dominant key currency in the 19th century.

The rôle of gold in all this was not too clear—perhaps deliberately, so each member could put its own interpretation on it. Parities were expressed in gold, as already noted; members might choose to pay for other members' currencies in gold; such transactions as occurred between members in gold were to be at parity; 25 per cent (sometimes less) of quotas, and most Fund charges, were payable in gold; the Fund could require a country whose currency was becoming scarce to sell it to the Fund for gold; but a member could sell newly mined gold in any market. However, no country undertook, as part of the Agreement, to redeem its currency in gold.

Nevertheless the system was linked to gold in an indirect and tenuous way. The U.S. government continued to buy and sell gold in transactions with other governments at $35.00 per fine ounce, subject to a handling charge of 1/4 of 1 per cent; no other country made any similar undertaking, but the Fund Agreement did commit them all (with some qualifications) to maintain their parities with the dollar; hence, technically, they were all on a *gold exchange standard* rather than a pure key-currency standard. This deference to an old fetish did not formally disappear until the Second Amendment to the Fund's Articles of Agreement (effective 1st April 1978), but as a practical matter it ended on 15th August 1971, as explained in the next section.

In its practical day-to-day operations during the first two-and-a-half decades after World War II the new system functioned substantially like the key-currency systems of the 1930's, or like the gold standard, in many respects. The need to maintain a sound balance-of-payments position and a fixed exchange rate had a useful disciplinary function. Producers in each country faced competition from producers in other countries, which put healthy pressure on them to remain efficient. Failure to do so meant a declining spending stream, a declining money supply, and a loss of reserve balances in the key currency, thus automatically penalizing the producers and inducing the authorities to undertake corrective actions.

However, there were four important differences between the Bretton Woods system and what had been known before. First, in a gold-standard system the supply of monetary gold at any given point in time is virtually fixed; if there is a sudden surge of attempts to convert holdings of foreign currencies into gold, the demand can not be met and the entire system of international payments may threaten to seize up—just like a run on gold coins in the domestic economy. In a well-managed key-currency system, however, an overall shortage of the reserve medium is inconceivable. The demand for the key-currency by member countries for reserve purposes is only a small part of the total demand for capital in its financial markets, and the total supply of the currency can be increased by its national authorities if necessary.

Second, the currencies of all Fund members were linked to the same key currency. Unlike the situation in the 1930's, when several key currencies were in competition and exchange rates among them were unpredictable, all currencies were interchangeable for current payments (or were expected to become so in due course).

Third, it was agreed that balance-of-payments discipline should not be enforced to the point of causing a serious reduction of output and employment.[7] This did not mean that discipline could be disregarded, it only meant that the internal adjustments necessary to correct an imbalance were to be effected less abruptly and painfully. The resources of the Fund were available to cushion the adjustment, and it was agreed that the exchange rate could be changed if necessary rather than subject the country to too-severe a deflation. The Fund's surveillance was expected to ensure that adequate corrective measures were indeed taken, and that any exchange-rate change (if more than 10 per cent cumulatively) was actually appropriate.

Fourth, it was hoped that the newly-evolving techniques of demand management would enable each member country to maintain a high level of employment at stable prices—and for a long time that hope seemed to be justified. In such an environment a country with a balance-of-payments deficit should be able to eliminate it in a reasonable length of time by shifting its resources from less-efficient to more-efficient industries, without unduly harming its trading partners, thanks to help and surveillance from the Fund

5. The Bretton Woods System in Operation, 1945-1973.

The Bretton Woods system worked reasonably well, or was made to work, for about 25 years. During this period the economies of war-damaged countries were repaired and the world as a whole experienced a growth in trade and in real income on a scale and with a persistence never seen before.

A great deal of the credit must of course go to the Marshall Plan and other forms of economic aid from the U.S.A., especially in the earlier years. This generous help to former friend and foe alike, including its keenest industrial rivals, was a tribute to the faith of successive U.S. administrations in the virtues of competition. Credit must also be given, however, to the still-evolving techniques of demand management; to the relative stability of the new international monetary system; and to the steady liberalization of trade thus fostered.

There were difficulties, to be sure, but in the early years it seemed reasonable to hope that they would gradually disappear as the distortions inherited from the war and The Great Depression (or perhaps going back to World War I) were overcome.

---

7 Supporters of the gold standard did not really advocate unemployment as part of the process of adjustment, they just saw it as a necessary but temporary side effect; they did not recognize that it could occur on a serious scale and persist for a long time.

As argued in Chapter 13, however, the early successes of demand management masked a serious weakness: inadequate defences against inflation.

Naturally, countries differed materially in the severity of their post-war problems and in their success in dealing with them, and therefore in the inflationary pressures they experienced. But even those countries in the most favourable circumstances (notably the U.S.A.) found themselves faced with persistent "creeping" inflation of one or two per cent per annum, and eventually most national inflation rates began to accelerate.

From the discussion of purchasing-power parity in section 5 of Chapter 15 you will see that it is impossible to maintain a given pattern of fixed exchange rates indefinitely if national price trends persistently diverge. Periodic realignments can of course be made, but if they become too frequent or too predictable they discredit the system. Nevertheless a substantial stability was in fact maintained for many years.

Also, there were other problems besides inflation. Many countries were less than enthusiastic about accepting the discipline of international competition. They resisted making internal adjustments that would upset established domestic industries, persisted with war-time exchange controls and other protectionist devices, and maintained overvalued currencies. When they did eventually have to devalue (perhaps as a condition of Fund assistance), it was therefore by a substantial amount. This tended to discredit the Fund's par values.

Britain inherited especially severe problems from the war; its balance of payments was chronically in deficit, and sterling suffered a series of crises. From 1958 on the U.S. balance of payments was also persistently in deficit, partly because by then many war-damaged industrial countries had substantially regained competitiveness in international markets. Thanks to the key-currency rôles of the pound and the dollar, this meant adding to the external reserves of other countries, relaxing balance-of-payments discipline for them, and feeding world-wide inflation.

Some countries (notably France) insisted on converting their dollar balances into gold. Others, noting that West Germany seemed to be doing better than the U.S.A. at restraining inflation, sought to convert them into deutschemarks. Speculative flights from the dollar began to vie with speculative flights from sterling as disturbers of the international scene.

Many economists had long criticized what they saw as the evils of a fixed-rate system, and had advocated fluctuating-rate systems of one kind or another; the implication was that domestic price stability was expendable and balance-of-payments discipline irrelevant, but this was seldom or never acknowledged. Various proposals appeared for reforming the international monetary system, designed to make exchange rates more flexible.

It was also widely argued that international reserves were inadequate, or were in danger of becoming so. Others argued that the problem was too much rather than too little international liquidity, due to the balance-of-payments deficits of the two key currencies. At least one voice asserted that the problem was not with the *quantity* of reserves but with their *quality*, meaning that confidence in the two major reserve currencies was being seriously undermined by their domestic inflations.

Successive international committees were appointed to recommend corrective measures, but their terms of reference were addressed to the mere *mechanics* of the system, not its fundamental problems. In 1967 proposals for amending the Fund's Articles of Agreement were presented to its annual meeting, based on four years of studies by the latest of many committees. A final text was agreed upon in 1968 and became effective on 28th July 1969, almost exactly 25 years after the Bretton Woods Conference. The principal change was to authorize the Fund to issue Special Drawing Rights (SDR's) as a supplement to existing reserve assets.

SDR's are rights to obtain the currencies of other Fund members, additional to the rights provided in the original Fund agreement. They are unconditional reserve assets, in that a participant[8] is entitled (subject to certain rules) to use them without obtaining the advance approval of the Fund, whereas normal drawings beyond certain limits do require approval. SDR's were originally *valued at* 0.888671 grams of fine gold (i.e., the par value of the U.S. dollar on 1st July 1944) for the acquisition of other currencies, but there was no suggestion of *convertibility into* gold.

SDR's are created by a bookkeeping entry in the Fund's accounts and distributed to members on the basis of their quotas. In return the members agree to provide their currencies in exchange for SDR's according to prescribed rules, and to buy back their original holdings of SDR's under certain conditions. Originally they were not used directly to make payments, hence were not a form of international money, even though they did count as official reserves. Since the Second Amendment to the Articles of Agreement (described in the next section), however, they have become a new form of international money.

The fundamental problems bedevilling the international monetary system were, of course, the persistence (later the acceleration) of inflation, and the basic incompatibility of fixed exchange rates with divergent national price trends.

---

8   Most, but not all, Fund members chose to participate in the SDR program.

Obviously the amendment to the Fund agreement could not solve these problems, since it was not even addressed to them.

After a period of relative calm in 1970, new speculations against the U.S. dollar and in favour of the Japanese yen and various European currencies broke out in 1971. On 15th August 1971 the President of the United States announced the "temporary" suspension of the convertibility of the dollar into either gold or SDR's, together with supplementary measures. Intense international negotiations brought agreement in December to devalue the dollar by about 9 per cent (i.e. to raise the price of gold from $35 to $38 per fine ounce).

New speculations soon broke out, and fourteen months later the price of gold was raised a second time, to $42.2222 per fine ounce. That rate, too, soon proved insupportable, and in March 1973 a new era began in which the exchange rates among virtually all major currencies were floating.

In sum, the Articles of Agreement of the International Monetary Fund were a carefully crafted attempt to redesign the international monetary system on a sound logical basis. The new grand design failed in the end because the international community did not live up to the precepts on which the agreement was based, not because of any logical flaw in the design.

Failure to appreciate the risk that the creeping inflation of the early years would eventually acquire a momentum of its own was the Achilles Heel of postwar economic policymaking. The main blame lies clearly at the door of the policymakers in the U.S.A. and Britain, the two major key-currency countries, precisely because of the responsibility that placed on them. "If golde rust, what shal iren do?"[10]

The U.S.A. bears special responsibility, because it suffered no direct war damage to its economy, and was therefore in a favourable position to live up to the spirit as well as the letter of the Articles of Agreement, which were largely based on its own precepts. Britain is entitled to greater sympathy, because the devastation it suffered in the war greatly complicated its postwar tasks; even so, it stubbornly pursued its own way through a series of largely-unnecessary crises.

This assessment benefits from the wisdom of hindsight, it is true. Nevertheless some of the minor players in these events proffered essentially the same criticisms even as history was unfolding.

---

10 That is how the simple village priest in Chaucer's *Canterbury Tales* explained his obligation to give his flock a good example.

6. Generalized Floating.

Until 1973 there had been only two rather brief experiences with generally floating exchange rates in modern times, and those were in abnormal circumstances: the early years of reconstruction after World War I, and the 1930's. Nevertheless it has always been clear that fluctuating rates do not prevent international trade, they merely make its nature more uncertain.

Some countries never did accept the gold standard even in its heyday, some have had persistently depreciating currencies (and domestic inflations) for periods of up to 100 years and more, and a few have experienced considerable periods in which their currencies persistently appreciated even though most currencies traded at fixed rates. But the period since 1973 has been unique in the extent and duration of fluctuating rates as a modern phenomenon.

The Fund made its first distribution of SDR's just before the new era of floating rates began, in three installments totalling 9.3-billion units[11] on 1st January 1970, 1971, and 1972. The goal was to eventually replace gold and national currencies by the SDR as the world's principal reserve asset. (This might have permitted the Fund to manage the international money supply in much the same way that a national central bank manages the domestic money supply.) Even though initially the SDR was not used directly in international payments, it did give the Fund much greater flexibility in transactions with its members: instead of dealing in national currencies, it could deal in SDR's.

The decision to make the first allocation of SDR's was made on much narrower and more questionable grounds, however; it was based on estimates that the world's need for reserves would grow by between US$4-billion and US$5-billion per annum for the three years, and that the supply from other sources would grow by only US$1-billion to US$1.5-billion per annum.

The projected rate of growth in the demand for reserves was far above the average growth of actual reserves in the preceding 30 years, which had been adequate to finance a tremendous expansion of both world income and world trade from their depression levels. Furthermore, some economists were arguing that the growth of reserves had already been excessive and was fuelling world inflation (it was mainly in the form of U.S.-dollar and sterling balances).

---

[11] The initial U.S.-dollar equivalent of the SDR was $1.00000; after the 1971 devaluation, $1.08571; from the 1973 devaluation till June 1974, $1.20635. Thereafter the basis of comparison was changed, in recognition of the new regime of floating rates; it is now calculated as the weighted average rate against a basket of major currencies.

However, the major miscalculation was the projected growth of reserves other than SDR's, at US$3-billion to US$4.5-billion over the next three years: official holdings of national currencies actually rose by US$71-billion between the end of 1969 and the end of 1972, while the nominal dollar value of official gold holdings remained virtually unchanged.

The next allocation of SDR's amounted to 12-billion in another set of three installments on 1st January 1979, 1980, and 1981. This time the decision was attributed to furthering the objective of making the SDR the principal reserve asset of the system, and procedural changes were also introduced to increase its usefulness. SDR's have continued to be a relatively small part of total world reserves, however; the largest and fastest-growing element by far has been holdings of national currencies.[12]

In the meantime two more international committees meeting between 1972 and 1978 eventually brought the Second Amendment to the Fund Agreement, effective 1st April 1978. One of the more dramatic changes was the virtual extirpation of gold and all its works from the Articles of Agreement: the Fund is now prohibited from managing the price of gold or establishing a fixed price for it.

Instead of endeavouring to maintain the values of their currencies within one per cent of their gold parities, members are merely committed to promoting orderly and stable exchange rates in some vague way. Each is in effect permitted to follow any exchange arrangements it chooses, with few limitations. The Fund *may* in due course determine that conditions permit the introduction of a widespread system of adjustable but stable par values, based on the SDR or such other common denominator (not gold or a currency) as it may prescribe, but that will take an 85 per cent majority.

On the positive side, the Second Amendment made changes in the nature and use of the SDR designed to assist it in becoming the principal reserve asset of the international monetary system and to increase its usability. Among other things, the SDR may now be used directly to make international payments, instead of merely to acquire other currencies; it has thus become a true international money, though only one among many, and not yet a very important one. Also, the revised Agreement is a pragmatic recognition of the facts of life at the time the amendment

---

12 The accrual of reserves after 1973 in the form of substantial unrealized profits on gold inventories, caused by the dramatic appreciation of its market price, is not relevant for present purposes. Gold has largely ceased to be used as an international money and has become simply a speculative commodity with a volatile price, which many central banks happen to hold for historical reasons. However, it does imply a further relaxation of balance-of-payments discipline and further inflationary potential.

came into effect. The Fund can only enforce rules that a majority of its members, perhaps a strong majority, are prepared to put into practice.

However, it is obvious that there is no longer a consensus about the principles on which the international monetary system should operate. That being so, the Fund's obligation to "exercise firm surveillance over the exchange rate practices of its members" is not likely to accomplish much.

Nevertheless the Fund has continued to go resolutely about its normal business of assisting its members in meeting their balance-of-payments problems, within the limits imposed by the overall economic climate. That climate has included, of course, the anti-inflation policies implemented under the leadership of the major industrialized countries, which have placed strains on many Fund members.

The economic climate has also included sharp fluctuations in the exchange rates among major currencies, sometimes dramatically reversed in a relatively short period of time. These fluctuations were long tolerated on the premise that a "clean float" (non-intervention by the authorities) was the best way to ensure that market forces were allowed to have their full effect on all exchange rates.

Recently, however, there have been encouraging signs of greater willingness by the major industrialized nations to coöperate in nudging rates towards what appear to be their equilibrium values. Perhaps both sides of the debate over fixed *versus* fluctuating rates can now agree that they must be flexible enough to accommodate divergent national price trends, but not so flexible as to generate adverse feed-back effects on those trends. Even so, it will surely be a long time before the international monetary system can be managed as well as a domestic monetary system can be managed by an efficient central bank.

Part Five

Some Contentious Issues

Chapter 17

Population, Resources, and the Ecology

1. Population Fears.

In the preceding chapters of this analysis, there is an unspoken assumption that economic growth is unquestionably a Good Thing, and furthermore that it can go on indefinitely and without restraint. At first blush it would seem that the only limits to the growth rate are the public's willingness to save, in order to invest in new productive capital facilities, and its ability to acquire new skills and to devise more productive techniques, although in Chapter 11 it turned out that there is also a risk of saving too much rather than too little. Also, persistent economic growth seems to promise ever-rising living standards.

This optimistic view has not been universal, however. Serious doubts have been raised from time to time on one aspect of the matter or another, usually centring on concerns about population trends.

From early in Chinese history, through ancient Greek civilization, and down to the present day, thoughtful observers have frequently been concerned with population problems. At the theoretical level, the main questions have been what determines the size of human societies, and what are the consequences of a persistent increase or a persistent decrease. At the practical level, the concern has sometimes been with overpopulation, sometimes with underpopulation.

In 1346 the Black Death invaded Europe from Asia, and successive outbursts of it are thought to have reduced the population of some countries by as much as 45 per cent between then and 1400. In the 17th and 18th centuries some of the same countries again lost population over several decades, though not on anything like the same scale, at a time when increased numbers were generally favoured in support of national power and territorial expansion.

In the 19th century fears of overpopulation became dominant, but then gradually faded in the face of contrary arguments and concrete evidence that contradicted earlier pessimistic projections.

In the final third of the 20th century overpopulation fears have again been raised by many writers, and the ability of the world economy to continue to expand much longer has been seriously questioned. Whereas 19th-century concerns focused on the adequacy of food supplies, the current concerns relate to supplies of resources in general, ecological disturbances, and pollution. These concerns tend to reinforce one another, but it is useful to look at them independently before considering their interactions.

The fear of overpopulation is generally associated with the views Thomas Malthus expressed in his *Essay on Population*. The first edition was published in 1798; what is called the second edition, but was really a second and different book, in 1803; the sixth and last in 1826.

Malthus made two initial postulates: that food is necessary to the existence of man, and that the passion between the sexes is necessary and will remain nearly in its present state. He then asserted that population increases in a geometric ratio (for example, 1, 2, 4, 8, ...), except when checked in some way, whereas subsistence can at best increase in an arithmetic ratio (for example, 1, 2, 3, 4, ...). He concluded that the availability of food supplies places an effective limit on population. (He clearly recognized that subsistence includes other things as well as food, but he evidently saw food as the main limiting factor in subsistence.)

According to Malthus, the limit on population operates through two kinds of checks only, preventive and positive. Preventive checks are rational acts by mankind designed to reduce the birth rate, such as postponement of marriage and avoidance of premarital sexual intercourse, but including certain activities that permit sexual gratification without procreation, of which he did not approve—infanticide, prostitution, homosexual acts, contraceptive practices, etc.

Positive checks include war, disease, pestilence, famine, natural disasters, and anything that prevents people from giving proper food and attention to their children. Malthus did not favour these either, of course, but considered them inevitable if people did not apply the positive checks he did approve. In his view, therefore, the checks on population came down to some combination of vice and misery.

Furthermore Malthus argued that wages were close to the level of subsistence in his own day, had been so almost without exception throughout history, and must necessarily remain so—a preview of what later came to be known as the Iron Law of Wages. His reasoning was that competition by members of the public for scarce supplies of food to feed their growing families will drive up its price until the worker can no longer feed them all.

Malthus was clearly wrong on a number of points, but there is no need to recount them all here or to try to set him right on them. Critics soon pointed out that wages in the richer countries were well above subsistence levels, and had long been so, yet his views became entrenched in the theories of British classical economists for 100 years or more. What finally discredited the case was the accumulation of irrefutable evidence that the populations of Europe and North America have been growing persistently and substantially since about 1750, accompanied by declining birth rates and rising standards of living.

The reasons that the wealthier nations (and in large measure the world as a whole) have been able to raise their standards of living so successfully are complex. In part, of course, it has been due to the expansion of European-style cultivation to new and extensive productive areas in North and South America and many parts of the Pacific—at the expense of the displacement and degradation of the aboriginal peoples. In part, too, it has been due to the enormous technological advances that have occurred in many fields, including agriculture. Malthus recognized that these factors were operating in the world, but clearly underestimated their force, especially that of the latter.

However, it is also clear that rising incomes give people the means and the incentive to defend their newly-won gains. In poor agricultural communities the main hope of support in old age or adversity may be numerous offspring, yet infant mortality is likely to be high, so there is a strong incentive for the individual family to maintain a high birth rate, even though the resources of the community may be already strained to the limit. In wealthier communities, on the other hand, the care and education of children to current standards becomes burdensome, and centralized systems of social insurance replace them as sources of security, so the incentives for having children are greatly reduced.

Also, the widespread dissemination of information on birth control has made it much easier to control family size. It therefore appears that, though a rise in the availability of food (and other consumer goods) may at first lead to an increase in the population, the rate of increase is likely to taper off as time passes—especially if the rise in income is rapid and sustained.

It does not follow, however, that the Malthusian ghost has been laid for ever. Malthus noted that death rates in Europe were falling because of better sanitation, cleaner water supplies, and better health care, but neither he nor his critics made much of it. The fact is that it was declining death rates and not increasing birth rates that explained the accelerating rise in the European population that set in about

1750. The improvements that gave rise to the decline soon spilled over to other parts of the world to some extent, especially those areas where European influence was strong.

After World War II, greatly improved medical care and public health measures spread rapidly throughout the developing world. Death rates plummeted and population soared. It is estimated that the world's population did not reach its first billion till about 1800 A.D., and its second till about 1930; but by 1975 it had doubled again, and it has recently passed 5 billion.

Presumably the European experience will be repeated elsewhere, and in due course the growth rate will decline substantially. Perhaps the world's population will actually stabilize eventually; but when, and at what level?

To add a little perspective, it may be useful to look briefly at two rough-and-ready attempts to calculate an optimum level of population for the world. Any such attempt raises many difficult questions, of course. For example, it has been suggested that the optimum level should yield the highest well-being per person. But, should it be solely in terms of economic well-being, or should it allow for such things as the quality of life and individual happiness? How would any of these be measured? Would an overall average suffice, or should account be taken of how fairly the benefits are distributed among the population? And so on.

Waiving all those questions, in 1963 Professor Brian Hocking of the University of Alberta gave a series of talks on biology on the Canadian Broadcasting Corporation's program University of the Air. In the course of this series he raised the question of an optimum population for the world, and came up with a figure of about one billion. His reasoning, as reported by J.R. Nursall in *Queen's Quarterly* [Kingston, Canada] for the Spring of 1965, may be summarized briefly.

One billion is estimated to have been the world's population about the middle of the 19th century, which is about when insect and other agricultural pests began to have truly serious effects. Today's agricultural practices are really contrary to nature, for they result in large areas devoted to a single crop, or grazed intensively by a limited selection of domestic animals. This is very different from the mixture of plants and animals in an uncultivated area, and it spreads an unnatural feast before pests that prey on that crop or those animals. Man has responded by attempting to eliminate these "weeds" and "vermin", but it has been a losing battle, with adverse effects on the ecology ever since.

In 1970 an American biochemist named H.R. Hulett published an article in *BioScience* in which he, too, attempted to calculate the population the world could support at the standard of living the U.S.A. then enjoyed. His reasoning was interestingly different. He noted that the production of food crops, forest products, and other outputs from renewable resources faces a definite limit, because it depends on photosynthesis, the process by which plants use the energy of the sun to produce carbohydrates. He also calculated world output of major metals and fertilizer, and observed that, while production could be increased in most cases, it would be a relatively slow and costly process.

On balance, Hulett concluded that a world population of about one billion could be supported by the then-existing agricultural and industrial system *and the existing world workforce*, at the U.S. standard of living. However, a smaller world population would provide a smaller workforce, so he concluded that the optimum population would be less than one billion.

These are both pretty imprecise estimates, of course. Nevertheless it is interesting to note that two serious thinkers arrived at very similar figures, by quite different routes. What is even more interesting is the sharp contrast—several orders of magnitude—between their conclusions and the present population of the world, let alone the figures now projected for a few years into the 21st century.

2. Resources and the Environment.

Obviously, the ability of Planet Earth to support its human population depends ultimately on its physical resources. These may be divided into those capable of producing outputs that may be maintained indefinitely, and those that are inevitably used up in the process of satisfying human needs or wants.

The first category includes the seas, the land areas on which plant and animal life can be grown, the annual runoff of water in rivers and streams, and the radiant energy supplied daily by the sun. The second consists of the currently-existing stock of all other useful or potentially-useful materials, meaning primarily the metallic and nonmetallic minerals, but also including such things as stone and gravel useful in construction.

Alternatively, we may identify the *products* of the first category as "renewable resources", and the second category as "nonrenewable resources". This is the most commonly used terminology. The principal renewable resources are the current world stock of plant and animal life—what biologists call the *biomass*—and the flows of water and radiant energy over and above what are currently being used in biomass production.

The distinction between these categories of resources is not absolute, of course. The productive capacity of soil may be depleted by erosion, or by failure to replenish the nutrients taken from it in continued cropping. The total stock of plant and animal life may be allowed to decline instead of being treated as a renewable crop, or the stock of any particular species may be completely used up or otherwise destroyed. Many minerals and other materials can be recycled to other applications when their usefulness in one application is ended. Nevertheless the distinctions are of great practical importance.

Naturally, the total output that can be produced from these resources—mankind's potential real income—will also be affected by the amount and types of capital goods inherited from the past, and by the size and acquired skills of the labour force. That is merely a recognition of the three factors of production introduced in Chapter 1—land, capital, and labour. However, we must now take account of additional complications.

Until now we have generally assumed that "the state of the arts" was unchanged, or in other words that there were no changes in either the technology used in the productive process or the body of skills possessed by the labour force. That was perfectly valid for our purposes: we did not really ignore technological progress, but there seemed to be little we could usefully say about it, so we just acknowledged its existence and let it go at that. Now that we want to look at the limits on the ability of Planet Earth to support human life, however, we must make some effort to recognize the contribution that technology may make.

Also, we have so far been able to assume that the market mechanism will take care of the allocation of resources among competing uses, without worrying about the choices this involves. Now we must explicitly recognize some of the trade-offs that must be made, even though we will not be able to be very specific about them.

For one example, the use of land to produce lumber and other forest products competes with its use for food crops; measures that would expand food production may limit the supply of wood for construction, fuel, and papermaking. For another, oil, coal, and natural gas may be burned to produce energy or used to produce important chemical products (including plastics); overcoming a shortage in one use may provoke a shortage in another use. Furthermore, we will soon find that expanding production in any given field may do unexpected and unintended harm to the environment.

Land and Soil. Let's start with land and soil resources, since they are fundamental to the food chain that links all living things.

New soil is generated primarily by the weathering of various kinds of rock, which is a very slow process, so for all practical purposes our current endowment is all we have to work with. But cultivatable land is continually being lost in various ways. Some is being lost by erosion through the action of wind and water or by the spread of deserts, as a result of either natural forces or human mismanagement.

Some is being lost by being paved over for the spread of towns and cities or the construction of new and better roads and highways—in this case, often consisting of the highest-quality and best-situated land.

According to a U.S. estimate made in 1967, the world's potentially cultivatable land area is about 32 million square kilometers, of which about 14 million was then actually cultivated. Grazing land was thought to account for about two thirds of the uncultivated portion, and accessible forests for the remainder.

However, a doubling of the land area under cultivation will not likely bring a doubling of world food production. The best land is already cultivated, it need hardly be said; that which will produce a crop with the least cost in terms of labour (by subsistence farmers) or money (by commercial farmers) will be used first. Most uncultivated but potentially usable land is marginal: it may lack water, it may be steep or rocky, it may be inaccessible, the soil may be poor, the growing season may be short, or the like. Grazing land is already producing food, so only a portion of the crops that could be obtained by cultivating it would count as a net increase.

Many of these shortcomings can of course be overcome in some measure. Dry areas can be irrigated, steep slopes can be terraced, poor soils can be fertilized, and so on. Moreover, output both from a great deal of presently-cultivated land and from potentially-cultivatable land can be greatly increased by employing the best techniques already in use by the most efficient producers.

However, all these remedies are costly. They require substantial amounts of working capital per hectare, large expenditures on mechanical equipment or fixed capital, or long and expensive education and training for farmers now using outdated techniques. They are not quickly available to the average farmer in many parts of the world.

Furthermore, some of these remedies may simply push the problem into another field, and may have unintended adverse effects on the environment. Irrigation may threaten scarce resources of water needed for other purposes. It may also destroy the productivity of the soil by waterlogging or by depositing alkaline salts due to the evaporation of some of the water. Conversion of forestland to cropland reduces the supply or potential supply of wood products, and may lead to the environmental damages that will be noted shortly. Many improvements in agricultural techniques involve substantially increased demands for energy, which as we will soon see raises other problems.

Looking ahead to the future, we may also count on technical progress to devise new, better, and more efficient productive techniques. The so-called "green revolution" gives many examples of what may be achieved: the development and introduction of high-yielding varieties of major foodcrops, and the increased use of irrigation, fertilizers, and pesticides have dramatically increased food production where they have been used.

However, these techniques require capital resources and current expenses that are beyond the reach of many individual farmers. In many cases they also make substantially greater demands on energy supplies. Also, some of the exotic new varieties have proven vulnerable to insect pests and plant diseases, some of them already known but others previously unknown or insignificant. Perhaps even more important, there is a risk that concentrating production on the new varieties may seriously reduce the reserves of older varieties and thereby deplete the pool of genetic material that is so necessary for the development of new strains.

Forests. Vast areas of the world were once covered by forests, but only a fraction remains. It has long been known that the clearing of forests often results in soil erosion, floods, and changes in local climates. It also results in the extinction of many species of plant and animal life (and their valuable genetic material), by the destruction of their sources of food and shelter or the physical conditions necessary for their survival. Nevertheless the process of deforestation still goes on, often with little regard for these adverse effects.

Nowadays the continuing destruction of tropical forests to meet growing needs for food and fuel is particularly serious. Unlike temperate-zone forests, tropical forests do not build up a large reserve of humus and nutrients in the soil; removing them leaves the soil vulnerable not only to erosion by wind or by heavy tropical rains, but also to the rapid leaching away of its scarce supply of nutrients through surface and underground runoff. Some iron-rich tropical soils turn to a brick-like substance when eroded and exposed to sun and oxygen, which is almost impossible to restore to productivity. Thus productive tropical forests may easily be turned into unproductive cropland.

Water. It has been calculated that the annual freshwater runoff from the major continents is about 46,000 cubic kilometers on the average. However, much of this is concentrated in thinly populated areas, such as the Amazon basin and the rivers flowing into the Arctic Ocean. Also, the annual and seasonal variations in rainfall (and therefore in runoff) in many areas are substantial, so floods and surpluses may alternate with droughts and shortages.

The main uses of water are for industrial and agricultural production, not necessarily near to abundant supplies. Some measures designed to deal with these problems, such as canals and storage dams, result in substantial losses by evaporation.

The principal alternative is to tap underground reserves by means of wells, but this too may run into problems. If the withdrawal of water exceeds the natural recharge from runoff, the water table sinks; eventually the cost of pumping from ever-deeper wells becomes prohibitive, and in any case it becomes a matter of mining a nonrenewable resource. In coastal areas salt water may replace fresh water in the underground reservoirs. Ground water containing certain alkaline salts is not suitable for irrigation.

Energy. Energy has been described as the ultimate resource. Simple hunter-gatherer societies depended almost entirely on the sun's radiant energy for meeting their needs, whether in the form of plant food, animal food derived from plant food, human muscle-power fuelled by those foods, or fuel of biological origin to cook with and keep warm by. In due course mankind found ways to harness animal power, water power, and wind power to supplement human muscle-power and thereby raise living standards, still within the scope of renewable energy resources. Then came the use of nonrenewable sources: first coal, then oil, and most recently atomic fission.

Nowadays energy is a major component in virtually everything that is produced or consumed in modern society. Quite aside from the sun's energy that is incorporated directly in plant life through photosynthesis, and indirectly in the animal life that feeds on the plant life, inputs of energy are required for the seeding, cultivation, and harvesting of all agricultural products.

The same is true of the production of raw materials from nonrenewable resources. Further energy is required for processing these materials into useful products, for transporting, storing, and packaging them, and for distributing them to the ultimate consumer—not to mention that required in the home to convert foodstuffs into palatable dishes, and for heat, light, etc.

The world use of energy has been growing rapidly for over 100 years, and the pace appears to be accelerating. Petroleum liquids and natural gas are presently the favoured sources for a great many uses. At any given time the supplies considered recoverable from currently-proven reserves are sufficient for only a relatively few years at recent use rates, but these figures are not very helpful, because new reserves are continually being found. Synthetic crude petroleum can be produced at considerable expense from the hydrocarbons in tar sands (mainly sand and asphalt) and oil shale (shale permeated by a bituminous material). Although the world total of these resources is substantial, it is uncertain how much can be recovered. It is thus unclear how much longer oil and gas can supply a major portion of our energy needs.

World supplies of coal could meet several times the present demand for hundreds of years, but would be exhausted in about a century if the growth rate were (say) 5 per cent per annum. Furthermore, expensive capital facilities would have to be provided if it were to replace oil in many applications.

Nuclear fission, using present-day technology, can replace other sources of energy primarily in producing electricity; it can not produce portable fuels, and only limited industrial use can be made of the heat it produces. The main raw materials are uranium and thorium; they are fairly widespread throughout the world, but exploration for them is still very incomplete. Energy production by this means is highly capital-intensive, entails serious risks, and raises difficult problems in the disposal of spent fuel.

Generating energy by burning fossil fuels (petroleum, natural gas, or coal) or by nuclear fission all produce pollution of one kind or another, as described in section 3 of this chapter. Controlled nuclear fusion offers the possibility of safer procedures, little or no radioactive wastes, and abundant fuel supplies. So far, however, it has not been possible to achieve it.

Other possible sources of energy are geothermal installations, and various applications of solar energy. The possibilities of tapping solar energy include not only directly using the sun's rays but also making use of the power in wind, tides, ocean currents, and other sun-based phenomena. The potential of these sources is enormous, though little has so far been accomplished. Realizing any substantial portion of this potential would be a great technological challenge, however, and in many cases would have adverse effects on the environment.

Nonrenewable Materials. Chemical fertilizers are widely and increasingly used in agriculture, and have contributed materially to increased outputs. They consist mainly of compounds of potassium, phosphorus, and nitrogen. Potassium compounds are in plentiful supply, and phosphorus compounds reasonably so. Nitrogen compounds are derived mainly from fossil fuels; the limitations on this source have already been noted.

However, the recycling of agricultural and human wastes appears to offer an adequate alternative source of these fertilizers, and a renewable one, making use of the natural cycle of growth, death, decay, and regeneration. Indeed, natural sources appear to be superior in many cases, especially for tropical soils, because of their humus content.

It is unlikely that the world will ever run out of iron or aluminum, because it is already feasible to mine ores with a metallic content only two or three times as high as the average in common rock. Supplies of a few other metals, including copper, are also relatively elastic: their ores range widely in richness, and are available in quantities that become greater as their metallic content decreases.

The supplies of most other metals are highly concentrated in a few localities, however, and are either not present at all or present in very minute proportions in common rock. Some, such as tungsten and mercury, are already in short supply. The recoverable supply of many others is insufficient to meet expected demand for more than a few years.

Shortages of any one material may be met in part by recycling, in part by the substitution of other materials, and in part by changes in product design that will economize on the use of material, but there are practical limits to all three processes. Economic considerations offer strong incentives for such actions, since growing shortages mean higher prices for the materials in question. However, economic considerations also impose limits on the effectiveness of these remedies, for rising costs may reduce the list of profitable products.

The anticipated shortages of many metals may be expected to increase the relative importance of iron and aluminum, the supplies of which are likely to prove more elastic. They may also increase the use of plastics, which for other reasons have already displaced metals in many uses. However, many plastics and chemicals are presently produced from petroleum and natural gas, and we have already seen that these and other fossil fuels are themselves threatened by supply shortages as sources of energy.

Plant materials offer an alternative to petroleum as a source of plastics and chemicals, but in turn this use competes with uses of scarce land resources for food, construction, and other purposes.

Thus the supply problems of food, energy, and materials are all interrelated.

Distribution and Equity Problems. The problems relating to the supplies of food, energy, and materials are complicated by the fact that existing supplies are unevenly distributed among the world's population, and their consumption is even more unevenly distributed. World food supplies in general are adequate or more than adequate at the present time, for example, but there is famine and starvation in some areas despite unwanted surpluses of major foodstuffs in other areas. This applies within nations as well as among nations: important sections of the population in even the richest countries are undernourished. The basic reason, of course, is lack of income by the individuals and families concerned, not a food shortage as such.

More generally, the per capita consumption of food, energy, and materials varies greatly both among nations and within nations, which in turn reflects enormous differences in income. One aspect of the matter is that the poorer (or developing) countries aspire to raise their standards of living towards those of the richer countries, which implies increasing pressure on the world's scarce resources.

However, more fundamental questions of ethics, morality, and equity are involved. How ought access to the world's resources be allocated among nations? Within nations? Is it proper for the already-developed nations to appropriate nonrenewable resources for their own immediate purposes, on a scale that pre-empts their eventual use by the developing countries as they raise their real incomes in the future? Is it proper for the present generation to appropriate nonrenewable resources for their own immediate use, on a scale that pre-empts their eventual use by future generations? If some or all of these actions are deemed to be improper, how should the economic rules be changed?

3. Pollution.

For the vast majority of mankind, history has seen a persistent trend of improvement in their quality of life and in their expectations of continuing improvements. This is particularly true of the last 200 years or so, thanks in large part to the technological advances that have occurred not only in the productive process in general but also in all fields of human endeavour.

It is of course true that there have been periods of retreats as well as periods of advances, both in particular geographic areas and for the world as a whole. It is also true that there are marginalized peoples in many parts of the world who have shared very little in these advances, and who live lives that are little improved over those of their forefathers several generations ago. Nevertheless even the poor (however we choose to define them) in virtually every country live incomparably better than their counterparts 200 or 100 (or even 50) years ago. Progress has indeed conferred many blessings on mankind, in the form of higher real incomes, better education, better health, and better opportunities for self-fulfillment and enjoyment.

However, there is a negative side to the story, too, quite distinct from the resource-depletion and other problems we have noted so far. The progress that has done so much to improve mankind's lot has done less-obvious but serious harm to the environment in which we live, in a wide variety of ways. Some of the harm has been the result of accidents, and some of it can be stopped or reversed, but much of it has consisted of almost inevitable side-effects of events or processes that have contributed to human progress.

The major evidence of this harm is pollution of various kinds—the addition of harmful substances to the soil, the water, or the air that are not naturally there, or the unnatural increase of substances that do occur naturally but are now being added in quantities that overwhelm the normal restorative powers of nature. The pollutants are many and varied. Individually and collectively they threaten the life, health, and well-being of humanity.

It must of course be acknowledged that nature is not unqualifiedly friendly and benign. The earth is continuously bombarded by ultraviolet solar radiation that would be injurious to plant and animal life alike if not screened out by the ozone layer that lies at altitudes of 15 to 40 kilometers above the earth. Natural forces from time to time have disastrous effects on human activities. Volcanoes erupt and not only create extensive local destruction but may also spew ash, carbon dioxide, and noxious gases into the atmosphere on a scale that affects the whole world. Storms, tidal waves, floods, droughts, earthquakes, and other natural disasters devastate large areas. Nevertheless the great variety of natural forces operating in the world long ago achieved a remarkably stable equilibrium, in which the effects of temporary disturbances were gradually eradicated and balance restored.

That continued to be the situation until comparatively recent times: mankind progressed primarily by learning to adapt to the forces of nature as he found them. Eventually, however, we learned to manipulate certain elements of our environment in ways that had cumulative effects of their own.

The first step was learning the use of fire. The evolution of settled agriculture as an improvement on simple hunting and gathering was another major development. The progressive exploitation of various energy sources was still another: the use of fossil fuels to supplement or replace wood and other plant products, the harnessing of domesticated daft animals, the steam engine, the internal combustion engine, electricity, and now nuclear power.

At first the scale of human activities was small enough so that these developments posed no serious threat to the restorative powers of nature. By the middle of the 19th century, however, and perhaps even earlier, this had ceased to be true, and pollution has accelerated dramatically since World War II.

The major pollutants in the air we breathe are oxides of sulphur, nitrogen, and carbon, hydrocarbons like methane, and small particles of solid matter discharged into the air. They come largely from the burning of fossil fuels (including automotive fuels), but also from industrial processes such as smelting, petroleum refining, and papermaking, and from the burning of trash. Some of them react with one another in the presence of sunlight to produce various types of smog (a combination of smoke and fog). They can seriously affect the health of human beings, animals, and plants, especially in heavy concentrations.

Oxides of sulphur and nitrogen combine with water droplets in the air to produce acid rain, which has damaged forests and lakes throughout the northern hemisphere. Some particles contain lead, mercury, cadmium, and other heavy metals, which can get into the food chain and adversely affect health.

Particular mention should be made of carbon dioxide. Most other forms of pollution can be sharply reduced if not eliminated (though usually at considerable cost), but ending emissions of carbon dioxide would be extremely difficult. It accumulates as a sort of blanket in the stratosphere, and inhibits the re-radiation of heat from the earth. It is widely believed that this will result in a "greenhouse effect", that is a persistent rise in the temperature of the atmosphere that will eventually cause widespread climate changes, the spread of deserts, and sufficient melting of the polar ice caps to flood many heavily-populated coastal areas.

Certain chemicals currently being released into the air are believed to be a serious threat to the ozone layer that, as mentioned previously, protects the earth from ultraviolet solar radiation.

Pollutants found in water include organisms that cause disease (often introduced in incompletely-treated sewage), chemical wastes from households, industry, and agriculture, mineral fibres and metals discharged by some mining and industrial operations or deposited from the atmosphere, and sediments from soil erosion.

Some of these chemicals and metals are highly toxic or are threats to health, and have invaded sources of drinking water and the food chain. Acid rain has depleted fish stocks (especially the more valuable species) in many lakes and rivers. The decomposition of some sewage wastes depletes the dissolved oxygen needed by fish. Fertilizer runoff stimulates the growth of undesirable forms of aquatic plant life, which make water unsuitable for recreation and may give it an unpleasant taste.

Water is also adversely affected by heat pollution—abnormal heating due to the use of water by power plants and some industries to get rid of waste heat. This reduces the oxygen content of the water, needed to support marine life and to decompose wastes. Increased water temperature will kill some forms of life, and interfere with the reproductive cycle of others.

Noise pollution is a fact of life in modern industrialized countries. It is a serious problem in many industrial activities, but is also prevalent in residential and recreational areas, thanks to such modern conveniences as small and large electrical appliances, power tools, power lawnmowers, motorcycles, and motor boats. Prolonged exposure to loud noise is known to impair hearing, and noise is believed to be a factor in many stress-related conditions.

Even getting rid of normal household trash raises serious pollution problems. A great many municipalities are experiencing increasing difficulty in finding suitable land-fill sites for garbage disposal. Burning any burnable components offers some advantages, including the production of heat that can be used to generate power, but it involves adding to air pollution by the discharge of carbon dioxide, noxious gases, solid particles, and toxic chemicals. Disposing of industrial wastes is even more of a problem, for they include various toxic substances. Finding safe ways of discarding spent fuel from nuclear power plants has yet to be accomplished.

4. Disputed Conclusions.

While there is some disagreement over the details, there is wide agreement regarding the essential facts about the world's present population, presently-exploitable resources, and current pollution problems. However, there is a wide range of views regarding future prospects in all three fields: population forecasts have proven notoriously unreliable in the past, and predictions in the other two fields depend heavily on the assumptions made about the contributions that technology may be able to make towards solving the many recognized problems. Consequently there is very wide disagreement concerning the conclusions to be drawn from the agreed facts, both with respect to what will happen if present trends are allowed to continue unimpeded and with respect to what can be done and should be done to influence the course of events.

A number of observers in recent decades have seriously questioned the ability of the world economy to continue indefinitely on a course of perpetual expansion. An important example is a report entitled *The Limits to Growth*, which was published in 1972 and immediately attracted a great deal of attention. It was prepared by a research team working at the prestigious Massachusetts Institute of Technology and sponsored by the Club of Rome. Using a complex computer model of the world economy, which endeavoured to simulate the relationships among population, food, natural resources, pollution, and other factors, they concluded that present trends could not be long continued.

Whereas Malthus largely confined himself to food as the limiting factor on population, the M.I.T. team found that pollution, resource exhaustion, or deteriorating health services would eventually bring a catastrophic decline even if food needs were fully met; if one limit were overcome in some way, another would become the controlling factor. Disaster would be inevitable sooner or later—and probably well before the year 2100—unless not only population growth but also pollution, resource consumption, and industrial expansion through capital investment were brought under control.

In 1977 Paul R. Ehrlich, Anne H. Ehrlich, and John P. Holdren published *Ecoscience: Population, Resources, Environment*—a monumental third edition of a work first published in 1970, in which they explored much the same relationships as the M.I.T. team. They endorsed much of latter's analysis, and reached basically similar conclusions, except that they were more optimistic about the possibility that remedial measures may be taken in time to bring human behavior into harmony with reality and thus avert a catastrophe. Their book has been a major source of information on resource and pollution problems in this chapter.

Many additional observers have reached similar conclusions, but many others have been unconvinced in greater or lesser degree. In fact there is a fairly continuous spectrum of views, from the highly pessimistic to the highly optimistic. The pessimists are commonly called neo-Malthusians, and the optimists refer to their writings as "doomsday literature". The pessimists sometimes call the optimists cornucopians, after the magic horn of plenty in Greek mythology, for they rely heavily on the belief that technological advances will save the day.

A detailed critique of *The Limits to Growth* was published in 1973 by a group at the University of Sussex in England, under the title *Thinking about the Future* (also published in the U.S.A. as *Models of Doom*, in this case including a reply by the M.I.T. team). They agreed that the problems addressed were serious, but offered technical criticisms of the procedures used and questioned the conclusions.

In a series of papers the British group examined the subsystems of the M.I.T. model in detail: population, agriculture, capital, pollution, and energy. With the exception of the first, they concluded that the assumptions in these subsections were unsatisfactory.

The group then reviewed the model as a whole, and tested its sensitivity to certain key assumptions. The collapse due to resource shortages is significantly postponed by introducing annual rates of increase of 1 per cent both for discovering new natural resources and for increasing technical capabilities. Raising both rates to 2 per cent postpones the collapse indefinitely, and makes the slowdown in population growth dependent on food shortages. Assuming a like improvement in food production removes even this limitation. However, the group did not attempt to construct an improved model with which to offer alternative calculations.

In evaluating these conflicting opinions, you may wish to briefly review the discussion of models in general in section 2 of Chapter 1. You should also note that a constant percentage growth rate is an exponential function, like compound interest; the value grows at an ever-faster pace, so sooner or later a variable that is growing at an exponential rate will overtake one that is not.

Limits to Growth uses exponential growth rates for some of its population-limiting factors, such as resource use, but not for population-supporting factors, such as improvements in technology. *Thinking about the Future* explores the effect of exponential growth rates for the population-supporting factors as well.

You must ask yourself whether it is appropriate to use an exponential growth rate in any given case, and consider possible alternatives. If you decide it is appropriate, you must still decide on a realistic numerical value. Finally, you should be aware that the annual growth rate of the world's population has been about 2 per cent in recent years; to assume the same growth rate for the discovery of new resources, the increase in technical capabilities, and the production of food would therefore be about equivalent to assuming all the problems away.

If you conclude that there is indeed a real danger that a catastrophic decline in the world's population will occur sooner or later unless corrective action is taken, more or less as the M.I.T. team warns, what do you think *should* be done about it? First, should anything be done to limit population growth? If so, what? What should be the policy target? (Some people think nothing should be done; some argue for zero population growth as the goal; others say the world's population should be reduced substantially below its present level.)

Second, should anything else be done, either instead or as well? Presumably we should at the very least do our best to eliminate pollution, or reduce it to the lowest possible level.

However, what about the questions raised at the end of section 2? What if anything should we do about sharing the remaining stock of nonrenewable resources among the world's nations, while supplies last? Should we let market forces operate unchecked, or should we interfere in some way to ration the stocks according to some concept of equitable sharing? Or perhaps give priority to the poorer nations, in an attempt to bring their standards of living up to some minimum level? What about sharply *reducing* the present standards of living in the wealthy nations? What about seeking more equal distribution of consumption *within* nations? And what about sharing the present stock of nonrenewable resources with future generations?

Next, what do you think *will in fact* be done? Will the international community find some way to limit population growth, and at what level will population eventually stabilize? What does this imply for the *average* standard of living in the world?

How, if at all, will the burden of the necessary adjustments be shared? Will the rich nations find some way to share access to resources with the poorer nations, and to help them control their populations? Or will they turn resolutely inwards, control their own populations as they see fit, pre-empt the use of the world's resources for their own use (perhaps by market power, perhaps by military intervention, perhaps in some other way), and let the rest of the world stew in its own juice? How will they share access to resources among themselves? By some form of mutual agreement, by armed force, or how?

If on the other hand you conclude that a population crisis will be avoided without the need for any intervention, many of the same questions remain. What will the eventual population of the world be, and what average standard of living will be sustainable thereafter? How *should* access to the world's resources be divided among and within nations? How *will* these problems be solved in fact?

Selected Readings

Bahr, Howard M., Chadwick, Bruce A., and Thomas, Darwin L., eds. *Population, Resources, and the Future: Non-Malthusian Perspectives.* Provo [Utah]: Brigham Young University Press, 1972.

Cox, Peter R., and Peel, John, eds. *Population and Pollution: Proceedings of the Eighth Annual Symposium of the Eugenics Society.* London: New York: Academic Press, 1972.

Dupâquier, Jacques, Fauve-Chamoux, A., and Grebenik, E., eds. *Malthus Past and Present.* London: Academic Press, 1983.

Ehrlich, Paul R. *The Population Explosion.* New York: Simon & Schuster, 1990.

Ehrlich, Paul R., Ehrlich, Anne H., and Holdren, John P. *Ecoscience: Population, Resources, Environment.* Third edition. San Francisco: W.H. Freeman and Co., 1977.

Cole, H.S.D., *et al. Thinking about the Future: A Critique of* The Limits to Growth. London: Chatto & Windus for Sussex University Press, 1973. [Also published as *Models of Doom: A Critique of* The Limits to Growth, New York, Universe Books, c. 1973.]

Malthus, Thomas Robert. *An Essay on the Principle of Population* [first edition, London: 1798]; and *A Summary View of the Principle of Population*; edited with an introduction by Anthony Flew. Hamondsworth [England]: Penguin Books, 1970.

Meadows, Donella H., *et al. The Limits to Growth: A Report for The Club of Rome's Project on the Predicament of Mankind.* Second edition. New York: Signet, 1974.

Meadows, Dennis L., ed. *Toward Global Equilibrium: Collected Papers.* Cambridge Mass.: Wright-Allen Press Inc., 1973.

Mesarovic, Mihajlo, and Pestel, Eduard. *Mankind at the Turning Point: The Second Report to The Club of Rome.* New York: E.P. Dutton & Co. Inc., 1974.

Robinson, H. *Population and Resources.* London: The Macmillan Press Ltd., 1981.

World Commission on Environment and Development [the Brundtland Comission]. *Our Common Future* [the Brundtland Report]. Oxford: Oxford University Press, 1987.

Chapter 18

Inflation and Unemployment

1. The Policy Issue.

Chapter 13 described the eclipse of demand management, because as presently practiced and under current conditions it can not achieve either of its main goals, but must be content with seeking the point of minimum combined discomfort from too much inflation and too much unemployment. Any combination of fiscal and monetary policies that would reduce unemployment would make inflation worse, and any combination that would reduce inflation would make unemployment worse.

Whereas unemployment rates were held around 3 per cent of the labour force in most industrialized countries for many years after World War II, they range from double to quadruple that now. Annual inflation rates, which had been 1 or 2 per cent in the best-regulated economies in the same period, are also double or quadruple or more—much more in some cases. And of course things are much worse in the developing countries. Yet governments are grateful that both rates are down from the far higher levels reached in the 1970's and early 1980's.

Make no mistake about it, both problems are serious. To give up on inflation and go all out for full employment, as some naïve critics propose, would soon bring an acceleration of the rate. That in turn would cause intolerable chaos in the decisionmaking process that is so vital to a money-and-market economy.

It is true that some economic agents can provide fairly well against the effects of an inflation rate that is correctly foreseen, but not everyone can do so. In any case future inflation rates are difficult to forecast accurately, and a rate that is accelerating or that threatens to do so compounds the difficulty. Even at relatively low rates—certainly at the rates of around 5 per cent annually that many governments now seem willing to tolerate—inflation introduces undesirable risks and uncertainties.

Unemployment is an equally serious problem, for it means not only the loss of potential real output but also, more importantly, damage to human values. For those who have had many years of rewarding and productive work, prolonged unemployment may so undermine their self-confidence that their future employability will be seriously impaired. For school-leavers and other would-be new entrants to the labour force, failure to learn the benefits and the discipline of productive and rewarding work experience at an early age may adversely affect their ability to hold a job for the rest of their lives. The discouraging prospects they see of ever winning a useful place in society is surely the main reason so many young people have become alienated and have turned to violent and anti-social behaviour.

Truly "full" employment is surely impossible, quite aside from seasonal factors in some activities. Shifting demand and supply conditions ensure that some old jobs will be disappearing even in the best of times, when still more new ones are being generated, so there will always be some transitional unemployment. In fact it has proven difficult for economists to agree on how close to full employment it is possible to get.

Shortages of particular skills may now show up even when the average unemployment rate is far above the 3 per cent level common in the early postwar years. However, this is not surprising under the present circumstances. Many young people have been denied work experience over the past 10 or 20 years, and have been discouraged from seeking vocational training because there seemed no point in it, so the supply of employable labour is weak.

Production has been well below the capacity of existing plant and equipment for the same length of time, so the inducement to invest has been too weak to generate the plant and equipment that would be needed to employ the potential labour force. Surely it is not unreasonable to hope that unemployment rates approximating 3 per cent could be achieved again, if inflation were controlled, adequate capital put in place, and the labour force properly trained.

2. The Case for Focusing on Inflation.

The economics profession has become divided more or less completely into a monetarist and a Keynesian (or a nonmonetarist) camp. So far neither camp has been able to come up with a convincing strategy that will control either inflation or unemployment without making the other worse.

Lacking anything better, the governments of most countries have chosen to focus primarily on controlling inflation and to limit their attempts at reducing unemployment. This strategy owes much to monetarist criticisms of Keynesian policies, though monetarists do not claim it as their own. Demand management has not been entirely abandoned, but it has been emasculated.

The methods now being used to combat inflation are the same as would have been used 50 or 100 or 200 years ago: tight money, and attempts to balance government budgets. The main difference is that these methods are not being applied as ruthlessly as the former orthodoxy would have prescribed. They could certainly end inflation quickly if they could be applied vigourously enough, as they have often done in the past, but public opinion will no longer permit such extreme measures, because of their intolerable social costs.

The case for this strategy rests on the hope that strictly limiting the growth of the money supply and eliminating or at least reducing government deficits will turn the situation around and restore sustainable growth. It relies on stimulating new private capital spending as the engine of expansion. The stimulus is to come partly from getting interest rates down, and partly from reducing business taxes.

Its proponents admit that it is responsible for the economic stagnation of recent years, the slump in world trade, and the plight of the developing countries. Nevertheless they argue that reversing these policies in an effort to reduce unemployment would prove mistaken: it would risk even higher rates of inflation that would in due course require even higher rates of unemployment to cure.

The argument also blames government deficits for much of the inflationary pressures, and for the high levels of nominal interest rates. Government borrowing and the consequent high interest rates are said to crowd out private borrowing from capital markets, hence eliminating or reducing these deficits is expected to reduce interest rates and make room for private capital spending that will revive the economy.

3. The Effects of a Cumulative Government Deficit.

Some advocates of the anti-inflation strategy currently in favour in so many countries seem to ignore or deny the stabilizing rôle government deficits can play in slack times. However, a logical case can be made for reducing or eliminating the deficit even in the face of continuing high unemployment. The argument entails, first, explaining precisely why drastic action is sometimes necessary; second, giving reasons for believing that those conditions now obtain in a given country; third, specifying how it can be done and what the effects will be; and, fourth, showing that the results will be better than those of the available alternatives.

An excellent explanation of the first point was given by Mr. J. de Larosière, then the Managing Director of the International Monetary Fund, in an address to the

Fortieth Congress of the International Institute of Public Finance in Innsbruck, Austria, on 27th August 1984. (His remarks were reported in the *IMF Survey* of 3rd September 1984.)

If government deficits were mostly cyclical, de Larosière said, or if a country's growth rate were high enough, the accumulation of government debt over time would not be serious; the total might even fall as a percentage of gross national product (GNP). But if deficits are persistent, if the growth rate slows down, and if real interest rates (after adjusting for inflation) are high, the debt will rise as a percentage of GNP—probably at an accelerating rate.

Rising government debt means that interest costs will absorb an ever-increasing portion of the budget, de Larosière continued, especially if interest rates rise or the growth rate of the economy falls, and may themselves become a major factor in generating ever-higher deficits. Eventually the time may come when inflating its way out of its problems may seem the only feasible solution for the government. Or, the financial markets may conclude that inflation is the inevitable result, confidence may evaporate, the government may no longer be able to borrow on money or capital markets, and the fear of inflation may prove to be a self-fulfilling prophecy.

De Larosière also noted the additional complications that arise if the debt is owed to foreigners and has been incurred for non-productive purposes. Whereas the burden of an internal debt is merely a transfer from one set of residents to another, and can be offset by domestic measures, the burden of an unproductive external debt must be paid to nonresidents and is a net drain on the real income of the economy.

However, he did not mention another serious side effect of a mounting internal government debt: the shift of income is regressive. Interest on government debt accrues mainly to the benefit of the well-to-do, but must be paid out of general revenue. If interest payments absorb a rising portion of the budget, there will be a net shift of real income to the holders of the debt.

This brings us to the second point in the argument for debt reduction. At the time of his address in Innsbruck de Larosière felt that the problem was already serious in most countries. It has got no better since. Whether it has yet become serious enough in any particular country to require drastic remedies is a matter of opinion, but there is no need to attempt to reach a definitive conclusion here and now. *The prospects are that the situation can only get worse*, since official and private projections are virtually unanimous in foreseeing a continuation of inflation and high levels of unemployment for years to come. Even if we conclude that drastic action is not yet needed, we had better start thinking about what to do when that time does come.

The only hope of escaping drastic budget cuts sooner or later seems to be that gradual growth as a result of "natural" economic forces will eventually raise the economy to something like the full-employment level. That would automatically increase government revenues and reduce expenditures on welfare and other social services, which would either balance the budget or make it much more manageable.

Any such hope looks pretty faint in most countries today, however. Inflation rates are stubbornly holding at uncomfortable levels after 20 years or so of official countermeasures; continuing economic recovery is likely to release renewed inflationary pressures, and necessitate renewed restraint. In any case the growth rate is vulnerable to a new cyclical downturn at any time.

Now for the third and fourth points: deciding how to reduce the budget deficit when the time for effective action can no longer be postponed, and evaluating the results.

The ideal solution would be to find a means of controlling inflation that does not sacrifice output and employment, so the techniques of demand management could once more be freely used to raise real income to its full potential; but that is still merely a hope for the future. Hardliners therefore say there will be nothing for it but to press the present strategy much harder, and make drastic cuts in government expenditures. (Raising taxes would of course be a logical alternative, but is seldom considered by hardliners, most of whom blame excessive social services for a large part of the deficit.) "Hew to the line, and let the chips fall where they may!"

A sharp reduction in the deficit, whether by cutting spending or by raising taxes, means a sharp increase in unemployment, already at painfully high levels. The implication is that materially reducing the rate of inflation would cause less net damage to society than the consequent increase in unemployment. At some point this might well become true; just where that point would lie, however, involves value judgements on which there might be substantial differences of opinion.

4. **The Case against Focusing on Inflation.**

Some critics would say that the harsh effects of deliberately depressing the spending stream as a means of controlling inflation might be justified if there were any hope not only that it could be pressed to a successful conclusion but also that so doing would usher in a new era of sustained prosperity and high employment at stable prices. However, they would deny that this would be the case. They would say that the all-but-universal acceptance of the strategy has not been because there is a consensus among economists that it will work, but because there is a poverty of new ideas and insights. Despite its obvious shortcomings, no-one has yet come up with an alternative that has won widespread acceptance as being clearly more promising.

As already noted, some supporters of the present strategy seem to ignore or deny the stabilizing rôle government deficits can play in slack times. But in such circumstances financing the deficit can not crowd out private investment that is not going to occur anyway.

Furthermore, a government deficit in slack times is essentially neutral with respect to interest rates. In good times and bad the money some people save must be borrowed and spent by others, or a self-reinforcing deflationary spiral like that of the 1930's will set in. The immediate effects on interest rates are pretty much the same whether it is businessmen who borrow to finance new capital spending or governments that borrow to support an ailing economy.

As also noted already, the current strategy relies on stimulating new private capital spending as the engine of expansion. This is a good approach as far as it goes, but some critics have said that it is doomed from the start, because the stimulants offered are inadequate. They consist partly of getting inflation down and thereby getting interest rates down, and partly of reducing business taxes. The strategy is certainly not working very well or very quickly. To be successful, it would have to cobble together a highly-improbable chain of events.

To get market interest rates down really low, the screws must be kept on until inflation has been reduced virtually to zero, so as to eliminate the inflation-premium component (i.e., compensation for the lost purchasing power of the money lent). This is clearly going to take a long time—after 10 or 20 years we are seeing some progress, but there is still a long way to go, and it is feared that hard-won ground will quickly be lost if the restrictive policies are relaxed.

However, there is also a risk-premium component in interest rates that must be eliminated if they are to fall—compensation for the risk that the borrower may default. But the long period of stagnation this scenario implies means continuing risks for even the soundest loans, so the risk premium is unlikely to decline until a business upturn is clearly under way.

Note that there is a "catch 22" problem here: interest rates must go down if capital spending is to revive and start an economic recovery; the risk premium must go down if interest rates are to go down; but recovery must begin before the risk premium will decline. No wonder fiscal and monetary restraint have had so much trouble getting interest rates to go down and stay down!

However, there is still another requirement for success, and it is the most important one of all: businessmen must become confident that they can sell sufficient additional output to justify the cost of new plant and equipment. In technical terms they need a positive "inducement to invest", i.e. the expected return on the investment must exceed the interest cost by an appreciable amount. Only then can the official strategy begin to succeed.

No new capital spending will occur without this crucial ingredient, regardless of any inducements such as low interest rates or tax concessions. But, as already pointed out, the depressed level of output this strategy has involved has meant that there has been a great deal of underutilized productive capacity that had to be either worn out or rendered obsolete by technical advances before there was much need for the creation of new capacity.

In the late 1980's there was at last some renewal of expansion in a number of countries, though interest rates remained relatively high and output was still well below potential. After all, *some* new investment opportunities are likely to occur even in slack times. But there was no assurance that the recovery would bring these economies to a high level of employment and a reasonable approximation to the full use of their productive resources, and in fact that did not occur. On the contrary, the 1990's started off with a new recession; recovery has been slow and uncertain.

As for the future, may not even the most prosperous countries find themselves still in a situation of chronic underemployment and continuing threats of a new recession? And what will prevent the reappearance of newly virulent inflationary price increases, despite substantial unemployment? Just the threat that their governments will reimpose restrictive fiscal and monetary policies? That will do little to encourage the stable rate of new capital formation necessary to support continued prosperity.

Doesn't this all sound distressingly like a recipe for the perpetuation of the boom-and-bust cycles of the 19th and the early-20th centuries, which were resumed in the 1970's?

5. Some Proposed Remedies.

Looking back over section 5 of Chapter 13, perhaps you could summarize the inflation problem by saying that there is no satisfactory mechanism for limiting the total of the community's money income to just the amount that will buy "tomorrow's" total potential output at "today's" prices. We are all free to set our asking prices at whatever level we think will be most advantageous, but there is nothing to put a limit on the total—nothing but the reluctance of the authorities to validate the resulting price increases, which in practice means nothing but how much unemployment the public will stand for.

Various forms of wage and price control have been tried in the past in an effort to limit the total money income of the community to a non-inflationary sum, but with only limited and temporary success. For one thing, it is extremely hard to devise a program that is clearly fair to everyone; as already observed, the Canadian effort in 1975-78 was better conceived than most, and was at least moderately successful in achieving its announced goals, yet its demise was widely welcomed.

However, controls have a much more serious fault still: they are not really compatible with a money-and-market system, which is essentially profit motivated.

Recall the discussion of pure profit and its rôle in sections 8 and 9 of Chapter 4, and the comments on price controls in section 3 of Chapter 13. Price controls are incompatible with the money-and-market system, because they are unable to recognize and respect pure profit. It is easy enough to recognize the idea in the abstract, but how could you ever identify what part of the businessman's "bottom line" is pure profit?

Some economists have proposed an "incomes policy" as a device to control inflation. This sounds as if it should be designed to limit money incomes to a non-inflationary total—just the thing we are looking for. In practice, however, most of these plans are addressed primarily to wages, salaries, and other forms of personal remuneration (or just "wages", for short); sometimes they are entirely so limited. This is both unfair and analytically unsound.

We saw in section 3 of Chapter 1 that "wages" is a type of factor return, but there are two other types as well, the "rent" of land and "interest" on capital. These two may be combined into "returns to property", which typically accounts for about 30 per cent of net national income in a modern economy. Restraints would have to apply evenhandedly to all factor returns in order to be fair, and in order to be effective in controlling inflation.

A variant known as a "tax-based incomes policy" (TIP) has won considerable support from professional economists. It proposes to give producers a tax inducement to keep costs down, through either a penalty for exceeding given guidelines or a tax credit for keeping within them. It is claimed that the plan need apply to only a relatively small number of the largest firms, with a supplementary plan for government employees and some special cases, and that it would be relatively easy to administer.

Some TIP proposals have been addressed mainly to wages, but it would seem that they could be made to apply to all costs, including capital-cost allowances (depreciation charges) and purchases of materials and services. TIP's have been criticized in other respects, however, including fears that they would interfere with functional price changes as well as merely inflationary changes, and that they could not clearly limit money-income claims to the value of potential output at stable prices.

Another proposal, the Market Anti-Inflation Plan (MAP), is intended to affect both wages and profits directly, and to use the market mechanism to promote an equilibrium. It claims to permit the money supply to be increased by just enough for economic health, and to leave individual prices and wages free to adjust while keeping the average price level stable.

The central bank would set up a MAP-Credit Office, open accounts for all firms, and credit each with 100 per cent of the previous year's net sales plus an allowance for increased productivity. Credit would be added for new employees hired, or deducted for employees let go; also for increasing or reducing capital. If its net sales exceeded its credit balance, the firm would have to buy equivalent credit from some other firm; if its net sales were less, it could sell the surplus credit. As you can see, and as critics were quick to point out, it sounds pretty complicated administratively.

All these schemes have faults, but most of them have useful features. For example, the TIP proposals suggest that business taxes might be applied to costs instead of profit or income. And the MAP proposal tries to enlist market-oriented incentives to combat inflation.

6. Ending the Budget Deficit.

Now suppose that the concerns about the budget that we discussed in section 3 prove inescapable: it becomes clear that drastic action must be taken to balance the budget, the hardliners insist on cutting government spending, others want to raise the income-tax and make it more progressive, but either course seems bound to cause a painful increase in unemployment. Can anything else be done?

Yes, there is an alternative, and it has been known for forty or fifty years. In the wide-ranging discussions flowing from the publication of Keynes's *General Theory of Employment Interest and Money* in 1936, it was eventually pointed out that fiscal policy could in principle promote full employment at any of a wide range of budget positions, *even if private capital-formation entirely failed to materialize.* At one extreme, a high budget deficit could obviously be used to stimulate the economy; but, at the other extreme, a *balanced* budget could also be used to support a high level of output and employment.

Low capital formation, a balanced budget, and high employment? How could that be?

Well, it was early noted that, if savings (and real income) were threatening to "go to waste" because of insufficient capital formation, there were three possible remedies: either supplement capital spending, or reduce saving, or do some of both. The first could be achieved by using government budget deficits as "savings offsets" or substitutes for private capital spending (which is why they were sometimes called "honourary investments" in those days). The second could be achieved by financing government spending out of taxes designed to reduce the flow of saving to no more than enough to cover the current flow of capital spending. The first alternative might be considered preferable under some circumstances (e.g., to cope with short recessions in a generally-buoyant economy), the second under other circumstances (e.g., persistent chronic depression).

The original zero-deficit full-employment budget proposals were designed in a non-inflationary context, to meet the possibility of a very low capital-spending propensity even at very low real interest rates. (Some economists at the time feared secular stagnation; others were less pessimistic, but were concerned that future economic growth might be slow.) In that context, high output and employment with little or no saving would be preferable to low output and employment due to unrealizable savings.

Also, the proposals were usually developed in terms of a closed economy, ignoring the complications introduced by international trade. However, the same idea can be easily adapted to present-day conditions in the real world.

The reality today is that most economies are condemned to operate well below their potential level of output and employment, for the reasons already explained. There can be little doubt that some potential capital spending is now being choked off by the high real interest rates that are deemed necessary to combat inflationary pressures. However, it is by no means clear that there would be enough viable private capital projects to make use of all the savings these economies would now generate at a high level of employment and low real interest rates.

Ending the growth of the national debt under these conditions will not be a painless operation. The major question is, how should the pain be apportioned? The unemployed now suffer the bulk of the pain imposed by present anti-inflation policies, and traditional budget-cutting measures would swell their ranks and increase their pain even more. Middle-income groups and the well-to-do have benefited from the current incentives to save, and from high market interest rates and other returns on their wealth. A good case can thus be made for putting all or most of the burden of debt reduction on investment income.

To repeat, it is clear that some potential real income and potential savings are currently unrealizable, whether because of an absolute shortage of viable capital projects or because otherwise-viable projects are uneconomic at present interest rates. Whenever we reach the point at which it is deemed imperative to end the increase in government debt, therefore, the proper solution is to impose a tax on saving designed to reduce the rate of increase in the national debt to whatever level the government and the public feel comfortable with. That level might be zero, or even negative, but on the other hand might approximate the rate of growth of GNP.

This would *not* give any net stimulus to the economy, of course, nor would it solve the inflation-unemployment dilemma, so in itself it would not bring any increase in output. But it would not bring any decrease either, and it *would* end the threat of an accelerating debt burden. It would also lower interest rates, since governmental demands for funds in the money and capital markets would be greatly reduced, so there might be an increase in private capital formation and some net expansion of the economy after all. However, any such expansion might have to be partly or wholly aborted in order to control inflationary pressures.

7. A Modest Suggestion.

Apparently the only way to escape the present policy dilemma that is compatible with a money-and-market economy is to find some means of combatting inflation that does not make unemployment worse. That will permit demand-management techniques to be used once more for their proper purpose, namely *supporting* output and employment at close to their potential levels, instead of perverting them to *depressing* output and employment in a vain effort to suppress inflation.

However, that in itself will not be enough. In addition, whatever measure or combination of measures is used to control inflation must be seen to be fair to all concerned, otherwise it will be difficult to get public acceptance for it.

A fully satisfactory solution may be a long time in the making, for we can not expect an instant and complete cure for a condition that has been building up for so long. Nevertheless, despite the lack of agreement among economists about the causes of inflation, perhaps sufficient common ground can be found to support a rough-and-ready approach that should be reasonably effective quite quickly and should create an environment in which a more refined long-run solution could be sought. The key point is to put a ceiling on the community's total money income without impairing the market mechanism.

Since all economic costs can be resolved into factor returns, focusing on them offers a promising basis for a winning anti-inflation strategy. It will permit money income to be tailored to real output without adverse effects on employment or on the profit motive. It will be basically fair, because all forms of income will be treated equally. It will be administratively feasible, because the basic information must already be reported to the income-tax authorities.

The authorities will take some chosen year as a base, and use that year's rates of pay and yields on property as standards. (Presumably the base year will be the year immediately preceding the start of the plan, or whatever recent year there are adequate data for.) By regulating any changes in these rates, the authorities will be able to limit the increase in total money income for the coming year to the same percentage as the increase in total production.

Some type of wage and salary controls on all forms of personal remuneration will of course be required, but the proposed strategy differs in two very important respects from the wage and price controls that have been so unsuccessful in the past. First, it eliminates the necessity to monitor all costs and markups through the maze of intermediate and final transactions that characterize the productive process—a Herculean task for any price-control office. Second, it applies to property income in exactly the same way as to wages: the same portion of what each would otherwise be is scooped out right at the start, thus ensuring equality of sacrifice.

Traditional wage and price controls are anomalous in that wages are prices too, and thus are regulated twice: first directly as factor returns, second indirectly as components of all the intermediate and final prices already mentioned. But returns to ownership are regulated only once, and that indirectly, as components of that multitude of markups. If there is any slack in the traditional system of controls, the benefit will certainly go to the owners of productive resources.

Working out the details and ensuring that everyone is fairly treated will be difficult, to be sure. We do have considerable past experience at devising systems of wage and salary controls, so there is no need to make detailed proposals here. Where we lack precedents is in putting controls on property income. We need a levy that will reduce them in exactly the same proportion that wages and salaries will be reduced by whatever form of wage restraint we impose.

Let's call it an Investment Levy. As a practical matter we might apply it as an interest-rate adjustment, on the reasonable assumption that all property returns include an interest component or the equivalent. It should be addressed to property income in the hands of those who ultimately benefit from it, so business would not treat it as a cost. Nevertheless it could be collected through the payers of interest and other returns to property (especially business firms) as a withholding tax, like the withholding tax on wages and salaries, to minimize evasion.

Perhaps a numerical example will help. Choosing figures that will make the arithmetic easy, suppose inflation is running at 5 per cent per annum when the new strategy is introduced, and suppose a typical and readily-identifiable interest rate stands at 10 per cent. Some form of wage and salary restraint would be applied, designed to hold money wages in the coming year at about 5 per cent lower than they would otherwise average. At the same time an Investment Levy of a flat 0.5 percentage points (i.e. 5 per cent of 10) would be deducted from all property income.

That's the basic idea, though year-end adjustments would have to be made that we needn't go into now. If for some reason this did not stop inflation in its tracks, new targets would be set each year for both wages and the Investment Levy.

The Investment Levy is the only real novelty in this proposed strategy. However, there are good reasons why investors should be prepared to accept it as part of a comprehensive plan to control inflation. For one thing, while they presently enjoy some degree of inflation protection in the form of historically-high market interest rates and other returns, those rates and returns are highly volatile—instruments that yielded 15 to 20 per cent in 1981 are currently yielding about half that.

Second, the current rates of return include not only an inflation premium but also a substantial though uncertain risk premium, as already noted. The first should decline if inflation falls further and the second if prosperity returns, which is exactly what this strategy is designed to accomplish; and investors would surely be glad to relinquish both in exchange for an end to the uncertainties that give rise to them.

Finally, the Investment Levy would automatically decline and expire with inflation. Hence investors are not asked to make much of a sacrifice, and can expect a substantial reward.

To end this section on a historical note, there is some parallel between this proposal and Keynes's 1925 proposal to correct the overvaluation of sterling by a reduction of 5 per cent in money wages, coupled with a tax of the same 5 per cent on all incomes other than from employment. If that suggestion had been followed, perhaps Britain would have been spared much subsequent grief.

8. Balance-of-Payments Problems.

So far we have ignored the balance-of-payments aspects of the inflation-unemployment dilemma. These aspects come into the discussion primarily in two places: section 6, which deals with drastic measures to cure a deficit in the government's budget, and section 7, which suggests a way to restore high levels of employment. We will find in the end that a single strategy will solve the two sets of problems at once. First, however let's look at the budget problem.

Equilibrium in an open economy is not a question of balancing capital formation neatly against domestic savings, but of balancing capital formation plus exports against savings plus imports. Export earnings are like capital spending in that they do not come directly out of domestic income (they come from the incomes of foreigners), and payments for imports are like saving in that they do not directly create domestic income.

Note also that a country can only import more than it exports if it borrows abroad or runs down its assets; and, conversely, the only way one country can transfer capital to another is by exporting more than it imports. Or, to put the same idea the other way around, a country that is running a deficit in the current account of its balance of payments is importing capital, and one that is running a current-account surplus is investing abroad.

Two important conclusions may be drawn from these relationships. First, deflationary pressure on the spending stream may come from weakness in export earnings instead of or as well as weakness in capital spending; we will have more to say about this later. Second, and more important for our immediate purpose, domestic saving need not equal domestic capital spending, for a country may import other people's savings to help finance its capital investment program, or may invest some of its own savings abroad.

Looking at the budget-deficit problem of section 6 as it applies to an open economy, we may say that *total* domestic saving consists of net private-sector saving *plus* any government budget surplus or *less* any budget deficit. In effect, the budget deficit is being financed at least partly by borrowing abroad.

Since total domestic saving equals net private saving minus the budget deficit, any tax strategy that reduces net private saving and the budget deficit by the same amount will leave total domestic saving unchanged. It should also have no direct effect on the volume of capital spending. With both saving and capital formation unchanged, the balance-of-payments deficit or surplus (the difference between imports and exports) will also be unchanged.

This is exactly what we would expect, since reducing private saving and the budget deficit by the same amount is designed to have no net effect on domestic income. That in turn means there should be no effect on purchases of imports, hence no change in the incomes of foreign exporters, hence no change in foreign purchases of domestic exports.

There would be some effect on the balance-of-payments deficit if the decline in interest rates that was indicated at the end of section 6 did materialize, and stimulated increased capital spending. This would imply increased income, and therefore increased imports. There might be adverse effects on the country's external reserves, or some disturbance in the exchange market, of a magnitude the authorities might feel it necessary to counteract. At worst, however, this would require a reversal (or perhaps only a partial reversal) of the decline in domestic interest rates that gave rise to the problem.

However, this remedy for the budget deficit would mean continuing to import foreign savings sufficient to cover not only all new capital investment but also any net dissaving that might occur; at best, little domestic saving would be available to finance domestic investment. Someone would still have to borrow abroad or sell off assets in order to finance the balance-of-payments deficit.

If export earnings were to rise for any reason, that would of course raise domestic income and tend to improve the balance of payments. There are limits to what any country can do to stimulate exports without arousing resistance, however, for most other countries are also experiencing more unemployment than they want, so any export push might well start a trade war that no-one could win.

The immediate effect even of making domestic export industries more efficient—surely the most orthodox of measures—is to take business away from competitors, and hence to induce counter-action of some kind. Successful export-led expansions usually depend either on new investment in those industries, which spreads the benefits abroad and generates income there, or on an independent increase in incomes in other countries.

Now for the suggestion made in section 7. A single country that found a successful strategy for ending inflation and re-expanding its economy would face a serious drain on its external reserves (or inappropriate pressures on its exchange rate) if its trading partners were still struggling with the inflation-unemployment dilemma. In principle, its import leakages would raise output and employment abroad, thus stimulating reciprocal effects on its exports. But even under the best of circumstances there might be such lags in these feedback effects that they could not be counted on to resolve the problem in good time, and under unfavourable circumstances the reciprocal effects might be negligible.

Unilateral measures to improve one country's balance of payments are normally counterproductive, as just noted. However, a country with a successful strategy for achieving a high level of output and employment at stable prices could implement a set of complementary measures that would permit it to pursue domestic expansion without an exchange drain, yet would leave uncoöperative trading partners no worse off.

The mainstay of the strategy would be to eschew any deliberate encouragement of exports and to rely on measures that would expand domestic output, combined with trade-diverting measures designed to just offset the external drain that would otherwise occur. The trade-diverting measures might take any of several forms—tariffs, quotas, or other devices—which would be protectionist in themselves but defensible as part of a broader strategy. They might well include trade preferences for any other country that chose to follow a similar set of domestic policies.

It is true that noncoöperating countries might ignore the expansionist aspect of the first country's domestic policies and attack the protectionist aspect in isolation. However, they would do themselves no good by pressing that claim and forcing an end to the combined measures: lower income in the first country would reduce its imports just as effectively as trade-diverting measures. This might well prove an adequate defence under international law and current international agreements.

On the other hand, if a strong country with a big domestic market took the initiative, it would be in a position to persuade others to join the exercise. In any case countries that chose to coöperate in such a strategy could support one another without giving a free ride to their uncoöperative partners.

Also, note that this strategy would simultaneously solve the government's budget problem in a very constructive way. An important side-effect of solving the inflation-unemployment dilemma would be higher government revenues and lower social-assistance costs, because of the increased national income it would mean. The government's budget deficits would be eliminated automatically, or at least reduced to manageable proportions. Drastic remedies would no longer be necessary.

9. Is This Argument Persuasive?

In the spirit of Part Five, you must not accept the foregoing argument without serious thought. Instead, you must use the analytical techniques described in the first four Parts of the book to help you decide. The object, after all, is not to promote any one remedy but to find a policy mix that will support renewed prosperity and growth (subject, of course, to such modifications as may be necessary to take account of the other issues discussed in this Part).

Begin by checking out the explicit and tacit assumptions on which the argument is based. Then consider the value judgements implicit in the presentation. Note that these ideas have already been presented to the public in a book and in several articles in journals devoted to public opinion, but have not won support from very many other economists. What do you conclude?

Finally, whether you agree or disagree, can you think of any way to improve the proposal, or can you devise a more promising one? I would like to appeal to all other economists, professional and amateur, to try their hands at this exercise. To repeat an argument I have used before, the most effective criticism of any model or theory or proposal is a better one. It is quite possible that *you* may be the person to come up with the winning strategy.

Selected Readings

Lerner, Abba P. "The Market Antiinflation Plan: A Cure for Stagflation", in James H. Gapinski and Charles E. Rockwood, eds., *Essays in Post-Keynesian Inflation*, pp. 217-229. Cambridge Mass.: Ballinger, 1979.

McLeod, Alex N. *The Fearsome Dilemma: Simultaneous Inflation and Unemployment*. Lanham Md.: University Press of America, 1984.

_____. "Levy against Inflation, for Jobs", *Policy Options* [Halifax N.S.], vol.5, no. 6, November 1984, pp. 47-52.

_____. "Deficit Cutting", *Policy Options* [Halifax N.S.], vol.8, no. 10, December 1987, pp. 9-11.

Weintraub, Sidney, and Wallich, Henry C. "A Tax-Based Incomes Policy", *Journal of Economic Issues*, vol. V, no.2, June 1971, pp. 1-19.

Weintraub, Sidney. "Proposals for an Anti-Inflation Policy", *Challenge*, vol. 21, no. 4, September/October 1978, pp. 53-54.

Chapter 19

Three Other Policy Issues

1. The Ownership of the Means of Production.

In section 3 of Chapter 2 we noted that the model of pure competition assumes, among other things, that productive resources are privately owned. This is sometimes described as "private ownership of the means of production". It is true that labour is also a means (or a factor) of production, and that labourers "own" their labour in the same way that landlords own their land and capitalists own their capital goods. Nevertheless "the means of production" is usually taken to mean the physical resources that are used in the productive process.

It is important to realize that it is strictly a matter of practical considerations, not any moral judgement, that justifies private ownership: it enlists the profit motive to harness the self-interest of producers to promote efficient productive practices, and to pass the benefits on to the consuming public, as explained in sections 8 and 9 of Chapter 4.

Of course, this motivation would operate at full efficiency only under the conditions spelled out in the model of pure competition. Conditions in the real world more closely resemble those of the model of imperfect or monopolistic competition, which is why a good deal of government intervention in economic affairs is considered necessary in most countries. Nevertheless this interpretation of the profit motive is the principal justification for the free-enterprise money-and-market system.

Indeed, it is commonly observed that the rewards given out by the market mechanism go disproportionately to the selfish, the pushy, the greedy, and the unscrupulous. These are not the qualities that endear people to others. Substantial incomes also go to those who have inherited wealth, without regard to their personal qualifications or any contribution they may personally make to the productive process. We accept the results partly because it has always been so, but primarily because we are prepared to pay this price in order to get the benefits that the money-and-market system undoubtedly provides.

As noted in section 3 of Chapter 9, reactions against the evils of the early industrial system led to the search for other forms of economic organization. The principal alternative appeared to be some form of the "social" ownership of the means of production, rather than "individual" ownership.

Criticisms of socialism have been primarily from a practical rather than a moral or judgemental point of view, just as the case for the market mechanism is a practical rather than a moral one: questions about the ability of a socialist society to allocate resources and manage the productive process efficiently. The main exceptions are (1) criticisms of certain variants, such as Marxism, which advocate the achievement of socialism though revolution rather than through peaceful processes,[1] and (2) criticisms of the political organization and political practices in some countries that have instituted socialism, or in proposals to implement it (e.g., as being undemocratic and relying on coercion). In these cases the judgemental criticism is properly directed at the means of achieving socialism, or at the political structure put in place or proposed, rather than at socialism as a form of economic organization.

Experience in countries that have tried social ownership, notably those in the Soviet bloc, has tended to confirm the difficulties of allocation and management, but socialist regimes have scored some notable successes too. Also, the public may well be prepared to pay a certain price in lost efficiency if the distribution of rewards is seen to be fairer. In some cases the average individual may be just as well off if a smaller output is shared more equally.

Nevertheless, some critics have launched frontal attacks on property ownership as such. The cry that "Property is theft!" has been heard down the ages in one form or another. It appears in the writings of Judah Ibn Tibbon in the late 13th century, Jacques-Pierre Brissot in the 18th, and Pierre-Joseph Proudhon in the 19th. In the preface to his *Major Barbara* George Bernard Shaw says, "Our property is organized robbery."

In general, property ownership may be traced back to the application of what William Wordsworth described as:

---

[1] Nevertheless it is widely acknowledged that revolution may be justified in some circumstances. For example, it was the opinion of a majority of the residents of Britain's thirteen North American colonies in 1776 that they were justified in rebelling, and that opinion is undoubtedly maintained by their descendants today.

> The good old rule
> ... , the simple plan,
> That they should take, who have the power,
> And they should keep who can.

Property titles in most of Europe date from feudal times, when they were clearly rooted in "the good old rule." (Land was then the principal form of property, of course.) It is true that these titles were usually granted, or subsequently validated, by letters patent from the sovereign, who in so acting was exercising his alleged divine right to rule, but it is clear that the recipient was largely dependent on his own resources to seize the property (if someone else was in possession) and to maintain his control over it. The sovereign himself depended on armed force to maintain his position against rivals or potential usurpers, and felt free to take over the domains of other rulers if he could.

Much the same appears to be true of other parts of the world, with local variations. In some cases, for example, land ownership seems to have been based on long-standing tradition. Even traditional tribal societies that did not practice settled agriculture jealously defended their customary rights to hunting or grazing areas against incursions by other tribes.

Once property titles became recognized in official legal codes, however, the full power of the governing authority was mobilized to maintain them and to ensure that ownership was transferred only by due legal processes.

Property in agricultural land is presumably the oldest form of substantial wealth, but commercial activities were long the major source of creations of new wealth. Commercial wealth is typically represented by the net worth of operating businesses, though of course some of it gets used to buy up landed properties or other assets. However, it has been the tremendous expansion of industrial activities in the past 200 years or so that has created most of today's great fortunes.

Many critics have concluded that the rules of the marketplace give capital an undue share of the net product; Karl Marx is a notable example, but by no means the only one. This is an interesting and highly debatable question, but an affirmative answer is not necessary to explain the growth of modern fortunes.

The fact is that any substantial accumulation of wealth in few hands tends to be self-perpetuating and cumulative. Wealth brings investment income independently of any economic activity on the part of its owner and regardless of whether the wealth arises from land-owning, from commercial activities, or from industrial enterprises. Aside from wanton extravagance, which has certainly wasted many an inherited fortune, there are practical limits to the ability of one person or one family to consume real income; a modicum of common prudence therefore ensures that most fortunes continue to grow because some of the annual income will be saved and invested in added wealth.

Perhaps it is the *concentration* of the ownership of the means of production in few hands, not private ownership as such, that should be at issue. This gives disproportionate power to a few individuals, which is addressed elsewhere in this chapter as a separate policy issue in its own right; the point to be made here is a different one, namely that it perpetuates an élite class whose privileges are not based on demonstrated merit.

In every generation there have been a few individuals who inherited wealth, whether in the form of a family business or otherwise, and proceeded to use it in ways that made independent contributions to the advancement of human welfare. Far more, however, have been content to live on the income from their inheritances without contributing directly to the productive process—the "idle rich" who were the object of criticism by some reformers in the past.

At one time a great many industrialized countries were moved to introduce relatively high taxes on the transfer of wealth from one generation to another: death duties, succession duties, inheritance taxes, or the like. It was thought that these measures would gradually equalize wealth and incomes and, in combination with universal education, ensure that all careers would be "open to talent" without the influence of special preference for anyone, but it is now clear that these hopes were far too optimistic.

Death duties have been quietly reduced or eliminated in many jurisdictions, mainly since the end of World War II, and their impact blunted in others because effective avoidance techniques were soon devised (for example, transferring assets to a trust fund). The reasons this has been permitted are doubtless complex. Failure to achieve any notable equalization of wealth may have been a factor. Also, the effects could be unduly severe in some instances, such as a rapid succession of deaths in one family; tax laws tend to be rather crude and insensitive in their application to particular cases.

The idea of "soaking the rich" by taxing them heavily undoubtedly used to have some appeal to the public, but experience has shown that even confiscatory taxes on high incomes would not give adequate revenues to modern governments. However, a cynic might suggest that a popular working definition of a rich person would be "someone with more money than I have", and add that the substantial rise in average incomes during the 20th century has made more and more people subject to death duties at the old rates, thereby weakening the enthusiasm for them.

Defenders of private ownership of property and large accumulations of wealth argue that it has been a major factor in the rise of civilization throughout the ages. Only as some individuals have been able to achieve a standard of living well above the average has it been possible to accumulate the savings that have financed the capital investment on which the increase in the average standard of living has depended. They have also contributed notably to the quality of life, through their patronage of science and the arts.

The matters at issue here are highly debatable, of course, and subject to a wide range of views. If after due thought you do conclude that changes should be made in the ownership of the means of production, however, there are many practical problems to be considered in proposing reforms. Abrupt changes may be very harsh on some individuals, may disrupt the smooth operation of the economy, and may bring very little immediate benefit.

Other problems stem from the national boundaries that separate the world's population. The prospect of change in any one country is likely to drive productive enterprises and able entrepreneurs to move to other countries, and to prompt wealthy individuals to shift their assets (and perhaps themselves) abroad too. And what should be done about the ownership of productive facilities in one country by residents of another?

The industrialized countries have appropriated control of the bulk of the world's resources in one way or another; if such a country nationalized the ownership of its means of production, should it share any of the ownership of its foreign investments with residents of the countries where they are situated?

If it were a developing country that did the nationalizing, would it be justified in taking over foreign firms without compensation? Why, or why not? Even if you feel it would have a moral right to do so, what would you advise it to do in practice, considering that it would probably want access to foreign capital and foreign technical help, not only for future development projects but even to continue operating its newly-nationalized facilities?

2. Concentration of Ownership.

The undue concentration of economic power has been a target of criticism throughout history. The power of wealthy landowners over poor tenants has often been a source of social unrest, especially if the landlords were absentee owners and their properties managed by hired officials with little authority to alter the terms of leases as conditions changed. Monopolies have also been a common cause of complaint, whether they were natural (for example, an industry in which a single plant of optimum size can serve an entire market) or artificial (such as an exclusive commercial right granted by a sovereign power); nowadays they are pretty well limited to the natural type, and the prices they may charge are usually regulated by some public authority.

The rise of commercial and industrial fortunes focused attention on corporate ownership, as economic power became increasingly concentrated in relatively few hands. The 19th century saw the enactment of legislation in many countries attempting to control the obvious abuses to which concentration gave rise, which were primarily seen as undue restraint of trade or reductions in competition in particular industries. Despite subsequent improvements in these laws, this remains the principal focus in most countries, though for the most part the law and its application are based on outdated economic theory.

As noted in section 1, the case for the effectiveness of competition in regulating the marketplace really requires conditions approximating those of pure competition, whereas competition in the real world more nearly resembles the model of imperfect or monopolistic competition. The more flagrant forms of collusion, market sharing, and other restraints on trade are now pretty well ruled out by law, and offenses that can be proven in court may incur severe penalties, but it is extremely unlikely that anything approaching the ideal degree of productive efficiency and consumer benefits envisaged in sections 8 and 9 of Chapter 4 is realized in practice.

In part, the problem arises from the mere increase in the size of the most efficient plant or organization in most industries, and from the realities of the nature of competition, not necessarily from the concentration of power in few hands to which modern industry and commerce are prone. In the ideal world of the purely competitive model, all decisions are decentralized and responsive to market pressures, right down to how many hours a week each individual worker chooses to work and how much he or she will be paid. In the real world of business, both the firms that employ workers and the unions that often represent them in wage-and-hour negotiations are run by bureaucracies.

Market pressures may indeed strongly influence the overall wage bargain, but the wage or salary of the individual worker is largely a bureaucratic decision, and may have little identifiable relationship to his or her net contribution to the firm's output. Similarly, the length of the work week is either a legal requirement or a bureaucratic decision, over which the individual worker has little influence. Inefficient firms are more likely to fail than efficient firms, but skill in promotion and salesmanship may be more important than efficiency in production.

Furthermore it is a fact of life that most industries in most countries are dominated by a very few large firms, which provides additional reasons why competition is not as efficient a regulator of the marketplace in the real world as restraint-of-trade laws seem to assume. The managers of these firms have substantial market power without having to do anything illegal. Their strong balance sheets give them preferred access to financing from banks, from other financial institutions, and from the money and capital markets, so they have important advantages over smaller firms in seizing opportunities for expansion, and can outbid them if necessary.

The managers of these firms can effectively influence political decisions, not merely or even primarily because of their contributions to political campaigns, but also through sheer persuasiveness and the ability to influence the behaviour of the economy. They can afford the best of legal, accounting, and other services when necessary, either for litigation or for appearances before regulatory authorities or for lobbying governments, and the costs are tax-deductible. Their purchases of goods and services from others are so substantial that they can often influence the actions and the pronouncements of their suppliers (including suppliers of legal and accounting services). They can offer valuable perquisites to those they wish to influence, including directorships, legal retainers, and consultancies.

Of course, big is not necessarily bad. There are many valid arguments in favour of large enterprises in many fields. Economies of scale are an obvious example. In some manufacturing industries the most efficient size of plant is very large indeed; so large in some cases that a single firm capable of competing in international markets would be able to supply the entire needs of a small or medium-sized country.

In such cases there need be little concern over the mere size of the firm, provided competitors from other countries are allowed free access to the domestic market; the number of effective competitors in an oligopolistic market is important, the absolute size of each firm is not. For similar reasons the authorities may allow domestic competitors to engage in joint ventures in *export* markets.

So far we have been talking primarily of concentration of ownership in a given industry. This includes both vertical integration (linking firms at different stages of production, like the mining of iron ore and the production of steel) and horizontal integration (linking firms at the same stage of production, like a hotel chain).

A more insidious form of concentration has attracted attention in recent years, namely the proliferation of conglomerates—enterprises that own or control firms in a wide variety of industries and activities. The ostensible reason in most cases is to diversify investment risks, but other factors are clearly involved as well. One is to minimize tax burdens, by offsetting losses in one subsidiary against profits in another. Another factor is the ability to control substantial cash flows and large pools of assets from a small base of equity capital. The end result is that a few huge financial empires have come to control a very large portion of the national economy in most countries.

Besides eroding the government's revenue base, techniques that offset losses in one firm against profits in another offend against one of the principal disciplinary functions of the marketplace: the elimination of inefficient firms and the survival of efficient firms.

Giving a few individuals, perhaps a single individual, control over a large block of assets with relatively little commitment of his or her own funds invites conflicts of interest: the manipulation of corporate assets in ways that enrich the manipulator but impoverish others (sometimes the shareholders or the creditors of the corporation, sometimes the taxpayer or the general public, sometimes all four). This is particularly true if a conglomerate (or in fact any commercial or industrial enterprise) gets control of a bank or other financial institution. One banker is reported to have said, "The easiest way to steal from a bank is to own one".

Most countries have laws against combinations in restraint of trade in any one industry or field of activity, which vary greatly in rigour and effectiveness. The anti-trust laws in the U.S.A. are perhaps the most stringent and the best known, but even these have not been able to prevent a substantial degree of concentration. (The term "anti-trust" comes from the use of a legal trusteeship, common in years past, as a binding device to control the voting stock of firms acting jointly to control a given market.) No country has yet shown effective leadership in controlling the expansion of conglomerates.

An outstanding feature of the growth of conglomerates in recent decades has been the mounting wave of takeovers and amalgamations. Some have been friendly, others unfriendly. Either way, they imply that the market has undervalued the target company: the acquirer believes it will be cheaper to enlarge the productive capacity under its control by buying up the shares (or equity stock) of an existing firm than by constructing a new plant. (Sometimes the acquisition proves to be a mistake, however, as we will see.)

Conceivably, a takeover may result in a rationalization of productive facilities that adds to overall productive efficiency. Typically, however, it adds nothing to productive capacity, and in fact is likely to disrupt the smooth operation of going concerns; in the process it runs up huge legal, accounting, and other expenses that must be paid for in some way out of future production.

Typically, also, a takeover adds to inflationary pressures, for it is virtually certain to be financed in large part by bank borrowing. Some of the debt may eventually be repaid (perhaps from the proceeds of the sale of some of the assets of the target firm), but in the meantime those who have sold out have a sudden windfall of liquid funds, which they will proceed to use either in conspicuous consumption or for the purchase of alternative investments. Since the supply of available equity stocks will have been reduced by the takeover, this adds up to increased inflationary pressures both in goods-and-services markets and in equity and capital markets.

The growth of conglomerates into financial empires has usually been by takeovers and buy-outs, which have richly rewarded their instigators. There have been instances, however, in which takeovers have crippled or bankrupted the acquiring firms, as when markets have turned adverse and left them with unsaleable assets bought with money borrowed at high interest rates.

However, other players in the game besides the builders of financial empires have also been able to make substantial profits. Target firms have devised a number of defences, including the buying back of their own shares. This has enabled so-called "greenmailers" to exact a substantial ransom: they buy up a sufficient block of shares to create a threat of a takeover (and may indeed be prepared to carry through with their threat), which they then sell back to the target company at a handsome profit. There is no increase in productive capacity or efficiency, but valuable time and effort has been diverted into mere manoeuvrings.

Nor is that the end of the story. The instigators of takeovers are not confined to people who are ambitious to build corporate empires, and greenmailers who imitate them. Lawyers and investment bankers pocket millions of dollars in fees in major takeover battles, whether operating for the would-be acquisitor or for the target company. This has led to the appearance of professional corporate raiders, who search out likely targets and promote takeovers for the fees they will generate.

However, it must be noted that there are defenders as well as critics of takeovers. Some firm believers in *laissez-faire* policies argue that they are in the public interest, because they create more efficient business entities. This argument is supported by the fact that, if it is cheaper to buy up an existing operation than to build a new plant, then the markets have evidently undervalued the target firms; and by the further fact that some takeovers have indeed resulted in more efficient operations. Both of these points have already been noted.

Finally, the concentration of economic power in relatively few hands is a world-wide phenomenon, not only in the sense that it occurs in virtually every country, but also in the sense that many of the largest firms and conglomerates operate in many different countries. The so-called multinationals or transnationals are often able to transfer their operations or their profits from one jurisdiction to another, as suits them. They can thus escape or minimize the tax burdens and the regulatory supervision to which they are subjected. Their operating budgets may compare favourably with those of a small or medium-sized country, and they can play one host country off against another by threatening to move their operations to a more favourable location. Little has so far been accomplished in devising ways of regulating such activities.

3. The Third-World Debt Problem: Who Should Pay the Piper?

By the 1970's international borrowing for balance-of-payments reasons had become eminently respectable—and quite rightly so, of course, within reasonable limits, since it gives the borrowing country time in which to effect necessary structural adjustments in its economy. International financial markets had become very liquid, and the International Monetary Fund (the IMF or the Fund) provided some assurance of both discipline on its members and support for them in case of need. In this context the major international commercial banks concluded that loans to sovereign nations to cushion structural adjustments were not only highly profitable but also virtually riskless, and they entered this field on a substantial scale.

By about 1980, however, the banks were becoming increasingly nervous about the security of some of their sovereignty loans. In 1982 it became public knowledge that many countries were facing difficulties in meeting their obligations, and that the problem was so serious as to constitute an immediate threat to the solvency of many banks and to the functioning of the international monetary system as a whole. Intensive negotiations between borrowers and lenders began, which brought a series of debt moratoria, reschedulings, and other adjustments, and have continued to this day.

Disaster has been avoided so far, and will probably continue to be avoided, for both borrowers and lenders stand to lose heavily if defaults become widespread. Nevertheless the Third-World Debt Problem has been a Sword of Damocles over many countries, and over the world as a whole, for many years. Perhaps a more apt metaphor would be to say that a relatively minor mishap could trigger an avalanche of trouble; the entire situation has been precarious.

How did this problem arise? Who is to blame? How can it be solved? Who should bear the costs?

When any borrower has trouble repaying a debt according to the contract, whether it is an individual, a business firm, or a national government, the first assumption is likely to be that the borrower's expectations were unrealistic and that he has acted irresponsibly. Certainly the lenders in the case of the Third World Debt Problem show few signs of accepting any of the responsibility. Whether they are national governments, international agencies, commercial banks, or private commercial or industrial firms, their formal stance is to expect the borrowers to repay in full, subject only to a willingness to negotiate reschedulings of repayment dates and the capitalization of some interest charges (that is, adding them to the debt rather than demanding immediate payment) on a case-by-case basis. The implication is that the borrowers' plight is their own doing, and that they must bear the cost of their mistakes.

Thus Mr. de Larosière, then the Managing Director of the International Monetary Fund, offered little comfort to the distressed borrowers in his address to the Fund's annual meeting in Toronto in 1982, when the problem first attracted widespread attention. He urged member governments to maintain strict limits on the growth of the money supply, and to intensify their efforts to reduce or eliminate their budget deficits, without any special concessions to the debtor countries.

De Larosière asserted that these policies would turn the situation around and restore sustainable growth, and argued against expansionary policies designed to reduce unemployment, which he thought would risk even higher rates of inflation that would in due time require even higher rates of unemployment to cure. Instead, he advocated measures to make labour costs more flexible, to allow labour to be more easily shifted from one industry to another as conditions changed, and to ensure that incentives to work were adequate.[2]

There are two sides to every story, however, and this case is no exception. No doubt some of the borrowing was irresponsible, or the proceeds were irresponsibly used. For example, the availability of loans permitted some countries to put off needed internal adjustments indefinitely. Even in these cases, however, irresponsible borrowing implies irresponsible lending as well, so the lenders must accept a share the responsibility too.

In any case borrowing always leaves the borrower vulnerable in case of an economic downturn. Evidently the majority of the loans that are now in trouble

---

[2] Mr. de Larosière apparently believed that a high rate of unemployment is a *desirable* feature of the deflationary strategy, presumably to discipline the labour force; the implication is that unreasonable wage and other demands by labour are the main cause of inflation. It does not follow that all advocates of this strategy share these views. Some may feel that unemployment is an *undesirable* but inevitable side-effect; the implication is that demands for wage increases and other benefits are no more at fault for the generation of inflation than demands for increases in other prices.

were judged economically viable by prudent lenders and responsible borrowers alike, in the context of the economic climate in which they were made. External developments, not misjudgements as such, have turned inherently-viable projects into generators of dead-weight debts (that is, debts that are not supported by income-producing activities).

Furthermore, there is no mystery about the nature of these external developments: they were the reduced levels of output in the major industrialized countries brought on by the anti-inflation measures that were applied with increasing rigour in the 1970's. These measures reached a peak of severity in 1981, when interest rates for the soundest borrowers reached 20 per cent or more. They had painful enough effects domestically, but their external repercussions were even more serious, for they dramatically reduced the incomes of Third-World countries.

For the most part, therefore, the loans and projects that are now at the centre of the debt problem were not put in jeopardy by inherent demerits as judged in terms of a sanely-operating international economic system, they were put in jeopardy by policy initiatives taken in the industrialized countries to deal with what are primarily their own domestic problems.

This causal sequence was explicitly acknowledged by Mr. de Larosière in his 1982 address. Britain and the U.S.A. were already applying with conviction the policies he advocated, many other countries were following them with varying degrees of enthusiasm (or resignation), and still others were (or were about to be) dragooned into doing so by their creditors either directly or through the influence of the Fund. He acknowledged that these policies explained the economic stagnation of recent years, the slump in world trade, and the plight of those developing countries that did not have oil reserves of their own.

In 1986 many oil-producing Third-World countries joined the ranks of distressed debtors, thanks to the collapse of oil prices. Since then a number of initiatives to alleviate the problem have been tried or proposed, but the basic situation remains unresolved.

Clearly, the anti-inflation strategy being followed by most countries is the main cause of the Third-World Debt Problem. The major industrialized countries no doubt sincerely believe it is not only in their own best interests but also in the best interests of the world as whole. But the painful effects are not confined to their own economies, they are also visited on the Third World.

Third-World countries are struggling to raise their living standards by harnessing the same two forces that have been so effective elsewhere: investment in productive capital, and international trade. They hope to accomplish in a generation or two what has taken 200 years in the industrialized countries, and are relying on imported financing and imported technology to speed up the process. International trade is therefore doubly important to them, since it must pay for borrowed money and borrowed technology, and it will let them specialize in products in which they have a comparative advantage.

The strategy of restraint adopted by the industrialized countries has thus hit the Third World a triple blow. First, the markets that many of their capital projects were intended to serve have been destroyed, so what should have been major contributors to increased real incomes have generated dead-weight debt instead. Second, the interest costs of the money borrowed to finance those projects have greatly increased; they have now receded from their 1981 peaks, but remain high. Third, not only have the expected increases in their real incomes been aborted, but also their previous real incomes have been sharply reduced by the contraction of world trade; they must therefore pay heavy debt-servicing costs out of greatly-reduced real incomes.

The Fund has come in for criticism for its rôle in these events, especially since its decisions are dominated by the major industrial countries. Not all these criticisms are justified: the Fund is not primarily an aid-giver as such, but a provider of specific cushioning credits to give its members time to make necessary adjustments to changes in their economic fortunes.

Nevertheless some criticisms of the Fund are surely proper. Its standard requirements for providing balance-of-payments aid include insistence on actions designed to ensure that the member country will soon be able to live within its income—an eminently sensible requirement if the world economy were operating at or near full capacity, and the member seeking aid were the only country (or one of a relatively few) experiencing balance-of-payments trouble. But these requirements become entirely improper when the world economy is operating well below capacity, and a substantial number of members are experiencing similar problems simultaneously, as has been the case for many years now.

This criticism gains added force from the fact that so many of the seekers after Fund help are developing countries in similar circumstances, including dependence on one or a few export staples. The result is a classic case of the error of composition: what would be a reasonable remedy for an isolated instance becomes unreasonable when applied to a large number of simultaneous instances, because adverse feed-back effects on the world economy that would be insignificant individually become highly significant collectively.

The Fund may also be criticized for the uneven domestic impact of its typical remedies, which usually include a substantial devaluation of the exchange rate and the ending or reduction of subsidies designed to keep down the cost of living, perhaps also a reduction in social services. These measures are highly regressive, for they impinge most heavily on the poor and weak; the governing élite can usually look after themselves pretty well. Surely there are other items that could be targeted instead, such as military expenditures. It is no defence for the Fund to plead the sensitivities of domestic policy priorities, since any conditions imposed in order to qualify for help constitute interference with those priorities.

An important implication of the foregoing argument is that the roots of the Third-World Debt Problem are to be found in the apparent inability of the major industrialized countries to find a remedy for their domestic inflations that does not make unemployment worse. In fact the roots of most of the world's economic problems today lie in the same troublesome policy dilemma. That problem was addressed in Chapter 18.

Despite the thousands of words written about the Third-World Debt Problem, however, there appears to have been surprisingly little explicit public discussion of who should bear the burden of the adjustments that must obviously be made if serious trouble is to be averted permanently. Most public discussion so far has focused on the fact that the lenders and their governments have graciously allowed many of the debts to be rescheduled and some of the interest to be capitalized, which simply means postponing and increasing the debt. As already noted, the implication is that the entire burden is to be borne by the borrowers; there is no suggestion that the creditors are in any way responsible, or that the governments of the industrialized nations are involved beyond ensuring the solvency of their financial institutions (preferably at no cost to the fisc).

It is true that a few governments have forgiven some loans to the governments of certain small and needy countries, but these are special cases and the amounts have been relatively small. For one thing, the loans in question have usually been politically rather than commercially based. For another, they have been forgiven on humanitarian or charitable grounds; there has been no acknowledgement by the creditor of any legal or moral responsibility for the situation.

Some major institutional lenders, especially some of the large international banks, have taken some action with respect to these debts. These actions have included the provision of substantial reserves against potential losses, and transactions whereby some Third-World debt contracts have been exchanged directly or indirectly for equity claims. Also, some Third-World debts are being traded at substantial discounts in secondary markets.[3]

However, there is little relief for the debtors in any of these actions. Exchanging debt for equity relieves them of immediate interest costs, and in some cases may bring some new foreign investment, but the equity thus given up may turn out to have been sold very cheaply if the global economy eventually revives. Sales of debt contracts merely replace one creditor by another.

Institutional lenders have always maintained reserves against the possibility of eventual losses on their loan portfolios, and ever since the debt crisis began they were quietly building them up to what seemed prudent levels in the light of the new uncertainties. In 1987 some major banks began to make substantial but sporadic write-offs, thereby posting major losses for the particular accounting period in question. By now their reserves have been raised to 40 or 50 per cent or more in many cases, and even as much as 100 per cent.

However, these provisions are merely bookkeeping entries, which provide offsets to the face values of the loans as recorded among their assets. They are explicit acknowledgements that some of the loans may never be repaid in full, but they do not in any sense constitute forgiveness of any particular loan or of loans in general; all debt contracts remain payable in full.

It is of course understandable that institutional lenders are extremely reluctant to write off any part of their sovereign loans explicitly, even though they may have already set up specific reserves against them. This is standard accounting practice, and has two good justifications: first, an acknowledged write-off for one debtor makes it hard to deny similar relief to others, perhaps less deserving; second, even those loans that appear most hopeless of recovery may some day prove recoverable. It will probably take official intervention by governments or regulatory authorities to effect a definitive adjustment of these loans.

Nevertheless it is imperative that effective action be taken soon to put an end to the present uncertainties. That is in the interests of all parties concerned: the distressed borrowers, the institutional lenders, the major industrialized countries, and the world economy as a whole.

Default on any serious scale would be disastrous for the borrowers, because it would cut them off from the capital they need for further development and because the probable repercussions would reduce world trade still further and depress their

---

3   There is some advantage to both parties. The seller gets liquidity, at a price; the buyer gains a substantial rate of return on his cost as long as interest charges continue to be met, and the possibility of a substantial capital gain if the loan is eventually repaid.

earnings even more. It would also be disastrous for the world at large, because it would mean serious losses if not bankruptcies for major banks and other lenders, which in turn would disrupt the economies of the major industrial nations and have seriously-adverse effects on their trading partners.[4]

This has been implicitly acknowledged by the initiatives taken or proposed by the governments of several industrialized countries in recent years. However, the relief which has been proposed (and provided in some measure) has consisted primarily of the infusion of additional credits in support of further economic development, and further debt reschedulings. These have been helpful, but they have not been enough to produce a definitive solution. Outright debt forgiveness has been limited to the poorest countries, mostly in Africa.

Most nations, even those with relatively low per capita incomes, have some internal measures designed to cushion the effects of adverse economic developments on particular individuals and sectors of the economy—unemployment insurance, social assistance, internal transfers for the benefit of the industries or regions concerned, and so on. But there is no systematic provision for cushioning the differential effects of international misadventures on individual countries; relief can only come from either voluntary concessions by the creditors, or involuntary concessions due to defaults by the debtors.

This is unconscionable under the best of circumstances, in a world that is increasingly interdependent because of the ties of mutual trade. It is intolerable when damage is done to one country by the deliberate domestic actions of another. There is not even the possibility of a civil suit for damages, as there is between individuals injured by the actions of other individuals, for the recognized body of international law does not extend to such matters.

Thus the major industrialized nations have inflicted severe damages on other nations by an anti-inflation strategy they have imposed for their own domestic reasons. They apparently believe it is also in the best interests the world as a whole, but they do not bear a fair share of the costs of carrying out their decisions.

The burden thus imposed is particularly severe for Third-World countries, and shows up most clearly in their current debt problems. Logic, equity, and morality all call for effective actions by the governments of the industrialized countries to offer adequate relief and compensation to other countries adversely affected by

---

4   To the extent that the increased loss-reserves recently set up by major commercial banks prove adequate, these risks for the world at large have been materially reduced. This in turn means that the bargaining position of the lenders has been improved.

their policy decisions when deliberately made for domestic reasons, subject to some internationally-agreed body of rules and procedures.

The case for relief and compensation is particularly strong with respect to the Third-World Debt Problem, since the selfish interests of the industrialized countries themselves would be served thereby: it would definitively forestall the disruptive threat of mass defaults on international loans.

It is not appropriate to leave the matter to negotiations between debtors and creditors, with or without participation by the creditors' governments, because the issues at stake go far beyond their narrow interests. Only governments, probably a group of governments of major countries acting together, can act effectively in the public interest. They could insist on a proper sharing of the cost by debtor governments and creditor financial institutions on a case-by-case basis where appropriate, and accept the residual liability on behalf of the general public as a reasonable way out of a situation that otherwise threatens disaster at any moment.

Fortunately, it is possible to end on two cautiously hopeful notes. First, there have recently been signs that the IMF is beginning to take a more sympathetic attitude to the problems of debtor countries when proposing domestic measures to meet their problems. Second, spokesmen for some major banks have spoken frankly about the need to find a permanent solution for the Third-World debt problem.

The bankers' suggestions have varied rather widely, but included some bold and innovative proposals. Several have spoken favourably of debt-equity exchanges, and of a proposal to have some debtor countries buy back debts at a discount and replace them with interest-bearing bonds backed by U.S. treasury bills. Others have said creditors should be prepared to negotiate interest payments according to the debtor's ability to pay. At least one has observed that it is time to "think the unthinkable", that is to consider forgiveness in order to reduce debts quickly to levels that can be serviced, subject to sanctions to ensure adequate performance subsequently by the debtors.

About the Author

ALEXANDER NORMAN McLEOD, B.A., M.P.A., Ph.D., is a monetary economist who is experienced in practical applications as well as in theoretical developments. He had a distinguished academic career, being medalist at Queen's University, Littauer Fellow at Harvard, and later a professor at Atkinson College of York University in Toronto, from which he retired in 1977 as Professor Emeritus.

Between these academic periods A.N.M. pursued the practical application of theory. He was employed in the Department of Finance in Ottawa during World War II, and was an early staff member of the International Monetary Fund. The Fund sent him to several Central American countries on financial missions, and in 1951-52 seconded him as a monetary adviser to the United Nations Commissioner in Libya in preparation for independence. On leave from the Fund, he was Director of Research for the Saudi Arabian Monetary Agency for two years. He became Chief Economist of The Toronto-Dominion Bank in 1955, and established its Research Department. While in that post he was chairman of the Economists' Committee of the Canadian Bankers' Association, which drafted the Association's influential presentation to the Royal Commission on Banking and Finance (the Porter Commission). In 1966 the International Monetary Fund's Central Banking Service provided him to Trinidad and Tobago as Governor of that country's central bank, and in 1969 he joined the faculty of Atkinson College. York University gave him leave of absence in 1973 to advise the Government of Botswana on monetary matters, which led to the establishment of their central bank.

Married, with four sons and a growing assortment of grandchildren, Professor McLeod now writes and works in support of national and international policies that are both socially responsible and economically sound.

Other Books by the Same Author

The Principles of Financial Intermediation. Lanham Md.; University Press of America, 1984. Pp. xiv + 237. Index.

The Fearsome Dilemma: Simultaneous Inflation and Unemployment. Lanham, Md.; University Press of America, 1984. Pp. xi + 197. Index.

Index

Index

Accelerator principle, 102, 104
Acceptance ratio, 206
Advertising, see Promotional activities
Agents of production, 5, 123n, 128
Austrian School, 197, 236
Automatic stabilizers, 225

Bagehot, Walter, 245
Bahr, Howard M., 312
Bailey, Samuel, 144f
Balance of international payments, 267-273, 327-330
Banks or banking, 200-208, 340
Banknotes, 206-208
Barone, Enrico, 142n
Biomass, 299
Bretton Woods System, 283-289
Brissot, Jacques-Pierre, 334
Brunner, Karl, 235
Budget Line, 156
Business cycles, 99-105, 136-141, 187f, 279f

Capital, 7f, 75f, 82f
Capital spending or capital formation, see Investment
Cassel, Gustav, 198
Catchings, W., 139
Central bank or central banking, 175, 200, 207-214, 242, 245, 276
Central planning, 8, 142f
Ceteris paribus, see "If..." assumption
Chadwick, Bruce A., 312
Chalmers, Thomas, 136
Chamberlin, Edward, 121
Charts and graphs, 11-13

Chequeable deposits, 206-208, 209
Circular flow, 19f, 111, 179, 204f
Closed economy, 114, 193
Club of Rome, 309f
Cole, H.S.H., 312
Commodity money, 200-205, 208
Commons, John Rogers, 150
Comparative advantage in trade, 251-257, 261
Competition: monopolistic or imperfect, see Model of monopolistic or imperfect competition; pure, see Model of pure competition; perfect, 21f, 61n, 108, 121n
Complementary goods, 40, 98f
Conglomerates, 339f
Consumer sovereignty, 20, 22, 130
Consumer spending, 101, 102
Consumption function or spending function, 179-181
Consumption-possibility curve or function, 156-162, 253-257
Cost curves or functions or schedules, 47-53, 59, 60, 128
Costs and benefits, private vs. social, 109f
Costs of production for a firm, 45-53, 58-61; sunk costs, 30, 45n, 59
Cox, Peter R., 312
Credit creation or expansion, 103, 201-208, 215, 216-221
Credit multiplier, 208, 210, 214, 216
Currency drain, 104, 216

Dalton, Hugh, 214n
Debt finance, 82f
Deflation, 139, 140f, 328
de Larosière, J., 317f, 343, 344

Demand, 25-40, 72-74, 98f, 102; derived, 72-74, 102 (acceleration of, 102); joint, 98

Demand curve *or* function *or* schedule, 31-40, 65-74, 80, 87, 121-123, 258-260, 261-266; community, 65-74, 80; for factors of production, 72-74; reciprocal, 258-263

Demand management, 100, 193-195, 223-233

Deposit expansion, 201-208, 216-221

Deposit multiplier, 208, 210, 214, 216

Depression, The Great: 19th century, 138, 177; 1930's, 105, 138, 179, 242, 280, 286

Deminishing returns, 42-45, 53, 55f

Disinvestment, 102, 104

Dismal science, the, 136

Dissaving, 179, 180n, 183, 190, 193

Douglas, Major C.H., 139

Duopoly, 85

Dupâquier, Jacques, 312

Econometrics, 4, 117-120

Economic problem, the, 10

Economies of scale, 48, 75

Effective demand, 193, 223

Effort-elasticity of demand, 160n

Ehrlich, Anne H., 310, 312

Ehrlich, Paul R., 310, 312

Elasticities, 32-38, 56f, 160n

Employment, 17, 224

Energy, 303f

Entrepreneur, 8, 41, 60n, 90

Entrepreneurship, 8, 41, 61

Equation of exchange, 169-174, 175

Equilibrium, 10, 18, 21, 67, 69, 78-80, 108, 123, 126, 130f, 142; general, 18, 80; long-run, 21, 67, 78-80, 108, 123, 130f; socialist, 142; stable, 69; unstable, 70f

Equities, 82f, 84, 341

Exchange rates, 252, 261-266, 274-292

Expectations, 102, 187, 189

Externalities, 109f

External drain, 216

External reserves, 209, 216, 273, 281, 287, 288

Fabian Society, 152

Factor costs, 5, 115, 123f

Factor returns, 5, 22, 81-84, 115, 128

Factors of production, 5-8, 20f, 22, 43n, 45

Factory Acts, 135

Fallacy of composition, 66, 74

Fauve-Chamoux, A., 312

Financial institutions *or* intermediaries, 19, 200-210, 209f, 340

Fiscal policy, 189f, 193f, 224f, 226f, 227

Fisher, Irving, 171-174, 175, 235

Foster, W.F., 139

Foreign-exchange market, 261-266

Foreign trade, 189, 190f, 251-273

Friedman, Milton, 235-248

Full employment, 140, 186f, 316; full-employment budgeting, 225

GNP, *see* Gross National Product

Graphs, *see* Charts and Graphs

George, Henry, 151f

Gold standard, 266, 277-280

Government deficits, 317-319, 323-325, 330

Grebenik, E., 312

Gross National Expenditure, 111n

Gross National Product, 110-117, 168f

Hamilton, Alexander, 148n

Hayek, Friedrich A. von, 236

Hildebrand, Bruno, 148

Historical School, German, 148f, 150f, 236

Hoarding, 198

Hobson, John A., 138
Hocking, Brian, 298
Holdren, John P., 310, 312
Hulett, H.R., 298f

"*If...*" assumption, 4
Income multiplier, 184-186, 192, 214-221 (*see also* Spending multiplier); double *or* compound, 214-221
Increasing returns to scale, *see* Economies of scale
Index numbers, 117, 168f
Inducement to invest, 187, 321
Infant-industry argument, 148n
Inferior goods, 38, 39
Inflation, 229-233, 238, 241, 315, 316-323, 325-327; non-accelerating rate of, 241
Innovation, 42, 103
Input-output analysis, 143
Institutionalism, American, 149-151, 236
Integration, 88n, 339
Interest rates, 166f, 197-200, 320; natural rate of, 198; real rates, 167
Internal drain, *see* Currency drain
International Bank for Reconstruction and Development (I.B.R.D), 283
International Monetary Fund (I.M.F.), 225, 272f, 283-292, 317f, 342, 344, 345f, 349
Investment, 163f, 174, 187-189
Investment Levy, 326f

Joint costs, 97f, 129
Joint demand, 98f
Joint products, 97f
Joint supply, 97f
Juglar, Clement, 105

Key currencies, 281-283

Keynes, John Maynard, 17, 136, 138, 173, 178, 187, 189, 199, 237, 239, 323, 327
Keynesian(s) *or* Keynesianism, 178, 223, 236, 244, 245
Keynesian Revolution, 177-195
Kitchin, Joseph, 105
Knies, Karl, 148
Kondratieff, Nikolai, 105
Kuznetz, Simon, 105

Labour, 5, 42f, 72f, 76-78, 81
Labour theory of value, 136, 144f
Labour unions, *see* Trade unions
Labour-power, 145
Laissez-faire, 63, 133, 236f
Land, 5, 6, 7f, 75, 81f, 300-302
Lange, Oscar, 142
Leakages, 192, 215, 216, 329
Leontief, Wassily, 143
Lerner, Abba P., 142, 331
Limits to Growth, 309-311, 313
Liquidity function, 199, 213f
Liquidity preference, 199
Liquidity trap, 213f
Long run, 21, 78-80
Lumpy data, 13, 28, 47

Malthus, Thomas R., 136f, 163, 296f
Marginal analysis, 26
Marginal-cost pricing, 93f
Marginal propensity to consume *or* to spend, 180, 181, 185n
Marginal propensity to import, 193n, 215
Marginal propensity to save, 180, 181, 185n
Markets, 65-71; *see slao* Money-and-market mechanism
Marshall, Alfred, 7f, 92
Marshall Plan, 283

Marx, Karl, 138, 144-148 *passim*, 149, 150, 335
Marxism, 142, 144-148, 334
Marx's sociology, 146f
McLeod, Alex N., 331
Meadows, Donella H., 313
Meadows, Dennis L., 313
Mergers, 88
Mesarovic, Mihajlo, 313
Meteoric stones, 7f
Mises, Ludwig von, 236
Mitchell, Wesley Clair, 150
Model of pure competition, 17-23, 61n, 62f
Model of monopolistic *or* imperfect competition, 88, 121-131, 179
Models of Doom, 310
Monetarism *or* monetarist(s), 137, 235-248
Monetary policy, 208-214, 223-228 *passim*, 240-242, 279f
Money, 137, 169-174, 200-208, 240
Monopoly, 18, 85-96
Monopsony, 85
Multipliers (*see also* Credit multiplier *and* Income multiplier): economic, 214f; instant, 186n; spending, 214-221
Mummery, A.F., 138

National Accounts, 110-117; *see also* Gross National Product
Natural resources, 6, 299-306
Net Economic Welfare (NEW), 117
New classical economics, 243
Non-accelerating rate of inflation, 241
Nursall, J.R., 298

Oligopoly, 121-131
Open economy, 114, 193, 327-330
Opportunity cost, 10

Overhead costs, 45n, 59
Overproduction, 136, 137, 146
Oversaving, 136, 138, 139
Owen, Robert, 141

Paradox of thrift, the, 183
Parameters, 118
Pareto, Vilfredo, 142n
Parkinson's Law of Costs, 61
Peel, John, 312
Pestel, Eduard, 313
Policy goals *or* objectives, 225, 227-229
Policy instruments, 227-229
Pollution, 306-309
Poor-man's goods, 38
Population theory, 136, 295-299
Price controls, 228f, 322f
Price level, 169-174
Price stability, 225f, 279f
Prices: asking, 178, 179, 231f; bid, 178, 179, 231f; realized, 232; sticky, 178, 179
Production curve *or* frontier *or* function, 156-162, 253-257
Productive property, 8
Profit(s), 60-64, 123; pure, 62-64, 123n; windfall, 81
Profit motive, 63f, 333
Promotional activities, 39, 56, 125, 126, 129-131
Proudhom, Pierre-Joseph, 142n, 334
Psychic income, 46n
Public Finance, 105-108
Public goods, 106
Purchasing-Power Parity, 265f, 287
Quantity theory of money and prices, 169-174
Quasi-rent, 7f

Rational expectations, 243

Reagan, President Ronald, 244
Real income, 9, 168f, 173, 174
Real output, 9
Reciprocal demand, 258-263
Real quantity of money, 241
Rent, 5, 6, 81f; differential, 81; pure, 6, 81; situation, 6, 82
Ricardo, David, 136, 137, 144f, 147, 151
Ricardian socialists, 145
Rich-man's goods, 38f
Robertson, Dennis H., 198
Robinson, H., 313
Robinson, Joan, 121
Roscher, Wilhelm, 148

Sanctity of contracts, 20
Saving function, 180, 181, 191
Saving(s), 31, 76, 165, 183
Say, Jean Batiste, 137
Say's Law of Markets, 137, 138
Schmoller, Gustav, 149
Schumpeter, Joseph A., 42, 103
Schwartz, Anna J., 242, 245
Shaw, George Bernard, 334
Short run *or* short term, 21, 67-69
Shut-down price, 55, 56, 59
Single tax, 151f
Sismondi, J.C.L. Simonde de, 137
Smith, Adam, 86, 106n, 136, 147
Social Credit, 139
Socialism, 141-144, 334; "scientific", 141; utopian, 141
Sombart, Werner, 149
Special Drawing Rights (SDR's), 272f, 288f, 290f
Spending function, 183
Spending stream, 19
Sterling Area, 281

Substitute goods, 99
Substitution effects, 39
Supplementary models, 73-90
Supply-and-demand analysis, 65-84, 145, 155
Supply curve *or* function *or* schedule, 56-58, 66f, 75-78, 80, 258-263; for factors of production, 75-78; industry, 66f, 75-78, 80
Supply-side economics, 243f
Surplus value, 145

T-accounts, 201
T-square accounts, 202
Taxation, 106-108, 115, 135.
Thinking about the Future, 310, 312
Thomas, Darwin L., 312
Tibbon, Judah Ibn, 334
Trade cycles, *see* business cycles
Trade unions, 134, 141, 150
Transfer payments, 81, 83, 111f, 190
Tripartite Agreement, 282

Unearned increment, 151
Underconsumption theories, 136-141, 146
Unemployment, natural rate of, 236, 240f, 246
Unproductive debt, 83f, 112n
Utility, 25-31

Validation thesis, 231
Value judgements, 4, 22, 91f, 129
Variables, economic, 80, 118; endogenous, 118; exogenous, 118
Veblen, Thorstein Bunde, 149f
Velocity of circulation, 171-174
Wages, 5f, 81
Wages of management, 6, 61
Wallich, Henry C., 331
Wasting assets, 6
Weinstock, Sidney, 331

Welfare, economic, 108-110, 117
Wicksell, Knut, 198
Wieser, Friederich von, 142n
Windfall profit, 81
Wordsworth, William, 334f